D0841467

HOPE AGAINST HOPE

Nadezhda Mandelstam

Hope Against Hope

A Memoir

Translated from the Russian by Max Hayward
With an Introduction by Clarence Brown
and "Nadezhda Mandelstam
(1899–1980): An Obituary"
by Joseph Brodsky

THE MODERN LIBRARY

NEW YORK

1999 Modern Library Paperback Edition

Copyright © 1970 by Atheneum Publishers
English translation copyright © 1970 by Atheneum Publishers
Introduction copyright © 1970 by Atheneum Publishers

All rights reserved under International and Pan-American
Copyright Conventions. Published in the United States by
Random House, Inc., New York, and simultaneously in Canada
by Random House of Canada Limited, Toronto.

Modern Library and colophon are registered trademarks of Random House, Inc.

Published in 1970 by Atheneum Publishers. This edition published by
arrangement with Simon & Schuster, Inc.

Grateful acknowledgment is made to Farrar, Straus & Giroux, Inc., for permission to
reprint "Nadezhda Mandelstam (1899–1980): An Obituary" from *Less Than One:
Selected Essays* by Joseph Brodsky. Copyright © 1986 by Joseph Brodsky. Reprinted
by permission of Farrar, Straus & Giroux, Inc.

LIBRARY OF CONGRESS CATALOGING-IN-PUBLICATION DATA
Mandel 'shtam, Nadezhda, 1899–1980
[Vospominania. English]
Hope against hope: a memoir / Nadezhda Mandelstam; translated from the Russian
by Max Hayward; with an introduction by Clarence Brown.
p.   cm.
Includes index.
ISBN 0-375-75316-8
1. Mandel 'shtam, Osip, 1891–1938. 2. Mandel 'shtam, Nadezhda, 1899–1980. 3. Soviet
Union—Politics and government. 4. Soviet Union—Intellectual life—1917–
5. Poets, Russian—20th century—Biography. I. Hayward, Max. II. Title.
PG3476.M355Z813   1999
891.71´3—dc21
[B]   98-47833

Modern Library website address:
www.modernlibrary.com

Printed in the United States of America

2   4   6   8   9   7   5   3   1

Nadezhda Mandelstam
(1899–1980)
AN OBITUARY

by Joseph Brodsky

Of the eighty-one years of her life, Nadezhda Mandelstam spent nineteen as the wife of Russia's greatest poet in this century, Osip Mandelstam, and forty-two as his widow. The rest was childhood and youth. In educated circles, especially among the literati, being the widow of a great man is enough to provide an identity. This is especially so in Russia, where in the thirties and in the forties the regime was producing writers' widows with such efficiency that in the middle of the sixties there were enough of them around to organize a trade union.

"Nadya is the most fortunate widow," Anna Akhmatova used to say, having in mind the universal recognition coming to Osip Mandelstam at about that time. The focus of this remark was, understandably, her fellow poet, and right though she was, this was the view from the outside. By the time this recognition began to arrive, Mme. Mandelstam was already in her sixties, her health extremely precarious and her means meager. Besides, for all the universality of that recognition, it did not include the fabled "one-sixth of the entire planet," i.e., Russia itself. Behind her were already two decades of widowhood, utter deprivation, the Great (obliterating any personal loss) War, and the daily fear of being grabbed by the agents of State Security as a wife of an enemy of the people. Short of death, anything that followed could mean only respite.

I met her for the first time precisely then, in the winter of 1962, in the city of Pskov, where together with a couple of friends I went to take a look at the local churches (the finest, in my view, in the empire). Having learned about our intentions to travel to that city, Anna Akhmatova suggested we visit Nadezhda Mandelstam, who was teaching English at the local pedagogical institute, and gave us several books for her. That was the first time I heard her name: I didn't know that she existed.

She was living in a small communal apartment consisting of two rooms. The first room was occupied by a woman whose name, ironically enough, was Nyetsvetaeva (literally: Non-Tsvetaeva); the second was Mme. Mandelstam's. It was eight square meters large, the size of an average American bathroom. Most of the space was taken up by a cast-iron twin-sized bed; there were also two wicker chairs, a wardrobe chest with a small mirror, and an all-purpose bedside table, on which sat plates with the leftovers of her supper and, next to the plates, an open paperback copy of *The Hedgehog and the Fox,* by Isaiah Berlin. The presence of this red-covered book in this tiny cell, and the fact that she didn't hide it under the pillow at the sound of the doorbell, meant precisely this: the beginning of respite.

The book, as it turned out, was sent to her by Akhmatova, who for nearly half the century remained the closest friend of the Mandelstams: first of both of them, later of Nadezhda alone. Twice a widow herself (her first husband, the poet Nikolai Gumilyov, was shot in 1921 by the Cheka—the maiden name of the KGB; the second, the art historian Nikolai Punin, died in a concentration camp belonging to the same establishment), Akhmatova helped Nadezhda Mandelstam in every way possible, and during the war years literally saved her life by smuggling Nadezhda into Tashkent, where some of the writers had been evacuated, and by sharing with her the daily rations. Even with her two husbands killed by the regime, with her son languishing in the camps for eighteen years, Akhmatova was somewhat better off than Nadezhda Mandelstam, if only because she was recognized, however reluctantly, as a writer, and was allowed to live in Leningrad and Moscow. For the wife of an enemy of the people big cities were simply off-limits.

For decades this woman was on the run, darting through the backwaters and provincial towns of the big empire, settling down in a new place only to take off at the first sign of danger. The status of nonperson gradually became her second nature. She was a small woman, of slim build, and with the passage of years she shriveled more and more, as though trying to turn herself into something weightless, something easily pocketed in the moment of flight. Similarly, she had virtually no possessions: no furniture, no art objects, no library. The books, even foreign books, never stayed in her hands for long: after being read or glanced through they would be passed on to someone else—the way it ought to be with books. In the years of her utmost affluence, at the end of the sixties and the beginning of the seventies, the most expensive item in her one-room apartment on the outskirts of Moscow was a cuckoo clock on the kitchen wall. A thief would be disillusioned here; so would those with a search warrant.

———

In those "affluent" years following the publication in the West of her two volumes of memoirs* that kitchen became the place of veritable pilgrimages. Nearly every other night the best of what survived or came to life in the post-Stalin era in Russia gathered around the long wooden table, which was ten times bigger than the bedstead in Pskov. It almost seemed that she was about to make up for decades of being a pariah. I doubt, though, that she did, and somehow I remember her better in that small room in Pskov, or sitting on the edge of a couch in Akhmatova's apartment in Leningrad, where she would come from time to time illegally from Pskov, or emerging from the depth of the corridor in Shklovsky's apartment in Moscow, where she perched before she got a place of her own. Perhaps I remember that more clearly because there she was more in her element as an outcast, a fugitive, "the beggar-friend," as Osip Mandelstam calls her in one of his poems, and that is what she remained for the rest of her life.

There is something quite breathtaking in the realization that she wrote those two volumes of hers at the age of sixty-five. In the Mandelstam family it is Osip who was the writer; she wasn't. If she wrote anything before those volumes, it was letters to her friends or appeals to the Supreme Court. Nor is hers the case of someone reviewing a long and eventful life in the tranquillity of retirement. Because her sixty-five years were not exactly normal. It's not for nothing that in the Soviet penal system there is a paragraph specifying that in certain camps a year of serving counts for three. By this token, the lives of

*Translated as *Hope Against Hope* and *Hope Abandoned,* and translated by Max Hayward.

many Russians in this century came to approximate in length those of biblical patriarchs—with whom she had one more thing in common: devotion to justice.

Yet it wasn't this devotion to justice alone that made her sit down at the age of sixty-five and use her time of respite for writing these books. What brought them into existence was a recapitulation, on the scale of one, of the same process that once before had taken place in the history of Russian literature. I have in mind the emergence of great Russian prose in the second half of the nineteenth century. That prose, which appears as though out of nowhere, as an effect without traceable cause, was in fact simply a spin-off of the nineteenth century's Russian poetry. It set the tone for all subsequent writing in Russian, and the best work of Russian fiction can be regarded as a distant echo and meticulous elaboration of the psychological and lexical subtlety displayed by the Russian poetry of the first quarter of that century. "Most of Dostoevsky's characters," Anna Akhmatova used to say, "are aged Pushkin heroes, Onegins and so forth."

———

Poetry always precedes prose, and so it did in the life of Nadezhda Mandelstam, and in more ways than one. As a writer, as well as a person, she is a creation of two poets with whom her life was linked inexorably: Osip Mandelstam and Anna Akhmatova. And not only because the first was her husband and the second her lifelong friend. After all, forty years of widowhood could dim the happiest memories (and in the case of this marriage they were few and far between, if only because this marriage coincided with the economic devastation of the country, caused by revolution, civil war, and the first five-year plans). Similarly, there were years when she wouldn't see Akhmatova at all, and a letter would be the last thing to confide to. Paper, in general, was dangerous. What strengthened the bond of that marriage as well as of that friendship was a technicality: the necessity to commit to memory what could not be committed to paper, i.e., the poems of both authors.

In doing so in that "pre-Gutenberg epoch," in Akhmatova's words, Nadezhda Mandelstam certainly wasn't alone. However, repeating day and night the words of her dead husband was undoubtedly connected not only with comprehending them more and more but also with resurrecting his very voice, the intonations peculiar only to him, with a however fleeting sensation of his presence, with the realization that he kept his part of that "for better or for worse" deal, especially its second half. The same went for the poems of the physically often absent Akhmatova, for, once set in motion, this mechanism of memorization won't come to a halt. The same went for other authors, for certain ideas, for ethical principles—for everything that couldn't survive otherwise.

And gradually those things grew on her. If there is any substitute for love, it's memory. To memorize, then, is to restore intimacy. Gradually the lines of those poets became her mentality, became her identity. They supplied her not only with the plane of regard or angle of vision; more important, they became her linguistic norm. So when she set out to write her books, she was bound to gauge—by that time already unwittingly, instinctively—her sentences against theirs. The clarity and remorselessness of her pages, while reflecting the character of her mind, are also inevitable stylistic consequences of the poetry that had shaped that mind. In both their content and style, her books are but a postscript to the supreme version of language which poetry essentially is and which became her flesh through learning her husband's lines by heart.

———

To borrow W. H. Auden's phrase, great poetry "hurt" her into prose. It really did, because those two poets' heritage could be developed or elaborated upon only by prose. In poetry they could be followed only by epigones. Which has happened. In other words, Nadezhda Mandelstam's prose was the only available medium for the language itself to avoid stagnation. Similarly, it was the only medium available for the psyche formed by those poets' use of language. Her books, thus, were not so much memoirs and guides to the lives of two great poets, however superbly they performed these functions; these books elucidated the consciousness of the nation. Of the part of it, at least, that could get a copy.

Small wonder, then, that this elucidation results in an indictment of the system. These two volumes by Mme. Mandelstam indeed amount to a Day of Judgment on earth for her age and for its literature—a judgment administered all the more rightfully since it was this age that had undertaken the construction of earthly paradise. A lesser wonder, too, that these memoirs, the second volume especially, were not liked on either side of the Kremlin Wall. The authorities, I must say, were more honest in their reaction than the intelligentsia: they simply made possession of these books an offense punishable by law. As for the intelligentsia, especially in Moscow, it went into actual turmoil over Nadezhda Mandelstam's charges against many of its illustrious and not so illustrious members of virtual complicity with the regime, and the human flood in her kitchen significantly ebbed.

There were open and semi-open letters, indignant resolutions not to shake hands, friendships and marriages collapsing over whether she was right or wrong to consider this or that person an informer. A prominent dissident declared, shaking his beard: "She shat on our entire generation"; others would rush to their dachas and lock themselves up there, to tap out antimemoirs. This was already the beginning of the seventies, and some six years later these same people would become equally split over Solzhenitsyn's attitude toward the Jews.

There is something in the consciousness of literati that cannot stand the notion of someone's moral authority. They resign themselves to the existence of a First Party Secretary, or of a Führer, as to a necessary evil, but they would eagerly question a prophet. This is so, presumably, because being told that you are a slave is less disheartening news than being told that morally you are a zero. After all, a fallen dog shouldn't be kicked. However, a prophet kicks the fallen dog not to finish it off but to get it back on its feet. The resistance to those kicks, the questioning of a writer's assertions and charges, come not from the desire for truth but from the intellectual smugness of slavery. All the worse, then, for the literati when the authority is not only moral but also cultural—as it was in Nadezhda Mandelstam's case.

—

I'd like to venture here one step further. By itself reality isn't worth a damn. It's perception that promotes reality to meaning. And there is a hierarchy among perceptions (and, correspondingly, among meanings), with the ones acquired through the most refined and sensitive prisms sitting at the top. Refinement and sensitivity are imparted to such a prism by the only source of their supply: by culture, by civilization, whose main tool is language. The evaluation of reality made through such a prism—the acquisition of which is one goal of the species—is therefore the most accurate, perhaps even the most just. (Cries of "Unfair!" and "Elitist!" that may follow the aforesaid from, of all places, the local campuses must be left unheeded, for culture is "elitist" by definition, and the application of democratic principles in the sphere of knowledge leads to equating wisdom with idiocy.)

It's the possession of this prism supplied to her by the best Russian poetry of the twentieth century, and not the uniqueness of the size of her grief, that makes Nadezhda Mandelstam's statement about her piece of reality unchallengeable. It's an abominable fallacy that suffering makes for greater art. Suffering blinds, deafens, ruins, and often kills. Osip Mandelstam was a great poet *before* the Revolution. So was Anna Akhmatova, so was Marina Tsvetaeva. They would have become what they became even if none of the historical events that befell Russia in this century had taken place: because they were *gifted*. Basically, talent doesn't need history.

———

Would Nadezhda Mandelstam have become what she became had it not been for the Revolution and all the rest that followed? Probably not, for she met her future husband in 1919. But the question itself is immaterial; it leads us into the murky domains of the law of probability and of historical determinism. After all, she became what she became not because of what took place in Russia in this century but rather in spite of it. A casuist's finger will surely point out that from the point of view of historical determinism "in spite of" is synonymous with "because." So much then for historical determinism, if it gets so mindful about the semantics of some human "in spite of."

For a good reason, though. For a frail woman of sixty-five turns out to be capable of slowing down, if not averting in the long run, the cultural disintegration of a whole nation. Her memoirs are something more than a testimony to her times; they are a view of history in the light of conscience and culture. In that light history winces, and an individual realizes his choice: between seeking that light's source and committing an anthropological crime against himself.

She didn't mean to be so grand, nor did she simply try to get even with the system. For her it was a private matter, a matter of her temperament, of her identity and what had shaped that identity. As it was, her identity had been shaped by culture, by its best products: her husband's poems. It's them, not his memory, that she was trying to keep alive. It's to them, and not to him, in the course of forty-two years that she became a widow. Of course she loved him, but love itself is the most elitist of passions. It acquires its stereoscopic substance and perspective only in the context of culture, for it takes up more space in the mind than it does in the bed. Outside of that setting it falls flat into one-dimensional fiction. She was a widow to culture, and I think she loved her husband more at the end than on the day they got married.

That is probably why readers of her books find them so haunting. Because of that, and because the status of the modern world vis-à-vis civilization also can be defined as widowhood.

If she lacked anything, it was humility. In that respect she was quite unlike her two poets. But then they had their art, and the quality of their achievements provided them with enough contentment to be, or to pretend to be, humble. She was terribly opinionated, categorical, cranky, disagreeable, idiosyncratic; many of her ideas were half-baked or developed on the basis of hearsay. In short, there was a great deal of one-upwomanship in her, which is not surprising given the size of the figures she was reckoning with in reality and later in imagination. In the end, her intolerance drove a lot of people away, but that was quite all right with her, because she was getting tired of adulation, of being liked by Robert McNamara and Willy Fisher (the real name of Colonel Rudolf Abel). All she wanted was to die in her bed, and, in a way, she looked forward to dying, because "up there I'll again be with Osip." "No," replied Akhmatova, upon hearing this. "You've got it all wrong. Up there it's now me who is going to be with Osip."

———

Her wish came true, and she died in her bed. Not a small thing for a Russian of her generation. There undoubtedly will surface those who will cry that she misunderstood her epoch, that she lagged behind the train of history running into the future. Well, like nearly every other Russian of her generation, she learned only too well that that train running into the future stops at the concentration camp or at the gas chamber. She was lucky that she missed it, and we are lucky that she told us about its route. I saw her last on May 30, 1972, in that kitchen of hers, in Moscow. It was late afternoon, and she sat, smoking, in the corner, in the deep shadow cast by the tall cupboard onto the wall. The shadow was so deep that the only things one could make out were the faint flicker of her cigarette and the two piercing eyes. The rest—her smallish shrunken body under the shawl, her hands, the oval of her ashen face, her gray, ashlike hair—all were consumed by the dark. She looked like a remnant of a huge fire, like a small ember that burns if you touch it.

1981

CONTENTS

INTRODUCTION

by Clarence Brown

Excellent books are slippery things. They slip through the fingers of policemen who want to prevent them being published, and once they are in print, they slip out of the categories into which tidy-minded critics long to fix them. This book is, for the most part, a memoir; but it is much more. To say of it that it relates the nineteen years, from May 1, 1919, to May 1, 1938, that Nadezhda Yakovlevna Mandelstam spent with her husband, the great Russian poet Osip Mandelstam, is to say, under the circumstances, a very great deal. But it is still not enough. For such a statement ignores many things that the curious reader will delight to find here. I shall try to name some of them.

The first is the author herself. "I played the role of 'poet's widow' with him," she once told me of her meeting with a visitor from the West. "It is a thing I can do when required." Indeed she could, but it was precisely that—a "role," something objectively different from herself, a kind of bedraggled plumage that she could, in case of need, snatch from the Victorian chiffonier and don in the nick of time to satisfy, with the addition of a few heart-rending phrases, some pilgrim's need to share the suffering and injustice of her life. When the coast was clear, the sweetly sad figure who had dispensed this and that fact of her husband's biography (even glancing at times, in her hammier moments, over her shoulder) would clear the general air with some spine-shattering Russian oath and revert to her true nature: a vinegary,

Brechtian, steel-hard woman of great intelligence, limitless courage, no illusions, permanent convictions and a wild sense of the absurdity of life.

And it is the true nature that one meets everywhere in this book. The style, in Russian, is an almost uncanny reproduction of her speaking voice. The toughness of the spirit that animates these pages will be familiar to anyone who has ever known her. The angle of vision is always hers.

But, for all of this, she herself, her person, the externals of her own life, are strangely absent. Her book is very much the book of her husband, to whom as man and poet she was utterly devoted throughout their years together and ever afterward; and where he is concerned she never has the slightest desire to make herself conspicuous. Her attitude is always that which she herself memorably expressed one May evening in 1965. The students of the Mechanical Mathematics Department of Moscow University had organized on their own initiative the first memorial evening of Mandelstam's poetry to be held in Russia. They invited Ilia Ehrenburg, an old friend of the poet and an even older one of his wife, to preside. Nikolai Chukovski, N. L. Stepanov, Varlam Shalamov and Arseni Tarkovski were among the writers and scholars who contributed reminiscences of Mandelstam and recited his poems. At one point Ehrenburg mentioned rather hesitantly, knowing that she would dislike his doing it, that Nadezhda Yakovlevna was in the auditorium. He continued, "She lived through all the difficult years with Mandelstam, went into exile with him, saved all of his poems. I cannot imagine his life without her. I hesitated whether I should say that the poet's widow was at this first evening. I don't ask her to come down here . . ." But here his words were smothered under thunderous applause that lasted for a long time. Everyone stood. Finally, Nadezhda Yakovlevna herself stood and a hush fell upon the house. Turning to face the audience, she said, "Mandelstam wrote, 'I'm not accustomed yet to panegyrics. . . .' Forget that I'm here. Thank you." And she sat down. But the applause would not die away for a long time.

In all fairness, the request was and is impossible. For all her diminutive size, she was colossally there in the hall (to murmur "Rot!" at the occasional statement with which she disagreed). And she is everywhere in this memoir of her husband. Her tone and her spirit, at least, are here.

In this note I shall set down some of the external facts of her life which she omits and which happen to be known to me.

She was born Nadezhda Yakovlevna Khazina—the daughter, that is, of Yakov Khazin—on October 31, 1899, in the town of Saratov. Her mother was a physician. I don't know what her father's occupation was, but I find in one of her letters the information that her parents were "nice, highly educated people." She had a sister, Anna, and a brother, Evgeni Yakovlevich, who became a writer. Though she relishes the slightly outré circumstance of having been born in Saratov—something like Balzac's having been married in Berdichev—the fact is that all her early life was passed in Kiev. There she studied art in the studio of A. A. Ekster, where one of her best friends was Ilia Ehrenburg's future wife, Liuba. Another was A. G. Tyshler, who later became a well-known artist. An acquaintance, but hardly a friend, was the extraordinary Bliumkin, the assassin of the German ambassador Count Mirbach and at times one of the most pestilential banes of Mandelstam's existence.

She learned the principal European languages to such an extent that she can still translate handily from French and German today. Her family traveled widely, nonchalantly, naturally, as used to be done, and she retains today a vivid familiarity with the now forbidden landscape of Europe. Her knowledge of English also began in childhood, for she has often mentioned her English governesses in letters to me ("they were all parson's daughters"), and she savors the slightly fusty Victorianism of some of her idioms. "Hope against hope" is one of these, which I count so often as I read back through her letters that it has practically become her slogan in my mind. The pun on her own name—Nadezhda means Hope in Russian—makes it eligible for this, and so does its expression of her obstinate courage. It doesn't make a bad title for her book, which has none in Russian.

Her knowledge of languages was very valuable in the twenties and thirties when she and her husband, like many of the old intelligentsia, were driven into a feverish spate of translating in order to live. She translated and edited numerous books—probably, I should think, under a pseudonym. At any rate, it would be impossible to determine what she translated, for those chores were no sooner finished than forgotten. She even collaborated with Mandelstam on many of the works, including those in verse, that carried his name as translator—an added reason, if any were needed, for putting little store by those pages in his canon. It must surely have been Nadezhda Yakovlevna who was mainly responsible for translating things like Upton Sinclair's *Machine* or editing the novels of Captain Mayne Reid, for she knew English far better than her husband, but when I asked her this she waved the question away with a gesture of distaste: "Who knows? What *didn't* we translate?"

As for her knowledge of English, it became her means of livelihood after Mandelstam's death, for she seems to have taught it in half the provincial towns of Russia before she was finally allowed to return to Moscow in 1964, when she began writing this book. In 1956, as a student of Mandelstam's old schoolmate, the great scholar Victor Zhirmunski, she earned the degree of "Kandidat nauk"—the equivalent of our doctorate—in English philology. Ten years later she presented me with a copy of the printed abstract of her dissertation, a brochure of thirteen pages, and since it is her principal acknowledged work before the present book, perhaps it should be noticed. The author is identified as "Head of the Department of English Language of the Chuvash Teachers' Training College," and the title of her work is *Functions of the Accusative Case on the Basis of Materials Drawn from Anglo-Saxon Poetic Monuments.* There is one tutelary reference to Engels, and one to Lenin. I do not suppose that she looks upon this with quite the contempt reserved for her translations, but the inscription in my copy reads, in part: "this thoroughly pleasant bit of rubbish."

Foreign visitors to the Soviet Union seldom realize how possible it is to meet people there without, in a sense, Meeting them. Very distinguished visitors have made this mistake. In fact, the more distinguished they are, alas, the more likely they are to be fooled, for the effort expended on them will be much greater. Nor does the effort cost very much. The roles of Poet's Widow, Rebellious Young Poet, Disloyal Journalist, etc., etc., are all too practiced to fail often of their goal. I say all this simply in order to remark that this is a book in which one can Meet the author of it. There are patches of reticence, true, but it is for the most part an utterly naked book, from its first page to its last an utterance from beyond the point of no return. Writing of her birthday on October 31, 1969, she said, "Everybody was astonished at my refusing to see anyone that day.... It was a most pleasant experience to be alone at seventy. I'm glad to be on my *vosmoi desiatok* [eighth decade]." It gave her, she said, the "freedom of the city," adding that I, living in England, would grasp what she meant. "Believe me, it is horribly good to be old and unable even to defend myself. Whoever wishes to knock me down will do it in no time." There is little reason, I am sure, to warn the reader of what Dostoyevski found: how dangerous such vulnerability can be, how powerful stark defenselessness.

II

But it would not be fitting to end this word of introduction on so heavy a note as that, for the fact is that Nadezhda Yakovlevna's book, however melancholy the sum total of its burden, is lightened time and again by an inexplicably buoyant sense of liberation, joy and even ... humor.

There is an occasional scene that might have derived from Gogol's *Inspector General*. Consider, for example, the official of the Ministry of Education who came to that Chuvash Teachers' Training College for a meeting. Hapless man! He could not have known that the Head of the English Department would laconically detail, years afterward, his pleas to the faculty to stop writing so many denunciations of each other and his warning that in future unsigned denunciations would not even be read. One tends to forget what a damned nuisance Stalinist officials must have found the system of ritual informing. In Voronezh an old Jewish grandmother raising her three grandsons was reported by some ill-wisher to be a prostitute. The Mandelstams, living nearby, were reported to be entertaining sinister guests at night and ... firing guns. Right up to 1937, Nadezhda Yakovlevna writes, a certain plausibility was still required.

Some of the humor has no barbs at all. The village of Nikolskoye had been settled by exiled criminals and fugitives in the days of Peter the Great. The street names had all been changed, of course, but Mandelstam eagerly noted down the names by which the locals still knew them: Strangler's Lane, Embezzler's Street, Counterfeiter's Row....

But the buoyancy of which I speak does not depend upon such passages as these. It depends upon the central figure of Osip Mandelstam himself. Nadezhda Yakovlevna calls him in one place "endlessly *zhizneradostny*." The word is usually rendered as "cheerful" or "joyous"— rather feeble counters for an original that means, in its two parts, "life-glad." Those who seek the roots of poetry in a close equivalency with life will find it perfectly astonishing that there are so few sad poems in Mandelstam. But while this or that fact of his tragic existence can explain the brute meaning of many lines, nothing can explain the poetry of them other than the wild joy that he took in the Russian language. It is not astonishing. *"Pechal moya svetla,"* Pushkin wrote, "My sadness is luminous"; and Mandelstam not only could but did use the line. The irrepressible Shakespeare could not restrain his pleasure in the antics of language even for Hamlet's bleakest soliloquies

>   it cannot be
> But I am pigeon-liver'd, and lack gall
> To make oppression bitter.

To all of which Yeats directly alludes when speaking of the essential gaiety of art in his "Lapis Lazuli":

> They know that Hamlet and Lear are gay
> Gaiety transfiguring all that dread.
> ———
> All things fall and are built again
> And those that build them again are gay.

In an early essay on Pushkin and Scriabin, of which only fragments remain, Mandelstam was evidently trying to find the source of this joy within the terms of Christianity. Christian art is joyous because it is free, and it is free because of the fact of Christ's having died to redeem the world. One need not die in art nor save the world in it, those matters having been, so to speak, attended to. What is left? The blissful responsibility to enjoy the world. Such, I take it, was the argument, as one can see it, from what is left. Whether in later years Mandelstam would have sought quite this underpinning for his innate gladness in life, I cannot tell. Perhaps the missing segments of this same essay might have modulated the statement in some way. But that is beside the essential point, which is that Mandelstam habitually converted not only the prose of life but even its truly darker moments into poems from which a sense of pleasure, even beatitude, is seldom absent.

Nadezhda Yakovlevna says in one place that he drew strength from what might drive others, herself included, into despair. But that is unfair. For her ample spirit, no less than the poet's creative gaiety, lends to her book its air of ultimate triumph.

III

It is one of the drabber commonplaces of literary history that the reputation of a poet generally suffers some diminution in the years just following his death. That Osip Mandelstam escaped this fate may be attributed in part to the peculiar circumstances of his demise. For years it was not even known for sure that he was in fact dead; and by the time the facts began to be more widely known—in the late fifties, more or less—the rise in Mandelstam's posthumous celebrity had already begun its phenomenal course. At the present moment there can be little doubt that among connoisseurs of Russian poetry he is the supreme verbal artist of this century.

This alone would make Nadezhda Yakovlevna's book absorbing enough, for she discusses the poetry of Mandelstam, especially the work of the exile years, with great sensitivity and with, needless to say, unimpeachable authority as regards the outward conditions of its origin.

His fame as a poet had been firmly established, however, in the decade before he met his future wife in 1919—a decade which, like all of his earlier life, she largely neglects, as she neglects everything of which she has no immediate knowledge. I shall therefore append the bare externals of that earlier life.

Osip Emilievich Mandelstam was born in Warsaw on January 15, 1891. His father was Emil Veniaminovich Mandelstam, a leather merchant, and his mother was born Flora Osipovna Verblovskaya. She was a teacher of piano, a woman of warm heart and cultivated intellect. Mandelstam grew up in St. Petersburg—the fact is by no means commonplace in the biography of Russian Jews of the period and argues his father's eminence in the guild that regulated such matters—and attended the Tenishev School. This was a progressive institution combining the classical disciplines with up-to-date commercial, scientific and even manual skills, and the roster of its graduates before the Revolution reads like a catalogue of Russian eminence for the first half of this century. When he finished in 1907, he went to Paris, took rooms across the street from the Sorbonne and read. The winter of 1909–10 he spent as a student in Heidelberg. He also attended the University of St. Petersburg for a brief time.

His earliest fame as a poet is connected with *Apollon,* one of the elegant journals of art and literature that adorned the revival of Russian taste around the turn of the century, and above all with a group of young poets who called themselves "Acmeists." They were in varying degrees willingly dominated by Nikolai Gumilev, a man of great fortitude (he died before a firing squad for complicity in a plot against the "new reality"), uncanny discernment in judging the poetry of his day, and himself not meanly gifted in the making of verses. He, with Anna Akhmatova and Osip Mandelstam, formed the trio whose work will save Acmeism from the transiency of many another such casual association and make it one of the permanent facts of Russian literary history.

He greeted Mandelstam's first book, *Kamen (Stone),* published in 1913, in the pages of *Apollon.* This little green brochure is today a great rarity, and even contemporary readers, as a matter of fact, tend to be more familiar with the second edition, considerably enlarged, of 1916. After the Revolution, a good part of which Mandelstam spent in the relatively humane environment of the Black Sea coast, his second book, *Tristia,* appeared in 1922 and again, under the title *Vtoraya kniga (Second Book),* in 1923—this time with a dedication to Nadezhda Yakovlevna. In 1925 he published a collection of autobiographical prose called *Shum vremeni (The Noise of Time).* Mandelstam's collected poems appeared in 1928 under the simple title *Stikhotvorenia (Poems)* and contained, in addition to the first two books, a section called "1921–1925." If one takes this as his "third book," one has accounted for all the poetry that he published in book form in his life. That same year there was also a book of criticism, *O poezii (On Poetry)* and a new edition of *The Noise of Time,* retitled *Egipetskaya marka (The Egyptian Stamp)* after a novella that had been added to it. The cumulative appearance of his work in verse, criticism and prose makes 1928 the "height" of his career. As Nadezhda Yakovlevna points out, this public summit was reached a few years after his real private position had begun to erode very dangerously.

Since 1955, owing to the truly heroic efforts of two Russian émigré scholars, Professor Gleb Struve and Mr. Boris Filippov, Mandelstam's texts, including not only all of the above but also a great treasure of works never published before, have been appearing in the United States. A collected edition of his poetry has existed in the Soviet Union for over a decade, but the authorities have so constantly postponed its publication that it has become something of a not terribly amusing international literary joke. When it appears, if it ever does, it will entirely vanish from the bookstores within a matter, quite literally, of minutes. Such is Mandelstam's stature among his countrymen at this moment. To attempt to characterize his art in so brief a note would be a waste of time, but to praise it without characterizing it would seem to me contemptuous of the reader's judgment. Faced with such indifferent alternatives, I shall simply postpone the whole matter for another place and ask that you take Mandelstam's status, for the moment, on faith. He is the greatest Russian poet of the modern period. Had the author of this book not lived, or had she been less valorous, intelligent and loving than she is, Mandelstam would no doubt have died several years earlier, and his work, that great concealed body of poetry and prose that never emerged in public print, would almost certainly have perished. In addition to everything else that it is, this splendid book is a record of how those things did not happen, and that is sufficient.

London / Easter 1970

Translator's Preface

All notes, except in the few cases where otherwise indicated, have been supplied by the translator, and the author bears no responsibility whatsoever for them. In order to keep footnotes to a minimum, most names of persons have been annotated in an Appendix, arranged in alphabetical order, at the end of the book. There is also a special note (page 419) on the various literary movements and organizations mentioned frequently in the text.

One short chapter of the original has been omitted in translation because it would make little sense for a reader unable to read Mandelstam's verse in Russian. The full Russian text of Mrs. Mandelstam's book has been published under the title *Vospominania* by the Chekhov Press (New York, 1970).

Mrs. Mandelstam refers to her husband throughout as O.M. (for Osip Mandelstam). In translation this has been reduced, for simplicity's sake, to M. Sometimes he is referred to in quoted conversation by his first name and patronymic: Osip Emilievich.

HOPE AGAINST HOPE

1
A MAY NIGHT

After slapping Alexei Tolstoi in the face, M. immediately returned to Moscow.* From here he rang Akhmatova every day, begging her to come. She was hesitant and he was angry. When she had packed and bought her ticket, her brilliant, irritable husband Punin asked her, as she stood in thought by a window: "Are you praying that this cup should pass from you?" It was he who had once said to her when they were walking through the Tretiakov Gallery: "Now let's go and see how they'll take you to your execution." This is the origin of her lines:

> "And later as the hearse sinks in the snow at dusk . . .
> What mad Surikov will describe my last journey?"

But she was not fated to make her last journey like this. Punin used to say, his face twitching in a nervous tic: "They're keeping you for the very end." But in the end they overlooked her and didn't arrest her. Instead, she was always seeing others off on their last journey—including Punin himself.

Akhmatova's son, Lev Gumilev, went to meet her at the station—he was staying with us at that time. It was a mistake to entrust him with

---

* See the note on Alexei Nikolayevich Tolstoi in the Appendix, where notes on most other persons mentioned by the author will also be found.

this simple task—he of course managed to miss her, and she was very upset. It wasn't what she was used to. That year she had come to see us a great deal and she was always greeted at the station by M. himself, who at once started to amuse her with his jokes. She remembered how he had once said angrily, when the train was late: "You travel at the same speed as Anna Karenina." And another time: "Why are you dressed like a deep-sea diver?"—it had been raining in Leningrad and she had put on boots and a rubber mac with a hood, but in Moscow the sun was shining and it was very hot. Whenever they met they were cheerful and carefree like children, as in the old days at the Poets' Guild.* "Stop it," I used to shout, "I can't live with such chatterboxes!" But this time, in May 1934, they had nothing to be cheerful about.

The day dragged on with excruciating slowness. In the evening the translator David Brodski turned up and then just wouldn't leave. There wasn't a bite to eat in the house and M. went around to the neighbors to try and get something for Akhmatova's supper. We hoped that Brodski might now get bored and leave, but no, he shot after M. and was still with him when he returned with the solitary egg he had managed to scrounge. Sitting down again in his chair, Brodski continued to recite the lines he liked best from his favorite poets, Sluchevski and Polonski (there was nothing he didn't know about both Russian and French poetry). He just went on and on, quoting and reminiscing, and it was only after midnight that we realized why he was being such a nuisance.

Whenever she came to see us, Akhmatova stayed in our small kitchen. The gas had not yet been installed and I cooked our semblance of a dinner on a kerosene stove in the corridor. In honor of our guest we covered the gas cooker with oilcloth to disguise it as a table. We called the kitchen "the sanctuary" after Narbut had once looked in there to see Akhmatova and said: "What are you doing here, like a pagan idol in a sanctuary? Why don't you go to some meeting or other where you can sit down properly?" Akhmatova and I had now taken refuge there, leaving M. to the mercy of the poetry-loving Brodski. Suddenly, at about one o'clock in the morning, there was a sharp, unbearably explicit knock on the door. "They've come for Osip," I said, and went to open the door.

Some men in civilian overcoats were standing outside—there seemed to be a lot of them. For a split second I had a tiny flicker of

* See page 426.

hope that this still wasn't it—my eye had not made out the uniforms under the covert-cloth topcoats. In fact, topcoats of this kind were also a sort of uniform—though they were intended as a disguise, like the old pea-green coats of the Czarist okhrana. But this I did not know then. All hope vanished as soon as the uninvited guests stepped inside.

I had expected them to say "How do you do?" or "Is this Mandelstam's apartment?" or something else of the kind that any visitor says in order to be let in by the person who opens the door. But the night visitors of our times do not stand on such ceremony—like secret-police agents the world over, I suppose.

Without a word or a moment's hesitation, but with consummate skill and speed, they came in past me (not pushing, however) and the apartment was suddenly full of people already checking our identity papers, running their hands over our hips with a precise, well-practiced movement, and feeling our pockets to make sure we had no concealed weapons.

M. came out of the large room. "Have you come for me?" he asked. One of the agents, a short man, looked at him with what could have been a faint smile and said: "Your papers." M. took them out of his pocket, and after checking them, the agent handed him a warrant. M. read it and nodded.

In the language of the secret police this was what was known as a "night operation." As I learned later, they all firmly believed that they were always liable to meet with opposition on such occasions, and to keep their spirits up they regaled each other with romantic tales about the dangers involved in these night raids. I myself once heard the daughter of an important Chekist,* who had come to prominence in 1937, telling a story about how Isaac Babel had "seriously wounded one of our men" while resisting arrest. She told such stories as an expression of concern for her kindly, loving father whenever he went out on "night operations." He was fond of children and animals—at home he always had the cat on his knees—and he told his daughter never to admit that she had done anything wrong, and always to say "no." This homely man with the cat could never forgive the people he interrogated for admitting everything they were accused of. "Why did they do it?" the daughter asked, echoing her father. "Think of the trouble they

---

* Member of the Cheka, the secret police. At later periods the Cheka was known successively as the OGPU, GPU, NKVD, MVD, MGB. It is now called the KGB.

made for themselves and for us as well!" By "us," she meant all those who had come at night with warrants, interrogated and passed sentence on the accused, and whiled away their spare time telling stories of the risks they ran. Whenever I hear such tales I think of the tiny hole in the skull of Isaac Babel, a cautious, clever man with a high forehead, who probably never once in his life held a pistol in his hands.

And so they burst into our poor, hushed apartments as though raiding bandits' lairs or secret laboratories in which masked carbonari were making dynamite and preparing armed resistance. They visited us on the night of May 13, 1934. After checking our papers, presenting their warrants and making sure there would be no resistance, they began to search the apartment. Brodski slumped into his chair and sat there motionless, like a huge wooden sculpture of some savage tribe. He puffed and wheezed with an angry, hurt expression on his face. When I chanced at one point to speak to him—asking him, I think, to get some books from the shelves for M. to take with him—he answered rudely: "Let M. get them himself," and again began to wheeze. Toward morning, when we were at last permitted to walk freely around the apartment and the tired Chekists no longer even looked searchingly at us as we did so, Brodski suddenly roused himself, held up his hand like a schoolboy and asked permission to go to the toilet. The agent directing the search looked at him with contempt. "You can go home," he said. "What?" Brodski said in astonishment. "Home," the man repeated and turned his back. The secret police despised their civilian helpers. Brodski had no doubt been ordered to sit with us that evening in case we tried to destroy any manuscripts when we heard the knock on the door.

2

CONFISCATION

M. often repeated Khlebnikov's lines: "What a great thing is a police station! The place where I have my rendezvous with the State." But Khlebnikov was thinking of something more innocent—just a routine check on the papers of a suspicious vagrant, the almost traditional form of meeting between State and poet. Our rendezvous with the State took place on a different, and much higher, level. Our uninvited guests, in strict accordance with their ritual, had immediately divided their roles between them, without exchanging a word. There were five people altogether—three agents and two witnesses. The two witnesses had flopped down on chairs in the hall and gone to sleep. Three years later, in 1937, they would no doubt have snored from sheer fatigue. Who knows by what charter we are granted the right to be arrested and searched in the presence of members of the public, so that no arrest should take place without due process of law, and it could never be said that anyone had just disappeared at dead of night without benefit of warrant or witnesses? This is the tribute we pay to the legal concepts of a bygone age.

To be present as a witness at arrests had almost become a profession. In every large apartment building the same previously designated pair would regularly be roused from their beds, and in the provinces the same two witnesses would be used for a whole street or district. They led a double life, serving by day as repairmen, janitors or plumbers (is this why our faucets are always dripping?) and by night as "witnesses," prepared if need be to sit up till morning in somebody's apartment. The money to pay them came out of our rent as part of the expense of maintaining the building. At what rate they were paid for their night work I do not know.

The oldest of the three agents got busy on the trunk in which we kept our papers, while the two younger ones carried on the search elsewhere. The clumsiness with which they went about it was very striking. Following their instructions, they looked in all the places cunning people are traditionally supposed to hide their secret documents: they shook out every book, squinting down the spine and cutting open the binding, inspected desks and tables for hidden drawers, and peered into pockets and under beds. A manuscript stuck into a saucepan would never have been found. Best of all would have been to put it on the dining table.

I particularly remember one of them, a young puffy-cheeked man with a smirk. As he went through the books he admired the old bindings and kept telling us we should not smoke so much. Instead, he offered us hard candy from a box which he produced from the pocket of his uniform trousers. I now have a good acquaintance, a writer and official of the Union of Soviet Writers,* who collects old books, showing off his finds in the secondhand book stores—first editions of Sasha Chorny and Severianin—and offering me hard candy from a tin box he

* See page 427.

keeps in the pocket of his smart stovepipe trousers which he has custom-made in a tailor shop exclusive to members of the Union of Writers. In the thirties he had a modest job in the secret police, and then fixed himself up safely as a writer. These two images blur into one: the elderly writer of the end of the fifties and the young police agent of the middle thirties. It's as though the young man who was so fond of hard candy had changed his profession and come up in the world: now dressed in civilian clothes, he lays down the law on moral problems, as a writer is supposed to, and continues to offer me candy from the same box.

This gesture of offering hard candy was repeated in many other apartments during searches. Was this, too, part of the ritual, like the technique of entering the room, checking identity papers, frisking people for weapons and looking for secret drawers? The procedure was worked out to the last detail and it was all quite different from the hectic manner in which it was done in the first days of the Revolution and during the Civil War. Which was worse I find it difficult to say.

The oldest of the agents, a short, lean and silent man with fair hair, was squatting down to look through the papers in the trunk. He worked slowly, deliberately and thoroughly. They had probably sent us well-qualified people from the section in charge of literature—this was supposedly part of the third department, though my acquaintance in the stovepipe trousers who offers me hard candy swears that the department responsible for people like us is either the second or the fourth. This is only a minor detail, but the preservation of certain administrative distinctions from Czarist days was very much in the spirit of the Stalin era.*

After carefully examining it, he put every piece of paper either on a chair in the growing pile of those to be confiscated, or threw it on the floor. Since one can generally tell from the selection of papers what the nature of the accusation will be, I offered to help the agent read M.'s difficult writing and date the various items; I also tried to rescue what I could—for example, a long poem by Piast that we were keeping, and the drafts of M.'s translations of Petrarch. We all noticed that the agent was interested in the manuscripts of M.'s verse of recent years. He showed M. the draft of "The Wolf" and, frowning, read it out in a low voice from beginning to end. Then he picked up a humorous poem about the manager of an apartment house who had smashed a harmo-

---

* Under Nicholas I, the secret police was called "The Third Section."

nium that one of the tenants was playing against the rules. "What's this about?" asked the agent with a baffled look, throwing the manuscript on the chair. "What indeed?" said M. "What is it about?"

The whole difference between the periods before and after 1937 could be seen in the nature of the two house searches we went through. In 1938 they wasted no time looking for papers and examining them— indeed, the police agents didn't even seem to know the occupation of the man they had come to arrest. When M. was arrested again in 1938, they simply turned over all the mattresses, swept his papers into a sack, poked around for a while and then disappeared, taking M. with them. The whole operation lasted no more than twenty minutes. But in 1934 they stayed all night until the early hours.

On both occasions, seeing me get M.'s things together, they made the same joking remark (also in accordance with instruction?): "Why so much stuff? What's the point? You don't think he's going to stay with us all that long? They'll just have a chat and let him go." This was the only relic from the era of "high humanism" in the twenties and beginning of the thirties. In the winter of 1937, reading a newspaper attack on Yagoda for allegedly turning the forced-labor camps into rest homes, M. said: "I didn't know we were in the paws of such humanists."

The egg brought for Akhmatova lay untouched on the table. Everybody—M.'s brother Evgeni, who had recently arrived from Leningrad, was also there—walked around the rooms talking and trying not to pay attention to the people rummaging in our things. Suddenly Akhmatova said that M. should eat something before he left, and she held out the egg to him. M. took it, sat down at the table, put some salt on it and ate it.

The two piles of papers on the chair and on the floor continued to grow. We tried not to walk on them, but our visitors took no such care. I very much regret that among the other papers stolen by Rudakov's widow we have lost some drafts of M.'s early poems—since they were not to be confiscated, they were just thrown on the floor and were marked with excellent impressions of military boots. I valued these pages very much and gave them for safekeeping into hands I thought would be safest of all: those of the young Rudakov, who in his devotion to us spent a year and a half in exile with us in Voronezh, where we shared every scrap of bread with him because he had no way of earning a living there. When he returned to Leningrad he also took with him for safekeeping the papers of Gumilev, which Akhmatova had trustingly delivered to him on a sleigh. Neither she nor I ever saw our papers again. Akhmatova occasionally hears rumors about people buying letters which she knows to have been among them.

"Osip, I envy you," Gumilev used to say to M., "you will die in a garret." Both had written their prophetic lines by this time, but neither wished to believe his own forecast, and they took consolation in the French idea of what happens to ill-starred poets. But a poet, after all, is just a human being like any other, and he is bound to end up in the most ordinary way, in the way most typical for his age and his times, meeting the fate that lies in wait for everyone else. None of the glamour and thrill of a special destiny, but the simple path along which all were "herded in a herd." Death in a garret was not for us.

At the time of the campaign in defense of Sacco and Vanzetti—we were then living in Tsarskoye Selo—M. sent a message to the hierarchy of the Russian Orthodox Church (through a certain churchman) proposing that the Church should also organize a protest against the execution. The answer came back at once: the Church would be willing to speak out in defense of the two men on condition that M. undertook to organize a similar protest if anything similar should happen to Russian priests. M. was quite taken aback and confessed himself defeated. This was one of the first lessons he learned in those days when he was trying to come to terms with the existing state of affairs.

When the morning of the fourteenth came, all the guests, invited and uninvited, went away and I was left alone with Akhmatova in the empty apartment, which bore all the marks of the night's ravages. I think we just sat opposite each other in silence. At any rate we didn't go to bed, and it never occurred to us to make tea. We were waiting for the hour when we could leave the building without attracting attention. Why? Where could we go, or to whom? Life went on. I suppose we looked a little like the "drowned maidens," if I may be forgiven this literary allusion—God knows, at that moment nothing was further from our minds than literature.

3

MORNING THOUGHTS

We never asked, on hearing about the latest arrest, "What was he arrested for?" but we were exceptional. Most people, crazed by fear, asked this question just to give themselves a little hope: if others were arrested for some reason, then they wouldn't be arrested, because they hadn't done anything wrong. They vied with each other in thinking up ingenious reasons to justify each arrest: "Well, she really is a smuggler, you know," "He really did go rather far," "I myself heard him say . . ." Or: "It was only to be expected—he's a terrible man," "I always thought there was something fishy about him," "He isn't one of us at all." This was enough for anyone to be arrested and destroyed: "not one of us," "talks too much," "a bad character" . . . These were just variations on a theme we had first heard in 1917. Both public opinion and the police kept inventing new and more graphic ones, adding fuel to the fire without which there is no smoke. This was why we had outlawed the question "What was he arrested for?" "*What for?*" Akhmatova would cry indignantly whenever, infected by the prevailing climate, anyone of our circle asked this question. "What do you mean, *what for?* It's time you understood that people are arrested *for nothing!*"

But even so, when M. was taken away, Akhmatova and I could not help asking the forbidden question "What for?" There were any number of possible reasons—by the standards of our laws, of course. It could have been for his verse in general, for what he had written about literature, or, more specifically, for the poem about Stalin. It could have been for slapping Alexei Tolstoi in the face. When this happened, Tolstoi had shouted at the top of his voice, in front of witnesses, that he would make sure M. was never published again, and that he would have him expelled from Moscow. . . . The same day, so we were told, he went to Moscow to complain to the boss of Soviet literature, Maxim Gorki. Before long we heard that Gorki had said—or at least the phrase was firmly attributed to him—"We'll teach him to strike Russian writers." People now tell me just as firmly that Gorki could not have said any such thing, and that he was really quite different from what we imagined him to be at the time. There is a widespread tendency to make Gorki out as a victim of the Stalinist regime, as a champion of free thought and a protector of the intelligentsia. I cannot judge, though I am sure Gorki had major disagreements with his master and was very hard-pressed by him. But from this it does not follow that he would have refused to support Tolstoi against a writer as deeply uncongenial to him as M. As regards Gorki's attitude to freedom of opinion, one only has to read his articles, speeches and books.

All things considered, our main hope was that M.'s arrest was indeed an act of vengeance for the slap in the face given to Alexei Tolstoi. However the charge was formulated, it could lead to nothing worse than banishment—and of this we were not afraid. Expulsion and exile had become a standard feature of our everyday life. In the years of the "breathing-space," before the terror began in earnest, there were always fairly widespread arrests, particularly among the intelligentsia, in the spring (mostly in May) and in the fall. They were meant to distract attention from our perennial economic failures. At that time there were scarcely any cases of people disappearing into thin air: they always wrote from exile, and returned at the end of their sentences—to be deported again. Andrei Bely, when we met him at Koktebel* in the summer of 1933, said he could scarcely keep up with the business of sending telegrams and writing letters to all his friends who had just "returned"—there had evidently been a clean sweep of theosophists, who were then released all at the same time in 1933. Similarly, in the spring before M.'s arrest, Piast had returned. After three or five years' absence all such exiles came back and were allowed to settle in small towns beyond a hundred kilometers from Moscow. If it happened to everybody else, why shouldn't it happen to us? Not long before his arrest, hearing M. talk rather carelessly with some people we did not know, I said to him: "You'd better watch out—it's almost May!" M. just waved his hand: "So what? Let them send us away. Others may be frightened, but what do we care?" And it was true: for some reason we really weren't worried about exile.

But it would be quite another matter if they had found the poem about Stalin. This was what had been in M.'s mind as he kissed Akhmatova goodbye before they took him away. We none of us doubted that for verse like this he would pay with his life. That was why we had watched the Chekists so closely, trying to see what they were after. The "Wolf" poems were not so bad—they would mean being sent to a camp, at the worst.

How might these potential charges be formulated? It was really all one! It is absurd to apply the standards of Roman law, the Napoleonic Code or any other legal system, to our times. The secret police always knew exactly what they were doing and they went about it systematically. Among their many aims were the destruction of witnesses who might remember certain things, and the creation of the unanimity needed to prepare the way for the millennium. People were picked up wholesale according to category (and sometimes age group)—

*A resort in the Crimea, popular with writers.

churchmen, mystics, idealist philosophers, humorists, people who talked too much, people who talked too little, people with their own ideas about law, government and economics; and—once the concept of "sabotage" had been introduced to explain all failures or blunders—engineers, technicians and agricultural specialists. "Don't wear that hat," M. once said to Boris Kuzin, "you mustn't attract attention—or you'll have trouble." And he did have trouble. But fortu-

---

MANDELSTAM'S POEM ON STALIN
(November 1933)[1]

We live, deaf to the land beneath us,
Ten steps away no one hears our speeches,

But where there's so much as half a conversation
The Kremlin's mountaineer will get his mention.[2]

His fingers are fat as grubs
And the words, final as lead weights, fall from his lips,

His cockroach whiskers leer
And his boot tops gleam.

Around him a rabble of thin-necked leaders—
fawning half-men for him to play with.

They whinny, purr or whine
As he prates and points a finger,

One by one forging his laws, to be flung
Like horseshoes at the head, the eye or the groin.

And every killing is a treat
For the broad-chested Ossete.[3]

---

[1] This poem, which Mrs. Mandelstam mentions on page 12 and at many other points, is nowhere quoted in full in the text of her book.

[2] In the first version, which came into the hands of the secret police, these two lines read:

> All we hear is the Kremlin mountaineer,
> The murderer and peasant-slayer.

[3] "Ossete." There were persistent stories that Stalin had Ossetian blood. Ossetia is to the north of Georgia in the Caucasus. The people, of Iranian stock, are quite different from the Georgians.

nately the attitude toward hats changed when it was decreed that Soviet scholars must dress even better than their foppish Western counterparts, and after serving his sentence Boris was appointed to a very good academic post. M.'s remark about the hat may have been a joke, but the nature of the head under it certainly determined its owner's fate.

The members of the exterminating profession had a little saying: "Give us a man, and we'll make a case." We had first heard it in Yalta in 1928 from Furmanov, the brother of the writer. A former official of the Cheka who had switched to film-making, he was still connected with the secret police through his wife, and knew what he was talking about. In the small boardinghouse where we were staying most of the people were TB patients, but Furmanov had come to restore his shattered nerves in the sea air. There was also a good-natured Nepman with a sense of humor who quickly got on friendly terms with Furmanov. Together they invented a game of "interrogation" which was so realistic that it gave them both quite a thrill. Furmanov, to illustrate the saying about it being possible to find a case against any man, "interrogated" the trembling Nepman, who always became entangled in the web of ingenious constructions that could be put on his every single word. At that time relatively few people had experienced at first hand the peculiarities of our legal system. The only ones who had so far really been through the mill were those belonging to the categories mentioned above, as well as people who had had their valuables confiscated, and Nepmen—that is, entrepreneurs who took the New Economic Policy* at its face value. That was why nobody, except for M., paid any attention to the cat-and-mouse game being enacted for their own amusement by the former Cheka interrogator and the Nepman. I wouldn't have noticed it either if M. hadn't told me to listen. I believe that M. was always intent on showing me things he wanted me to remember. Furmanov's game gave us a first glimpse of the legal process as it was while the new system was still only taking shape. The new justice was based on the dialectic and the great unchanging principle that "he who is not with us is against us."

Akhmatova, who had carefully watched events from the first, was

---

* The New Economic Policy (NEP) was launched by Lenin in 1921 to allow the country to recover after the Civil War. Limited private enterprise (including private publishing) was allowed. NEP ended in 1929.

wiser than I. Sitting together in the ransacked apartment, we went over all the possibilities in our minds and speculated about the future, but we put very little of it into words. "You must keep your strength up," Akhmatova said. By this she meant that I must prepare for a long wait: people were often held for many weeks or months, or even for more than a year, before they were banished or done away with. This was because of the length of time needed to "process" a case. Procedure meant a great deal to our rulers, and the whole farrago of nonsense was always meticulously committed to paper. Did they really think that posterity, going through these records, would believe them just as blindly as their crazed contemporaries? Or perhaps it was just the bureaucratic mind at work, the demon from the ink pot, feeding on legal formalities and consuming tons of paper in the process? If the formalities in question could be called "legal" . . .

For the family of an arrested man the period of waiting was taken up by routine steps (what M. in his "Fourth Prose" calls "imponderable, integral moves") such as obtaining money and standing in line with packages. (From the length of the lines we could see how things stood in our world: in 1934 they were still quite short.) I had to find the strength to tread the path already trodden by other wives. But on that May night I became aware of yet another task, the one for which I have lived ever since. There was nothing I could do to alter M.'s fate, but some of his manuscripts had survived and much more was preserved in my memory. Only I could save it all, and this was why I had to keep up my strength.

We were roused from our thoughts by the arrival of Lev. Because his mother was staying with us and we hadn't enough room for both, he had been put up for the night by the Ardovs. Knowing that M. was an early riser, he came almost at the crack of dawn to have early-morning tea with us, and we told him the news as he came in through the door.

He was still a boy, but so alive with ideas that wherever he appeared in those years he always caused a stir. People sensed the dynamic strength fermenting in him and knew that he was doomed. Now our house had been stricken by the plague and become a death trap for anyone prone to infection. For this reason I was overcome by horror at the sight of Lev. "Go away," I said, "go away at once. Osip was arrested last night." And he obediently went away. That was the rule among us.

4

THE SECOND ROUND

My brother Evgeni was still asleep when we rang to tell him the news. On the phone, of course, we used none of the taboo words like "arrested," "picked up" or "taken away." We had worked out a code of our own and we understood each other perfectly without having to spell anything out. Both he and Emma Gerstein quickly came over to the apartment. All four of us then left, one after the other at short intervals, each with a shopping basket in his hand or a wad of manuscripts in his pocket. In this way we managed to save part of M.'s papers. But on the prompting of some sixth sense, we did not remove everything. We even left the pile of stuff on the floor lying where it was. "Don't touch it," Akhmatova had said to me when I had opened the trunk to put back this eloquent heap of papers. I obeyed, not knowing why. It was simply that I trusted her instinct.

That same day, after Akhmatova and I had returned from running errands around the city, there was another knock at the door, but this time a rather delicate one. Once more I admitted an uninvited guest—it was the senior of the three police agents who had come the night before. He glanced with satisfaction at the pile of papers lying on the floor. "Ah, you still haven't tidied up," he said, and started on a second search. This time he worked by himself, and he was interested only in the trunk which contained the manuscripts of M.'s verse. He didn't even bother to look at the manuscripts of prose works.

Hearing about this second search, Evgeni, who was the most reserved and tight-lipped person in the world, frowned and said: "If they come once more, they'll take both of you with them."

What was the explanation of this second search and the removal of further papers? Akhmatova and I exchanged glances—always enough for Soviet citizens to understand each other. Clearly, the official in charge of the case had examined the manuscripts confiscated the night before (none of the poems was very long, and not much time had been needed to read them), but had not found what he was looking for. They had therefore sent this agent to have another look, fearing that some essential document might have been missed in the haste of the search. We could see from this that they wanted some one particular thing and would not rest content with verses such as the "Wolf" poem. But the thing they were looking for wasn't in the trunk—neither M. nor I had ever written it down on paper. This time I didn't offer to help, and Akhmatova and I just sat drinking tea, with an occasional sidelong glance at our visitor.

The agent had appeared exactly fifteen minutes after our arrival. In other words, he must have been informed about it. But who had tipped him off? It could have been a police spy living in the building, one of our neighbors who had been instructed to keep an eye on us, or a "tail" keeping watch in the street. We had not yet learned to identify these people—that was to come with later experience when we saw them all the time in front of Akhmatova's house: they stood there without the least pretense at disguise. Why were they so open about it? Was it just plain clumsiness, or was it their crude way of intimidating us? Perhaps there was an element of both. By their whole behavior they seemed to be saying: You have nowhere to hide, you are always under surveillance, we are always with you.... On more than one occasion, good acquaintances whom we had never suspected dropped a casual phrase to let us know who they were and why they had honored us with their friendship. Presumably this kind of openness was calculated to play its part in the whole system of conditioning: such innuendos, with all the vistas they opened up, had the effect of making us quite tongue-tied, and we retreated into our shells even more. Later on, in Tashkent, I was often advised, for example, not to go on carrying around with me the remnants of M.'s manuscripts, to forget the past, and not to try to get back to Moscow—"They approve of your living in Tashkent." There was never any point in asking *who* approved of it. The question would be met with a smile. Such hints and cryptic phrases spoken with a smile always produced a furious reaction in me: suppose it was all the idle talk of a despicable wretch who in fact knew nothing, but was just putting on the mannerisms of one close to the rulers of our destiny? There was no end of such people. But this was not all. In Tashkent, again, when I was living there with Akhmatova, we often returned home to find our ashtrays filled with someone's cigarette ends, a book, magazine or newspaper that had not been there before, and once I discovered a lipstick (of a revoltingly loud shade) on the dining table, together with a hand mirror that had been brought in from the next room. In the desk drawers and suitcases there were often traces of a search too conspicuous not to be noticed. Was this in accordance with the instructions given to those who rummaged in our things, or was it simply their idea of amusing themselves? Did they laugh out loud and say: "Let them have a good look"? Both explanations are possible. Why not give them a fright, they must have reasoned, so they don't get too complacent? However, they used this technique against Akhmatova more than against me.

As regards the "tails," I particularly remember one from the period after the war. The weather was very cold and he was trying to keep warm by stamping his feet and swinging his arms very energetically, as the cabbies used to. Several days running, Akhmatova and I went past this dancing "tail" every time we left the house. Then he was replaced by another one who was not quite so lively. Another time we were walking through the courtyard back to the apartment when a flashbulb suddenly went off behind us: they had evidently decided to take a photograph to find out who was visiting Akhmatova. To get into this courtyard one had to go through a lobby in the main building, and the door into it was guarded by a doorman. On this occasion we were held up at the entrance for rather a long time. The excuse was an idiotic one: the doorman had lost the key or something like that. Had the "photospy" begun to load his camera only when he was told we had returned? All this happened not long before the Decree on Akhmatova and Zoshchenko,* and these signs of a special interest in her made my flesh creep.

I did not myself receive this kind of attention and was almost never honored with my own individual "tail." I was generally surrounded not by regular agents, but only by common informers. Once, however, in Tashkent I was warned by Larisa Glazunov, whose father was a high official of the secret police, against one of the private pupils sent to me by a woman student in the Physics faculty. This one, the woman student had insisted, didn't want lessons from anyone except me. One day Larisa happened to run into her on my doorstep and told me that the girl worked for her father. I assured Larisa that this had been plain to me for some time already: the girl never came for her lesson at the agreed hour, but always at some odd time, evidently in the hope of catching me unawares, but ostensibly to ask whether she could postpone her lesson because she was so busy. Apart from this, she had the characteristic mannerisms of a minor agent: she could never refrain

---

* The Party decree of 1946—see the note on Zhdanov in the Appendix.

from watching me out of the corner of her eye as I moved about the room. It was not hard to guess why she wanted these lessons that she was always skipping. She soon stopped coming, and the student who had pressed her on me, a decent girl who had obviously got caught in the web, was clearly very upset and anxious to explain things to me. I managed to avoid this confrontation, but I will never forget how the girl sent to spy on me kept sighing and repeating: "I adore Akhmatova and your hubby"—the vulgar tone was typical of her milieu. All this relates to a much later stage; in 1934 we hadn't even heard the word "tail," and therefore we did not suspect who had informed the police agent about our return to the apartment.

5
SHOPPING BASKETS

While rummaging in our trunk and going through all the manuscripts for the second time, the agent did not even notice that Piast's poems were missing—it was this that might have alerted him to the fact that we, too, had removed a few things. Akhmatova's shrewdness in advising me not to tidy the room had paid off—if I had put all the papers back in the trunk, the agent might have got suspicious.

Piast's poems were very long, and it was these we had had to take away in shopping baskets. They were divided into chapters called "Fragments." M. liked them—perhaps because of the way in which Piast denounced the concept of the lawful wedded life. He referred to his own wife as his "wedded" one, and refused to live with her. When we settled for the first time in a normal apartment, tiny as it was, M. too was minded to rebel against the trammels of married life and began to praise Piast inordinately. Noting his enthusiasm, I asked: "And who is your 'wedded' one? Not I, surely?"

To think that we could have had an ordinary family life with its bickering, broken hearts and divorce suits! There are people in the world so crazy as not to realize that this is normal human existence of the kind everybody should aim at. What wouldn't we have given for such ordinary heartbreaks!

Piast had given me two of his poems to keep, after writing them out in long hand: typewriters were expensive and neither of us could afford one. He had given me the only fair copies and refused to believe me when I tried to convince him that he could hardly have chosen a worse place to keep them in. After his exile our apartment seemed to him the epitome of stability, security and calm, almost like a fortress. When he saw our night visitor pick up the "Fragments," M. sighed sadly, fearful of what might happen to Piast. It was at this point that "the strength came over me," as Akhmatova put it, to retrieve from the agent and thus virtually preserve for posterity Piast's curses on "wedded wives" and his paeans to the illicit beauties of the kind he preferred—for some reason, they were all as tall as guardsmen. He had brought the most recent of these female giants to our apartment to hear him recite his "Fragments." Is it possible that she kept a copy of the manuscript? Actually, I believe she was less interested in Piast than in the fees he was then extorting from the State Publishing House for a translation of Rabelais. I also remember Piast complaining at that time about his wayward stepdaughter; I am told that she is still living, though somewhere far away, and has fond memories of her rather eccentric stepfather. Perhaps she still has the poems that I rescued?

Just before M.'s arrest we had constant visits from the ordinary police because of Piast: he had given our address when he registered with them and got permission to spend a few days in Moscow to straighten out his literary affairs. His permit had expired and the police were now looking for him to make sure he left the city for the place he was allowed to live in. Luckily for him, he was not with us during the searches—as he would have been if he hadn't been frightened off by the visits from the ordinary police. If he had fallen into the hands of our agents, they would have hauled him off together with our manuscripts. He was lucky. Just as he was also lucky not to survive till the next wave of arrests and die in his bed or a hospital ward in Chukhloma or some other such place he was allowed to live in. Like the dramas of family life, this was normal and hence could be regarded as happiness. To understand this one had to go through a certain schooling.

As to M.'s manuscripts, we rescued a small number of drafts from various years. After this we never kept them in the apartment again. I took some of them out to Voronezh in small batches in order to establish the texts in final form and to compile lists of the unpublished items. I gradually got this done together with M. himself, who had now changed his attitude toward manuscripts and drafts. Previously he had no time at all for them and was always angry when, instead of destroying them, I threw them into the old yellow trunk that had belonged to my mother. But after the search of our apartment and his arrest, he understood that it was easier to save a manuscript than a man, and he no longer relied on his memory, which, as he knew, would perish with him. Some of these manuscripts have survived to the present day, but the bulk of them disappeared at the time of his two arrests. What do they do in the bowels of our Halls of Justice with all the papers which in the early days they took away in briefcases and then, later on, in sacks? But why speculate about the fate of papers when we don't know what happened to their owners? It is a miracle that a few witnesses and a handful of manuscripts have survived from those times.

6

"INTEGRAL MOVES"

There was no third search and we were not arrested. We therefore started the same routine as everybody when their relatives have been picked up. After running around the city all day, we came back exhausted and, instead of making a proper dinner, opened a can of corn. This went on for three days. On the fourth day my mother arrived from Kiev. She had vacated her apartment there, sold off the unwieldy family furniture, and come to spend the rest of her days with her daughter and son-in-law now that they had at last settled in a nice apartment of their own. Nobody met her at the station, and she was very angry and hurt. But when she learned what had happened, all her resentment vanished and she was once again the student radical of prerevolutionary days who knew exactly what to think about the Government and its police activities. Throwing up her hands, she gave us a piece of her mind on the theory and practice of Bolshevism, made a rapid survey of our household resources, and, declaring that even in her day the doctors attributed the high incidence of pellagra in Bessarabia to the excessive consumption of corn, took some money out of her purse and ran off to buy provisions. Now that we had someone to look after us, we pursued our routine with even greater energy.

I had gone to see Bukharin right at the outset. When he heard what had happened, he changed color and bombarded me with questions. I had not realized that he was capable of getting so upset. He paced rapidly up and down his huge office, occasionally stopping in front of me to ask another question. "Have you been to see him?" I had to explain to him that visits to relatives in prison were no longer allowed. Bukharin did not know this. Like all theorists, he was not good at drawing practical conclusions from his theory.

"He hasn't written anything rash, has he?" I said no—just a few poems in his usual manner, nothing worse than what Bukharin knew of already. It was a lie, and I still feel ashamed of it. But if I had told the truth, we should not have had our Voronezh "breathing-space." Should one lie? May one lie? Is it all right to lie in order to save someone? It is good to live in conditions where one doesn't have to lie. Do such conditions exist anywhere? We were brought up from childhood to believe that lies and hypocrisy are universal. I would certainly not have survived in our terrible times without lying. I have lied all my life: to my students, colleagues and even the good friends I didn't quite trust (this was true of most of them). In the same way, nobody trusted me. This was the normal lying of the times, something in the nature of a polite convention. I am not ashamed of this kind of lying and I misled Bukharin quite deliberately, out of a calculated desire not to frighten off my only ally. How could I have done otherwise?

Bukharin said that M. could not have been arrested for slapping Tolstoi in the face. I replied that people could be arrested for anything. What could be more convenient than Article 58 of the Criminal Code,* which was always applied to everything?

My account of Tolstoi's threats and the phrase "We'll teach him to strike Russian writers" had their effect. He almost groaned. Probably this man who had known the Czarist jails and believed in revolutionary terror as a matter of principle had at this moment a particularly keen premonition of what lay in store for himself.

I went to see Bukharin frequently during those days. His secretary, Korotkova, described by M. in his "Fourth Prose" as a "squirrel who chews a nut with every visitor," greeted me every time with an affectionate and frightened look and immediately went in to announce me. The door of the office was at once flung open and Bukharin ran out from behind his desk to meet me: "Anything new? Nor have I. Nobody knows anything."

These were our last meetings ever. On the way from Cherdyn to Voronezh I went to *Izvestia* to try and see him again. "What terrible telegrams you've been sending from Cherdyn," Korotkova said and

---

* The notorious article (covering "anti-Soviet propaganda" and "counter-revolutionary activity") under which all "political" prisoners were charged.

disappeared into his office. When she came out again, she was almost in tears. "Nikolai Ivanovich doesn't want to see you—because of some poem or other." I never saw him again. Later on he told Ehrenburg that Yagoda had recited the poem on Stalin by heart to him, and this so frightened him that he gave up his efforts. By then he had done everything in his power, and we had him to thank for getting a revision of M.'s sentence.

A visit to Bukharin took no more than an hour, but the general process of "going the rounds," trying to get people to intervene, meant running around the city the whole day long. The wives of arrested men (even after 1937 men far outnumbered women in the jails) all trod a well-beaten path to Peshkova in the "Political Red Cross." The only real point in going there was to talk and unburden oneself, thus creating an illusion of activity that was quite essential in these periods of anxious waiting. The "Red Cross" had no influence whatsoever. Very rarely it would forward a package to a prisoner in a labor camp or notify relatives of the result of a trial or a death sentence carried out. In 1939 this strange institution was abolished and the last link between the prisons and the outside world was thus cut. The very concept of assistance for political prisoners is, of course, quite incompatible with our system: one only has to think of the number of people who have been sent to forced labor and solitary confinement just because they were acquainted with others arrested before them. The closing down of the "Political Red Cross" was hence perfectly logical, but it meant that the relatives of prisoners now lived only on rumors, some of them deliberately put about to frighten us.

The "Red Cross" had been headed by Peshkova from the very beginning. However, I went not to her, but to her deputy, a brilliant man called Vinaver. His first question was: What was the rank of the senior police agent who had gone through the papers in our trunk? I now learned that the higher the rank of the senior agent during such searches, the more serious the case and the worse the fate in store for the victim. Since I had not known at the time about this form of divination, it had not occurred to me to note the stripes on the man's uniform. Vinaver further told me that material conditions "inside" were not at all bad—the cells were clean and the prisoners well fed: "The food is probably better than what we eat at home." I didn't have to explain to Vinaver that one would rather starve and be free, and that there was something unbearably ominous about this "civilized treatment" in prison. He knew and understood this just as well as I did. A little later he told me what to expect in the future, and he turned out to be right. He had enormous experience and knew how to draw the proper conclusions from it. I went to see him regularly and always kept him informed of developments. I didn't do this only to have the benefit of his advice, but rather from the need to maintain contact with one of the last people in those confused times to keep a sense of law and to fight stubbornly, if vainly, against the use of brute force.

Though he did, in fact, have some good advice for me as well. It was he who told me to persuade M. to take things as easily as possible, not asking for a transfer to another place, for example, or drawing attention to himself in any way—in other words, to keep mum and show no signs of life at all. "Don't sign any more pieces of paper. The best thing is to let them forget all about you." In his view, this was the only way to save oneself, or at least to keep alive a little longer. Vinaver could not follow his own advice because he was already far too exposed. He disappeared during the terror of 1937. There are rumors that he lived a double life and wasn't what he seemed to be. I do not believe this and never will. I hope his name will be cleared by posterity. I know that stories of this kind are put around by the secret police themselves to compromise people who have fallen foul of them. Even if there are documents in the archives that show him in a bad light, this would still not be proof that he betrayed his visitors to the police. Even if Peshkova was led to believe Vinaver had been attached to her as a police spy, that is no reason for us to believe it. It is easy enough to fabricate documents; people signed the most incredible statements under torture, and nothing would have been easier than to put alarming ideas about police spies and provocateurs into the head of an old woman like Peshkova. But how will the historians ever get at the truth if every minute grain of it is buried under huge layers of monstrous falsehoods? By this I mean not just the prejudices and misconceptions of any age, but deliberate and premeditated lies.

7

PUBLIC OPINION

Akhmatova also played her part in all these moves. She managed to get an interview with Yenukidze, who listened to her carefully but said not a word. Next she went to Seifullina, who at once rushed to the phone and rang a friend of hers in the secret police. His only comment was: "Let's hope they don't drive him out of his mind—our fellows are very good at it." The next day this "friend in the secret police" told Seifullina that he had made inquiries, and that it was better not to get involved in the case. When she asked why, he didn't reply. Seifullina was discouraged—as we always were, beating a hasty retreat when advised not to "get involved" in some case or other.

This is an extraordinary feature of our life: none of us ever submitted petitions and pleas, expressed our opinion about something or took any other action before finding out what people thought "at the top." Everybody was too conscious of his helplessness to try and assert himself. "I can never get anywhere with these things," Ehrenburg used to say in explanation of his refusal to help people over such matters as pensions, housing or residence permits. The trouble was that though he could ask for favors, he could never insist. Nothing could make things easier for the powers-that-be. Any initiative from below can be halted by the mere hint that it will meet with disapproval "at the top." Both the middle and the higher reaches of the bureaucracy turned this attitude to their advantage and declared certain questions "untouchable." From the second half of the twenties the "whisper of public opinion" became fainter and fainter until it ceased to be the prelude to action of any kind. All cases involving somebody's arrest were, needless to say, "off limits," and only relatives were supposed to try and do anything about them—that is, visit Peshkova and the office of the public prosecutor. It was quite exceptional for an outsider to involve himself in activity on behalf of a prisoner, and anybody who did deserves all due credit. Since M.'s poem had given cause for offense to the most awesome person in the land, there was very good reason to keep right out of the whole business. I was grateful to Pasternak, therefore, when he volunteered to help. He came to see me with Akhmatova and asked me whom he should approach. I suggested he see Bukharin, whose attitude to M.'s arrest I already knew, and Demian Bedny.

I had good reasons for suggesting Demian Bedny. Through Pasternak I was now able to remind him of a promise he had made in 1928. In that year M. had learned from a chance conversation in the street with his namesake Isaiah Mandelstam that five bank officials, specialists left over from the old regime, had been sentenced to death by shooting for embezzlement or negligence. Much to his friends' and his own surprise, and despite the rule against intervening in such matters, M. raised such a hue and cry all over Moscow that the five old men were spared. He mentions this episode in his "Fourth Prose." Among his "integral moves" was an approach to Demian Bedny. Their meeting took place somewhere in the backyard of the "International Bookstore," which, as a passionate book-lover, Demian was always visiting. He probably also used it to meet his friends—people living in the Kremlin no longer dared invite anybody there. Demian refused point blank to intervene on behalf of the old men. "Why should you worry about them?" he asked when he realized that they were neither relatives nor friends of M. But at the same time he promised that if anything ever happened to M. himself, he would come to his help without fail. For some reason M. was very gratified by this promise, though at that time we were firmly persuaded that "they'll neither touch nor kill us." When M. came down to join me at Yalta shortly afterward, he told me about this conversation with Demian. "It's really very good to know. He won't keep his word, you think? I think he will." This was why in 1934 I advised Pasternak to speak with Demian Bedny. Pasternak called him on the day after M.'s arrest, the day on which our trunk was examined for a second time, but Demian seemed to have got wind of the case already. "Neither you nor I can get involved in this," he said. Was it that he knew of the poem about Stalin, with whom he was already in trouble himself, or was he simply responding with the usual Soviet formula on the need to avoid those stricken by the plague? Whichever it was, Demian was in any case in disgrace himself. It was his passion for books that had got him into trouble: he had been unwise enough to note in his diary that he didn't like to lend books to Stalin because of the dirty marks left on the white pages by his greasy fingers. Demian's secretary had decided to curry favor by copying out this entry in Demian's diary and sending it to Stalin. Though the secretary apparently gained nothing by his treachery, Demian was reduced to dire straits for a long time and even had to sell off his library. By the time his works began to appear in print again, the fifteen years required under law before anyone can inherit had gone by, and I myself have seen his heir, a puny youth from his last marriage, going to Surkov and trying to beg a little money in his father's name. I also heard Surkov refuse outright—as though visiting a final insult on Demian through his offspring. What had he done to deserve this? Nobody ever worked so wholeheartedly for the Soviet regime. With me it was a different matter: I could scarcely be surprised if I was trampled on from time to time. What else could I expect?

In the middle of May 1934, Demian and Pasternak met at some gathering (probably in connection with the Union of Writers that was then being set up) and Demian offered to take Pasternak home in his car. If I remember rightly, he got rid of his driver and for a long time they drove around Moscow alone. At that time many of our big shots were not yet afraid of talking in automobiles, though later on there were rumors that they also had microphones planted in them. Demian told Pasternak that Russian poetry was being "shot dead" and mentioned Mayakovski as a case in point. In Demian's view, Mayakovski had died because he had trespassed on territory to which he was a stranger—the same political territory in which he (Demian) was so much at home.

When he had unburdened himself, Demian drove Pasternak not to his home, but to our apartment in Furmanov Street, where Akhmatova and I were sitting, distraught after the two searches.

At a congress of journalists taking place in Moscow just at that time, Baltrushaitis frantically made the rounds of the delegates and, invoking the memory of Gumilev, begged them to save M. from a similar fate. I can imagine how this combination of names sounded to the ears of our hard-bitten journalists of those years, but Baltrushaitis was a citizen of a foreign country and they could scarcely expect him to be impressed by the suggestion that it was better not to "get involved."

Baltrushaitis had long before had a presentiment of what M.'s end would be. At the very beginning of the twenties (in 1921, before the execution of Gumilev) he had urged M. to take out Lithuanian citizenship. This would have been quite feasible, since M.'s father had once lived in Lithuania and M. himself had been born in Warsaw. M. even went so far as to hunt out some papers and take them round to Baltrushaitis, but then he thought better of it: you can't escape your fate and better not to try.

The slight stir created by M.'s arrest evidently had some effect, since the whole affair did not develop according to the usual pattern. At least, that's what Akhmatova thought. And, indeed, even this muted reaction, this faint murmur, was in itself something quite out of the ordinary and a matter for astonishment. But if one had tried to interpret this whispering, it is not clear what one would have found. In my naïveté I had thought that public opinion always sided with the weak against the strong, with the oppressed against the oppressor, with the quarry against the hunter. My eyes were later opened by the more up-to-date Lida Bagritski. In 1938, when her friend Postupalski was arrested, she complained bitterly to me: "Things were different before. When Osip was arrested, for instance, some were against it, and others thought it was all right. And now look what's happening: they're arresting their own people!"

One must admire the way Lida put it. With Spartan bluntness she was simply defining the basic moral law of those who were supposed to constitute our intelligentsia and were, hence, presumably the foundation of public opinion. The distinction between "one of us" and "not one of us" (or "alien elements," to use the phrase then current) went back to the Civil War with its iron law of "Who whom?"* After victory and the surrender of the other side, the winners always claim rewards, decorations and privileges, while the defeated are subject to extermination. But it soon becomes evident that the right to count as "one of us" is neither hereditary nor even granted for life. The right to style oneself thus is a matter for constant struggle, and has been from the beginning. A person who was yesterday "one of us" can be degraded with lightning speed to the opposite status. What is more, by the very logic of this division, you become "not one of us" from the moment you lose your footing and start to slip downward. 1937 and all that followed were possible only in a society where this division has been taken to its logical conclusion.

The usual reaction to each new arrest was that some retreated even further into their shells (which, incidentally, never saved them) while others responded with a chorus of jeers for the victim. In the late forties my friend Sonia Vishnevski, hearing every day of new arrests among her friends, shouted in horror: "Treachery and counterrevolution everywhere!" This was how you were supposed to react if you lived in relative comfort and had something to lose. Perhaps there was also an element of primitive magic in such words: what else could we do but try to ward off the evil spirits by uttering charms?

---

* Lenin's famous phrase summarizing the issue between the Bolsheviks and their enemies.

8
INTERVIEW

Two weeks later a miracle happened, the first of several: the official interrogating M. rang me and suggested a meeting. A pass was issued to me with unprecedented speed. I went up the broad staircase of the Lubianka,* then along a corridor and stopped at the interrogator's door, as I had been instructed. Just as I got there something quite extraordinary happened: I saw a prisoner being led along the corridor. The guards had evidently not expected to run into an outsider in this inner sanctum. I saw that the man was a tall Chinese with wildly bulging eyes. I had no time to observe any more than his fear-crazed eyes and the fact that he had to hold up his trousers with his hands. Seeing me, the guards made a quick movement and they hustled the prisoner into a room. I just had time to get a glimpse of the faces of these members of the "inner" guard who were a very different type from those on the outside. It was a fleeting impression, but it left me with a feeling of horror and a strange chill running down my spine. Ever since I have always felt the same chill and a trembling sensation at the mere approach of such people, even before seeing the look on their faces: they follow you with their eyes, never moving their heads. Children can get this look from their parents—I have seen it in schoolboys and students. I know, of course, that it is a purely professional mannerism, but with us, like everything else, it has been taken to horrible extremes, as though everybody with this sleuth's look were a model pupil eagerly trying to show teacher how well he has learned his lesson.

I had only a momentary glimpse of the Chinese, but whenever I hear of people being shot, I see his eyes again. How was this meeting possible? According to all accounts, the most elaborate precautions are taken to prevent such mishaps. The corridors are supposedly divided into separate sections, and guards are alerted by a special system of signals if the way ahead is not "clear." But do we really know what goes on in these places? We lived on rumors and trembled. Trembling is a physiological response which has nothing in common with ordinary fear as such. But Akhmatova was angry when I once said this to her.

---

* Political prison and headquarters of the secret police in Moscow.

"What do you mean, it isn't fear? What is it, then?" She said it was not just a physical reflex, but a result of holy terror of the most ordinary and agonizing kind—she had suffered from it through all the years right up to Stalin's death.

Stories about various kinds of special technical equipment in the prisons—apart from the signaling system in the corridors—stopped only at the end of the thirties when methods of interrogation were simplified and became so comprehensible in their old-fashioned way that there was no more call for myths. "Everything is straightforward now," to quote Akhmatova again. "They stick a fur cap on your head and send you straight to the taiga."* Hence the line in "Poem Without a Hero":

> There, behind the barbed wire,
> In the very heart of the dense taiga
> They take my shadow for questioning.

I just don't know what section it was—the third or the fourth—to which I was summoned for this meeting, but if it was the one that dealt with literature, the interrogator certainly had a name hallowed in Russian literary tradition: Christophorovich.† Why didn't he change it, if he worked in the literary section? Perhaps the coincidence appealed to his fancy. M. was always very angered if one even pointed such things out: he was very much against the frivolous mention of anything connected with Pushkin. Once, when I was ill, we had to spend two years in Tsarskoye Selo and we actually took one of the apartments in the old Lycée,‡ which were quite good and comparatively cheap. But M. was terribly upset by what for him was almost sacrilege, and at the first pretext he insisted we clear out and revert to our usual homeless existence. So I was never able to summon up the courage to discuss the name of his interrogator.

---

* Taiga: virgin forest.
† Christophorovich was the patronymic (middle name) of the notorious Chief of Police and head of the Third Section under Nicholas I, Count Alexander Christophorovich Benkendorff (1783–1844). Benkendorff was responsible for the official persecution of Pushkin and Lermontov.
‡ Famous school for the sons of the aristocracy created by Alexander I at Tsarskoye Selo ("Czar's Village"), the Imperial summer residence near St. Petersburg.

Our meeting took place in the presence of Christophorovich—I have to refer to him by this taboo patronymic because I have forgotten his last name. He was a large man with the staccato, overemphatic diction of an actor of the Maly Theater school, and he kept butting into our conversation, not to tell us things in a normal way, but to read us pompous little lectures. To all his sententiousness there was an ominous and threatening undertone. The effect on me as a person from the outside was to arouse disgust rather than fear. But two weeks without sleep in a cell and under interrogation would have radically changed my attitude.

When M. was brought in I at once saw that he was as wild-eyed as the Chinese, and that his trousers were slipping down in the same way. This is a precaution against suicide—belts and suspenders are taken away and all fasteners are removed.

Despite his distraught appearance, M. immediately noticed I was wearing someone else's raincoat. He asked whose it was, and I told him: Mother's. When had she arrived? I told him the day. "So you've been at home all the time?" At first I didn't understand why he was so interested in this wretched raincoat, but now I saw the reason: he had been told that I was under arrest too. This is a standard device used to break the prisoner's spirit. When prisons and interrogations are as shrouded in mystery as in this country and there is no possibility of public control over them, such techniques work without fail.

I demanded an explanation from the interrogator, but the futility of demanding anything in such a place is self-evident. One could only do it out of naïveté or extreme anger. In my case it was both. But of course I got no answer.

Thinking we should not meet again for a long time, if ever, M. hastened to tell me the things he wanted me to convey to the outside world. We are all exceedingly well "prison-trained"—whether or not we have actually been in jail—and we know how to seize "the last chance of being heard"—a need which in his "Conversation About Dante" M. attributed to Ugolino. To us it comes naturally, and you are bound to bring it to a fine art if you have to live our sort of life. I have several times had this "last chance of being heard" and tried to take advantage of it, but it so happened that the people I was talking to didn't catch the implication of my words and failed to register what I was trying to convey. They evidently thought that our acquaintance, only just begun, would go on forever and that there would be plenty of time to learn, gradually and at leisure, everything they wanted to know. This was a fateful mistake from their point of view, and my efforts to communicate went for nothing. During our meeting M. was in a better position—I was very well prepared to take in his meaning. Nothing had to be elaborated and not a word was wasted.

M. managed to tell me that his interrogator had the text of his poem about Stalin and that it was the first draft with the word "peasant-slayer" in the fourth line: "All we hear is the Kremlin mountaineer, the murderer and peasant-slayer." This was a very important clue to the identity of the person who had denounced M. to the police. Next, M. was eager to tell me how the interrogation was being conducted, but Christophorovich constantly interrupted him and tried to take advantage of the occasion to intimidate me as well. By listening carefully to the heated words passing between the two, I tried to glean every scrap of information that would be of interest to people outside.

The interrogator described M.'s poem as a "counter-revolutionary document without precedent," and referred to me as an accessory after the fact. "How should a real Soviet citizen have acted in your place?" he asked. It appeared that in my place any real Soviet person would immediately have informed the police, for otherwise he made himself liable to be charged with a criminal offense. Almost every third word uttered by the interrogator was "crime" or "punishment." I discovered that I had not in fact been charged only because they had decided "not to proceed with the case." Then, for the first time, I heard the phrase "isolate but preserve": such was the order that had come down to him, the interrogator implied, as a supreme act of clemency from the very highest level. The sentence originally suggested—that M. should be sent to a forced-labor camp on the White Sea Canal*—had been commuted, by this same supreme authority, to exile in the town of Cherdyn. Christophorovich added that I could accompany M. if I wished. This was a further unprecedented act of clemency, and I naturally agreed at once. But I am still curious about what might have happened if I had refused.

What a rush there would have been if—say, in 1937—all who wanted had been told they could go into voluntary exile with their families, children, belongings and books! All would have flocked to wait in line—wives side by side with their husbands' lovers, daughters with their stepmothers.

---

* A showpiece built by forced labor in the 1930's.

But maybe not. People only keep going because they don't know their future and hope to avoid the fate of others. As their neighbors perish one after the other, the survivors take hope from the famous question "What were they arrested for?" and discuss all their indiscretions and mistakes. It is the women, as the real mainstays of the household, who are always the most frantic in their efforts to keep the small flame of hope from going out. In 1937 Lilia Yakhontov, for instance, said after a visit to the Lubianka: "I shall always feel safe as long as that building stands." Her pious expression of devotion may even have delayed her husband's end for a few years—he later threw himself out of a window in a fit of wild fear that he was about to be arrested. And in 1953 a Jewish woman biologist, a true believer, tried to convince another Jewish woman (who had come from the West and was therefore completely shaken by what was going on) that nothing would happen to her "if you have committed no crime and your conscience is clear." Then there was the woman I met in a train in 1957 who explained to me that one must be very careful about rehabilitated persons, since they were being released on humanitarian grounds, not because they were innocent: "Say what you like, there's no smoke without fire." Casuality and expediency are the basic articles of faith in our ready-made philosophy.

9

THEORY AND PRACTICE

The gist of what I had learned by the time I went home from the meeting was that the interrogator had charged M. with the authorship of the poem on Stalin, and that M. had admitted it, together with the fact that about ten people in his immediate circle had heard him recite the poem. I was angry that he had not denied everything, as a good conspirator might have done. But it was impossible to think of M. in such a role: he was too straightforward to be capable of any kind of guile. He was utterly without deviousness. Besides, I am told by people of experience that in our conditions it is essential to admit to some basic minimum, otherwise such "persuasion" is applied that the prisoner, at the end of his tether, will incriminate himself in the most fantastic way.

In any case, how on earth could we be expected to behave like good conspirators? A political activist, a revolutionary or a member of an underground organization is always a person of a special outlook. But although that kind of activity was just not for us, we were constantly forced by the circumstances of our life to behave like members of a secret society. When we met we spoke in whispers, glancing at the walls for fear of eavesdropping neighbors or hidden microphones. When I returned to Moscow after the war, I found that everybody covered their telephones with cushions, because it was rumored that they were equipped with recording devices, and the most ordinary householders trembled with terror in the presence of the black metal object listening in on their innermost thoughts. Nobody trusted anyone else, and every acquaintance was a suspected police informer. It sometimes seemed as though the whole country was suffering from persecution mania, and we still haven't recovered from it.

I must say that we had every reason to be afflicted in this way: we all felt as if we were constantly exposed to X-rays, and the principal means of control over us was mutual surveillance. "There is nothing to fear," Stalin had said, "one must get on with the job." So the employees of all Soviet institutions duly took their offerings to their superior, to the secretary of the Party cell or to the personnel department. In the schools a system of "self-government" in the classroom, with monitors and Komsomol representatives, made it very easy for the teachers to get everything they needed out of their pupils. Students were instructed to spy on their professors. The penetration of the world at large by the secret police was organized on a grand scale. In any institution, particularly in the universities and colleges, there is always a large number of people whose careers have begun in the security service. They are so superbly trained that they have no difficulty getting promotion in any field of activity. When they are given "study leave," they receive all kinds of incentives and are often allowed to stay on and do graduate work. Another link with the secret police is maintained through informers who are even more dangerous because, merging with the rest, they are indistinguishable from their colleagues. To advance themselves, they are quite capable of framing people—something the professionals rarely do. This was part of our everyday life, a dreary routine relieved only by a neighbor telling you at dead of night how "they" had summoned him to bully him into working for them, or by friends warning you which other friends to beware of. All this happened on a vast scale and affected everybody indiscriminately. Every family was always going over its circle of acquaintances, trying to pick out the provocateurs, the informers and the traitors. After 1937 people stopped meeting each other altogether, and the secret police were thus well on the way to achieving their ultimate objective. Apart from assuring a constant flow of information, they had isolated people from each other and had drawn large numbers of them into their web, calling them in from time to time, harassing them and swearing them to secrecy by means of signed statements. All such people lived in eternal fear of being found out and were consequently just as interested as regular members of the police in the stability of the existing order and the inviolability of the archives where their names were on file.

This system of mass surveillance came into being only gradually, but M. was one of the first to be singled out for individual treatment. His status in Soviet literature was defined as early as 1923, when his name was crossed off the list of people allowed to work for the various magazines, and from then on he was always surrounded by swarms of agents. We learned to distinguish several varieties of the breed. The most easily identifiable were the brisk young men of military bearing who, without bothering to feign interest in the author, immediately asked him for his "latest work." M. generally tried to get rid of them by saying he had no spare copy. They would thereupon offer to type it out for him and return it "with a copy for yourself." With one such visitor M. argued for a long time, refusing to let him have "The Wolf"—this was in 1932. The young man insisted, saying that it was in any case widely known. Failing to get it, he came back the next day and recited the poem by heart. After giving this proof of how "well known" it was, he got the author's copy he needed. Agents of this kind completely disappeared from the scene as soon as they had done their job. The good thing about them was that they were always in a hurry and never tried to "make friends." It was evidently not part of their assignment to spy on the other people who came to see us.

The second type of agent was the "admirer"—generally a member of the same profession, a colleague or a neighbor. In apartment buildings housing members of the same institution, one's neighbors are always colleagues too. People like this would appear without calling beforehand, just dropping in out of the blue. They would stay for a long time, talking shop and attempting minor provocations. Whenever we were visited by one of these, M. always asked me to serve tea: "The man is working, he needs a cup of tea." To ingratiate themselves, they tried all kinds of little tricks. S., for instance, first came to us with tales about the East—he said that he was himself originally from Central Asia and had studied in a madrasah there. As proof of his "Eastern" credentials he brought along a small statuette of the Buddha, which could have been bought in any junk store. It was supposed to bear witness to his expert knowledge of the East and his serious interest in art. The connection between the Buddha and an Islamic madrasah never became clear to us. S. soon lost patience with us and, after making a scene, left us to be taken care of by someone else—or so it appeared, to judge from the equally sudden appearance of another neighbor who also tried to cultivate our acquaintance by bringing us a Buddha! This time it was M. who lost his temper: "Another Buddha! That's enough! They must think of something new!" and he threw out the hapless replacement, without even giving him tea.

The third and most dangerous kind of agents we called "adjutants." These were young devotees of literature, sometimes doing graduate work at the university, who were extremely keen on poetry and knew everything there was to know about it. When they first came they often had the purest intentions, but then they were recruited. Some of them openly admitted to M.—as they did to Akhmatova as well—that they were "called in to report." After making this kind of admission they generally disappeared from the scene. Others also suddenly stopped coming to see us, without any explanation. In some cases I found out many years later what had happened—namely, that they had been "summoned" by the police. This was the explanation in the case of L., for example, whom Akhmatova told me about. Not daring to approach her in Leningrad, he had managed to see her during one of her visits to Moscow, and he said to her: "You cannot imagine how closely they watch you." It was always painful when somebody one had become friendly with mysteriously broke off relations, but this, alas, was the only thing that honorable people could do if they refused to play the role of an "adjutant." "Adjutants" had to serve two gods at once. With all their love of poetry, they were mindful of their own careers as writers or poets, of the need to get into print and find their feet. It was this side of them that the police generally played on. To be on close or friendly terms with Mandelstam or Akhmatova, or to have any kind of truck with them, opened no doors in the world of literature, but an "adjutant" only had to submit a candid report on an evening's conversation (of the most innocent kind, needless to say) at our apartment and they would help him to get into the coveted pages of the literary magazines. There was always a crucial point at which the young devotee of literature would break down and agree to embark on a double life.

Finally, there were some real lovers of evil who had a taste for their dual role. Some of them were quite famous: Elsberg, for example, who was undoubtedly an outstanding figure in his field. He was active in different circles than the ones we moved in, and I only know about him from what others have told me, but I was struck by the refinement of the man's methods when I happened to see an article of his entitled "The Moral Experience of the Soviet Era." It appeared at a moment when there was a possibility of his being publicly exposed, and by writing an article under this title he was, as it were, suggesting to his readers that, as an authority on the moral standards of our age, he could scarcely be in any jeopardy. In fact there were some revelations about him, but only some time later, and even so it proved impossible to apply such a mild sanction as expulsion from the Union of Soviet Writers. He lost nothing at all, not even the devotion of his research students. It was typical of Elsberg that, after getting his friend S. sent to a concentration camp, he continued to visit S.'s wife and gave her advice. She knew about his role, but was frightened of betraying her disgust: to expose informers was not done, and you paid a very high price for doing so. When S. returned after the Twentieth Congress, Elsberg met him with flowers, shaking his hand and congratulating him.

We lived among people who vanished into exile, labor camps or the other world, and also among those who sent them there. It was dangerous to have any contact with people who still tried to go on working and thinking in their own way; for this reason Alisa Gugovna Usov was quite right not to let her husband visit M. "You can't go there," she would say, "they see all kinds of riffraff." She reasoned that it was wiser not to run the risk: who knew what sort of people you might antagonize in the heat of a literary argument? This caution, however, did not save Usov: he went to a labor camp with his fellow linguists as a result of the "dictionary case." All roads led there. The old Russian proverb that prison or the poorhouse waits for every man has never been more true, and the verb "to write" took on an additional meaning in the Russian language. The old scholar Zhirmunski once said to me about a group of his best graduate students: "They all write"—i.e., reports for the secret police—and Shklovski told us we should be careful with his little dog because it had learned to "write" from the bright young "adjutants" who came to see him. . . . When Alisa Usov and I later taught at Tashkent University, there was no point in trying to pick out informers, because we knew that everybody "wrote." And we tried to become adept in Aesopian language. At parties with graduate students we always raised our glasses first "for those who have given us such a happy life," and both the initiated and the students understood us in the required sense.

It was quite natural for the "adjutants" and all the rest of them to "write," but the odd thing was how we were still able to joke and laugh. In 1938 M. even declared he had invented a device for the suppression of jokes as a dangerous thing: he would move his lips silently and point at his throat to indicate the position of the cut-off device. But the "device" didn't help and M. couldn't stop telling jokes.

10

LEAVING FOR EXILE

As soon as I came home, the apartment began to fill with people. Men would not come near our plague-stricken house, but sent their wives instead—women were less exposed. Even in 1937 most women were arrested because of their husbands, not on their own account. No wonder, then, that men were more cautious than women. On the other hand, even the most prudent men were surpassed by their wives when it came to "patriotism." I quite understood why no husbands had come, but I was astonished to see so many wives: persons sentenced to exile were usually shunned by all. Akhmatova gasped: "What a lot of them!"

I packed our baskets—the same ones which had so irritated the staff at CEKUBU,* as M. tells in his "Fourth Prose"—or, rather, threw everything into them at random: saucepans, linen, books. M. had taken his Dante to prison with him, but didn't insist on keeping it when they told him that once a book had been taken to the cells, it could not be allowed out again and had to be left in the prison library. Not yet knowing the conditions in which a book becomes an eternal hostage, I threw in another edition of Dante. I had to think of everything—going

---

* Acronym for "Commission for the Improvement of the Living Conditions of Scholars," created in 1921. See the note on Gorki in the Appendix.

into exile was not like setting off on an ordinary journey with a couple of suitcases. This I had every reason to know, having spent all my life moving from place to place with my wretched belongings.

My mother gave me all the money realized from the sale of her furniture in Kiev. But it was very little, a wad of worthless paper. Our women visitors went off in all directions to raise money for us. This was in the seventeenth year after the creation of our system. Seventeen years of persistent indoctrination had been to no avail. These people who collected money for us, as well as those who gave it, were breaking the rule that governed relations with victims of the regime. In periods of violence and terror people retreat into themselves and hide their feelings, but their feelings are ineradicable and cannot be destroyed by any amount of indoctrination. Even if they are wiped out in one generation, as happened here to a considerable extent, they will burst forth again in the next one. We have seen this several times. The idea of good seems really to be inborn, and those who sin against the laws of humanity always see their error in the end—or their children do.

Akhmatova went to the Bulgakovs and returned very touched by the reaction of Elena Sergeyevna, Bulgakov's wife, who burst into tears when she heard about our exile and gave us everything she had. Sima Narbut ran around to see Babel, but did not come back. But all the others kept arriving with contributions and there was soon a sum so large that it lasted us for the journey to Cherdyn and the first two months of our life in Voronezh. Admittedly, we didn't have to pay for our tickets (except for a small supplement on the return journey)—this is the one convenience of being an exile. In the train M. noticed what a lot of money I had, and asked where I had got it. When I explained, he laughed: what a roundabout way of getting the means to travel. All his life he had been eager to travel, but never could because of lack of money. The sum we had now was enormous for those days. People like us had never at any time been rich, but before the war nobody in our circle could even say that he was comparatively well-off. Everybody lived from hand to mouth. Some of the "Fellow Travelers"* started doing quite well as early as 1937, but this was only by comparison with the rest of the population, which could barely make ends meet.

At the end of the day Dligach came with Dina, and I asked him whether he could lend me some money. He went off to get some and

* See page 427.

left Dina with us. I never saw him again—he vanished for good. I didn't expect him to lend me money, I just wanted to see whether he would disappear like this. We had always suspected that he was an "adjutant," and, as such, it would have been natural for him to clear off when he heard I had been to see M.—for fear that I might have learned about his role. This is indeed what it looked like, but it is still not final proof. He might simply have taken fright—this cannot be ruled out.

I was seen off to the station by Akhmatova, M.'s brother Alexander and my own brother, Evgeni Khazin. On the way there I stopped at the Lubianka, as had been agreed with the interrogator, by the same entrance I had used that morning to come to the meeting with M. The officer on duty let me in and a moment later the interrogator came down the staircase with M.'s suitcase in his hands. "You're off?" he said. "Yes," I replied and forgetting who he was, automatically held out my hand as I said goodbye. We were not, I repeat, revolutionaries, underground plotters or politically minded people at all. But we suddenly found ourselves having to act as though we were, and I had now nearly sinned against time-honored tradition by shaking hands with a member of the secret police. But the interrogator saved me from disgrace by not responding—he did not shake hands with people like me—that is, with his potential victims. It was a good lesson for me—my first political lesson in the spirit of the old revolutionaries: never shake hands with a policeman. I was very ashamed that I had to learn it from a police interrogator. Since then I have never forgotten it.

We went into the station building, and I was about to go to the ticket office when I was intercepted by a short, fair-haired man in a baggy civilian suit—it was the agent who had searched our trunk and thrown the papers in a pile on the floor. He handed me a ticket, but didn't take my money. Some porters—not the ones we had hired, but some new ones—picked up my baggage. They told me I needn't worry and that everything would be taken right through to the train. I noticed that the first ones didn't come up to beg for tips, but just vanished.

We had to wait for a long time, and Akhmatova was forced to leave me, because her train to Leningrad was already due to depart. At last the fair-haired man reappeared, and, relieved of all the usual burdens and worries of getting on a train, we went through to the platform. The train drew in and I caught a glimpse of M.'s face through the window. I showed my ticket to a conductress, who asked me to go right to the end of the train. My brother and brother-in-law were not admitted.

M. was already in his compartment and there were three soldiers with him. With our guards we occupied all six berths, including the two on the side. The stage manager of our departure, the fair-haired agent, had arranged everything so perfectly that he seemed to be showing off the marvels of a Soviet Thousand and One Nights.

M. pressed up against the window. "It's a miracle!" he said, glued to the pane. Our two brothers were standing on the platform. M. tried to open the window, but a guard stopped him: "It's against the rules." The fair-haired man came back once more to check that everything was all right and gave final instructions to the conductress: the door into this compartment from the rest of the coach was to be kept locked during the whole journey, and only the toilet at our end could be used. At stopping points only one of the guards was allowed to leave the coach; the other two were to stay with us all the time. Wishing us a good journey, the fair-haired man left us, but I saw him standing on the platform until the train started to leave. He was obeying his instructions to the letter, no doubt.

The coach gradually filled with other passengers. The door to our compartment was guarded by a soldier who turned back passengers eager to find places—the rest of the coach was crammed. M. stayed by the window, desperate for contact with the two men on the other side, but no sound could penetrate the glass. Our ears were powerless to hear, and the meaning of their gestures hard to interpret. A barrier had been raised between us and the world outside. It was still a transparent one, made of glass, but it was already impenetrable. The train started for Sverdlovsk.

11

On the Other Side

At the moment when I entered the coach and saw our brothers through the glass, my world split into two halves. Everything that had previously existed now vanished to become a dim memory, something beyond the looking-glass, and the future opening up before me no longer meshed with the past. I am not trying to be literary—this is just a modest attempt to put into words the mental dislocation that is probably felt by all the many people who cross this fateful line. Its first result was utter indifference to what we had left behind—an indifference due to our knowledge that we had all set out on a path of inescapable doom. One of us might be granted a week's grace or even a year, but the end would be the same. It would be the end of everything—friends, relatives, my mother, Europe. . . . I say "Europe" advisedly, because in the "new" state I had entered there was nothing of the European complex of thought, feelings and ideas by which I had lived hitherto. We were now in a world of different concepts, different ways of measuring and reckoning. . . .

Until a short time before, I had been full of concern for all my friends and relatives, for my work, for everything I set store by. Now this concern was gone—and fear, too. Instead there was an acute sense of being doomed—it was this that gave rise to an indifference so overwhelming as to be almost physical, like a heavy weight pressing down on the shoulders. I also felt that time, as such, had come to an end—there was only an interlude before the inescapable swallowed us with our "Europe" and our handful of last thoughts and feelings.

How would it come, the inescapable? Where, and in what form? It really didn't matter. Resistance was useless. Having entered a realm of non-being, I had lost the sense of death. In the face of doom, even fear disappears. Fear is a gleam of hope, the will to live, self-assertion. It is a deeply European feeling, nurtured on self-respect, the sense of one's own worth, rights, needs and desires. A man clings to what is his, and fears to lose it. Fear and hope are bound up with each other. Losing hope, we lose fear as well—there is nothing to be afraid for.

When a bull is being led to the slaughter, it still hopes to break loose and trample its butchers. Other bulls have not been able to pass on the knowledge that this never happens and that from the slaughterhouse there is no way back to the herd. But in human society there is a continuous exchange of experience. I have never heard of a man who broke away and fled while being led to his execution. It is even thought to be a special form of courage if a man about to be executed refuses to be blindfolded and dies with his eyes open. But I would rather have the bull with his blind rage, the stubborn beast who doesn't weigh his chances of survival with the prudent dull-wittedness of man, and doesn't know the despicable feeling of despair.

Later I often wondered whether it is right to scream when you are being beaten and trampled underfoot. Isn't it better to face one's tormentors in a stance of satanic pride, answering them with contemptuous silence? I decided that it is better to scream. This pitiful sound, which sometimes, goodness knows how, reaches into the remotest prison cell, is a concentrated expression of the last vestige of human dignity. It is a man's way of leaving a trace, of telling people how he lived and died. By his screams he asserts his right to live, sends a message to the outside world demanding help and calling for resistance. If nothing else is left, one must scream. Silence is the real crime against humanity.

That evening, guarded by three soldiers in the coach to which I had been taken in such comfort, I had lost everything, even despair. There is a moment of truth when you are overcome by sheer astonishment: "So that's where I'm living, and the sort of people I'm living with! So this is what they're capable of! So this is the world I live in!" We are so stupefied that we even lose the power to scream. It was this sort of stupefaction, with the consequent loss of all criteria, standards and values, that came over people when they first landed in prison and suddenly realized the nature of the world they lived in and what the "new era" really meant. Physical torture and fear are not enough to explain the way people broke down and confessed, destroying others in the process. All this was only possible at the "moment of truth," during the madness which afflicted people when it looked as though time had stopped, the world had come to an end and everything was lost for ever. The collapse of all familiar notions is, after all, the end of the world.

But what was so terrible about moving to a small town on the Kama, where, it seemed, we should have to live for three years? Was Cherdyn any worse than Maly Yaroslavets, Strunino, Kalinin, Muinak, Dzhambul, Tashkent, Ulianovsk, Chita, Cheboksary, Vereya, Tarusa or Pskov, in all of which I was cast up in the homeless years after M.'s death? Was this a reason for going out of one's mind and expecting the end of the world?

Yes, I think so. Now that I have regained my sense of despair and am capable once more of screaming, I can say this quite emphatically. And I think that the superb way in which our departure was organized, with the stop at the Lubianka for M.'s suitcase, the porters who didn't have to be paid, and the polite fair-haired escort in civilian clothes who saluted as he wished us a happy journey—nobody had ever gone into exile like this before—was more terrible and sickening, and spoke more eloquently of the end of the world, than the plank beds in the forced-labor camps, the prisons and shackles, and the brutal cursing of policemen, torturers and killers. It was all done with the greatest style and efficiency, without a single harsh word. And there we were, the two of us, guarded by three well-briefed peasant youths, sent off by an unseen and irresistible force to some place in the east, and forced to live in exile, where, as they had seen fit to tell me, M. was to be "preserved." This I had been told in that large, clean office where, at that very moment perhaps, they were now interrogating the Chinese.

12

THE IRRATIONAL

Our encounter with the irrational forces that so inescapably and horrifyingly ruled over us radically affected our minds. Many of us had accepted the inevitability—and some the expediency—of what was going on around us. All of us were seized by the feeling that there was no turning back—a feeling dictated by our experience of the past, our forebodings about the future and our hypnotic trance in the present. I maintain that all of us—particularly if we lived in the cities—were in a state close to a hypnotic trance. We had really been persuaded that we had entered a new era, and that we had no choice but to submit to historical inevitability, which in any case was only another name for the dreams of all those who had ever fought for human happiness. Propaganda for historical determinism had deprived us of our will and the power to make our own judgments. We laughed in the faces of the doubters, and ourselves furthered the work of the daily press by repeating its sacramental phrases, by spreading rumors about each new round of arrests ("that's what passive resistance leads to!") and finding excuses for the existing state of affairs. The usual line was to denounce history as such: it had always been the same, mankind had never known anything but violence and tyranny. "People are shot everywhere," the young physicist L. once said to me. "More so here, you think? Well, that's progress." "But look, Nadia," L.E. used to argue with me, "things are just as bad abroad."

In the middle of the twenties, when the atmospheric pressure began to weigh more heavily on us—at critical periods it was heavier than lead—people all at once started to avoid each other. This could not be explained only by fear of informers and denunciation—we had not yet had time to get really scared of these. It was rather the onset of a kind of numbness, the first symptoms of lethargy. What was there to talk about when everything had already been said, explained, signed and sealed? Only children continued to babble their completely human nonsense, and the grown-ups—everybody from bookkeepers to writers—preferred their company to that of their peers. But mothers prepared their children for life by teaching them the sacred language of their seniors. "My children love Stalin most of all, and me only second," Pasternak's wife, Zinaida Nikolayevna, used to say. Others did not go so far, but nobody confided their doubts to their children: why condemn them to death? And then suppose the child talked in school and brought disaster to the whole family? And why tell it things it didn't need to know? Better it should live like everybody else.... So the children grew, swelling the ranks of the hypnotized. "The Russian people is sick," Polia X. once said to me, "it needs to be treated." The sickness has become particularly obvious now that the crisis has passed and we can see the first signs of recovery. It used to be people with doubts who were considered ill.

Mikhail Alexandrovich Zenkevich was one of the first to sink into a hypnotic trance or lethargy. This did not prevent him from going to work, earning money and bringing up his children. Perhaps it even helped him to stay alive and look so utterly normal and healthy. But on a closer look it was clear that he had passed the point of no return: he could not smash the looking-glass. Zenkevich lived in the knowledge that everything he had once lived by was irretrievably lost, gone for good, left on the other side of the glass. It was a feeling that could have been transmuted into poetry, but Zenkevich, the sixth Acmeist,* had firmly decided that there could be no such thing as poetry without the Poets' Guild and all the talk which had so captivated him as a very young man. He now wandered about the ruins of his Rome, trying to persuade himself and others that it was essential to surrender not only one's body, but one's mind as well. "Don't you understand," he said to M., "that it's all finished, that everything's different now?" . . . This argument applied to everything: poetry, honor, ethics, the latest political conjuring trick or act of violence, the show trials, purges, or deportation of the kulaks.... It was all justified because "everything's different now." . . . Sometimes, however, he excused himself by saying that he

* See page 426.

had swallowed so much bromide that his memory had gone. . . . But in fact he had forgotten nothing and was touchingly devoted to M., even though he expressed astonishment at M.'s obstinacy and mad persistence in holding to his own. All that Zenkevich wanted to take with him from the past into his new "life after death" were a few original manuscripts. Begging M. to give him one of his rough drafts, he said: "Gumilev has gone, and I haven't a single page of anything written by him!" This angered M. and he wouldn't give him anything—"He's already preparing for my death!"

At the beginning of the fifties—a ghastly time!—I met Zenkevich in the courtyard of Herzen House,* and though this was the first time I had seen him in fifteen years, he at once started his usual talk about manuscripts: "Where are Osip's papers? I never got anything from him and I haven't a single line in his hand. Maybe you could let me have something?" Remembering that M. could not stand this cadging of his, I gave him nothing, but he managed to get what he wanted all the same. He had kept from the past not books or living verse, but only scraps of paper with a few lines written in their own hand by old comrades who had perished—documentary evidence, as it were, of a literary life that had once been. "And poetry too isn't what it was, you know," he complained.

Zenkevich was one of the first to go to the White Sea Canal and carry out orders by writing a piece of doggerel in praise of the "transformers of Nature." For this M. conferred on him the title Zenkevich-Canalski—just as the great explorer Semionov had once been styled Semionov-Tianshanski, after his discovery of the Tian Shan mountain range. In 1937 Lakhuti arranged for M. to go to the Canal under the auspices of the Union of Soviet Writers. The well-meaning Persian had hoped that M. would write something about it and thus save his life. When he came back M. neatly wrote down a few glib lines and said, showing them to me, "Shall we present them to Zenkevich?" M. went to his death, but these lines have survived, their purpose unfulfilled. Later on, in Tashkent, I once happened to come across them and I asked Akhmatova what I should do with them: "Should I throw them in the fire?" This was in a balakhana† where we were both living as evacuees. "Nadia," Akhmatova replied, "Osip gave you the right to do

---

* A center for writers and journalists set up in Moscow in 1920.
† A kind of mezzanine in houses in Central Asia.

what you wish with absolutely all his papers." This was totally disingenuous: we were all against falsification, the destruction of manuscripts or any other kind of tampering with anyone's literary remains, and it was not easy for Akhmatova to give her blessing to my suggestion. But now, quite unexpectedly, she had given me in M.'s name a right that M. himself had never given me: to destroy or keep what I saw fit. She did this so that we could get rid of the Canal poem, and without more ado it was at once reduced to a little pile of ash.

If anybody happens to have kept a stray copy of this poem, I beg and pray him, by virtue of the right that Akhmatova and I bestowed upon ourselves, to set aside his love of original manuscripts and throw it in the fire. A poem like this could be of use only to the Union of Soviet Writers as something to be shown to any foreigners who might be curious enough to make inquiries: "Mandelstam's literary remains? Look at this: what's the point of publishing this?" They have no compunction, after all, about falsifying details of a person's life or the date of his death. Who started the rumor that M. was killed by the Germans in Voronezh? Who has postdated the deaths of all who perished in the camps to the beginning of the forties? Who publishes the works of poets, both living and dead, deliberately omitting the best of what they wrote? Who holds up for years and years manuscripts by dead and living writers and poets, long after they have been got ready for publication? One could never even begin to list it all—too much has been hidden away and buried in all kinds of secret depositories, and even more has been destroyed.

Another reason I was so angry about the poem describing the beauties of the Canal was that M. himself would have been sent there to work on it if it hadn't been for the order to "isolate but preserve" him. Forced labor on the Canal had been commuted to exile in Cherdyn, since nobody could be "preserved" once he was sent to the Canal. The young and healthy linguists Dmitri Usov and Yarkho were so broken by their few years at the Canal that they died almost immediately after their release—though they had scarcely been employed on hard physical labor. If M. had gone to the Canal, he would have died in 1934 instead of 1938—the "miracle" gave him a few extra years of life. All the same, miracles send a shiver down my spine. Not that I wish to appear ungrateful, but miracles are an Eastern thing and are ill-suited to the Western mind.

Nowadays I have a different feeling about Misha Zenkevich, the self-appointed Roman who, in the ruins of his Colosseum, preserves a few manuscripts by the poets who have been killed. I now find his life touching and, even though it has been free of great disasters—he has never been in prison or gone hungry—almost tragic. Frail by nature, Zenkevich succumbed earlier than others to the plague that infected all our minds; with him, however, it was not the acute attack I suffered in the railroad car, but a long-drawn-out chronic form from which nobody ever recovered. Can one explain the susceptibility of our intellectuals to this sickness only by reference to conditions after the Revolution? Weren't the first microbes already lurking in the pre-revolutionary malaise with all its frantic searchings and false prophecies?

There was a special form of the sickness—lethargy, plague, hypnotic trance or whatever one calls it—that affected all those who committed terrible deeds in the name of the "New Era." All the murderers, provocateurs and informers had one feature in common: it never occurred to them that their victims might one day rise up again and speak. They also imagined that time had stopped—this, indeed, was the chief symptom of the sickness. We had, you see, been led to believe that in our country nothing would ever change again, and that it was now up to the rest of the world to follow our example and enter the "New Era," after which all change would cease everywhere. And the people who accepted this doctrine worked sincerely for the greater glory of the new morality which followed from a historical determinism taken to its extreme conclusion. They thought that everybody sent to the next world or to the camps had been eliminated once and for all. It never entered their heads that these ghosts might rise up and call their grave-diggers to account. During the period of rehabilitations,* therefore, they were utterly panic-stricken. They thought that time had gone into reverse and that those they had dubbed "camp dust" had suddenly once more taken on flesh and reassumed their names. They were seized by terror. It so happens that during that time I was able to observe one wretched woman informer who lived next door to Vasilisa Shklovski. She was constantly being summoned to the Prosecutor's office, where she retracted testimony given many years before, thus clearing the names of persons both living and dead. On returning home, she came running to Vasilisa—whose apartment it

---

* The period after 1956 when some of Stalin's victims were officially cleared of the charges once made against them.

had once been her job to watch—and stammered that, as God was her witness, she had never said anything bad about Malkin or anybody else, and that her only reason for going to the Prosecutor's office now was to say good things about all the dead people so they would be cleared as soon as possible. The woman had never had anything remotely resembling a conscience, but this was more than she could stand, and she had a stroke that left her paralyzed. She must at some moment have got so scared that she really believed these rehabilitations were serious and that all the slanderers and other minions might be brought to trial. This, of course, didn't happen; but, all the same, she's better off as she is now—paralyzed and senile. For her, time has stopped once more.

And in Tashkent one of the most senior secret-police officials, who was pensioned off after the changes but was occasionally summoned to interviews with former victims who had by some miracle survived and returned from the camps, could not stand it and hanged himself. I was able to read a draft of his suicide letter addressed to the Central Committee. His reasoning was quite simple: As a completely dedicated young Komsomol,* he had been assigned to the secret police and had constantly been decorated and promoted for his work. During all his years of service he had never seen anybody but his colleagues and the prisoners he interrogated; he had worked day and night without pause and it was only after he was retired that he had the time to stop and think about what had been going on. Only then did the thought cross his mind that he might have been serving not the people, but "some kind of Bonapartism." He tried to put the blame on others: on the people he had interrogated for signing all kinds of bogus confessions, thereby misleading the officials in charge of their cases; on the officials sent from Moscow with instructions concerning "simplified interrogation procedure" and demands that the quotas be fulfilled; and, last but not least, on the informers who volunteered the denunciations which forced the secret police to act against so many people—a secret policeman was prevented by his class consciousness from disregarding information of this kind. . . . He had finally made up his mind to commit suicide after reading Victor Hugo's "Last Day of a Condemned Man."

He was buried and the case was hushed up—it couldn't be other-

* Member of the Young Communist League.

wise, since he had named all the officials who had come from Moscow to brief him, and the informers who had brought him denunciations. The daughter of the dead man—she was called Larisa, after Larisa Reisner—stormed and raged for a long time, thinking only of getting even with those who had caused her father's death. Her anger was directed against the ones who had stirred up this nightmarish business. "They should have shown some consideration for the people in official positions at that time! They didn't start all this, they were just carrying orders." To this Larisa kept adding that she would not "let the matter rest here," and she even said she was going to get the whole story out of the country so that people abroad would know how her father had been treated. I asked her what exactly she proposed to complain about. For Larisa it was all quite clear: one could not make such sudden changes because it was so "traumatic." One could not inflict traumas on people such as her father and his colleagues. "Who is going to sympathize with you?" I asked, but she didn't understand the question. People had been promised that all change was at an end, and further changes were inadmissible. "All right, let them no longer arrest people, but things should stay as they were." Let time stand still. The stopping of time means peace and stability. They need it so much, the leaders of our age.

Larisa wanted time to be halted again, and to a considerable extent her plea has been heeded. The sons of her father's deposed colleagues have gone to Moscow to learn new methods, and before they went they put flowers on his grave. They will fill the same jobs and move into the same offices, always ready to act in accordance with instructions from above. The only question now is: What will these instructions be?

Larisa and I had nothing in common, but, looking at her, I always wondered why all lives in this country are equally ill-fated. What do you have to be to escape? In what burrow can one hide? Larisa and her friends had made a burrow of sorts for themselves, stocking it with all the things which for them symbolized the good life: sideboards, wineglasses, standard lamps, Bohemian cut glass and old Russian china, embroidered dressing gowns and Japanese fans. But all the furnishings they traveled to Moscow to buy only served, like tombstones, to bury them. Their burrow had not been deep enough either: some were destroyed at a wave of Stalin's hand, others destroyed themselves.

13
THE NAMESAKE

In the train I did not at first realize that anything was wrong with M. He greeted me with joy and took my appearance for a miracle. Indeed, it was a miracle. He said that he had been expecting all the time to be shot: "It happens to people for much less, you know." This was true enough. We had never doubted that he would be shot if they found out about the poem. Vinaver, a very well-informed man of enormous experience who was privy to many secrets, told me several months later when I came from Voronezh to see him and read him the poem about Stalin at his request: "What do you expect? He got off very lightly: people are shot for much less than that." At the same time he warned me not to place too much hope in mercy from on high: "It might be withdrawn as soon as the fuss has died down," he said. "Does that happen?" I asked. He was staggered by my naïveté. "I'll say it does!" And he added: "Just try not to attract attention. Perhaps they'll forget about you then." But we didn't follow this advice. M. was not one to keep quiet and he went on making a fuss to the very end.

In the train M. said that this merciful sentence to three years in exile meant only that his execution had been put off to a more convenient time—just what Vinaver told me later. I wasn't in the least surprised by this reading of the situation: by 1934 we were already a little wiser about what was going on. When M. said that there was no escape anyway, he was absolutely right—a sober view of the situation could lead to no other conclusion. And when he whispered to me: "Don't trust them," I could only nod in agreement. Who indeed could trust them?

Yet this talk was actually a result of the severe psychotic state to which M. had been reduced in prison. At first, however, it was not M. who appeared unbalanced to me, but the senior guard (called Osip, like both M. and the target of his poem)* when he took me aside and said, his kindly, sheepish eyes popping out of his head, "Tell him to calm down! Tell him we don't shoot people for making up poetry." He had heard us mention the poem in our conversation, and he wanted us to know that people were shot only for spying and sabotage. In the bour-

---

* Osip is a form of Joseph.

geois countries, he went on, it was quite a different matter: there you could be strung up in no time for writing some stuff they didn't like.

To some degree or another we all, of course, believed what was dinned into us. The young people—whether students, soldiers, writers or guards—were particularly credulous. "No elections could be fairer," a demobilized soldier said to me in 1937. "They put up candidates, and we elect them." M. also fell for it and proved gullible on this occasion: "This is the way they're doing it now, but they'll gradually learn better, and then we shall have proper elections," he said as he left the polling booth, awed by the novelty of the first and last elections in which he was ever to vote. Even we, with all our experience, were not able to form a proper judgment of all the changes, so what could we expect of younger people? . . . I remember how in Kalinin the woman next door who used to bring me milk just before the war once said with a sigh: "At least we get a little salted herring, or sugar, or kerosene now and again. But what must it be like in the capitalist countries? I suppose you can just starve to death there." Even today the students believe that education for all is possible only under socialism, and that "over there" people are sunk in ignorance. Once, while we were having a meal with Larisa, the daughter of the Tashkent official who had killed himself, there was a fierce argument about whether in large foreign towns like London or Paris they would refuse to give a residence permit to an airman who had been invalided out of the service. There had just been such a case in Tashkent (this was in 1959) and Larisa was saying that an airman must be given a permit, particularly if he was a test pilot. I tried to explain that "over there" you didn't need a permit to reside in a city, but nobody would believe me: since everything was so much worse "over there," the difficulties with residence permits were bound to be tremendous. How could anybody live in a city without a permit? You'd be caught straight away! If we all believed what our mentors told us, how could we wonder that our guard Osip believed them?

I had brought a small volume of Pushkin with me. Osip was so taken by the story of the old gypsy that he read it out loud to his bored comrades. "Look at what those Roman Czars did to old men," Osip said to the others. "It was for his poems they sent him away." The description of Ovid's northern exile* affected him greatly: he thought it was a terrible thing, and he decided to reassure me that we were not in for any-

---

* In Pushkin's poem "The Gypsies."

thing as bad as this. Accompanying me, as per instructions, to the toilet, Osip managed to whisper to me that we were going to Cherdyn—where the climate was good—and that our first change of train would be in Sverdlovsk. When I told him that the interrogator had already told us this, Osip was crestfallen: he had been instructed to keep our destination and route a secret, and only the guards were supposed to know such things. In his fondness for us, Osip had broken the rules and told us where we were going, only to learn that I knew already. But I made him feel better by saying that if it hadn't been for his confirmation of the interrogator's words, I should have had all kinds of wild ideas.

This was not the only exception Osip made for us. Every time we had to change trains—and it happened often—he got the other guards to carry our things for us, and when we transferred to a river steamer at Solikamsk, he whispered to me to take a cabin at our own expense ("So your man can have a rest"). He kept the other guards away from us and they stayed up on deck. I asked why he was disobeying orders like this, but he just waved his hand: up to now he had always traveled in charge of common criminals and "saboteurs" who had to be watched very carefully—"but your man's different, he doesn't need watching!" But none of the guards would touch any of our food, try as I would to offer them a bite: it was forbidden. Only when they had handed M. over to the commandant in Cherdyn did they say at last: "Now we are free, you can treat us!"

In the whole of my life I was to meet only two more people of Osip's profession. One of them just ground his teeth all the time and kept on saying that we could have no idea of what it was like. He dreamed of the day when he would be demobilized, and I was glad when I heard that he had regained his freedom. "Even a state farm is like paradise now," he told me when we met. The other man was a brutish creature with a low forehead who had once let a prisoner escape and hence lost a job which had seemed full of promising possibilities and had obviously suited him very much. For years, drunk or sober, he cursed the "counter-revolutionary German fascist saboteur" who had ruined his career. His one dream was to catch the swine and kill him. He also harbored a grudge against the Soviet regime: why was it soft on these criminals, sending them to camps instead of shooting them like that— He snapped his fingers expressively. We should have had a very poor time if this man, rather than Osip, had been given the task of taking us to Cherdyn.

14

A Piece of Chocolate

During the first change of trains at Sverdlovsk we had to wait for many hours at the station, and the guards kept a very close watch not only on M. but on me as well. I wasn't allowed to send a telegram, buy bread or go near the newsstand. Neither had I been permitted to get out at intermediate stops ("It's against the rules"). M. noticed this at once: "So they're treating you the same as me." I tried to explain to the guards that I hadn't been exiled, that I was traveling of my own free will. "Not allowed. Those are the orders."

In Sverdlovsk we had to sit for many hours, from morning till late at night, on a wooden bench flanked by two armed guards. At our least move—we weren't allowed to get up and stretch our legs or change our position in the slightest—the guards at once sprang to the alert and reached for their pistols. For some reason they had put us on a seat right opposite the station entrance, so we faced the endless stream of people coming in. The first thing they saw was us, but they looked away immediately. Even little boys decided not to notice us. We weren't allowed to eat, either, because our food was in our suitcase and we were not supposed to touch our things—it was against the rules. There was no water within reach. Osip didn't dare disobey his orders here: Sverdlovsk was a station not to be taken lightly.

In the evening we were transferred to the narrow-gauge line from Sverdlovsk to Solikamsk. We were taken to some sidings and put aboard a car with ordinary seats, a few rows of which were left empty to separate us from the other passengers. Two soldiers stood next to us all night while a third one guarded the empty seats to keep away passengers who stubbornly tried to sit in them. In Sverdlovsk we had sat side by side, but now we were facing each other by a window of the unlighted car. The white nights had already started, and we could glimpse the wooded hills of the Ural as they flashed by. The railroad went through thick forest, and M. stared out of the window all night long. This was his third or fourth sleepless night.

We traveled in crowded cars and on river steamers, we sat in busy stations swarming with people, but nowhere did anybody pay any attention to the outlandish spectacle of two people, a man and a woman, guarded by three armed soldiers. Nobody gave us so much as a backward glance. Were they just used to sights like this in the Ural, or were they afraid of getting infected? Who knows? Most probably it was a case of the peculiar Soviet etiquette that has been carefully observed for several decades now: if the authorities are sending someone into exile, all well and good, it's none of our business. The indifference of the people around us hurt and upset M. "They used to give alms to convicts and now they don't even look at them." With horror he whispered in my ear that in front of a crowd like this they could do anything to a prisoner—shoot him down, kill him, torture him—and nobody would interfere. Bystanders would just turn their backs, not to be upset by the sight. During the whole journey I tried to catch somebody's eye, but never once succeeded.

Perhaps only the Ural was so stony-faced? In 1938 I lived in Strunino, in the permitted zone a hundred kilometers from Moscow. This was a small textile town on the Yaroslavl railroad and in those years trainloads of prisoners passed through it every night. People coming in to see my landlady spoke of nothing else. They were outraged at being forbidden to give the prisoners bread. Once my landlady managed to throw a piece of chocolate through the bars of a broken window in one of the prison cars—in a poor working-class family, chocolate was a rare treat and she had been taking it home for her little daughter. A soldier had sworn at her and swung the butt of his rifle at her, but she was happy for the rest of the day because she had managed to do at least this much. True, some of her neighbors sighed and said: "Better not get mixed up with them. They'll plague the life out of you. They'll have you up in front of the factory committee." But my landlady didn't go out to work, so she wasn't afraid of any factory committee.

Will anybody in a future generation ever understand what that piece of chocolate with a child's picture on the wrapper must have meant in a stifling prison train in 1938? People for whom time had stopped and space had become a prison ward, or a punishment cell where you could only stand, or a cattle truck filled to bursting with its freight of half-dead human beings, forgotten outcasts who had been struck from the rolls of the living, stripped of their names, numbered and registered before being shipped to the black limbo of the prison camps—it was such as these who now suddenly received for the first time in many months their first message from the forbidden world outside: a little piece of chocolate to tell them that they were not yet forgotten, and that people were still alive beyond their prison bars.

On the way to Cherdyn I consoled myself with the thought that the dour people of the Ural were simply afraid to look at us, but that every one of them, on returning home, would tell his family about the two people, a man and a woman, being taken somewhere to the north by three soldiers.

15

THE LEAP

I had realized that M. was ill the first night, when I noticed that he was not sleeping, but sitting with his legs crossed and listening very intently to something. "Do you hear?" he asked me whenever our eyes met. I listened—but there was only the hammering of wheels and the snoring of passengers. "You have bad hearing. You never hear anything." He really had extremely fine hearing, and he could catch the slightest sounds that I never heard. But this time it was not a question of hearing.

He spent the whole journey listening like this, and from time to time he would shudder and tell me that disaster might strike any moment, and that we must be ready, not be caught unawares. I realized that not only was he expecting to be put to death, but that he thought it would happen any moment—right now, during the journey. "On the way?" I asked. "You must be thinking of the twenty-six commissars."* "And why not?" he answered. "You think our own people couldn't do the same thing?" We both knew perfectly well that our own people were capable of anything. But in his madness M. hoped to cheat his executioners, to run for it, to break away or be killed in the attempt—anything rather than die at their hands. It is strange that all of us, whether mad or not, never give up this one hope: suicide is the last resort, which we keep in reserve, believing that it is never too late to use it. Yet so many people who were determined never to fall alive into the hands of the secret police were taken by surprise at the last moment.

The thought of this last resort had consoled and soothed me all my life, and often, at times when things were quite unbearable, I had pro-

---

* The twenty-six Bolshevik commissars of Baku who were shot in 1921, allegedly on British orders.

posed to M. that we commit suicide together. M. had always sharply rejected the idea.*

His main argument was: "How do you know what will come afterward? Life is a gift that nobody should renounce." And there was the final and most telling argument: "Why do you think you ought to be happy?" Nobody was so full of the joy of life as M., but though he never sought unhappiness, neither did he count on being what is called "happy."

Generally, however, he dismissed the idea of suicide with a joke: "Kill ourselves? Impossible! What will Averbakh say?" Or: "How can I live with a professional suicide like you?" The thought of suicide first came to him during his illness on the way to Cherdyn as a means of escaping the death by shooting that he believed was inevitable. It was then that I said to him: "Very well, if they shoot us, we shan't have to commit suicide." At this, already ill and obsessed as he was, he suddenly burst out laughing: "There you go again." From then on our life was such that the suicide theme recurred frequently, but M. always said: "Wait . . . not now. . . . We'll see. . . ." In 1937 he even consulted Akhmatova, but she said: "Do you know what they'll do? They'll start taking even better care of writers and even give some Leonov or other a dacha. Why do you want that to happen?" If he had made up his mind to do it then, he would have been spared his second arrest and the endless journey in a cattle car to Vladivostok, to horror and death in a camp, and I should not have had to live on after him. I am always struck that people find it so difficult to cross this fateful threshold. There is something in the Christian injunction against suicide which is profoundly in keeping with human nature—this is why people don't do it, even though life can be far more terrible than death, as we have seen in our times. When M. had gone and I was left alone, I was sustained by the memory of his words "Why do you think you ought to be happy?" and by the passage in the "Life" of the Archpriest Avvakum when his exhausted wife asks him: "How much further must we go?" and he replies: "Until the very grave, woman." Whereupon she gets to her feet and walks on.

If these notes of mine survive, people reading them may think

---

* *Author's Note:* Georgi Ivanov's story about how M. had tried to kill himself as a young man in Warsaw is, I believe, completely without foundation, like many other romantic tales by this writer.

they were written by a sick person, by a hypochondriac. . . . By then all will have been forgotten and nobody will believe the testimony of a witness. One only has to think of all the people abroad who still do not believe us. Yet they are contemporaries, separated from us only by space, not by time. I recently read the following reasonable-sounding words by a foreign author: "They say that *everybody* was afraid there. It cannot be that everybody was afraid. Some were and some weren't. . . ." It sounds so reasonable and logical, but in fact our life was far from logical. And it wasn't just that I was a "professional suicide," as M. had called me teasingly. Many other people thought about it, too. Not for nothing was the best play in the Soviet repertory entitled *The Suicide.**

So it was in the train to Cherdyn, traveling under the eye of three guards, that M. first thought of killing himself, but this was the result of illness. He was a man who always noted everything in the minutest detail and his powers of observation were extraordinarily acute. "Attention to detail," he noted in one of his rough drafts, "is the virtue of the lyric poet. Carelessness and sloppiness are the devices of lyrical sloth." But now, on the journey to Cherdyn, this feral perceptiveness and acute sense of hearing had turned against him, exacerbating his illness. In the hectic throng of crowded stations, and in railroad cars, he constantly registered each little detail, and, thinking it all referred to him personally—isn't egocentrism the first symptom of mental illness?—he decided it all added up to one thing: the fateful moment was at hand.

In Solikamsk we were put in a truck to be taken from the station to the pier. On the way we drove through a forest clearing. The truck was full of workers and M. was frightened by the appearance of one of them, a bearded man in a dark-red shirt with an ax in his hand. "They're going to behead me, as in Peter's time," he whispered to me. But on the river steamer, in the cabin we had got thanks to Osip, M. started making fun of his own fears and clearly saw that he was frightened of people who were no threat to him—such as the workers in Solikamsk. And he added bitterly that they would lull his suspicions and then "grab" him when he was least expecting it. This is indeed just what happened four years later.

In his dementia M. understood perfectly well what was coming, but

---

* By Nikolai Erdman.

when he recovered he lost this sense of reality and began to believe he was safe. In our sort of life people of sound mind had to shut their eyes to their surroundings—otherwise they would have thought they were having hallucinations. To shut your eyes like this is not easy and requires a great effort. Not to see what is going on around you is not just a passive activity. Soviet citizens have achieved a high degree of mental blindness, with devastating consequences for their whole psychological make-up. This generation of people who chose to be blind is now disappearing for the most primitive of reasons—they are dying off—but what have they passed on to their children?

We were glad to see Cherdyn with its pleasant scenery: it reminded one of what the country was like before the time of Peter the Great. We were taken to the local Cheka and handed over to the Commandant together with our papers. Osip explained that he had brought "a very special bird" whom they were ordered to "preserve" without fail. He was evidently very anxious to impress this on the Commandant, a man with the typical appearance of one who had served on the "inside"—that is, who had shot and tortured prisoners and had then been posted to this remote place because of his brutality: in other words, because he had seen too many unmentionable things. I sensed that Osip must have made a certain effort on our behalf—to judge from the mixture of curiosity and venom with which the Commandant looked at us, and from the ease with which I was able to enlist his help to get us a place in the local hospital. As other exiles in Cherdyn told me later, he did not usually "pamper" people who had been brought there under guard. In the hospital we were given a large empty ward with two creaking beds set up at right angles to the wall.

As it says in M.'s poem, I really hadn't slept for five nights as I watched over him on the journey. But in the hospital, tired by the endless white night, I fell into a troubled, wakeful kind of sleep through which I could see M., legs crossed and jacket unbuttoned, sitting on the shaky bed and listening to the silence.

Suddenly—I sensed this through my sleep—everything changed place: M. was all at once on the window sill and I was there beside him. He put his legs outside, and I just had time to see him begin to lower his whole body. The window sill was a high one. I reached out desperately with both hands and managed to grab the shoulders of his jacket. He wriggled out of the sleeves and dropped. I could hear the sound of his falling—a dull thud and a cry. His jacket was left hanging in my hands. I ran screaming along the hospital corridor, down the stairs and outside. Some nurses raced after me. We found M. on a pile of earth that had been plowed up to make a flower bed. He was lying there all huddled up. Shouting and cursing, they carried him upstairs. They swore mostly at me for not having kept an eye on him.

A woman doctor, very disheveled and very angry, came running and quickly examined him. She said he had dislocated his right shoulder, but there was no other damage apart from this. He was lucky: he had thrown himself from a second-floor window of an old district hospital which would equal at least a third-floor window of any modern one.

From somewhere a crowd of hospital orderlies appeared. M. lay on the floor of a completely empty ward, which they called the operating room, and struggled with the men holding him while the woman doctor set his shoulder to the accompaniment of loud curses: a substitute for the anesthetic lacking in this hospital. The X-ray equipment was not working because the generator was switched off to save fuel during the white nights, and the mechanic had gone on vacation. This was why the doctor did not notice the fracture in M.'s shoulder bone. It was not discovered till much later, in Voronezh, where we had to consult a surgeon because M. had lost the use of his right arm. He was under treatment for a long time and partially recovered the use of his arm, but he could not raise it—to hang up his coat, for instance. This he had to do with his left hand.

After his leap that night he calmed down. As he says in his poem: "A leap—and my mind is whole."

16

CHERDYN

Unshaven, with the beard of a Biblical patriarch, M. lay for two weeks in Cherdyn, looking closely at everything around him with a studious and, for some reason, very serene gaze. I thought that he had never looked so alert and so calm as during this illness. He was not upset by the peasants, as bearded as he was himself, who wandered along the corridors. As he now told me, the experience in Solikamsk had done him good: peasants are peasants, and there's no reason to fear them—

you could tell them straightaway from "those others" (that is, police-men). The peasants in the hospital had festering sores and they were treated in the same rough-and-ready fashion as M. had been. They talked slowly among themselves and were always smirking for no apparent reason. A lot of things about human behavior are hard to understand, but this smirk made no sense at all. It was easier to explain their sores: the hideous conditions in which they had been transported here, lifting loads too heavy for them, injuries . . . A thin woman with the face of a radical intellectual from the 1860's—an exile like us, who worked as housekeeper in the hospital and considered herself remarkably lucky to have the job—said she would gladly sacrifice her life for the sake of these peasants. From this remark M. realized at once what kind of a person she was.

I cannot now remember how these bearded peasants were referred to at the time. The word may have been "resettled"; all I remember is that it was forbidden to describe them for what they were: peasants deported as kulaks.* We do not like to call a spade a spade. Those bearded men with their festering sores have long been dead and buried. There is never any mention of them anywhere. Are we afraid to touch those sores?

At that time the tradition of comradeship and mutual help still lingered on both in the forced-labor camps and in remote places of exile such as ours. In the world beyond, all this was a thing of the past, but Cherdyn was faithful to the old ways, and the housekeeper showed warm concern for us. She insisted that I buy some fur boots for winter—they would be unobtainable later on—and start growing vegetables if we wanted to eat properly. Exiles were given plots of land to grow food on, but they had to find their own accommodation. In Cherdyn, as everywhere else, there was a desperate shortage of housing, and the exiles rented corners of rooms where they could. The housekeeper took us to see a little man with short legs who had managed to do quite well for himself. He had curtained off a corner in someone's house with plush curtains and made some bookshelves which were filled from top to bottom with the works of Marx and Engels. Behind these curtains he lived with his wife, and both of them went every three days to report to the Commandant. M. was expected to do the same, even

---

* Kulak: a pejorative term for a rich peasant. During collectivization it was used indiscriminately for all small holders.

though he was in hospital. They had given him a document that did not qualify as a residence permit, and every three days the Commandant put a stamp on it. The other exiles were worried in case the Commandant decided to send M. away to some place in the surrounding district. He tried to keep as few people as possible in the town because "there are too many as it is." "Does he have the right?" I asked, saying that M.'s document mentioned only Cherdyn itself, not the district. "You are in his hands. He'll send you wherever he wants. He's always making people leave the town." At the beginning of that spring there had been many more political exiles, but they had all had to leave for the countryside, where there was nothing for them to do except manual labor. "And some of the comrades were quite ill," the housekeeper added. In the camps and places of exile the word "comrade" had a special ring all its own that had long been forgotten in the world outside.

The housekeeper's husband was always arguing with the short-legged Marxist who lived behind the plush curtain. They were former members—marginal ones at that—of parties now destroyed, and their arguments had begun way back in the revolutionary underground of Czarist times. Their wives were more concerned with their jobs than with this kind of talk, and they obviously missed their children, which both couples had left with relatives. "How are they getting on, I wonder?" they kept sighing, but they couldn't bring themselves to send for them. "We are done for, but we must give them a chance to live." Their own future was perfectly clear to them: on the first pretext they would be finished off here on the spot, or sent to rot in the camps. "Perhaps things will ease off," we once said to the Marxist. "Not a hope!" he replied. "They're only just beginning to warm up." But I didn't believe him. It's only natural, I thought, that they take such a gloomy view of the future: there's not much room for optimism in their situation. And things really can't go on forever like this. . . . In my long life I have often imagined that we had reached the limit and that things would "ease off," as I put it. Nobody likes to part with his illusions.

The other exiles tried to set my mind at rest as to M.'s health. "They all come out of there in his state, but it will be all right later on—they get over it." "Why are they in such a state?" I asked. They didn't know how to explain it to me. "Was it like that in the old days?" They had all been in Czarist jails, and should have been able to enlighten me. But all they could tell me was that in the old days people's mental state was not affected so much by prison. At the same time I was not to be alarmed:

"it" always cleared up completely. The illness lasted from two to three months. The main thing was a certain self-control: it was important not to think about the future—which boded no good anyway. We should make the best of Cherdyn as a last breathing-space. Expect nothing and be ready for anything—that was the key to sanity.

They urged us to resign ourselves to fate and not throw away our little remaining money on telegrams. Once they are out of prison, all exiles, dazed by the fantastic nature of their treatment there, always started bombarding the Government with protest telegrams. Nobody ever received an answer. My new friends were people of enormous experience. They had spent more than ten years already in various places of exile and in labor camps (where at first the men were separated from their wives, but were later reunited with them). I thought of G., an old country doctor whom I had met at the very beginning of the twenties in Moscow. He had come to plead on behalf of his family, but achieved nothing. "I have nobody left," he told me, "they have sent all of them away, even the youngsters," and he gave me the names of all his sons and grown grandchildren. "This never used to happen." The old man knew that in the old days, if someone's eldest son was exiled, the grandchildren were always handed over to the care of their grandparents. The arrest of a son never affected the other members of a family—they remained free, and lived where they liked. The old man was now trying to get back one of his grandsons who was still under age, but nothing came of it.

I told the other exiles in Cherdyn about the formula that had been applied in M.'s case: "isolate but preserve." What did they think it meant? Perhaps the Commandant wouldn't dare to make M. leave the town and live in even worse conditions? Perhaps it would enable us to get some improvement in his lot and proper medical treatment for him? They doubted it. There were many people in their circles who had been personally acquainted with those who later rose to power, Stalin among them. They had had dealings with them in the underground and in exile in Czarist times. Now, going into exile again, they had often heard assurances that they were only being "isolated" and that they would be given "all the conditions" needed for life and work. However, these promises were never kept, and the petitions and letters with which they bombarded the Government just vanished into a bottomless pit. Isolation, they said, promised not "preservation" but the most ordinary kind of destruction, quietly, without witnesses, "at the right moment." The only things one could trust in were one's own patience and discipline. The only thing to do was to expect the worst and cling to one's human dignity. It was difficult to do this, and you needed all your strength. Such was the conclusion they had drawn from their experience and a sober analysis of their situation. But we couldn't help feeling that they were not quite objective in their pessimism: life had treated them so badly that they were bound to see everything in the darkest light. Was three years' exile in Cherdyn really the end? Everything would come out all right, things would ease off, and life would go on. . . .

People always clutch at straws, nobody wants to part with his illusions, and it is very difficult to look life in the face. To see things as they are demands a superhuman effort. There are those who want to be blind, but even among those who think they are not, how many are left who can really see? Or, rather, who do not slightly distort what they see to keep their illusions and hopes alive?

Our Cherdyn friends had only one aim in life—to preserve their human dignity. For this they had given up any kind of activity, condemning themselves to total isolation and the prospect of an early death. This was undoubtedly passive resistance of a kind, but the movement known by this term in India is by comparison a very active form of political struggle. In a certain sense they had now adopted the idea of self-perfection once proposed by the Vekhi (Landmarks)* group and indignantly rejected by them at that time. It must be said, however, that they had little choice. The only other thing they could have done was to scream, but no one would have heard anyway.

I later heard quite by chance what happened subsequently to the housekeeper at the Cherdyn hospital. She was sent to Kolyma† and there told the story of M.'s illness to a fellow prisoner, a woman writer from Leningrad called E. M. Tager. After jumping out of the window, M. went on believing he would be shot, but he no longer tried to run away from it. He had decided that his executioners would come at some particular time, and at the appointed hour he waited for them in fear and agitation. In the hospital ward where we were living, there was a large clock on the wall. One day M. said he expected to be put to death at six o'clock that evening, and the housekeeper advised me to

* See note on Berdiayev in the Appendix.
† A forced-labor camp area in the Soviet Far East.

move the hands on the clock without his noticing. She and I managed to do this, and this time M. was not overcome with fear as the fateful hour approached. "Look," I told him, "you said six, but it's already quarter past seven." Oddly enough, this trick worked and he no longer had bouts of terror associated with certain hours of the day.

The housekeeper had remembered this episode in exact detail and told it to E. M. Tager, who was her neighbor in the camp barrack. After twenty years in the labor camps Tager was rehabilitated after the Twentieth Congress* in 1956 and returned to her native city. She was given an apartment in the same building as Akhmatova, and it was there that I met her. And I, who also owe it to chance that I have survived with my memories, recognized the woman who told her the story of the clock as the housekeeper from Cherdyn. It is thus only through a chain of pure chance that I am able to write down (will it ever find its way to other readers?) the story of how the worst expectations of one of our fellow exiles in Cherdyn proved only too true. My nameless Cherdyn sister died in Kolyma from total exhaustion. I have been able to discover nothing about the fate of her children whom she had left behind "to give them at least a chance. . . ." Did they escape the fate that usually befell the children of exiles and prisoners? Did they have to pay the price of prison and camp on account of the parents who had wanted only to preserve their human dignity? And have they themselves kept the human dignity for which their parents paid so dearly?

This I do not know, and shall never learn.

17

HALLUCINATIONS

We walked around Cherdyn, talked with people and spent our nights in the hospital. I was no longer afraid of keeping the window open. There was only the sling on M.'s arm to remind me of that first night when I had been left holding an empty jacket. When the secret police came to take M. away for the second time in 1938, I was again left with an empty jacket in my hands: in all the hurry M. forgot to take it.

---

* The Party Congress at which Khrushchev made his "secret speech" denouncing Stalin.

During the few days in Cherdyn M. became very much calmer. The crisis had passed, but his illness was not over. As before, he was waiting for the death sentence to be carried out, but his mental state had improved to the point where he had regained a certain sense of reality. After the business with the clock he said that there was obviously no escaping the end in store for him, but that there was nothing to be done about it—even committing suicide wasn't so simple, "otherwise nobody would come into their clutches alive. . . ."

His agitation had passed, but he still had auditory hallucinations. They took the form not of inner voices, but of violent and utterly strange ones which seemed to come from without. M. spoke about them almost objectively, trying to understand what they meant. He explained that these voices he was hearing could not come from inside because they used a vocabulary that wasn't his. "I couldn't say such things even to myself"—this was his argument in favor of the real existence of these voices. In a way his ability to analyze them made it harder for him to fight his hallucinations. He couldn't believe in their internal origin because he thought that a hallucination was necessarily some kind of reflection of one's own inner world.

"Perhaps it's something you've repressed?" I asked him. He insisted that things he'd repressed would be quite different, and that what the voices said was foreign to him. "Even their worries are quite different from mine." M. revealed himself so fully in his verse that for me at least there were very few "dark corners" in him. If I mention "dark corners" at all, it was because he was a reserved man and there were subjects that he scarcely ever talked about. For instance, he never said how he arrived at the associations in his poetry—which, indeed, he never commented on in any way—and always had very little to say about things and people dear to him—his mother, for instance, or Pushkin. In other words, there was an area which he thought it was almost sacrilegeous to touch on—this is what I mean by saying he was a reserved man. But it would be wrong to put this reticence down to "inhibitions." He was not inhibited in his thoughts and feelings—rather the contrary. And in any case, how could inhibitions have been involved when his illness was caused by an over-reaction to external factors?

"Whose vocabulary is it? Whose words can you hear?" I asked. This he could not say. It could have been the words of the guards who had led him along the corridors of the Lubianka when he was called out for interrogation at night. They sometimes winked at each other, snapped their fingers in a symbolic gesture meaning death by shooting, and also exchanged occasional remarks calculated to terrify the prisoner. All this was deliberately intended to help the interrogator in his task, as everybody who has ever been in the Lubianka knows. M. also kept remembering the voice of the man who had let him out of the "iron gates of the GPU." M. referred to him as the prison commandant, but perhaps he was simply the duty guard. M. couldn't actually see him because he was sitting in the "Black Maria," but he could hear someone checking his papers before allowing it to go through the gates. This voice, together with the whole ritual, had produced a strong impression. But most of all he had been affected by the interrogator's solemn monologues with their stress on "crime and punishment."

"The voices," M. said to me once, "are like a composite quotation of everything I heard." ("Composite quotation" is an expression coined by Andrei Bely, who said that for him every writer was represented not by a series of separate, word-for-word quotations, but by a kind of "composite quotation" that summed up the essentials of his thoughts and words.)

To test M.'s sense of reality, I asked him whether he also heard the voices of the guards who had brought us to Cherdyn, such as Osip, or those of the bearded men who had come to the hospital for treatment. M. was indignant: those guards had been simple village youths doing this horrible job by way of duty—"babes in the wood," he called them. As for the bearded men, he saw them as just what they were: peasants who had been deported as kulaks—"ordinary people could never say or think this kind of thing." There was in his mind a total contrast between "ordinary people" and the sort he had encountered in the Lubianka. More than once, in Cherdyn and later on, he told me: "You can't imagine what a special type they are there." In saying this, he made a distinction between the guards "on the outside" (as well as some of the officials we had dealings with in Voronezh) and the very specific personnel who did their work at night. The first were run-of-the-mill Red Army types, but the second—those "on the inside"— were quite out of the ordinary: "To do that job," M. said, "you have to have a particular vocation—no ordinary person could ever stand it." In Cherdyn the only person who struck him as belonging to this "inner" category was the Commandant. This was what the other exiles thought, too. They warned us to watch our step with him and to keep out of his way as much as possible: "You never know what ideas he might get into his head." He was one of those who had been in the Civil War: "He always follows his class instinct," the short-legged Marxist told me with horror, "and no good ever comes of that—you can never tell where it will lead a man." The poor fellow was completely at the Commandant's mercy and M.'s instinctive fear of him was well-founded.

What M. heard were the coarse voices of men trying to frighten him by describing his "crime" and enumerating all kinds of possible punishments in the language of our newspapers during Stalin's campaigns against "enemies of the people." They cursed him in the foulest language and blamed him for the ruin he had brought on all those to whom he had read his poem. The names of these people were reeled off as those of defendants at a forthcoming trial, and appeals were made to his conscience as the one who had brought them to this pass. Strange to say, the word "conscience," which had gone out of ordinary use—it was not current in newspapers, books or in the schools, since its function had been taken over first by "class feeling" and later by "the good of the state"—was still doing service in prison, where people under interrogation were constantly warned of the "pangs of conscience" they would suffer. Boris Sergeyevich Kuzin had told us that when they tried to recruit him as an informer he was threatened not only with arrest, difficulties in his work, the spreading of rumors among his friends and colleagues that he was already a police spy, but also with the "pangs of conscience" he was bound to suffer for all the misery he would bring on his family if he refused to cooperate. This word, occurring in such a specific context in M.'s hallucinations, was a direct indication that they originated in those nighttime interrogations. Neither had M. imagined or dredged up from some obscure recesses of his own mind the idea of a trial with a list of defendants accused of conspiracy against Stalin. During my interview with M. in prison I had myself heard the interrogator allude to this possibility when he told me he was not "proceeding with the case" only on orders from above. But how, he had then asked by way of a rhetorical question, could one explain M.'s whole case except as a conspiracy?

Where is the borderline, in times such as ours, between the normal and the sick? M. and I thought about the same things, but with him they assumed a tangible quality: he not only thought about them, but saw in his mind's eye what they could lead to. He would wake me during the night to say that Akhmatova had been arrested and was at that moment being taken for questioning. "Why do you think so?" I asked. "I just do." Walking round Cherdyn, he would look for her corpse in the ravines. Of course it was madness, but once I had recovered from the torpor that had come over me in the train, I too couldn't sleep at night for wondering which of our friends had already been arrested and what they would be accused of—they would be lucky if the charge was only failure to denounce us, but there was nothing that couldn't be pinned on them. The real madness would have been to believe that the interrogator had meant it when he said he was not going to "proceed with the case." To be so trusting could even be despicable: I remembered, for instance, how I had recoiled from Adalis when she told me how she had been summoned for questioning about one of her husbands and, believing everything the interrogator said, at once disowned him, even though he was totally innocent.

Was I sick when I lay awake during those nights, imagining the way in which all my friends were being questioned and tortured, even if such tortures were as yet only psychological, or at least left no traces on the body? No, there was nothing sick about this—any normal person in my place would have tormented himself with similar thoughts. Who of us has never pictured himself in the office of the interrogator? Who of us has never thought up answers to the questions he might be asked? Not for nothing did Akhmatova write these lines:

> There, behind the barbed wire,
> In the very heart of the dense taiga
> They take my shadow for questioning. . . .

M. was, of course, a person of unusual sensitivity who was more vulnerable to psychological damage than others, and always reacted very strongly to external stimuli. But does one need to be all that hypersensitive to be broken by this life of ours?

When I asked that M. be examined by a specialist, the woman doctor refused point blank to arrange it. Her reply reminded me of Osip's "it's against the rules." When I persisted, she avoided talking with me and used bad language. At last she broke down and said: "What do you expect me to do? They're always in this state when they come 'from there.' "

With my old-fashioned view of things I thought it was wrong—indeed criminal—to exile a person suffering from hallucinations, and I denounced the doctor as a murderess because of her indifference. But I soon noticed that the bearded peasants did not think so badly of her. "There's no sense in badgering her," one of them said. "What can she do? Nothing at all." When I asked them what she was like, they said she was "no worse than anybody else." There are indeed circumstances in which it is not possible to display high moral qualities. When I'd seen more of her, I realized that she was just an ordinary country doctor. Unluckily for her, she had come to a place where they sent people "from there," and she was thus forced to have constant dealings with the secret police and act "on instructions." She had learned to hold her tongue and not to disobey orders. Day after day she changed the pus-covered bandages of the peasants, shouting and cursing at them, but at least doing her best for them. And she gave me a good piece of advice: not to try and have M. sent to Perm for a medical examination, or to put him in a clinic. "People get over this, but in one of those places he'd be done for—you know what they're like." I took her advice and it was as well I did so: people really do get over "it." But I would like to know what its medical name is, why it affects so many people held for inter-rogation, and what conditions "inside" make it so widespread. I repeat that M. was unusually sensitive and may have been prone to mental ill-ness, but I was struck not so much by it having happened to him as by everybody telling me how commonplace this sickness was. People who had known the Czarist jails, which were scarcely distinguished by their humaneness, confirmed my suspicion that prisoners held out much better and kept their sanity a great deal more easily in those days.

Many years later, in a train traveling east, I happened to share a compartment with a young woman doctor who had the same kind of bad luck as the one in Cherdyn: she had been assigned to a hospital in a labor camp. Times were not now so terrible—this was in 1954—and the girl started to tell me her troubles: How could she get out of it? It was more than flesh and blood could stand. "The worst is that you're helpless. What sort of doctors are we? We say and do what we're told." By this time I knew only too well that no doctor dares to show inde-pendence and is all too often forced to go against his conscience, though some are not even aware of breaking the Hippocratic oath when they refuse to give certificates of illness or disability. But what's the point of picking on the doctors? We all do only what we are told. We all act "on instructions," and there is no sense in closing our eyes to the fact.

18
PROFESSIONAL SICKNESS

I imagine that for a poet auditory hallucinations are something in the nature of an occupational disease.

As many poets have said—Akhmatova (in "Poem Without a Hero") and M. among them—a poem begins with a musical phrase ringing insistently in the ears; at first inchoate, it later takes on a precise form, though still without words. I sometimes saw M. trying to get rid of this kind of "hum," to brush it off and escape from it. He would toss his head as though it could be shaken out like a drop of water that gets into your ear while bathing. But it was always louder than any noise, radio or conversation in the same room.

Akhmatova told me that when "Poem Without a Hero" came to her, she was ready to try anything just to get rid of it, even rushing to do her washing. But nothing helped. At some point words formed behind the musical phrase and then the lips began to move. The work of a poet has probably something in common with that of a composer, and the appearance of words is the crucial factor that distinguishes it from musical composition. The "hum" sometimes came to M. in his sleep, but he could never remember it on waking. I have a feeling that verse exists before it is composed (M. never talked of "writing" verse, only of "composing" it and then copying it out). The whole process of composition is one of straining to catch and record something compounded of harmony and sense as it is relayed from an unknown source and gradually forms itself into words. The last stage of the work consists in ridding the poem of all the words foreign to the harmonious whole which existed before the poem arose. Such words slip in by chance, being used to fill gaps during the emergence of the whole. They become lodged in the body of the poem, and removing them is hard work. This final stage is a painful process of listening in to oneself in a search for the objective and absolutely precise unity called a "poem." In his poem "Save My Speech," the last adjective to come was "painstaking" (in "the painstaking tar of hard work"). M. complained that he needed something more precise and spare here, in the manner of Akhmatova: "She knows how to do it." He seemed to be waiting for her help.

I noticed that in his work on a poem there were two points at which he would sigh with relief—when the first words in a line or stanza came to him, and when the last of the foreign bodies was driven out by the right word. Only then is there an end to the process of listening in to oneself—the same process that can prepare the way for a disturbance of the inner hearing and loss of sanity. The poem now seems to fall away from the author and no longer torments him with its resonance. He is released from the thing that obsesses him. Io, the poor cow, escapes from the gadfly.

If the poem won't "go away," M. said, it means that there is something wrong with it, or something "still hidden in it"—a last fruitful bud from which a new shoot might sprout. In other words, the work is not finished. Whenever M.'s "inner voice" ceased, he was always very eager to read the new poem to someone. I wasn't enough for this: I witnessed his throes at such close quarters that M. always thought I must also be able to hear the "hum." He even reproached me sometimes for not having caught part of it. In his last Voronezh period (when he wrote the verse in his Second and Third Notebooks) we went round to Natasha Shtempel, or invited Fedia Marants, an agronomist of the utmost charm and integrity who in his youth had studied to be a violinist but had had to give it up when he damaged his hand in an accident. Fedia had some of the inner harmony which comes to people who listen to music, and though this was his first encounter with poetry, his musical sense made him a better judge than many a specialist would have been.

The first reading rounds off, as it were, the process of working on a poem, and the first listener is felt to be a contributor to it. From 1930 M.'s "first listeners" were Boris Sergeyevich Kuzin, a biologist, to whom M. dedicated his poem "To the German Language," and Alexander Margulis—it was he who circulated the poems of the first two Notebooks. Memorizing them as he listened, or getting copies of them, he read them to his innumerable friends and acquaintances. M. wrote an endless number of "margulets," as he called the couplets about him which had to begin with the words "Old man Margulis . . ." and be submitted for his approval. M. used to say that the poverty-stricken "old man Margulis" (he was no more than thirty at the time) kept an even poorer old man in his apartment and secretly supported him. Margulis was a real "one-man orchestra" who could whistle even the most difficult symphonies. It is a pity that the best "margulets," those about how the "old man" performed Beethoven in the streets of Moscow, have been lost. Margulis married the beautiful Iza Khantsyn, famous for her performances of Scriabin. Most of all in life he loved music, poetry and tales of adventure. I have been told that when he was dying in a camp in eastern Siberia he told yarns and adventure stories to the common criminals, who gave him food in return.

M.'s first listener was often Lev Gumilev, who lived with us in the winter of 1933–34. The beginning of the first Voronezh Notebook was read to Rudakov, who was exiled to Voronezh together with other ex-members of the aristocracy from Leningrad, but soon was allowed to return to the city.

It so happens that all of M.'s "first listeners" came to a tragic end. Apart from Natasha, they all went through prison and exile. Fedia Marants, for instance, was in prison for two years during the Yezhov terror, but he stuck it out without signing any confession and was therefore one of the people fortunate enough to be released after Yezhov's fall. Ill and broken after this ordeal, he was again arrested and exiled during the war merely because he happened to have been born in Vienna, from where he had been brought home to Kiev at the age of three weeks.

It might seem logical to conclude that if all M.'s "first listeners" suffered persecution, there must have been a link between their cases. But in fact there was no such link. Even before we met him, Kuzin had been "hauled in" for questioning, in connection with some affair involving biologists. He actually first got in trouble for some humorous verse he always carefully avoided showing us. He was summoned to various private apartments with rooms specially reserved for a secret police official whose job was to recruit informers. He was arrested for the first time in 1932, and then again for a second time together with his fellow biologist Vermel—both of them were regarded as neo-Lamarckists and had already been expelled from the Timiriazev Academy. The biologist Kuzin, the agronomist Fedia Marants, the son of an executed general Rudakov, and the son of an executed poet Gumilev did not even know each other. The only thing they all had in common was their love of poetry. Evidently this went with qualities of the mind which in our country doomed people to death or, at the best, to exile. Only translators were exempt.

The process of doing a translation is the exact opposite of work on original verse. I am not speaking here, of course, of the miraculous meeting of poetic minds that one finds in Zhukovski, whose translations brought a new element into Russian poetry, or of other translated verse that has become a valid part of Russian literature—such as A. K.

Tolstoi's rendering of Goethe's "Bride of Corinth," which we liked so much. Only real poets can achieve this kind of thing—and then very rarely. But an ordinary translation is a cold and calculated act of versification in which certain aspects of the writing of poetry are imitated. Strange to say, in translation there is no pre-existing entity waiting to be expressed. The translator sets himself in motion like an engine and then grinds out the required melody by a laborious mechanical process. He is deficient in what Khodasevich so aptly called "secret hearing." A real poet should beware of translation—it may only prevent the birth of original poetry.

In his "Conversation About Dante" M. speaks of "translators of ready-made meaning" to express his attitude toward translation and those who use poetic forms as a medium of ideas. M. always distinguished between this and real poetry. There was a time when people in this country stopped reading poetry altogether. "The thing about poetry," said Akhmatova, "is that once somebody swallows a substitute he will feel poisoned forever after." Poetry is now in fashion again and people are reading it as never before—but only because they have learned to tell the difference between it and all the glib products of "translators."

A poem is like a word. A consciously made-up word lacks all vitality. This is shown by the failure of all the attempts to create one's own vocabulary—these idiosyncratic games with man's divine gift of speech. When you attach an arbitrary meaning to the phonetic unit known as a word, the result is jargon, or the kind of verbal chaff used for selfish purposes by high priests, soothsayers, heads of state and other charlatans. Both words and poetry are desecrated in this way and made to perform the function of a hypnotist's crystal. Sooner or later the deception will be shown up for what it is, but people are always in danger of falling for every new imposter who turns his crystal in a different direction.

19

"Inside"

What happened to M. in the Lubianka during his interrogation? Later on, in Voronezh, he talked to me a great deal about it, trying to distinguish between his hallucinations and the facts. During the whole time his acute powers of observation never deserted him. This I saw when at our meeting he at once asked me about my coat and drew the right conclusion when I told him it was my mother's: "So you haven't been arrested." But he was ill, and not all his observations and conclusions proved well founded. Together we carefully sifted out the grains of fact, but it was not an easy task.

We had one fairly good way of judging whether something he remembered was true. During our meeting the interrogator touched on a great number of points. His obvious purpose was to impress on me his view of the case as a whole and various aspects of his inquiry into it. I was, as it were, being given authoritative guidance on how the whole thing should be seen. There were many women, such as Adalis, who gratefully accepted such guidance—most of them out of an instinct of self-preservation, but some quite sincerely. During the interview, then, I served as a kind of phonograph disc on which the interrogator recorded his version of events for me to make known to the world outside. He was deliberately trying to frighten me and, through me, those I would talk to about it. But he miscalculated, like other functionaries of our times, to whom it never occurs that their victims may dare to apply their own, rather than official, criteria to what they are told. Terror and depotism are always short-sighted.

Because of his acute sensitivity M. was no doubt easy game for his jailers and they were not, therefore, particularly subtle in their treatment of him. They kept him in a cell for two persons. The interrogator said that solitary confinement was "forbidden for reasons of humanity." I knew this was a lie. If it had ever been forbidden, it was only on paper. At every period we met people who had been kept in cells all alone. But whenever there was a shortage of prison space these tiny cells were filled to bursting point. Generally, however, the second place in a cell for two was used in a way of which in 1934, before M.'s arrest, we had never heard: M.'s cellmate tried to frighten him with the thought of his trial, assuring him that all his family and friends had been arrested and would appear in the dock together with him. He went through all the articles of the criminal code under which M. might be accused, as though giving him "legal advice," but in fact trying to alarm him at the prospect of being charged with terrorism, conspiracy and the like. M. would return from his nighttime interrogation to the clutches of his "fellow prisoner," who gave him no respite. But the man's approach was very crude, and M. once cut him short by asking: "Why are your nails so clean?" He had stupidly claimed to be a "veteran" of several months' standing, but his nails were neatly mani-cured. Early one morning he returned to the cell, supposedly from an interrogation, a little later than M., who noticed that he smelled of onion—and told him so.

The interrogator, countering M.'s remark at our interview that he was being held in a cell by himself, mentioned the humane ban on soli-tary confinement and added that M. had been with another prisoner whom it had been necessary to transfer because of M.'s "rudeness" to him. "How considerate!" M. managed to get in by way of the last word in this exchange.

At the very first interrogation M. had admitted to being the author of the poem on Stalin, so the stool pigeon's task could not have been merely to find out something that M. was hiding. Part of the function of these people was to unnerve and wear down prisoners under inter-rogation, to make their lives a misery. Until 1937 our secret police made much of their psychological methods, but afterward these gave way to physical torture, with beatings of the most primitive kind. After 1937 I never again heard of anyone being held in solitary-confinement cells, with or without stool pigeons. Perhaps people picked out for such treatment after 1937 did not leave the Lubianka alive.

M. was put through the physical ordeal which had always been ap-plied. It consisted mainly of not being allowed to sleep. He was called out every night and kept for hours on end. Most of the time was spent not in actual questioning, but in waiting under guard outside the in-terrogator's door. Once, when there was no interrogation, he was wak-ened all the same and taken to see a woman who kept him waiting at the door of her office for many hours, only to ask him at the end of it whether he had any complaints. Everybody knew how meaningless it was to make complaints to the prosecutor, and M. did not avail himself of this right. He had probably been called to her office simply as a for-mality, and also to keep him awake even on a night when the inter-rogator was catching up on his own sleep. These night birds lived a preposterous life, but all the same they managed to get some sleep, al-though not at the times when ordinary mortals did. The ordeal by de-privation of sleep and a bright light shining right in the eyes are known to everybody who has gone through such interrogations.

At the interview I had noticed how sore M.'s eyelids looked and asked what the reason was. The interrogator hastened to reply that it was through too much reading, but it later came out that M. was not allowed to have books in his cell. His eyelids never got better and he had trouble with them for the rest of his life. He told me that the inflammation was caused not only by bright lights but also by a stinging liquid which he believed was squirted through the spy-hole in the door whenever he went near it—since any anxiety made him very restless, he naturally paced his cell when he was left alone there. I have been told that the spy-hole is protected on both sides by thick glass so that no liquid could possibly be sprayed through it. This is perhaps one of the things that M. imagined, but one cannot help wondering whether a strong light was enough to bring about such a chronic infection of the eyelids.

M. was given salty food, but nothing to drink—a common practice in the Lubianka. When he went up to the spy-hole and demanded water from the guard outside, he was dragged off to a punishment cell and put in a strait-jacket. He had never before seen a strait-jacket, and as a check, he wrote down what it was like and we went to the hospital to look at one. His description fitted exactly.

At the interview I saw that M. had bandages on both wrists. When I asked him what was wrong with them, he just waved his hand, but the interrogator delivered himself of an angry speech about how M. had brought forbidden objects into his cell—an offense punishable under such-and-such an article. It turned out that M. had slashed his veins with a razor blade. He had been told by Kuzin, who in 1933, after two months in jail, had been released on the intervention of a Chekist friend with a passion for entomology, that the thing you want most in prison is a knife or at least a razor blade. He had even thought of a way of providing for an emergency by hiding one in the sole of his shoe. Hearing this, M. persuaded a cobbler he knew to secrete a few blades in this way for him. Forethought of this kind was second nature to us. In the mid-twenties Lozinski had shown us the bag which he kept packed in readiness for his arrest. This was something commonly done by engineers and members of other "exposed" professions, and the remarkable thing was not the fact itself, but the way in which everybody thought it was the most natural thing in the world. Such things were just part of our daily life, and with the blade he had so opportunely hidden in his shoe M. was able to slash his wrists. Bleeding to death is not the worst way of getting out of this life of ours. . . .

The work of undermining a person's sanity was carried on quite systematically in the Lubianka, and since our secret police is a bureaucratic institution like any other, all the procedures involved were probably governed by precise instructions. Even though the personnel were specifically selected for the job, one cannot ascribe what went on to their wicked nature, since the same people could overnight have become kindness itself—if so instructed. There were rumors among us that Yagoda had set up secret laboratories and staffed them with specialists who were carrying out all kinds of experiments with drugs, hypnosis, phonograph records and so forth. It was impossible to check such stories, and they may have been a product of our morbid imaginations, or tales deliberately put about to keep us all on tenterhooks.

In his cell M. sometimes heard a woman's voice coming from a distance and thought it was mine. It sounded as though I was complaining, groaning or talking very quickly about something, but it was so indistinct that he could make out no words at all. He concluded that the interrogator's hints that I too had been arrested must be true. When we later discussed this, we were not sure whether or not it had been an auditory hallucination. Why hadn't he been able to make out any words? In a state of hallucination the words he heard were all too distinct. Moreover, many other people who went through the Lubianka in those years also thought they heard their wives talking or screaming, only to learn later that they had never been arrested. Could they all have had hallucinations? And if so, how were they caused? There was some talk of the secret police having among their special equipment phonograph records with the voice of a "standard" wife, mother or daughter which were used to break a prisoner's spirit. After these more subtle torments and psychological methods had been replaced by exceedingly primitive ones, nobody complained any more that he had heard his wife's voice. Among the cruder methods, I know, for instance, that they would arrange for a woman prisoner to catch a glimpse of a man hideously beaten up and covered in blood, and then say that it was her son or husband. But there was no more talk of voices coming from a distance. Were there such recordings? I do not know and have no means of finding out. In view of the hallucinations from which M. suffered on leaving prison, I am inclined to think that this woman's voice was of the same order as the inner voices that plagued him in Cherdyn. There are still rumors about a laboratory for experiments with drugs.

Methods like these are possible only if a prisoner's links with the outside world are broken from the moment of his arrest. Apart from the signatures in the receipt book for packages, he is left completely in the dark about the people he has been torn from—and by no means everybody is allowed to receive packages. The first means of pressure brought to bear on a prisoner is the withdrawal of his right to receive packages—the last thread that binds him to the world outside. This is why it is better in our sort of life to have no ties. A man feels so much stronger if he doesn't have to watch out all the time during his interrogation for hints and pretended slips of the tongue about the fate of members of his family. It is harder to unhinge a single man, and he is better able to look after his own interests and conduct a systematic defense of himself. Even though the sentence was decided beforehand, a shrewd self-defense could still make some difference. One friend of mine was able to outwit his interrogator—admittedly a provincial one—in an extraordinary way. After a long battle he agreed to go back to his cell and write down all the nonsense required of him. He was given paper and he put down everything the interrogator wanted, but without signing it. The interrogator was so pleased that he didn't notice this. My friend was obviously born under a lucky star, because about this time Yezhov was dismissed. His case hadn't yet come before the tribunal, no sentence had been passed and he was able to get a reversal on the grounds that his deposition was not valid without a signature. He belongs to those few who were released after Yezhov's fall. But to be born under a lucky star is not enough—it is also advisable not to lose one's head, and this is easiest for people with no family ties.

20

CHRISTOPHOROVICH

M.'s interrogator, the celebrated Christophorovich, was not without his arrogant side, and he seemed to take pleasure in his work of intimidating a prisoner and reducing him to a nervous wreck. By his whole appearance, the way he looked at you and his tone of voice, he seemed concerned to show up his prisoner as a nonentity, a miserable creature, a disgrace to mankind. "Why is he so stuck up?" we would have asked if we had met him in the ordinary way of things, but during his nightly interrogations the prisoner was supposed to squirm under his gaze, or at least to feel utter impotence. Christophorovich behaved like a person of superior race who despised physical weakness and the pathetic scruples of intellectuals. This he made clear during the interview by the whole of his well-practiced manner, and I too, though not frightened by him, could feel myself growing smaller under his gaze. Yet I already had a suspicion that such latter-day Siegfrieds, the heirs to the supermen, cannot themselves stand up to the ordeals they inflict on others. Magnificent before the defenseless, they are only good at savaging victims already caught in a trap.

The interrogator's arrogance was reflected not only in his manner, but also in occasional very superior remarks that smacked of the literary drawing room. The first generation of young Chekists, later to be removed and destroyed in 1937, was distinguished by its sophisticated tastes and weakness for literature—only the most fashionable, of course. In my presence Christophorovich said to M. that it was useful for a poet to experience fear ("you yourself told me so") because it can inspire verse, and that he would "experience fear in full measure." Both M. and I noted the use of the future tense. In what Moscow drawing rooms had Christophorovich heard this kind of talk?

Both M. and I had the same general impression that, as M. put it, "this Christophorovich has turned everything upside down and inside out." The Chekists were the avant-garde of the "new people" and they had indeed basically revised, in the manner of the Superman, all ordinary human values. They were later replaced by people of a completely different physical type, who had no values at all, revised or otherwise.

It turned out, however, that the technique used by the interrogator to frighten M. was an utterly primitive one. Mentioning somebody's name—mine, Akhmatova's or my brother's—he would say that he had obtained certain statements from us. When M. inquired whether whoever it was had been arrested, the interrogator gave no definite answer, but dropped a casual-sounding hint that "we have them here," only to deny a few minutes later that he had said any such thing. Uncertainty about such matters always has a devastating effect on the prisoner, and it is only possible under a prison system like ours. In playing this cat-and-mouse game with M. and only hinting that his family and friends had been arrested, Christophorovich was behaving like a top-level interrogator, since it was more usual to inform the prisoner straightaway, without any beating about the bush, that everybody had already been arrested, or questioned and shot. Then you could go back to your cell and wonder whether it was true or not.

Christophorovich, as a "literature specialist," made great play with his "inside knowledge," claiming to know everybody and everything that was going on. He tried to create the impression that all our acquaintances came to see him, and that he knew all our little secrets. He referred to many people only by their nicknames or by some telltale feature: one was "the bigamist," another "the ex-Party member" and a woman acquaintance of ours "the actress." These three examples I heard during the interview, but M. told me he had called many other people by nicknames like this. Apart from showing how well informed he was, this had another purpose. Since police informers are always referred to only by code names, he was trying to cast a shadow on all these people. The high police official in Tashkent who committed suicide, according to his daughter, also always knew everybody's nickname, and himself invented them for people. Realizing what the intention behind the use of them was, M. paid no attention to his interrogator's innuendoes.

M. told me that the interrogator's methods constantly betrayed the influence of stereotyped official procedure. Our authorities assumed that for each class and even sub-group of the population there were certain standard remarks that were often made in conversation. It is said that the research section of the Lubianka had compiled reams of such "typical" remarks. Christophorovich tried some of them out on M., for example: "You said to So-and-so that you would rather live in Paris than in Moscow." The theory was that M., as a bourgeois writer and ideologist of a dying class, must surely be eager to return to its bosom. The name of the person to whom he was supposed to have made such remarks was always a common one, such as Ivanov or Petrov (or, if need be, Ginzburg or Rabinovich). The guinea pig on whom this type of approach was tried out was supposed to quake in his shoes and begin frantically going over in his mind all the Ivanovs or Rabinoviches to whom he might have confided his dream of going abroad. In the eyes of Soviet law, such a dream was, if not an outright crime, at least an aggravating circumstance for which you could even be charged under some convenient article of the criminal code. In any case, an accused person's class nature was fully revealed by his ambition to go to Paris, and in our classless society, account must always be taken of one's class allegiance. . . . Another example of this kind of questioning was: "You complained to So-and-so that before the Revolution you earned much more by your writings than now." M. was obviously not to be caught out by such things. The whole approach was indeed crude, but they had no need of subtlety. Why bother? "Give us a man, and we'll make a case."

Christophorovich had been conducting the interrogation in preparation for a trial, as was implicit in his words "We have decided not to proceed with the case" and similar remarks. By our standards he had more than enough to go on, and a trial would have been a more natural outcome than what actually happened. The interrogator's approach was to seek an explanation for every single word in the poem on Stalin. He was particularly concerned to find out what had prompted the writing of it. He was flabbergasted when M. suddenly told him in reply to his question that more than anything else he hated fascism. M. had not intended to speak so frankly to the interrogator, and he blurted this out despite himself—he was by then in such a state that he just didn't care. As he was in duty bound to, the interrogator stormed and shouted, demanding to know what M. thought was fascist about our system. This question he repeated in my presence during the interview, but, astonishingly enough, he didn't pursue the matter when M. replied evasively. M. later assured me that there was something ambiguous about the interrogator's whole behavior, and that behind his blustering manner one could constantly sense his hatred for Stalin. I didn't believe M., but in 1938, when Christophorovich was also shot, I began to wonder. Perhaps M. had spotted something that a more balanced and worldly-wise person would not have seen—such people are always too conventional in their reasoning. It is difficult to believe that the mighty Yagoda and his awesome organization surrendered to Stalin without a struggle. In 1934, when M.'s poem was being investigated, it was widely known that Vyshinski was intriguing against Yagoda. In our incredible blindness—what better example of conventional reasoning?—we had eagerly followed the rumors of a struggle between the Prosecutor General and the head of the secret police, thinking that Vyshinski, a lawyer by training, would put an end to the excesses and terror of secret tribunals. To think that we believed this— we who knew what to expect from the Vyshinski of the trials in the twenties! For Yagoda's followers, however, and in particular for Christophorovich, it was clear that a victory for Vyshinski would do them no good at all, and, of course, they knew better than anyone else what tortures and humiliations to expect in their final days. When there are two groups fighting for the right to unlimited control over the fate of their fellow citizens, the losers are doomed to die, and perhaps M. really was able to read the secret thoughts of his iron-willed interrogator. But the extraordinary thing about those times was that all these "new people," as they killed and were destroyed themselves, thought that only they had a right to their views and judgments. Any one of them would have laughed out loud at the idea that a man who could be brought before them under guard at any time of the day or night, who had to hold up his trousers with his hands and spoke without the slightest attempt at theatrical effects—that such a man might have no doubt, despite everything, of his right to express himself freely in poetry. As we were to discover, Yagoda liked M.'s poem so much that he even learned it by heart—he recited it to Bukharin while we were still in Cherdyn—but he would not have hesitated to destroy the whole of literature, past, present and future, if he had thought it to his advantage. For people of this extraordinary type, human blood is like water and all individuals, except for the victorious ruler, are replaceable. The worth of any man is measured by his usefulness to the ruler and his henchmen. The skilled propagandists who help to rouse the people to expressions of enthusiasm for the leader deserve to be better paid than the rest. Our rulers may sometimes have bestowed favors on their cronies—they all liked to play the Haroun al Rashid—but they never allowed anyone to interfere in their business, or to have an opinion of his own. From this point of view, M.'s poem was a real crime—a usurpation of the right to words and thoughts that the ruling powers reserved exclusively for themselves, whether they were enemies or friends of Stalin. This astonishing presumption has become second nature to our rulers. Your right to an opinion is always determined by your rank and status in the hierarchy. Not long ago Surkov explained to me that Pasternak's novel is no good because its hero, Dr. Zhivago, has no right to make any judgments about our way of life— "we" had not given him this right. Christophorovich was no more able to grant such a right to M.

Christophorovich referred to the poem as a "document" and to the writing of it as a terrorist "act." At our interview he said he had never before set eyes on such a monstrous "document." M. did not deny that he had read it to a number of people—eleven all told, including me, our brothers and Akhmatova. The interrogator had extracted their names one after another by going through all the people who came to see us, and it was evident that he really was very well informed about all those closest to us. At the interview M. told me all the names that had cropped up during the interrogation so that I could warn everybody concerned. None of them suffered, but they all got a terrible fright. I do not wish to give all the names here, otherwise someone may be tempted to speculate as to the identity of the traitor. Christophorovich was anxious to know how each of his listeners had reacted to the poem. M. insisted that they had all begged him to forget it and not bring ruin on himself and others. Apart from the eleven named during the interrogation, seven or eight other people, including Shklovski and Pasternak, had heard the poem, but the interrogator did not mention them, and they did not therefore figure in the case.

M. signed the record of his interrogation without even reading it over—something for which I gave him no rest during the next few years. Even the interrogator rebuked him for this in my presence. "I suppose he trusted you," I said angrily. In fact, I believe that in this respect there was no reason not to trust him: by our standards it was a perfectly real case, there was enough material for ten trials and therefore it would have made no sense to invent anything.

At the beginning of the interrogation, M. noticed, the interrogator had behaved much more aggressively than toward the end. He even stopped describing the poem as a "terrorist act" and threatening that M. would be shot. At first he threatened not only M. with the firing squad but all his "accomplices" as well—that is, everybody who had heard the poem. When we later discussed this softening in the interrogator's attitude, we decided it had been brought about by the instruction to "preserve" M. I did not see Christophorovich in the early stage, when he had used threats against M., but I must say that at the interview his manner still seemed to me monstrously aggressive. But this is in the nature of the job—probably not only in our country.

The interrogator probed into M.'s feelings about the Soviet system and M. told him that he was willing to co-operate with any Soviet institution except the Cheka.

He said this not out of daring or bravado, but because of his total inability to be devious. I believe this quality of M.'s was a puzzle to the interrogator, one he could not fathom. His only explanation for such a statement, particularly when it was made to his face, would have been stupidity, but stupidity of this kind he had never encountered before, and he had a baffled look when he quoted M.'s words at our interview. M. and I recalled this detail at the height of the Yezhov terror, when Shaginian wrote a half-page article in *Pravda* saying how gladly persons under investigation unburdened themselves to their interrogators and "co-operated" with them at their interrogations. This she explained by the great sense of responsibility common to all Soviet citizens. Whether Shaginian wrote this article of her own free will or on instructions from above, it is something that should not be forgotten.

In their depravity and the depths to which they sank, some writers exceeded all bounds. In 1934 already Akhmatova and I heard that Pavlenko was telling people how, out of curiosity, he had accepted an invitation from Christophorovich, who was a good friend of his, to hide in a cupboard, or between double doors, and listen to one of the nighttime interrogations. In the interrogator's room I noticed several identical doors—far too many for one room. We were later told that some of these doors opened into cubby-holes, and others into emergency exists. Premises like these are scientifically designed in the most up-to-date fashion with the aim of protecting the interrogator against prisoners who might try to attack him.

According to Pavlenko, M. cut a sorry figure during his interrogation: his trousers kept slipping down and he had to hold them up with his hands; his replies were confused, incoherent and beside the point, he talked nonsense and was very nervous, squirming "like a fish in a frying pan." Public opinion here has always been conditioned to take the side of the strong against the weak, but what Pavlenko did surpassed everything. No Bulgarin would ever have dared to do this. Moreover, in the official literary circles to which Pavlenko belonged, it had been completely forgotten that the only thing with which someone in M.'s position could be reproached was giving false evidence to save his own skin; certainly he could not be blamed for being bewildered and frightened. Why are we supposed to be brave enough to stand up to all the horrors of twentieth-century prisons and camps? Are we supposed to sing as we fall into the mass graves? Face death in the gas chambers with courage? Travel cheerfully to prison in a cattle car? Engage our interrogators in polite conversation about the role of fear in poetry, or discuss the impulses that lead to the writing of verse in a state of fury and indignation?

The fear that goes with the writing of verse has nothing in common with the fear one experiences in the presence of the secret police. Our mysterious awe in the face of existence itself is always overridden by the more primitive fear of violence and destruction. M. often spoke of how the first kind of fear had disappeared with the Revolution that had shed so much blood before our eyes.

21
WHO IS TO BLAME?

The interrogator's first question was "Why do you think you were arrested?" Receiving an evasive answer, he suggested M. try to think which of his poems might have led to his arrest. M. recited, one after another, "The Wolf," "Old Crimea" and "The Apartment." He hoped he could fob Christophorovich off with these, though any one of them would have been enough to send him to a labor camp. The interrogator knew neither "Old Crimea" nor "The Apartment," and copied both of them down. M. suppressed eight lines from "The Apartment," and it was in this truncated form that the poem later turned up among Tarasenkov's copies. Next the interrogator took a sheet of paper from a file, read out a description of the poem about Stalin and several lines of the text. M. admitted he was the author. The interrogator then asked him to recite the whole poem. When M. had finished he remarked that the first stanza in his copy was different, and he read out what he had:

> We live, deaf to the land beneath us,
> Ten steps away no one hears our speeches.
> *All we hear is the Kremlin mountaineer,*
> *The murderer and peasant-slayer.*

M. explained that this was the first version. M. then had to copy the poem out in his own hand, and the interrogator put it in his file.

M. saw the copy produced by the interrogator, but could not remember whether he was actually allowed to hold it in his hand and read it. At that moment he was so flustered that he didn't know what he was doing. We cannot therefore be certain of the form in which the poem had been passed on to the police—whether in full or only partially, whether in an accurate copy or not.

Among the people who had heard it there were a number who could have memorized these sixteen lines even after hearing them only once. People who are themselves writers are particularly good at this, but they nearly always garble the text slightly, substituting one word for another or leaving something out. If M. had seen such minor changes, he would have known that the poem had been given to the police by someone who had only heard it recited, and he would thus have been able to clear the one person he had allowed to make a copy (in the first version, moreover). But M. did not have enough presence of mind to make this check. It was all very well for us to discuss later on in Voronezh what he should have done and how he should have behaved. I am always hearing accounts of how some bold spirit or other foxed his interrogator or gave him hell, but aren't these perhaps the product of reflections after the event?

There was another reason, too, for M.'s lack of initiative in this matter: he was by no means anxious to discover who the traitor was, even if he had the opportunity. We lived in a world where people were always being "hauled in" and asked for information about our thoughts and feelings. They summoned people who were compromised by their background or by psychological deficiencies, threatening one because he was the son of a banker or Czarist official, and promising favors or protection to another. They summoned people who were afraid of losing their jobs or wanted to make a career, those who wanted nothing and feared nothing, and those who were ready for anything. The object of all this was not just to gather information. Nothing binds people together more than complicity in the same crime: the more people could be implicated and compromised, the more traitors, informants and police spies there were, the greater would be the number of people supporting the regime and longing for it to last thousands of years. And when it is common knowledge that everybody is "summoned" like this, people lose their social instincts, the ties between them weaken, everybody retires to his corner and keeps his mouth shut—which is an invaluable boon to the authorities.

Once they played on Kuzin's feelings as a son by telling him: "Your mother won't stand it if we arrest you." To this he replied that he wished his mother would die, and the official was quite shaken by such heartlessness. (This was the same man who had threatened to start rumors that "we have recruited you, and you'll never be able to look people in the face again.")

The artist B., a man of absolute purity whom we all loved, always used to arrive late for these interviews—nobody dared cut them altogether, even though they were unofficial and generally arranged on the telephone, as in a Kafka novel. When they rebuked him for being late, B. would say: "I always fall asleep when I have trouble." A woman friend of mine, in the twenties when she was still a pretty young girl, used to be stopped on the street and hauled off by police agents—as though they were staging a new abduction of Europa. There was nothing they wouldn't do.

They generally invited people for these interviews not to the Lubianka, but to apartments specially allotted for the purpose. The uncooperative were kept for hours on end and urged to "think again." No secret was made of all this—it was an important element in the general system of intimidation, as well as being a good way of testing a person's "loyalty." The stubborn became marked men and were "dealt with" as opportunity arose. The cooperative, on the other hand, were helped in their careers, and whenever there were dismissals or purges, they could count on the good will of the personnel department.

The way in which people reacted to proposals to cooperate depended on their generation. The older people suffered if they were merely panicked into signing an undertaking not to divulge anything about the interview. Of all my friends only Zoshchenko ever refused to sign such a statement. Younger people did not even understand what was wrong about this. They preferred to stall by saying: "If I were to learn anything, I'd come and tell you, but I never hear anything—I never go anywhere except to work." This is the sort of boast made by people who refused to "cooperate"—a word with a very wide meaning in this country. But what percentage refused? There's no way of knowing. Presumably their number increased in periods when the terror slackened off. Apart from people who were forced into cooperating, there were hosts of volunteers. Denunciations poured into every institution on a quite unmanageable scale. Before the Twentieth Congress I heard an inspector of the Ministry of Education address a meeting at the Chuvash Teachers' Training College, where I was then working, and ask the staff to stop writing denunciations, warning them that anonymous ones would no longer be read at all. Can it be true that they no longer read anonymous denunciations? I find it hard to believe.

Because of this system of "interviews," people developed two kinds of phobia—some suspected that everybody they met was an informer, others that they might be taken for one. Quite recently a certain poet was moaning to me that he had no copies of M.'s poems. When I offered him a copy of one of them, he was horrified in case I might get the idea that he was asking for it on behalf of the Lubianka! S., when I offered him the same poem, thought it his duty to inform me that for decades the secret police had been calling him in and harassing him. In 1934, when M. and I were in Voronezh, I was visited by X., who was gloomy and upset. "Tell me," he said, "that it wasn't me." He had come to find out whether we regarded him as the person responsible for M.'s arrest. He had not even heard the poem about Stalin, and was a good friend. When I told him what we thought of him, he was enormously relieved.

We often stopped people who talked too freely by saying: "Good God! What are you doing? What will people take you for if you talk like that?" And we were always being advised not to meet people at all. Misha Zenkevich, for example, told me I should not allow anyone into the house unless I had known him all my life, to which I always replied that even such friends might have changed into something different. This is how we lived, and this is why we are not the same as other people.

An existence like this leaves its mark. We all became slightly unbalanced mentally—not exactly ill, but not normal either: suspicious, mendacious, confused and inhibited in our speech, at the same time putting on a show of adolescent optimism. What value can such people have as witnesses? The elimination of witnesses was, indeed, part of the whole program.

2 2

THE ADJUTANT

We got to know Dligach in the middle twenties in Kiev when a group of young journalists there managed to talk the dim-witted editor of a local newspaper into publishing a few articles by M. This would have been quite out of the question in Moscow. Dligach's wife, a limpid blonde of a type M. always found touching, had gone to the same school as I. They lived not far from my parents, and we often met them on our visits to Kiev. A few years later Dligach turned up in Moscow to work, like M., on the newspaper *Moscow Komsomol.* He didn't get on very well and, as a provincial, was given a hard time by his Moscow colleagues. One day he came to us, beaming all over his face, to say he had at last had a piece of good luck: he had found on the floor a letter written by one of his enemies, an editor of the newspaper. It was a typical letter from a village youth who had come to the town to earn his living. He sent greetings to his friends and neighbors, and told his mother that, thank God, he was on good terms with his superiors, would soon settle in a more permanent way, get some kind of award and a room to himself, after which he would invite one of his younger brothers to join him and help him get on his feet as well.

The letter was a perfectly human one in which the young man talked about his personal interests in a way unbecoming to someone occupying an official position on a Komsomol newspaper. What was worse, he mentioned God—something no Komsomol official could afford to do. Even such hackneyed expressions as "thank God" were regarded as a concession to religion. It was clear that the youth was leading a double life, and talked two different languages. At what point do people switch from bureaucratic and ideological jargon to ordinary everyday speech? Our leading playwright was always longing to write a play about this linguistic dualism and the critical moment at which people pass from one idiom to the other. "When does it happen, out on the street or only at home?" he would ask, itching to start work. But, being a man of the older generation, he never went ahead with it. Many years later another writer,* much younger, dealt with this question in a story about a meeting of a village Soviet, when the kolkhozniks started speaking in official jargon the moment the chairman rang his bell.

Dligach intended to make full use of his find to expose his enemy to the higher authorities. He had come to us to brag about his good luck, and he showed the letter to M. M. snatched it from him and threw it into the stove.

Dligach's behavior was typical of that period—the end of the twenties and the beginning of the thirties. In their struggle for ideological purity, the authorities did everything to encourage "fearless unmaskers" who, "without respect for persons," showed up "survivals of the old psychology" in their colleagues. Reputations were pricked like soap bubbles, and the "unmaskers" quickly climbed the ladder of promotion. Every official who moved up the scale in those years was bound to use this method at least once—that is, "unmask" his immediate superior, as the only way of taking his place. Dligach might have found his letter very useful in this way, but, to our surprise, he agreed with M.'s comment on his behavior and left us more in sorrow than in anger after his hopes for a better future had gone up in smoke in our stove. But perhaps he really was angry, because we didn't see him again for several years.

---

* See the note on Alexander Yashin in the Appendix.

He reappeared at our apartment in Furmanov Street in the winter of 1933–34. He was brought to us by Dinochka, a tiny actress, scatterbrained but very nice, whom we had inherited from Yakhontov. We remembered the letter and Dligach thanked M. for having saved him from doing such a despicable thing. He now quickly gained our confidence; the old business of the letter was forgiven and forgotten as something that any youngster might have done in those years: how could one hold such a thing against him for the rest of his life?

In 1933 Dligach also saw a lot of Bezymenski, trying to fix up some of his newspaper business through him. He was always telling M. he should consult Bezymenski about various matters (such as the affair with Amir Sagidzhan and Alexei Tolstoi over which M. was still fuming). Almost on the very eve of his arrest M. was being urged by Dligach to go and see a woman prosecutor, a friend of Bezymenski's, to tell her what had made him slap Tolstoi in the face. I do not know what the purpose of all this fuss was, but I do know that M. had read his poem on Stalin to Dligach.

The morning after M.'s arrest, at a very early hour, we had a phone call from Bezymenski. I told him, of course in the guarded language that everybody understood, what had happened during the night. He whistled through his teeth and hung up. This was the one and only phone call we ever had from Bezymenski. Had Dligach told him about M.? Perhaps he had heard something about the arrest and had just phoned to check? But who could have told him? How could he have known? The warrant had been signed by Yagoda himself, and too little time had gone by—it was only a few hours since M. had been taken away—for any rumors to spread. Why did he call?

The last time I saw Dligach was in the hall of our apartment in Furmanov Street when I returned from the meeting with the interrogator. Dligach went away to get the money I asked him for and never came back. When Dinochka wanted to come and see us in Voronezh, Dligach made a violent scene, forbidding her to do any such thing. Dinochka was indignant and left him. Still in a state of shock, she told us in Voronezh about her boyfriend's sudden fit of hysteria and the breaking-off of their relationship, which had apparently lasted several years. After the war I heard that Dligach had hanged himself. He did this out of sheer panic during the campaign against "cosmopolitans." He was not known for his courage.

As I have said, M. was not concerned to try and find who had betrayed him. He said that he had only himself to blame: it was wrong, in our times, to lead people into temptation. Not for nothing had Brodski—the one who sat in the room during M.'s arrest—once asked M. not to read him any dangerous poems, since he would only have to go and report them. When I nagged M. about Dligach, he just said with amazing indifference: "If it wasn't him, it was another." I was very anxious to put all the blame on this insignificant person because the very thought of all the other possibilities was intolerable. It was easier to put it all on the wretched Dligach than to suspect somebody we thought of as a real friend. Yet I am not sure it was Dligach who denounced M. During the interrogation Dligach's name never came up. This may have been to protect him, but it is also possible that the informers who had given the names of our visitors never met Dligach because he generally came in the daytime with Dinochka—she was busy at the theater in the evenings and in any case avoided our friends, preferring to catch us alone. Informers always told the police about the whole circle of one's friends, not just picking out one isolated individual. Christophorovich knew of practically everybody who came to see us regularly.

Was Dligach capable of memorizing sixteen lines after one hearing? I never heard him repeat verse he had heard in these conditions. M. read the poem on Stalin only once in his presence and broke his usual rule by doing so in front of a second person—the artist T., whose name was not mentioned by the interrogator either. And—most important of all—we could not recollect whether Dligach had heard the poem in the "peasant-slayer" version or not. Probably not. T. was a rare visitor who came to see us not long before M.'s arrest, by which time the first version had been completely discarded. The only person M. had allowed to write the poem down had done so in the first version, but, judging by his whole life, this man is above suspicion. Perhaps someone stole it from him? The suggestion has a certain appeal, but I believe that things always passed from private hands to the secret police in a much more direct fashion.

Dligach's behavior after M.'s arrest could be explained by cowardice, or by the well-known phobia about being taken for a police spy. By his past he was fitted more than anyone else for this role, but the horror was that the same part could be played by people from whom one least expected it. So many informers were eminently respectable ladies, or young men from good families—the very picture of honesty!—or highly intellectual people utterly devoted to scholarship and art who were able to win you over by their refined, elegant, clever conversation. One of these would have fitted the part very much better than the humdrum Dligach. But he scarcely matters. He was just a poor wretch who happened to live in terrible times. Can a man really be held accountable for his own actions? His behavior, even his character, is always in the merciless grip of the age, which squeezes out of him the drop of good or evil that it needs from him.

Another puzzle is: when did the poem about Stalin become known to the police? It was written in the autumn of 1933, and the arrest took place in May 1934. Perhaps after he had slapped Tolstoi in the face, the authorities had stepped up their surveillance of M. and learned about the poem only in the course of making inquiries among their agenst? Or had they kept it for six months without taking any action? This seems inconceivable. As for Dligach, he appeared on the scene fairly late—in the middle of the winter—and wormed his way into our confidence in the spring.

One final question: was it my fault for not getting rid of all our friends and acquaintances, as did most good wives and mothers at that time? My guilt is lessened only by the fact that M. would in any case have given me the slip and found a way of reading his outrageous poem—and in this country all real poetry is outrageous—to the first person he met. He was not one to put a gag on himself and lead a life of voluntary seclusion.

23

ON THE NATURE OF THE MIRACLE

Vinaver, who often had to go to the Lubianka, was the first to learn that something odd was going on in connection with M.'s case: "There's a kind of special atmosphere about it, with people fussing and whispering to each other." As we soon learned, the case had been suddenly revised and M.'s sentence commuted to "minus twelve."* All this happened in record time—in no more than a day, or only a few hours. The very pace of events was testimony to their miraculous nature: when the right button was pressed above, the bureaucratic machine functioned with astonishing speed.

The greater the degree of centralization, the more impressive the

---

* A form of banishment which allowed people to live anywhere except in twelve major cities.

miracle. We were overjoyed by miracles and accepted them with the innocent credulity of an Oriental mob. They had become part of our life. Which one of us had never written letters to the supreme powers, addressed to the most metallic of names?* And what is such a letter but a plea for a miracle? If they are preserved, these mountains of letters will be a veritable treasure trove for historians: the life of our times is recorded in them far more faithfully than in any other form of writing, since they speak of all the hurts, humiliations, blows, pitfalls and traps of our existence. But to go through them and sift out the tiny grains of real fact will be a Herculean labor. The trouble is that even in these letters we observed the special style of Soviet polite parlance, speaking of our misfortunes in the language of newspaper editorials. But even a cursory look at these letters to the "powers-that-be" would show at once how much we needed miracles—to live without them was impossible. Only one must remember that even if they got their miracles, the writers of such letters were doomed to bitter disappointment. This they were never prepared for, despite the warning of popular wisdom that miracles are never more than a flash in the pan, with no lasting effect. What are people left with in the fairy tales after their three wishes have come true? What becomes, in the morning, of the gold obtained in the night from the lame man? It turns into a slab of clay, or a handful of dust. The only good life is one in which there is no need for miracles.

The affair of M.'s arrest gave birth to a whole cycle of stories, spread by word of mouth, about miracles which had suddenly come from on high, bursting on us like benevolent thunderclaps—if this is not a contradiction in terms. And it is indeed true that we were saved by a miracle that gave us the three years' lease of life in Voronezh.

It was my brother, Evgeni Khazin, who first told us by telegram about the commuting of M.'s sentence to "minus twelve." When we showed it to the Cherdyn Commandant, he shrugged his shoulders and said: "We'll see about that. By the time I hear, it'll be winter." And he thereupon reminded us that it was time we cleared out of the hospital and found winter quarters for ourselves: "Find something without cracks in the walls—it gets cold in these parts."

The official telegram came the next day. The Commandant might not have told us straightaway if, before he came to work, we hadn't got

* Stalin's name is derived from the Russian for "steel."

to know about it from the girl clerk in the telegraph office with whom M. gossiped and joked during his morning walk. We went to the Commandant's office, but had to wait a long time for him to appear. He read the telegram in our presence and could not at first believe his eyes. "Perhaps this was sent by your relatives," he said. "How am I to know?" For two or three days he kept us waiting in great anxiety until at last he got confirmation from Moscow that the cable was an official one and had not been fabricated by the cunning relatives of the exiled man who had been given into his charge. He now summoned us and told us to choose the town we would like to go to. The Commandant insisted that we decide at once—there was nothing in the telegram about giving us time to think it over. "Right now!" he said, and we chose our town under his gaze. We did not know the provinces and we had no friends anywhere outside the twelve forbidden towns. Suddenly M. remembered that Leonov, a biologist at Tashkent University, had said good things about Voronezh, where he was born. Leonov's father worked there as a prison doctor. "Who knows, perhaps we shall need a prison doctor," said M., and we decided on Voronezh. The Commandant then duly made out a travel warrant for us. He was so shaken by the turn of events—that is, by the speed with which our case had been reviewed— that he did us the unheard-of favor of letting us use an "official" horse and cart to take our belongings to the pier. (We should never have been able to hire a horse privately—all private horses had been wiped out by the recent collectivization.) At the last minute the Commandant wished us luck—as one of the first witnesses of the miracle that has so suddenly happened to us, he must even have felt in some ways a kind of intimate of ours.

With the housekeeper at the hospital, on the other hand, it was the opposite—she lost all faith in us. What sort of people could we be if the authorities treated us like this? was the unspoken reproach I read in her eyes. Needless to say, she now had no doubt that M. had earned this favor in some unspeakable way—they never otherwise allowed anyone to escape their clutches. The housekeeper had greater experience than we, and, like all our fellow countrymen, she was peculiarly (though quite understandably) egocentric in trusting only to her own experience. As an exile M. had been automatically "one of us" for her (though three years later she was to learn that not all exiles could be so regarded and you had to hold your tongue in their presence, too), but now he had been pardoned—for to an inhabitant of Cherdyn,

Voronezh sounded like paradise—he was alien and suspect in her eyes. I imagine that after we had left, all the exiles in Cherdyn spent a long time trying to remember what indiscreet things they had said to us, and wondering whether we hadn't been sent there specially to ferret out their inner thoughts and secrets. It would have been pointless to feel any resentment toward the housekeeper—I should have felt exactly the same in her place. The loss of mutual trust is the first sign of the atomization of society in dictatorships of our type, and this was just what our leaders wanted.

The housekeeper was as much an outsider to me as we were to her, and a lot of the things she said made no sense to me. In that memorable year I had already come to understand one or two things, but it was still not enough. The housekeeper was always saying that she and the others had been exiled quite illegally. For example, by the time of her arrest she had stopped working for her party, and when they picked her up, she was already a private person—"and they knew it too!" But in my barbarism or, rather, barbarized by what had been dinned into my ears, I couldn't follow her reasoning. If she herself admitted having belonged to one of the parties that had been liquidated, how could she complain about being kept in exile? It was only what could be expected under our system. . . . This was how it struck me then. Our system, I felt, was harsh and brutal, but that was life, and a strong regime could not tolerate avowed opponents who, even though out of action, might make a comeback. I was not easily taken in by official propaganda, but I had swallowed some of their barbaric ideas of justice. Others were even more receptive to the "new law"—Narbut, for example, thought there had been no choice but to exile M. "The state has to protect itself, doesn't it? What would happen otherwise, I ask you?" I did not argue with him. What was the point of trying to explain that unpublished verses have the same status as thoughts, and that nobody should be banished for his thoughts? It always needed a personal misfortune to open our eyes and make us a little more human—and even then the lesson took a little time to sink in.

There had been a time when, terrified of chaos, we had all prayed for a strong system, for a powerful hand that would stem the angry human river overflowing its banks. This fear of chaos is perhaps the most permanent of our feelings—we have still not recovered from it, and it is passed on from one generation to another. There is not one of us—either among the old who saw the Revolution or the young and innocent—who does not believe that he would be the first victim if ever the mob got out of hand. "We should be the first to be hanged from a lamppost"—whenever I hear this constantly repeated phrase, I remember Herzen's words about the intelligentsia which so much fears its own people that it prefers to go in chains itself, provided the people, too, remain fettered.

What we wanted was for the course of history to be made smooth, all the ruts and potholes to be removed, so there should never again be any unforeseen events and everything should flow along evenly and according to plan. This longing prepared us, psychologically, for the appearance of the Wise Leaders who would tell us where we were going. And once they were there, we no longer ventured to act without their guidance and looked to them for direct instructions and foolproof prescriptions. Since we could offer no better prescriptions of our own, it was logical to accept the ones proposed from on high. The most we dared do was offer advice in some minor matter: would it be possible, for example, to allow different styles in carrying out the Party's orders in art? We would like it so much. . . . In our blindness we ourselves struggled to impose unanimity—because in every disagreement, in every difference of opinion, we saw the beginnings of new anarchy and chaos. And either by silence or consent we ourselves helped the system to gain in strength and protect itself against its detractors— such as the housekeeper in Cherdyn, or various poets and chatterboxes.

So we went on, nursing a sense of our own inadequacy, until the moment came for each of us to discover from bitter experience how precarious was his own state of grace. This could only come from bitter personal experience, because we did not believe in other people's. We really are inadequate and cannot be held responsible for our behavior. And we are saved only by miracles.

24

JOURNEY TO VORONEZH

Our documents were made out and stamped by the most influential institution in the Soviet Union, and we were authorized to buy tickets for reserved seats in the military booking office. This was an unheard-of privilege in those days, when all the railroad stations and piers in the country were besieged by sullen, grimy mobs who had to wait for weeks on end to buy a ticket. It looked as though a whole people were on the move or being evacuated. At the pier in Perm, exhausted and ragged people with blackened faces had encamped in whole families, or perhaps tribes, sitting on bundles and piles of rags next to their wooden trunks with crude lacquer patterns on them. All over the river-bank, charcoal fires were glowing in pits dug in the sand where they were making a stew for their children. The grown-ups chewed crusts of bread which they carried with them in bags—bread was still ra-tioned at that time and they had stored up these iron reserves for the journey. Collectivization had uprooted vast hordes of people and they were roaming the country, desperately searching for somewhere to live and still sighing for their boarded-up huts.

Strictly speaking, these were not dispossessed kulaks—those had long ago been deported to new places—but marginal groups who had fled in panic and were now wandering aimlessly—anything to get away from their native villages. We have seen many forced mass migrations and several voluntary ones: during the Civil War, during the famines in the Volga region and the Ukraine, during collectivization, wartime evacuation. Right up to the last war, the railroad stations were still crowded with uprooted peasants. After the war, people again began to wander in search of food and work, but on a smaller scale. Every fam-ily in which an able-bodied man had survived was desperate to find a place where there was bread and a demand for labor. Sometimes they traveled in organized fashion—that is, going to jobs for which they had been hired beforehand. But, finding that things were no better else-where, they tried to get back home again or move on to some new place. Every mass deportation—whether of whole classes or ethnic groups—was accompanied by waves of voluntary migration. Children and old people died like flies.

Mass deportation is something quite new, for which we have the twentieth century to thank. Or perhaps the conquering despots of an-cient Egypt or Assyria? I have seen the trains taking bearded peasants from the Ukraine and the Kuban, and the closed cattle cars transport-ing prisoners to the forced-labor camps of eastern Siberia. Then there were the trainloads of Volga Germans, Tartars, Poles, Estonians. . . . And again cattle cars with prisoners for the camps—sometimes more of them and sometimes less, but never ceasing. The departure of the former aristocracy from Leningrad was a little different. Coming after collectivization, this was the second of the mass deportations. In 1935 Akhmatova and I went to the Paveletski station to see off a frail woman with three small boys who was being exiled to Saratov. They were not, of course, going to be given a permit to live in the town itself—people as helpless as this were expected to make out as best they could in the country somewhere. The station presented the usual sight—it was impossible to move in the milling throng, but this time the people were sitting not on bundles, but on quite respectable-looking trunks and suitcases still covered with old foreign travel labels. As we pushed our way through to the platform, we were constantly greeted by old women we knew: granddaughters of the Decembrists,* former "ladies" and just ordinary women. "I never knew I had so many friends among the aristocracy," said Akhmatova. "Why all the fuss about them? Why should Leningrad be cluttered up with them?" said the non-Party Bolshevik Tania Grigoriev, the wife of M.'s younger brother, Evgeni.

I have read somewhere that in the history of all nations there is a time when people "wander in body and spirit." This is the youth of a nation, the creative period of its history that affects it for many centuries and sets its cultural development in motion. We also appear to be wanderers, but will our migration bring the fruits promised by the philosopher? Our ordeal has been too great for us to keep our faith in these fruits, yet I cannot say that the answer to the question is "no." We have all, from top to bottom of society, learned something, even though we have destroyed our culture in the process and reverted to savagery. Still, what we have learned is very important.

We traveled from Cherdyn to Kazan by river steamer, but had to change in Perm. This meant a wait of twenty-four hours. We could not get into a hotel because M. had no identity papers—they had been taken from him at the time of his arrest. Identity papers are the privilege of the city dweller. Peasants do not have papers and are hence barred from the hotels, as are townspeople in our sort of plight. In any case there is never any room in the hotels, even for ordinary citizens with papers.

It was impossible to sit down anywhere on the pier because of the vast number of migrants. We wandered around the town all day until we were totally exhausted. We sat on benches in the town park with its

---

* Noblemen who attempted to overthrow the Czar in December 1825.

sparse shrubs and were surprised to see how pale the children were, even though they were from the better-off families of the city. We remembered how struck we had sometimes been by the sallow skin of the children in Moscow—this was always so during each of the successive famines. The last time had been in 1930 when we returned from Armenia to Moscow just after they had put up prices and not long before rationing and special stores were introduced. This was the price Moscow was paying for collectivization. By the time we left Moscow, things had greatly improved, but Perm still looked in frightful shape. We got a meal in a restaurant, but had to hurry over it because there was a line at each table—there was no food in the stores, and it was possible to get some kind of a meal only at the restaurants.

As he grew more tired, M. also became more and more worked up, and I was sure his illness would come back. These two journeys—the one under guard to Cherdyn, and now this one to Voronezh—only made his morbid condition worse. That night, as we continued to wander the streets, he kept wanting to go to the inquiry window at the MGB* building "to talk about my case." When he finally did so, the officer on duty would not listen. "Go away . . . people like you are coming here all the time." At this M. suddenly came to his senses. "That damned window is like a magnet," he said, and we went back to the pier. In Akhmatova's phrase, these were still comparatively "vegetarian" times, but the "magnet" already had a great hold on everybody's mind. Was there nobody who was not bothered by thoughts of interrogations, trials and shootings? There may have been a few such blissful people among the very young.

The steamer arrived in the middle of the night. With the tickets we had bought in the military booking office, feeling not like exiles but more like pampered protégés of the country's most feared institution, we made our way through the murmuring crowds and were almost the first to board. The crowd followed us with envious and hostile glances: the ordinary people take a poor view of privilege, and this crowd on the pier at Perm could not know why we had been able to buy our tickets without waiting in line. In our times, when it has often been possible to obtain one's daily bread only by special favor, hatred for the privileged has grown particularly intense. For at least ten out of the first forty revolutionary years we had rationing, and even in the supply

---

* MGB: Ministry of State Security—i.e., secret police.

of bread there was no egalitarianism—some got next to nothing and others more than enough. As my brother Evgeni explained to us in 1930 when we returned from Armenia, "We have a famine, but things are done quite differently nowadays. They've divided everybody into categories, and we all starve, or eat, according to rank. Everybody gets just as much as he deserves." Then I remember a young physicist—this was after the war—saying to his startled mother-in-law as he ate a steak which had been bought in the special closed store to which his father-in-law had access: "It's very good, and what makes it particularly nice is that other people can't get it." People were proud of their ration category and of their other rights and privileges, and carefully concealed the amount of their earnings from their inferiors. By an irony of fate, we were traveling on tickets bought in the booking offices for the most privileged, and this aroused universal envy. Yet at the same time we did not look at all like members of the elite, and this only increased people's resentment of us.

We took a berth for two, walked around the deck and had a bath—just like real tourists. These few days were a turning point for M. I was quite astonished at how little he needed to get over his illness—only three days of peace and quiet. He calmed down, read Pushkin and began to talk in a completely normal way. His auditory hallucinations and paroxysms of fear, agitation and egocentric view of what was going on around him—all this had almost ceased, or at least he had learned to cope with any slight relapse. But it was not over altogether—until the late autumn he still had a tendency to be oversensitive, and he tired easily (this had always been so because his heart was abnormally small and during that summer it became much weaker). I also noticed that, unusually for him, he was very easily hurt and—something unheard of before—he was intellectually listless. He had begun to read again almost at once, but he avoided anything strenuous, scarcely looking even at his Dante.

It is possible that his recovery was slowed down by a new misfortune: in Voronezh I fell ill, at first with spotted typhus that I must have picked up on some railroad station or pier. National calamities in Russia are always accompanied by spotted typhus, and until very recently it has been endemic. In the hospitals its incidence was concealed by giving it a number instead of calling it by its name—it was either 5 or 6, I don't remember exactly. Even this was made into a state secret, so that the "enemies of socialism" should not know what illnesses afflicted us. After recovering from spotted typhus I made a trip to Moscow and came down afterward with dysentery (which was also disguised under some number or other). I was sent back to the isolation hospital, where the use of germicides was unknown, except for patients belonging to the highest categories. Vishnevski happened to be in the hospital at the same time, and it was from him that I learned of the existence of new drugs which would have helped me recover much more quickly. But even the medicine you get depends on your status. I once complained about this in the presence of a Soviet official who had held high rank before his retirement. I said medicine was something everybody needed. "What do you mean, everybody?" he asked. "Do you expect me to get the same treatment as a cleaning woman?" He was a kind and perfectly decent person, but nobody was unaffected by the "fight against egalitarianism."

25

THOU SHALT NOT KILL

Among all the ways in which the state could destroy people, M. most of all hated the death penalty, or the "highest measure," as we delicately called it. The fact that it was death by shooting which he so much feared in his delirium was not accidental. While he was quite calm about exile, deportation and forced-labor camps ("This we are not afraid of," he would say), he shuddered at the very thought of death by execution. We had often read announcements about the shooting of people, and sometimes notices were posted up in the cities about such things. We read about the execution of Bliumkin (or Konrad) in Armenia—the news was plastered on every wall and post. M. and Boris Sergeyevich [Kuzin] returned to the hotel shaken, depressed and sick. Neither of them could stomach it. It was probably not only that the death penalty symbolized violence of every kind for them, but that they could also imagine it far too vividly. The rationalist feminine mind is less affected, and for me the idea of instant death seemed less abhorrent than that of mass deportation, prison, forced-labor camps and other such outrages against human dignity. But for M. it was different, and his first clash with the new regime (when it was still very young indeed) arose out of his feelings about capital punishment. The story of his encounter with Bliumkin is known from Georgi Ivanov's inaccurate second-hand account. There is also a mention of the episode in Ehrenburg's memoirs. Ehrenburg was present once when Bliumkin threatened M. with a revolver. Bliumkin was always brandishing his revolver in public places, as I once had occasion to see myself.

This was in Kiev in 1919. M. and I were standing on a balcony on the second floor of the Hotel Continental when we suddenly saw a cavalcade sweeping down the broad Nikolayev Street. It consisted of a horseman in a black cloak surrounded by a mounted escort. As it approached, the horseman in the black cloak looked up and, seeing us, he turned around sharply in the saddle, and the next thing we saw was a hand pointing a revolver at us. M. was about to duck, but instead he bent over the edge of the balcony and waved in greeting to the horseman. When the group drew level with us, the hand which had pointed the revolver was already hidden in the folds of the cloak. All this lasted only a second. It reminded me of a killing I once witnessed in the Caucasus: the driver of a tram leaned out while it was moving down the main street, and shot a bootblack. This was by way of blood revenge. The scene with Bliumkin was just the same, except that he did not actually shoot and bring his vendetta to a conclusion. The cavalcade swept past and turned off toward Lipki, where the Cheka had its headquarters.

The horseman in the cloak was Bliumkin, the man who shot the German Ambassador, Count Mirbach. He was probably on his way to Lipki. We had heard that he had been given very important secret work connected with counter-espionage. The cloak and the cavalcade were simply self-indulgence on the part of this mysterious man. What I fail to understand is how such ostentation could be reconciled with the secrecy demanded by his work.

I had occasion to meet Bliumkin even before I got to know M. I had once lived with his wife in a tiny Ukrainian village where several people wanted by Petliura were hiding among a group of young artists and journalists. When the Reds took over, Bliumkin's wife suddenly came to see me and gave me a certificate made out in my name, guaranteeing the safety of our house and property. "What's this for?" I asked in astonishment. "We have to protect the intelligentsia," she replied. In the same way, on October 18, 1905, women from the "workers' patrols" had gone disguised as nuns to distribute ikons to Jewish homes. They hoped that the pogrom mob would be misled by this. During the many searches of our house my father never once produced this obviously fake certificate made out to me (I was then only eighteen). It was from this woman, who tried to save the intelligentsia with such methods, that I first heard of Mirbach's assassin. I also met him several times in person during one of his brief visits—he was always coming and going in mysterious fashion.

The similarity of the balcony incident in Kiev to an act of blood vengeance was not accidental. Bliumkin had sworn to take vengeance on M. and had already brandished a revolver at him several times before, but he had never actually fired. M. thought it was all an empty threat and put it down to Bliumkin's love of melodramatic effects: "What's to stop him from shooting me? He could have done it long ago if he wanted." But even so, M. couldn't help ducking every time Bliumkin drew his revolver. The final episode in this Caucasian game was in 1926 when M. was leaving the Crimea and happened to get into the same train compartment as Bliumkin. Seeing his "enemy," Bliumkin demonstratively unhitched his holster, put his revolver in his suitcase and held out his hand. They then talked amicably for the rest of the journey. Not long after this we learned of Bliumkin's execution by shooting. Georgi Ivanov, pandering to the tastes of his least discriminating readers, has given such a highly colored account of the whole story that it becomes meaningless—yet respectable people continue to quote his version, ignoring its logical flaws. This is only possible because we are so cut off from each other.

Not long before their clash, Bliumkin had proposed to M. that he work in a new organization which was then being set up, and which he said would have a great future. In Bliumkin's view, this organization was bound to give shape to the new era and become the focus of power. M. took fright and refused to work for it—this at a moment when nobody yet knew exactly what the nature of the new institution would be. M. only had to learn that it was powerful to keep right away from it. He had always, in an almost childish way, shunned any contact with power. When he arrived in Moscow in 1918, for instance—he had traveled by Government trains—he had to stay with Gorbunov in the Kremlin for a few days. One morning when he came to breakfast in the common dining room, the waiter, a former court flunkey who now waited on members of the Revolutionary Government in the same obsequious fashion, said that Trotski himself would shortly be coming in to take coffee. M. seized his raincoat and fled, thus losing a unique opportunity to have a proper meal in the hungry city. He found it impossible to explain what prompted him to flee like this: "I just didn't want to breakfast with him." A similar thing happened when he was summoned to the People's Commissariat of Foreign Affairs to discuss the possibility of a job there. Chicherin came out to see him and asked him, as a test, to draft an official telegram in French. He left him alone to do it, and M., seeing his chance to escape, just made off without even trying to draft the telegram. "Why did you run away?" I asked him. He dismissed the question in the same way—if it had been some minor official he might have stayed and taken a job in the Commissariat, but it was better to keep away from people invested with power. It was perhaps this instinctive, almost unconscious abhorrence of power that saved M. from many false and disastrous paths which opened up before him at a time when even the most experienced people had no idea what was going on. What would have happened to him if he had joined the Commissariat of Foreign Affairs, let alone the "new organization" which Bliumkin was so keen he should work for?

M. first understood the functions of this "new organization" during his clash with Bliumkin. The scene was the Poets' Café in Moscow—the only detail correctly reported by Georgi Ivanov. But it is not true that Bliumkin used to go there as a bloodthirsty Chekist looking for new victims—as has been written in the West. Rather he was a welcome visitor; he was close to the center of power, and such persons are always sought after in literary circles. M.'s quarrel with Bliumkin took place a few days before the assassination of Mirbach. At that early date the term "Chekist" still meant very little. The Cheka had only just been organized, and up till then terror and shootings had been carried out by other organizations—by military tribunals, I believe. In his conversation with Bliumkin, M. perhaps clearly understood for the first time the precise functions of this "new organization" which Bliumkin had asked him to join a few days previously.

Bliumkin, in M.'s words, began to boast that he had powers of life and death in his hands, and that he was about to shoot some "wretched intellectual" who was being held under arrest by the "new organization." It was fashionable in those years to speak with contempt of the "spineless intelligentsia" and to talk blithely about shooting people. Bliumkin was not just following the fashion, he was one of those who created it. He was referring to an art historian, a Hungarian or Polish count, whom M. had never heard of before. When he later told me the whole story in Kiev, M. could not remember either the name or the nationality of this man he had stood up for. In just the same way he was unable to remember the names of the five old men he saved from execution in 1928. It is now easy to find out the count's name from published materials about the Cheka, which include a report on the murder of Mirbach, where Dzerzhinski mentions that he had already heard of Bliumkin.

Bliumkin's boast that he was going to put this "wretched intellectual" up against the wall and shoot him enraged M., who said that he would not stand for it. To this Bliumkin said he would not tolerate any interference in his business and that he would shoot M. too if he dared to "meddle." It appears that Bliumkin threatened M. with his revolver during this first argument between them. This was something Bliumkin did at the slightest provocation—even, I was told, at home with his family.

According to the story as it has been told abroad, M. next managed to seize Bliumkin's warrant and tear it up. What kind of a warrant could it have been? The art historian was already in the Lubianka, so the warrant for his arrest must already have been filed away and could not have been in Bliumkin's possession. Nor would it have made sense for M. to do this—a piece of paper can always be replaced. Knowing M.'s temperament, I can well believe he would have been capable of snatching something and tearing it up, but he would not have left it at that. That would not have been like him—it would have meant that, frightened by Bliumkin's threats, he washed his hands of the business after making a fuss merely as a sop to his conscience. If that had been the case, the story would only be worth recalling as an illustration of how badly standards of behavior had declined. But in fact the story had a sequel.

M. went straight from the Poets' Café to Larisa Reisner and made such a row that Raskolnikov phoned Dzerzhinski and arranged for him to see Larisa and M. In the published account it says that Raskolnikov also went with M. to the meeting, but this is not true—only his wife, Larisa, went. I doubt whether anything in the world would have induced Raskolnikov to go to the Cheka on such an errand, particularly together with M., whom he did not like. He was always irritated by his wife's literary infatuations.

Everything else in the published account is more or less true: Dzerzhinski listened to M., asked for the file on the case, accepted M.'s assurances about the art historian and ordered his release. Whether his order was actually carried out I do not know. M. thought it was, but a few years later he learned that in a similar case an order for someone's release given by Dzerzhinski in his presence was not followed up. In 1918 it never occurred to M. to check whether this promise given by such a high official had actually been kept. He did, however, hear from someone that the Count had been released and allowed to return to his own country. This also seemed to be borne out by Bliumkin's subsequent behavior.

Dzerzhinski showed interest in Bliumkin himself and began to question Larisa about him. She didn't know very much, though M. later complained about how garrulous and indiscreet she was—qualities for which she was celebrated. At all events, her loose talk did Bliumkin no harm, and M.'s complaint about his threats to kill prisoners remained, as could be expected, the voice of one crying out in the wilderness. If closer attention had been paid to Bliumkin, the murder of the German Ambassador might have been prevented. But, instead, Bliumkin was allowed to carry out his plans without the slightest hindrance. Dzerzhinski remembered M.'s visit only after Mirbach's assassination and evidently mentions it in his report only to show how well informed he was. He couldn't even remember who was with M. After the assassination Bliumkin was suspended from work for a time, but he was soon allowed to return to it and remained with the Cheka until his downfall and execution.

One may ask: Why didn't Bliumkin carry out his threat to take vengeance on M. for interfering in his "business" and even getting the better of him? In M.'s opinion, Bliumkin, terrible as he was, was by no means an utter savage. M. always said that Bliumkin never had any intention of killing him—on all the occasions when he threatened him, he allowed himself to be disarmed by other people present, and in Kiev he himself put away his revolver. Brandishing a revolver, shouting and raving like one possessed, Bliumkin was simply indulging his temperament and his love of external effects—he was by nature a terrorist of the flamboyant type which had existed in Russia before the Revolution.

Another question is: How could Bliumkin's revolting braggadocio about killing people and the contemptuous words about a "wretched intellectual" marked down for destruction be reconciled with the activity of his wife, who, however absurdly, had tried to save the intelligentsia? It may be, of course, that the woman I knew in the Ukranian village was only one of Bliumkin's mistresses and did not share his views. But with people of Bliumkin's type one can never be sure of appearances, and there are people who think that he may have been playing a double game, and that all this talk about the shooting of "spineless intellectuals" was intended to cast doubt on the "new organization" which he had joined as a representative of the Left Social Revolutionaries.* If this was so, M.'s reaction was precisely the kind of effect he hoped to achieve—which could be why he never took vengeance on him. But only the historians may be able to make sense of this when they come to study this strange time and this outlandish man.

For my own part, I think that he was not playing a double game, but that the people who were making history in those days had all the cruelty and inconsistency of the children they were. Why is it so easy to turn young people into killers? Why do they look on human life with such criminal frivolity? This is particularly true in those fateful periods when blood flows and murder becomes an ordinary everyday thing. We were set on our fellow men like dogs, and the whole pack of us licked the hunter's hand, squealing incomprehensibly. The headhunting mentality spread like a plague. I even had a slight bout of it myself, but was cured in time by a wise doctor. This happened in Ekster's studio in Kiev when some visitor or another (it was either Roshal or Cherniak) read out some couplets by Mayakovski about how officers were thrown into the Moika Canal in Petrograd to drown. This brash verse had its effect and I burst out laughing. Ehrenburg, who was also there, at once fiercely attacked me. He gave me such a talking-to that I still respect him for it, and I am proud that, silly as I was at the time, I had the sense to listen to him and remember his words forever afterward. This happened before my meeting with M., so that he did not have to cure me of the head-hunting mentality and explain to me why he stood up for the art historian.

This is something that hardly anyone here understands, and I am still always being asked why M. did it—that is, why he intervened for a stranger at a time when people were being shot on every side. They understand if it is for a relative or a friend, a chauffeur, or a secretary—

---

* Non-Marxist Russian revolutionaries who collaborated with the Bolsheviks in the days after the October Revolution.

even in the Stalin era this sometimes happened. But where there is no personal interest, one is not supposed to interfere. People living under a dictatorship are soon filled with a sense of their helplessness, in which they find an excuse for their own passivity. "How can I stop executions by speaking up? It's beyond my control. Who will listen to me?" Such things were said by the best of us, and the habit of not trying to pit oneself against superior force meant that any David who attacked Goliath with his bare hands met with puzzlement and shrugs of the shoulders. This was the case when Pasternak, at a most dangerous time, refused to sign a collective letter by the Soviet writers approving the latest shooting of "enemies of the people." No wonder it was so easy for the Goliaths to destroy the last of the Davids.

We all took the easy way out by keeping silent in the hope that not we but our neighbors would be killed. It is even difficult to tell which among us were accomplices to murder, and which were just saving their skins by silence.

26

THE WOMAN OF THE RUSSIAN REVOLUTION

"We must create a type of Russian revolutionary woman," said Larisa Reisner on the one occasion when we visited her at her home (this was after her return from Afghanistan). "The French Revolution created its own type. We must do the same." This did not mean that Larisa wanted to write a novel on the subject, but that she hoped to establish herself in this role. This was the purpose of her journeys back and forth across the battle fronts, and her visits to Afghanistan and Germany. She had found her vocation in life in 1917 and it was made easier for her by family tradition. Her father, Professor Reisner, had formed close links with the Bolsheviks in his Tomsk days, and Larisa thus found herself in the camp of the victors.

During our meeting Larisa overwhelmed M. with stories and they all had about them something of the same light-headedness with which Bliumkin reached for his revolver or otherwise strove to create a sensation. Larisa also built up her image of the "Russian revolutionary woman" in a way reminiscent of Bliumkin. She had no time for those who sat at home moaning about their helplessness—she belonged to circles in which the cult of power reigned supreme. The right to use power has always been justified by reference to the good of the people: the people must be reassured, the people must be fed, the people must be protected. Larisa despised such arguments and had even cut the word "people" out of her vocabulary—it too seemed to smack of the prejudices of the old intelligentsia, against which the whole of her anger and the fire of her eloquence were directed. Berdiayev is mistaken when he says that the intelligentsia was destroyed by the people for which it once made such sacrifices. The intelligentsia destroyed itself, burning out of itself, as Larisa did, everything that conflicted with the cult of power.

At this meeting with M., Larisa at once remembered how she had betrayed her principles by going to see Dzerzhinski with him: "Why did you want to save that count? They're all spies." To me she complained rather coyly that she had "got into this business" because M. had rushed her into it against her better judgment. One may indeed ask why she went against her own beliefs by going to plead for a "wretched intellectual" whom she did not even know. M. thought it was out of a desire to show how influential she was, and how close to the new regime. But in my opinion she did it simply to humor M., whose verse she liked so much that she was ready to do anything for him. The one thing Larisa could not overcome was her love of poetry—though this too she was bent on doing, since it scarcely suited her image of the "Russian revolutionary woman." In the first few years after the Revolution there were many such poetry-lovers among the victors. How did they manage to reconcile it with their Hottentot ethic: "If I kill, it's good; if I'm killed, it's bad"?

Larisa not only loved poetry, but she also secretly believed in its importance, and for her the only blot on the Revolution's record was the shooting of Gumilev. She was living in Afghanistan at the time this happened, and she believed that if she had been in Moscow she would have been able to put in a good word and prevent it. During her meeting with us she kept coming back to this subject, and we were thus witnesses to the birth of the legend about Lenin's supposed telegram ordering a stay of execution. That evening Larisa gave us the legend in the following version: her mother, hearing what was about to happen in Petrograd, went to the Kremlin and persuaded Lenin to send a telegram. Nowadays it is Gorki who is credited with having informed Lenin about the impending execution. But there is no truth in either version. While Larisa was abroad we several times went to see her mother, who bitterly lamented that she had not taken Gumilev's arrest seriously and tried to reach Lenin—which might have made all the difference. As regards Gorki, it is true that people asked him to intervene—Otsup, for one, went to see him. Gorki had a strong dislike of Gumilev, but he nevertheless promised to do something. He could not keep his promise because the sentence of death was announced and carried out with unexpected haste, before Gorki had got round to doing anything.

When we began to hear touching stories about a telegram from Lenin, M. often remembered how we had heard the legend take shape in Larisa's apartment. Until her return from abroad there had been no such stories in circulation and everybody knew that Lenin had shown no concern for a poet of whom he had never even heard. But when one thinks of all the blood shed in this country, why is it that this legend has proved so persistent? I am always meeting people who assure me that the telegram has been printed in such-and-such a volume of Lenin's works, or that it is still preserved in the archives. The story has even reached the ears of the writer in stovepipe trousers—the one who always carries a box of hard candy in his pocket. He has even promised to bring me the volume in which he has read it with his own eyes, but he has never kept his promise. The myth invented by Larisa to cover up her own weakness will still have a long life in our country.

She had less luck with her image of the "Russian revolutionary woman" than with her myth about Lenin's telegram. This was probably due to the fact that, though she belonged to the victorious side, she was not really much of a fighter. M. told me how she and her husband Raskolnikov lived a life of luxury in hungry Moscow—keeping a town house, with servants and magnificently served meals. In this they were different from the Bolsheviks of an older generation, who stuck to their modest way of life much longer. Larisa and her husband justified themselves by saying that, as people engaged in building a new order, it would have been sheer hypocrisy for them to deny themselves their due as incumbents of power. Larisa was ahead of her time in fighting "egalitarianism" even before it was denounced.

I remember one story that M. told me about Larisa. At the very beginning of the Revolution there was need to arrest some high-ranking officers—admirals, or other "military specialists," as they were called. Raskolnikov and Larisa offered to help. They invited the admirals to come and stay with them, and the admirals duly accepted. They were royally entertained by their beautiful hostess, and then arrested at breakfast by the Chekists, without a shot being fired. This really was a dangerous operation, and it passed off smoothly, thanks to the trap cunningly laid by Larisa.

Larisa was capable of anything, but I am somehow convinced that if she had been in Moscow when Gumilev was arrested, she would have got him out of jail, and that if she had been alive and still in favor with the regime during the time when M. was being destroyed, she would have moved heaven and earth to try and save him. But in fact one cannot be certain of anything, people can be so changed by life.

M. was on friendly terms with her, and she wanted to take him to Afghanistan with her, but Raskolnikov wouldn't hear of it. At the time we went to see her she had already left Raskolnikov, and after that we lost touch with her completely: M. had clearly decided to have nothing more to do with this "woman of the Revolution." When we heard about her death, he sighed, and in 1937 he said how lucky Larisa had been to die in time: all the people in her circle were now being destroyed wholesale.

With Raskolnikov we had nothing in common at all. He once showered M. with telegrams—this was when he took Voronski's place as editor of *Krasnaya Nov* [*Red Virgin Soil*]. Extraordinary as it may seem, the so-called "Fellow-Traveling" writers who had been published by Voronski boycotted the journal under its new editor when he took over after the sudden dismissal of its creator. Raskolnikov so badly needed material that he even approached M., whose comment on his telegrams was: "I don't care who the editor is: I won't be published either by Voronski or Raskolnikov." The "Fellow Travelers" soon forgot their former protector and never again worried about changes in editorship. As for M., he would never have had his *Noise of Time* published if it had not been for Georgi Blok, who worked in the private publishing house Vremya [Time] before it was closed down.

All the people Larisa had known when she was still a professor's daughter (when she edited an absurd little magazine and visited poets to show them her poems) perished before their time—as did everybody she got to know later when she was trying to become the "woman of the Russian Revolution." She was beautiful in a heavy and striking Germanic way. Her mother watched over her as she lay dying in the Kremlin hospital, and committed suicide immediately after her death.

We were so unused to people dying a natural death from illness that I still find it hard to believe that this beautiful woman could have been carried away by something as ordinary as typhus. Contradictory and unrestrained, she paid for all her sins with an early death. I sometimes feel that she may well have invented the story about the admirals in order to enhance her status as the "woman of the Russian Revolution" by taking credit for a killing. All these people building a "new world" were so vehement in denouncing as hypocrisy all the commandments, including "Thou shalt not kill." But then this same Larisa, when she visited Akhmatova at the height of the famine, was horrified to find what poverty she was living in, and a few days later reappeared with a bundle of clothing and a food parcel which she had managed to buy with special vouchers. In those days it was just as hard to get such vouchers as to free someone from jail.

27

TRANSMISSION BELTS

A miracle is a two-stage affair. The first stage is to get a letter or petition to the totally inaccessible person it is addressed to—if it is sent by ordinary official channels, there is no hope at all that the miracle will come to pass. Millions of letters have been sent, but the number of miracles can be counted on one's fingers. Here there is certainly no question of "egalitarianism."

My telegrams to the powers-that-be would have been as futile as the housekeeper in Cherdyn said, if I had not sent copies to Nikolai Ivanovich Bukharin. If it had not been for this detail, my Cherdyn friend would have been quite right. Nikolai Ivanovich was as impulsive as M. He was not the sort to ask himself what business it was of his, or to start calculating his chances of success. Instead he sat down and wrote a letter to Stalin. This was an act completely at variance with our normal code of behavior, and by that time there were very few people left in the country who were capable of such impulsiveness: they had long ago been destroyed or "re-educated."

In 1930 in a small rest home in Sukhumi for high officials, which we had got into owing to a blunder on the part of Lakoba, I had a conversation with the wife of Yezhov. "Pilniak comes to see us," she said.

"Whom do you go to see?" When I indignantly passed this on to M., he tried to calm me: "Everybody goes to see someone. There's no other way. We go to see Nikolai Ivanovich."

We had first started "going to see" Bukharin in 1922 when M. had asked him to intercede for his brother, Evgeni, who had been arrested. M. owed him all the pleasant things in his life. His 1928 volume of poetry would never have come out without the active intervention of Bukharin, who also managed to enlist the support of Kirov. The journey to Armenia, our apartment and ration cards, contracts for future volumes (which were never actually published but were paid for—a very important factor, since M. was not allowed to work anywhere)—all this was arranged by Bukharin. His last favor was to get us transferred from Cherdyn to Voronezh.

In the thirties Bukharin was already complaining that he had no "transmission belts." He was losing his influence, and was in fact very isolated. But he never hesitated to help M., worrying only about whom it would be best to approach. At the height of his glory at the end of the twenties—he was hardly yet forty—he was at the very center of the world Communist movement and used to drive up to his gray headquarters, where he received representatives of all races and nations, in a black automobile escorted by three or four others carrying his guards. Already he was saying things which gave some hint of the future. When, from a chance conversation in the street, M. learned about the impending execution of the five old men and went around the city in a fury, demanding that they be reprieved, everybody just shrugged their shoulders, and he pleaded with Bukharin for all he was worth, as the only man who listened to his arguments without asking "What business is it of yours?" As a final argument against the execution he sent Bukharin a copy of his recently published volume of *Poems* with an inscription saying: Every line here is against what you are going to do. I have not put these words in quotation marks, because I do not remember the exact phrasing, only the general sense. The sentence was repealed and Bukharin informed M. by sending him a telegram in Yalta, where he had come to join me after he had done everything he could in Moscow. At first Bukharin had tried to fend M. off with words like "We Bolsheviks have a simple approach to these things: we each know that it could happen to him as well. There's no point in swearing that it can't." And as an illustration he mentioned the recent shooting of a group of Komsomols in Sochi for debauchery. M. remembered these words during Bukharin's trial.

From what quarter did Bukharin think the danger came? Did he fear the return of his defeated enemies, or did he sense the threat from his own side? We could only guess; to a direct question this slight man with the red beard would have replied with a joke.

In 1928, sitting in an office which was at the pivot of some of the most grandiose developments of the twentieth century, these two doomed men talked about capital punishment. Both were going to their own death, but in different ways. M. still believed that his "oath to the fourth estate" obliged him to come to accept the Soviet regime—everything, that is, except the death penalty. He was reconciled to the new state of affairs by Herzen's doctrine of *prioritas dignitatis,* which had powerfully undermined all his notions of popular rule. "What is a mechanical majority!" M. would say, trying to justify the abandonment of the democratic forms of government. Unfortunately, the idea of indoctrinating the people also went back to Herzen, though he added the proviso that it must be done "through the laws and institutions." Isn't this the basic error of our times, and of each one of us? What do the people need to be indoctrinated for? What satanic arrogance you need to impose your own views like this! It was only in Russia that the idea of popular education was replaced by the political concept of indoctrination. When M. himself became a target for it, he was one of the first to revolt.

Bukharin's path was quite different. He clearly saw that the new world he was so actively helping to build was horrifyingly unlike the original concept. Life was deviating from the blueprints, but the blueprints had been declared sacrosanct and it was forbidden to compare them with what was actually coming into being. Determinist theory had naturally given birth to unheard-of practitioners who boldly outlawed any study of real life: Why undermine the system and sow unnecessary doubt if history was in any case speeding us to the appointed destination? When the high priests are bound together by such a bond, renegades can expect no mercy. Bukharin was not a renegade, but he already felt how inevitable it was that he would be cast into the pit because of his doubts and the bitter need which one day would drive him to speak out and call things by their real name.

M. once complained to him that in the Land and Factory Publishing House* one felt the lack of a "healthy Soviet atmosphere." "And what," asked Bukharin, "is the atmosphere like in other organizations?

---

* See the note on Narbut in the Appendix.

The same as in a cesspool—it stinks!" And another time, when M. told him: "You have no idea how people can be persecuted here," Bukharin just gasped: "*We* have no idea?" and together with T., his secretary and friend, he burst out laughing.

The fundamental rule of the times was to ignore the facts of life. Holders of high office were supposed to see only the positive side of things and, once ensconced in their ivory towers (it was they, not we, who were shut off like this!), to look down indulgently at the writhing human masses below. A man who knew that you cannot build the present out of the bricks of the future was bound to resign himself beforehand to his inevitable doom and the prospect of the firing squad. What else could he do? We were all prepared for the same end. When M. said goodbye to Akhmatova in the winter of 1937, he said, "I am ready for death." I have heard the same phrase, in slightly different words, from dozens of people. "I am ready for anything," Ehrenburg said to me once as I was leaving his apartment—this was at the time of the "Doctors' Plot"* and the campaign against "cosmopolitans," and his turn was coming. As one era followed another, we were always "ready for anything."

Thanks to Bukharin, M. got a vivid impression of the first fruits of the "new world" as it was created in front of our very eyes, and was hence one of the first to learn where the threat lay. In 1922 when he was trying to help his arrested brother, M. approached Bukharin for the first time. We went to see him in the Metropole Hotel. Bukharin at once phoned Dzerzhinski and asked him to see M. A meeting was fixed for the next morning, and M. now made his second visit to the organization for which Bliumkin had foretold such a great future—he was thus able to compare the period of revolutionary terror with the age in which a new concept of government was being born. Dzerzhinski had not yet given up the old ways. He received M. in simple fashion and suggested he stand surety for his brother—a solution actually proposed by Bukharin. Dzerzhinski picked up the phone and gave the necessary instructions on the spot. The next morning M. went to see the interrogator in charge of his brother's case and returned full of im-

---

* In 1952 a large group of Kremlin doctors, mostly Jewish, were accused of trying to poison the Soviet leaders. They were all released shortly after Stalin's death. "Cosmopolitans" was a frequent euphemism for "Jews" in the anti-Semitic campaigns of the last years of Stalin's life.

pressions. The interrogator wore a uniform and was flanked by two bodyguards. "I got the instruction," he said, "but we cannot let you stand surety for your brother." The reason he gave was: "It will be awkward to arrest you if your brother commits a new crime." The implication of this was that some crime had already been committed. "A new crime?" M. said when he got back home. "What can they have cooked up now?" We had no illusions, and we were afraid that they were going to try and frame Evgeni Emilievich. It also occurred to us that Dzerzhinski might have given his instruction over the phone in a manner suggesting that the interrogator did not have to take it seriously.

It is true that the refusal to comply was made to sound like a favor ("We don't want to arrest you, too"), but the general tone, the armed guards, the air of mystery and hint of intimidation ("He'll commit a new crime") all struck a new note. The forces conjured up by the older generation were getting out of hand, and a future was brewing that had little resemblance to the terror of the early revolutionary days. There was even a new language coming into being—a language of state. Fearful as it was, the terror of the early days could not be compared with the systematic mass extermination which the all-powerful "state of a new type" practiced on its subjects in accordance with laws, instructions, orders and directives issued by all kinds of committees, secretariats, special tribunals—if they were not simply handed down "from above."

When M. told him how he had been received by the interrogator, Bukharin flew into a rage. We were quite taken aback by the violence of his reaction. A few days later he came to tell us that no crime had been committed—either an old or a new one—by M.'s brother, and that he would be released in two days' time. These two days were needed for the formal winding up of a case involving an uncommitted crime.

Why did Bukharin react like this? He was, after all, a proponent of terror, so why should he have got so worked up? A youth had been picked up as a warning to his fellow students, and he wasn't even in danger of being shot—a very ordinary case. So why was Bukharin so upset? Did he too have a foreboding of the "new" spirit that was beginning to threaten us all? Did he remember the magic broom of the sorcerer's apprentice in Goethe's poem? Did it occur to him that neither he nor his colleagues would now be able to contain the forces awakened by them, any more than the poor apprentice could halt the magic broom? No, the most likely thing is that Bukharin was indignant because a wretched interrogator had got out of line and failed to obey an order passed down by his seniors in the hierarchy. The machine, he must have thought, was not yet properly tuned, and did not always work as it should.

He had always been a man of passionate temperament, quick to anger, but his way of venting his indignation changed with the times. Until 1928 he would shout "Idiots!" and pick up the phone, but after 1930 he just frowned and said: "We must think whom to approach." He arranged our trip to Armenia through Molotov, and also our pension. The pension was given "for services to Russian literature and in view of the impossibility of finding employment for the writer in Soviet literature." This formula was close to the realities of the situation, and we suspected that Bukharin was responsible for it. In the case of Akhmatova they could think of nothing better than to give her a pension on the grounds of old age, though she was only thirty-five. As an "old-age pensioner" she received seventy roubles a month—enough to keep her in cigarettes and matches.

At the beginning of the thirties Bukharin, in his search for "transmission belts," was always talking of going to see Gorki to tell him about M.'s plight—the way nobody would publish him or give him work. M. vainly argued with Bukharin that no good would come of such an approach to Gorki. We even told him the old story about the trousers. When M. returned to Petrograd from Wrangel's Crimea by way of Georgia, he was half dead and had no warm clothing by the time he arrived in the city. In those days clothing could not be bought, but was supplied only against vouchers. The issue of such vouchers for writers had to be authorized by Gorki. When he was asked to let M. have a pair of trousers and a sweater, he crossed out the word "trousers" on the voucher and said, "He'll manage without." The many writers who later became "Fellow Travelers" still recall Gorki's fatherly concern for them, but this was the only time he ever denied someone a pair of trousers. The trousers were a small matter in themselves, but they spoke eloquently of Gorki's hostility to a literary trend that was foreign to him: here too it was a question of "spineless intellectuals" who were worth preserving only if they were well equipped with solid learning. Like many people of similar background, Gorki prized learning but had a quantitative view of it: the more, the better. Bukharin did not believe M., and decided to take soundings. Soon, however, he was telling us: "There's no point in going to Gorki." However much I pestered him, he wouldn't tell me why.

When our apartment was searched in 1934, they took away all Bukharin's notes to us. They were a little flowery, with a sprinkling of Latin tags. He begged our pardon for not being able to see us at once, but *nolens volens* he could only see us at the times arranged by his secretary: "Please don't think me bureaucratic, but otherwise I could never get anything done. Would tomorrow at nine be convenient? The pass will be ready. If it's inconvenient, perhaps you can suggest another time."

I would give a great deal to be able once more to ask Korotkova, the squirrel-like secretary mentioned in "Fourth Prose," for an interview, and then to come and talk with Nikolai Ivanovich about all the things we didn't manage to say at the time. Perhaps he would again ring up Kirov and ask him what was going on in Leningrad and why they were not publishing Mandelstam there—"the book has been scheduled ages ago, but you keep putting it off year after year." And now it's twenty-five years since M. died. . . .

Fate is not a mysterious external force, but the sum of a man's natural make-up and the basic trend of the times he lives in—though in our age a great many tortured lives have been cut to the same hideously standard patterns. But these two men, with their particular endowments, themselves defined their relations with their times.

28

VORONEZH

M.'s identity papers were taken from him at the time of his arrest. When we arrived in Voronezh, his only document was the travel warrant issued to him by the Cherdyn GPU Commandant which enabled him to buy tickets in the military booking offices. M. now handed it over at a special window in the shabby premises of the Voronezh GPU and was given a new document which only entitled him to a temporary residence permit. He had to make do with this while it was being established whether he would be kept in Voronezh itself or sent off into the countryside somewhere. Moreover, our new overlords had not decided which category of exile we belonged to. There are several types, of which the two main ones known to me are "with reporting" and "without reporting." In the first case, one had to make regular visits to the GPU offices. In Cherdyn M. had to go and report every three days. If one does not have to report, one may be either permitted or forbidden to travel in the region to which one has been exiled. In the autumn M. was called to the police and given identity papers with a permit to reside in Voronezh. The type of exile was thus the easiest—with identity papers! It was now that we learned what a privilege it is to have identity papers, a privilege not granted to everybody.

The granting of identity papers is an enormous event in the life of an exile, since it gives the illusion of having some rights as a citizen. The first few months of our life in Voronezh were marked by constant visits to the police to get a piece of paper known as a "temporary permit." Seven or eight months running we had to renew this permit, which was valid for only one month at a time. A week before it expired, M. had to begin collecting the necessary documents needed for its renewal: a note from the local housing department to certify that he had been properly registered to live in such-and-such a house, references from the GPU and his place of work. There was no problem about the note from the GPU, since his standing with them was clear enough, but what was he to do about the second reference? At first he had to ask the local branch of the Union of Soviet Writers. This was never a straightforward procedure. The officials of the Union would gladly have made out any kind of certificate, but they were frightened, and some of them trembled at the thought of exercising their right to put the Union's stamp on a scrap of paper, in case they found themselves issuing a certificate to a bad writer. Every time the heads of the local branch applied to some higher authority for permission to issue a paper stating that M. really was engaged in literary work. At first there was whispering, dark looks and much scurrying about, but once they received clearance from higher up, the Voronezh writers were all smiles: they, too, were glad when all ended well. Those were still comparatively innocent days.

Each piece of paper meant at least two visits to the relevant office: first to apply for it, and then to collect it. Often one had to come again because it wasn't yet ready. When they were ready, all these references had to be handed to the head of the identity-papers section of the local police, where there was always a long line. Two or three days later M. again had to stand in line there to collect his temporary identity paper, which then had to be taken next day and stamped with the residence permit. This meant standing in line once more at the appropriate window in the police station. Fortunately, the girl clerk who entered residence permits was very kind to M. Ignoring the murmurs of concierges fretting in the line with their enormous registers under their arms (all arrivals and departures had to be entered in them), she always called M. to the window straightaway and took his identity paper so that she could return it to him next morning, duly stamped, without his having to wait in line.

In the summer of 1935 M. was granted the favor of receiving an identity paper valid for three months, accompanied by a residence permit for the same period. This made our lives much easier, particularly since the lines for papers had lengthened considerably after the purge in Leningrad: the lucky ones, who had been sent no farther than Voronezh, now had to go through the lengthy ordeal of getting permits and papers to live there.

People who live in countries without identity papers will never know what joys can be extracted from these magic little documents. In the days when M.'s were still a precious novelty, the gift of a benevolent fate, Yakhontov came to Voronezh on tour. In Moscow M. and he had amused themselves by reading from the ration books which were used in the excellent store open only to writers. M. refers to this in his poem "The Apartment": "I read ration books and listen to hempen speeches." Now Yakhontov and M. did the same thing with their identity papers, and it must be said that the effect was even more depressing. In the ration book they read off the coupons solo and in chorus: "Milk, milk, milk . . . cheese, meat . . ." When Yakhontov read from the identity papers, he managed to put ominous and menacing inflections in his voice: "Basis on which issued . . . issued . . . by whom issued . . . special entries . . . permit to reside, permit to reside, permit to reside . . ." Ration books reminded one of the literary fare that was doled out to us in the magazines and by the State publishing houses, and every time he opened *Novy Mir* [*New World*] or *Krasnaya Nov,* M. would say, "Today they're dishing out Gladkov" (or Zenkevich or Fadeyev). The line quoted above was intended in this double sense. Allusions to his identity papers are also to be found in M.'s verse: "Clutching in my fist a worn year of birth, herded with the herd, I whisper with my bloodless lips: I was born on the night between the second and third of January in the unreliable year of eighteen ninety something or other, and the centuries surround me with their fire."

Another amusement of this type (it was rather like a schoolboy thumbing his nose behind the teacher's back) took the form of a public stage performance by Yakhontov. In a turn entitled "Traveling Poets" he read passages from Pushkin's "Journey to Erzrum" and from Mayakovski in such a way as to suggest that poets could travel abroad only under the Soviet regime. The audience reacted with total indifference: nobody then imagined that anybody could travel abroad and as they left at the end of this baffling evening, the only comment they could manage was: "That's what comes of living too well." To keep his spirits up in the face of such an impassive audience, Yakhontov had to keep playing little tricks. At one point he would recite from Mayakovski's poem about the "Soviet Passport" and, taking his own identity papers from his pocket, brandish them in front of the audience, looking all the time straight at M. M. took his brand-new papers out of his pocket, and they exchanged knowing glances. The authorities would have taken a poor view of such antics, but they are very literal-minded, and there were no instructions to cover cases of this kind.

Another thing about identity papers was that they gave rise to guessing games. Since every general renewal of people's papers was also the occasion for a quiet purge, I decided not to go to Moscow to renew mine, but to do it in Voronezh. The result of this was that I lost my right to live in the capital and did not recover it until twenty-eight years later. But in any case I had no hope of getting my Moscow papers renewed—where would I have got a reference about my employment, how would I have explained the whereabouts of my husband, in whose name the title to our Moscow apartment was made out? When we both got our brand-new Voronezh papers, we noticed that they had the same serial letters before the numbers. It was thought that these letters were a secret-police code indicating the category to which one belonged—i.e., that one was an exile or had been convicted of some offense. "Now you are really trapped," M. said, examining the numbers and serial letters. Our more optimistic friends consoled us by saying that it wasn't so, but rather that the police had forgotten that M. was an exile and failed to mark his papers accordingly. We were so convinced that all citizens were numbered and registered according to categories that it never occurred to any of us to doubt the significance of these letters and numbers. Not until a few years after M.'s death did it turn out that these serial numbers had no special significance—apart from showing that my frightened fellow citizens had imaginations more lively than even the GPU and the police.

We were not too upset by the loss of my Moscow residence permit. "If I return," M. said, "they'll register you as well. But until then they won't let you live there in any case." Sure enough, I was thrown out of the capital in 1938 and after that was allowed to come back only for brief periods of a month or so on academic business. At last Surkov proposed that I return ("you've been in exile long enough"). Throwing up my work, I returned to Moscow to move into the room offered me by the Union of Writers. I was kept hanging around for six months, and then Surkov informed me that there would be neither a room for me nor a permit to reside in the city. "They say that you left it of your own free will," he explained to me, adding that he had no time to "talk with the comrades about you." And it is only now at last, in 1964, that I have suddenly been granted the right to live here. No end of people have written letters and pleaded on my behalf, but perhaps it has only happened now because a certain magazine* is about to print some of M.'s poems. This means that he has at last returned to Moscow. During thirty-two years not a line of his work has appeared in print. It is twenty-five years since his death, and thirty since his first arrest.

It really was a great relief when M. was given proper papers in Voronezh. The business of renewing the temporary ones not only took up a great deal of time, but was accompanied by constant anxiety and speculation as to whether it would be issued or not. In the GPU office and the police station one heard the same conversations all the time: some complained to the man behind the window that they had been refused a permit to reside, others begged for it to be granted. But the official never argued—he just stretched out his hand for your application and told you when it had been turned down. Those who were refused permits to live in Voronezh had to move into the countryside, where it was impossible to earn one's living and conditions were unbearable. And every time we joined all the other people making the rounds of offices to get our bits of paper, we trembled in case we should be unlucky and be forced to move on in some unknown direction for reasons not revealed to us. "And clutching in my fist a worn year of birth, herded with the herd . . ." When M. read these lines to Mikhoels, he took out his papers and held them in his clenched hand.

---

* The monthly literary magazine *Moskva* [*Moscow*] published nine of Mandelstam's poems in August 1964.

29

DOCTORS AND ILLNESSES

When we first got to Voronezh, we stayed in the hotel. Those in charge of us evidently permitted this to exiles arriving at their destination, even when they had no papers. We were not actually given rooms, only beds in rooms (separate for men and women) shared by a number of people. We were put on different floors, and I had to keep running up the stairs because I was worried about M.'s condition. But every day it got harder to climb the stairs. After several days my temperature shot up, and I realized I must be falling ill with spotted typhus, which I had no doubt picked up on the journey. The first symptoms of spotted typhus are unmistakable and cannot be confused with anything else, certainly not with flu. But this meant many weeks in the hospital, in the isolation wing, and I kept picturing the scene of M. throwing himself out of the window. Hiding my temperature from him—it was still going up—I begged him to see a psychiatrist. "If that's what you want," he said, and we went together. M. described the whole course of his illness himself, and there was nothing for me to add. He was completely objective and lucid. He told the doctor that at moments of tiredness or distraction he still had hallucinations. Most of all this happened when he was falling asleep. He said he now understood the nature of the voices and had learned to stop them with an effort of the will, but that in the hotel there were many irritants that made it difficult for him to fight his illness—it was very noisy, and he couldn't rest during the day. But the most unpleasant thing was the constant closing of doors, even though he knew they closed from the inside, not the outside.

Prison was ever-present to our minds. Vasilisa Shklovski cannot stand closed doors—because of all the time she spent in prison as a young woman, when she learned at first hand what it means to be closed in. And even people who had no experience of prison cells were not always free of this kind of association. When Yakhontov stayed in the same hotel during his visit to Voronezh a year and a half later, he immediately noticed how the keys ground in the locks. "Oho," he said, as we closed the door on leaving his room. "It's a different sound," said M., reassuringly. They understood each other perfectly. This is why M. is so insistent in his verse on the right to "breathe and open doors"—it was a right he was terrified of losing.

The psychiatrist was careful about what he said to us. We all suspected each other of being police spies, and there were many among people who had suffered like M.—a man who had undergone a psychological trauma was often incapable of resistance. But without waiting for M. to finish, the psychiatrist said that such "complexes" were very often observed in "psychostenic types" who spent any length of time in prison.

I then told the doctor about my own illness (at this moment M. understood my purpose in bringing him here and became terribly alarmed) and asked whether it wouldn't be best for M. to go into a clinic while I was in the hospital. The doctor replied that it would be perfectly all right to leave M. where he was since there were scarcely any traces left of his traumatic psychosis. He added that he had often observed the same condition among people exiled to Voronezh. It was caused by a few weeks, or even days, of imprisonment, and always cleared up, leaving no trace. M. then asked him why it was that people got into this state after a few days in prison, whereas in the old days prisoners spent years in dungeons without being affected like this. The doctor only shrugged his shoulders.

But is it true that they were unaffected? Perhaps prison always causes mental trouble, if not psychological damage. Is this really a specific feature of our prisons? Or is it perhaps that before we go to prison our mental health is undermined by anxieties and brooding on "prison themes"? Nobody here is able to go into this question—and abroad the facts are not known, because we are only too good at keeping our secrets from the outside world.

I have heard that somebody abroad recently published his memoirs about life in a Soviet camp, and that the author was struck by the large number of mentally sick people he encountered among the prisoners. As a foreigner, he had lived in the Soviet Union in somewhat special conditions, and his knowledge of our life was very superficial. The conclusion he reaches is that certain psychotic conditions are just not treated in this country, and that people suffering from them get sent to camps for infringement of discipline and other offenses caused by their illness. The percentage of mentally unbalanced people in the country is indeed enormous, and among those sentenced for hooliganism and petty theft there are, I believe, many psychotics, not to mention psychopaths. They are given several years for breaking into a store and stealing a few bottles of vodka, and when they come out they immediately do the same thing again and are sent back to prison and the labor camps for a good ten years. Under Stalin much less attention was paid to them, and far fewer of them went to the camps than nowadays. But the question remains as to why so many intellectuals and nervous or sensitive people in general are so strongly affected by their arrest and often fall prey to this mysterious trauma which quickly passes after their release. The foreign author of the book about the camps does not say *where* the prisoners he saw had become mentally sick, in prison or "outside." Nor does he say who they were—youths who had stolen to buy drink, or peaceful citizens. And were they psychopaths or were they suffering from the prison trauma I have described? All these questions will remain open, both for foreigners and for ourselves, until we are able to speak up about our past, present and future.

After I came out of the hospital, M. again went to see a psychiatrist, an eminent specialist who had come from Moscow to inspect the local lunatic asylum. M. went on his own initiative to tell him the story of his illness and to ask whether it might not be the consequence of some organic trouble. He mentioned that he had earlier noted in himself a tendency toward obsessive ideas—for instance, at times when he was in conflict with the writers' organization he could think of nothing else. Moreover, he actually was very sensitive to external shocks. I had noticed the same thing, incidentally, in M.'s two brothers. Though they were both of a very different make-up, they also tended to become obsessional about any difficult event in their lives.

The Moscow psychiatrist did an unexpected thing: he asked M. and me to walk around the wards with him. Afterward he asked whether M. thought he had anything in common with the patients he had seen in the clinic, and if so, how he would describe it: senility? schizophrenia? hysteria? They parted friends.

Nevertheless, without telling M., I went back to see the doctor myself next morning. I was worried in case the fearful things he had shown us the day before might produce a new shock in M. The doctor reassured me, saying that he had deliberately shown his patients to M. because better knowledge of these things would help him to get over the painful memories of his own illness. As for M.'s nervous sensitivity and inability to withstand traumas, the psychiatrist saw nothing pathological about this: the traumas had been pretty severe, and one could only wish that there were fewer of them in our life.

I was now struck by the light-heartedness with which M. made fun of his illness and how quickly he managed to forget the days he had spent in a state of delirium. "Nadia," he said a month and a half after our arrival in Voronezh, complaining about a bad meal I had made for him, "I just can't eat stuff like this—I'm not out of my mind now, you know."

The only thing that seemed to me an aftereffect of his illness was an occasional desire he now had to come to terms with reality and make excuses for it. This happened in sudden fits and was always accompanied by a nervous state, as though he were under hypnosis. At such moments he would say that he wanted to be with everybody else, and that he feared the Revolution might pass him by if, in his short-sightedness, he failed to notice all the great things happening before our eyes. It must be said that the same feeling was experienced by many of our contemporaries, including the most worthy of them, such as Pasternak. My brother Evgeni Yakovlevich used to say that the decisive part in the subjugation of the intelligentsia was played not by terror and bribery (though, God knows, there was enough of both), but by the word "Revolution," which none of them could bear to give up. It is a word to which whole nations have succumbed, and its force was such that one wonders why our rulers still needed prisons and capital punishment.

Fortunately, M. was only seldom overcome by these bouts of what is now called "patriotism," and once he had come to his senses he himself dismissed them as madness. It is interesting to note that in the case of people concerned with art or literature, total rejection of the existing state of affairs led to silence, while complete acceptance had a disastrous effect on their work, reducing it to mediocrity. Unfortunately, only their doubts were productive, but these brought down the wrath of the authorities on their heads.

Another factor which made for reconciliation with reality was simple love of life. M. had no taste for martyrdom, but the price one had to pay to live was much too high. By the time M. had decided to pay a first installment, it was in any case too late.

To come back to my own illness, I was put in the wing for spotted-typhus cases. I overheard the head doctor saying to some superintendent or other that I was very sick, and that I was "in the charge of" the secret police. At first I thought I must have imagined this in my delirium, but the doctor, who was to prove a good friend, later confirmed to me after my recovery that he really had said these words. Subsequently, during my wanderings around the country, I was often told by people connected (whether openly or secretly) with the secret police—officials of personnel departments and informers—that I was "in the charge of Moscow." What this meant I do not know. To understand it, one would have to learn more about the structure of the agency in whose charge I was. Personally, I think it is better not to be in anybody's charge, but I just cannot imagine how to achieve this. It would be interesting to know whether we were all accounted for in the same way, or only a select few of us.

The kindly woman doctor who looked after our ward told me that her husband, an agronomist, was at that time coming to the end of his sentence in a camp, to which he had been sent, together with many others of his profession, for allegedly poisoning the wells in his village. This is not the invention of a lively mind, but a fact. Later on, when I was better, and began making trips to Moscow, she gave me packages to mail to him in his camp. In those years such food parcels could be mailed only from Moscow, whereas nowadays they can be sent only from small provincial towns. For a number of years Emma Gerstein used to go out to all kinds of outlandish places, lugging heavy parcels which Akhmatova wanted mailed to her son Lev.

When the "poisoner of the wells" returned at the end of his sentence, we were invited to a party in his honor and toasted him in sweet wine while he sang songs in his soft baritone and rejoiced in his freedom. In 1937 he was arrested once more.

I got a lot of attention in the hospital from a nurse called Niura. Her husband worked at a flour mill. Once he had brought home a handful of grain for his hungry family and been sentenced to five years. The nurses greedily ate anything the typhus and dysentery patients left on their plates, and they were always talking about their misfortunes and poverty.

I came out of the hospital with a shaved head, and M. said that I looked like a real convict.

30

THE DISAPPOINTED LANDLORD

I came back not to the hotel, but to a "room" which M. had managed to find to serve us as a temporary accommodation. It consisted of a glassed-over veranda in a large tumbledown house that belonged to the best cook in town. He had managed to hang on to it as a private owner because he was the chef in a "closed" restaurant in the exclusive category. In this connection, M. said to me that we might at last be able to find out who actually used these mysterious "closed" restaurants. In the spring of 1933, during a trip to the Crimea, we had been refused admittance to restaurants in Sebastopol and Feodosia, on the grounds that they were "of the closed type." But from the cook we learned nothing about it—for him it was no joking matter. He was a tired, sick old man who no longer had any appetite for food, and lived in one room of his house—all the others were occupied by tenants who for a long time had been paying him the nominal rent fixed by law. As the owner, he had to do all repairs at his own expense, and in summer he let the veranda just to make ends meet. His one hope was that the place might be pulled down or taken over by the housing department of the local Soviet, but no local Soviet in its right mind would want to saddle itself with a ruin like this. So the last private owner of a large house in Voronezh was miserably going to the dogs, and his only dream was to become an ordinary tenant in his own house, which would in any case soon be pulled down.

The Voronezh of 1934 was a grim place, badly off for food. Dispossessed kulaks and peasants who had fled the collective farms begged in the streets. They stood by the bread stores and stretched out their hands. They had long since eaten their supplies of dry crusts brought with them in bags from their native villages. In the cook's house there was an old man called Mitrofan who was frantic with hunger. He wanted to get a job as a night watchman, but nobody would take him. He put this down to his name: "With a name like this they think I must have something to do with the church." In the middle of the city there was a half-ruined cathedral of St. Mitrofanius, and he was probably right. When we moved out of the house that winter, the old man hanged himself. With our departure his last means of earning a little money had gone: he had helped us to find our new room by bringing along old women who acted as go-betweens for owners of rooms, or corners of rooms (or simply beds), and potential customers.

One had to search for such accommodation in houses that were still privately owned or owned by the housing department of the local Soviet. This was illegal and counted as speculation. Owners and tenants always hated each other even before they met. The tenants wanted to pick a quarrel as soon as possible so they would have an excuse to refuse to continue paying rent at a rate twenty times higher than what the housing department would have charged, and the owners, once they had made a few urgent repairs out of the rent money, suddenly began to feel they had sold their birthright for a mess of pottage and took fright in case their tenants might stay on for good. This, in fact, is what generally happened. Once he had his residence permit and had reached the end of the few months originally agreed on, the tenant would make his own agreement with the housing committee (this often involved a little greasing of palms) and was given permanent title to the accommodation in question. This was in the case of housing run by the local Soviet. In a privately owned place, the tenant just refused to move out, and since it was never possible to get a court order against him, he simply stopped paying rent. This was how most people eventually got a permanent place to live, and it was, so to speak, a natural process of re-distribution of living space. As such, it was a much more passionate affair than the earlier phase of outright confiscation had been. It was attended by constant rows and scenes and the writing of mountains of denunciations, by means of which both tenants and owners sought to get rid of each other. Nowadays such things cannot happen because living-space is rented out privately like this only to people who have no residence permit—a tenant in such a situation, living like a bird in a tree, cannot easily make any claims. The only scope left for trouble-making is for a neighbor to denounce a tenant who lives without a permit, but the authorities have begun to take a lenient view of such cases. Times have changed.

In Voronezh the most favored tenants were exiles. Since they were always under threat of being forced to move to some remoter place, the owner of the room they rented could always, in case of conflict, help this to come about. For this reason we got plenty of offers and M. was run off his feet looking at rooms in all kinds of hovels. But in fact it was a long time before we actually moved, because everybody wanted a year's rent in advance. The water was already freezing in our veranda when I went to Moscow to get some translating work to do. I obtained it with astonishing ease. Luppol had heard about our "miracle" and, certain he could give M. work without running any great risk, he was very glad to do so. We gave the advance on the translation to the owner of a small house on the outskirts of the city who had agreed to be paid for only six months ahead. Every journey into the city center was a nightmare—and we had to go in frequently to obtain references for the renewal of M.'s papers, to find jobs for him, and so forth. There were endless waits at the tram stops, and people hung from the cars like clusters of grapes. Before the war, city transport was in a terrible state, even in Moscow. That winter we also got to know the winds blowing from the steppes in all their fury. People in our sort of plight are particularly sensitive to cold, as we realized during all the recurrent periods of famine, war or exile.

It soon appeared that the owner of the house, an agronomist who wore high leather boots, had only taken us in because he thought he might make interesting contacts through us. "I thought you'd have writers like Kretova and Zadonski* coming to see you, and we'd all be dancing the rumba together," he complained in a hurt tone. To give expression to his disappointment in us, he burst into our room when we were visited by friends, such as Kaletski and Rudakov, and demanded to see their papers: "You're holding meetings here, and as the owner of the house I'm responsible." We threw him out and he went away sighing sadly. Once he cornered me and bemoaned his fate: "If only more decent people would come to see you." He could not return the money we had paid him in advance, and we just had to stay on for the whole six months. M. took it all with good humor: exiles had traditionally suffered at the hands of their landlords. In the old days they denounced you to the police, and now it was to the GPU. But it seemed that our agronomist only threatened, and never actually went to report us. We had to be thankful for small mercies.

Our next room, which we occupied from April 1935 to February 1936, was in the city center, in a former lodging house where all kinds of shady types had settled. The police raided the place several times, looking for illegal vodka stills. Our young neighbor, a prostitute, adored M. because he always bowed to her on the street, and she often came with a pail of water to wash our floor. But she wouldn't take any money: "I'm doing it because I like you." An old Jewish woman who was bringing up three young grandchildren used to come in and complain about life in general. The owner of the place was trying to get rid of her and kept writing denunciations in which he accused her of prostitution. The old woman denied it, pointing to her age ("Who would need me?") and the small size of her room, where the three grandchildren slept all huddled together.

* Voronezh writers.

It was lucky that people who wrote denunciations were so unconcerned about plausibility and reported whatever came into their heads—until 1937 there had to be some element of truth. Denunciations were in fact a reflection of their writers' level, illustrating what flights of fantasy they were capable of. Our second Voronezh landlord was on the very lowest level. Once we were summoned to the GPU office, confronted with one of his denunciations, and asked to write an explanation. He had reported that we had been visited during the night by a suspicious type, and that the sound of shots had come from our room. The first part might just have got by, but the second part was hopeless. The visitor in question was Yakhontov, whose name was plastered up all over town on the billboards, and when he simply confirmed that he had sat up with us all night, that was the end of the matter.

The mere fact of being summoned in connection with a denunciation meant that it was not going to be used against you. This was shown by something that happened to me later—admittedly, after the fall of Yezhov when the terror had subsided. I was called out to the GPU section of the police station in Moscow, where after M.'s death I had managed to get a temporary permit to live in our old apartment. I was asked to explain a denunciation to the effect that I held meetings in my apartment during which there was counter-revolutionary talk. The only person who had visited me was Pasternak—he came to see me immediately on hearing of M.'s death. Apart from him, nobody had dared to come and see me, as I explained to the secret-police official. In the upshot nothing much happened, except that I was asked to leave Moscow before my temporary permit had run out. This time I was being eased out by my temporary lodger, who had been moved in with us by the Union of Writers on the recommendation of Stavski. The man, whose name was Kostyrev, called himself a writer and sometimes hinted that he had rank equivalent to that of a general.

When after the Twentieth Congress they were going to give me a place to live in Moscow again, I was called to the Union of Writers and asked how I had come to lose my original apartment. I told them about Kostyrev. Ilyin, the official of the Union dealing with me, spent a long time going through lists of writers, but he could find no one of this name. Whether Kostyrev was a writer or a general, the fact is that he had used the standard technique of getting an apartment for himself. I believe that Kostyrev was trying to get out of the secret police into literature, but he probably didn't make it. The time when he moved into our apartment was a transition period for people with double careers and double missions.

Our landlord in Voronezh who thought he heard shooting in our room at night saw nothing shameful in his activities as an informer. He probably regarded himself as a useful member of society, a keeper of the peace. What his work was we could never make out. He never talked about it and we preferred not to inquire. He described himself as an "agent" and was always going out into the countryside on matters "concerning collectivization." At any event, he was very small fry— though even people like him were carefully chosen.

His wife, who was very young, almost a girl, and whom he had married to save her from the hard life of her dispossessed kulak family, had let the room to us during one of his prolonged absences in the countryside. She herself moved to the kitchen and sent the money received from us to her parents. Her husband thus had two tenants around his neck, but got no benefit from it. Though she had been "saved" by him, she kept him pretty firmly in hand. Judging by some of the talk that passed between them, she knew something about him that even in those brutal times would not have been taken lightly. Both to his face and behind his back she referred to him in the traditional way as a "Herod," and when she cursed him in choice language, he cringed in front of her. But, all the same, he could not put up with us, his tenants, and he played all the nasty tricks he could think of. For instance, he once came into our room holding a live mouse by the tail—the house swarmed with all kinds of vermin—and, greeting us from the doorway in brisk military fashion, he said: "Allow me to roast this." Then he started to walk over to our electric toaster, which had an open grill. He thought this kind of toaster was despicable—a bourgeois plaything which should be done away with, like the kulaks, and opposed by any honest Soviet citizen. Rudakov and Kaletski, who were always sitting around in our room, sprang to the mouse's defense, and the landlord, who was a fearful coward, retreated. From the neighboring room we could then hear his jibes about the intellectuals and their weak nerves—"I'll give them a real scare—I'll grill a cat on that toaster of theirs." The extraordinary thing was that he wasn't a drunkard and did all these things in a completely sober state. The mouse was his star turn.

When M. went to the rest home in Tambov, the "agent" threw all our things out of the room. They were gathered together and kept by the prostitute. When he returned, M. couldn't get into his room and had to go out and wait in the offices of the newspaper next door. Somebody rang up the nameless institution in which our landlord worked. In the evening he came to the newspaper office and said to M.: "You can go back—I've been told not to make trouble." This brought home to us the advantage of renting a room from a member of an institution which imposed military discipline on its employees. From that time on, the "agent" behaved like a lamb. When we moved out, he himself loaded our belongings into the cab. He was so delighted that he even crossed himself: he had never thought he would get rid of his unwelcome tenants so easily.

It was said that in 1937 he got rid of another tenant, but he didn't enjoy his triumph for long, because he was transferred to guard duty in a forced-labor camp.

During our three years in Voronezh we changed rooms five times. After leaving the "agent," we moved to an apartment belonging to a widow in a luxurious new building for engineers and technicians. She let two rooms simultaneously—one to us and the other to Dunayevski, a young journalist. It was he who had arranged this splendid new place for us, but the widow had only agreed to it because she calculated that he would marry her. When it appeared that he had no intention of doing so, we had to move out to make room for another prospective husband.

The last of our rooms was in the tiny house of a seamstress who worked for the local theater. It seemed like heaven to us, a dream from a vanished past, a reward for all our tribulations. M. had taken them all quite calmly, but living at the seamstress' house, he came back to life.

The seamstress was a most ordinary sort of woman, friendly and good-humored. She lived with her mother, whom she called "Grandma," and her son Vadik, who was like all boys of his age. Her husband, a cobbler, had died a few years previously and some actors who had their shoes repaired by him had got his widow a job in the theater so she could feed her family. Since the cobbler had been a Party member, she managed also to get an allowance for her son. They lived, like everybody, on potatoes and "Grandma" kept a few hens in the outhouse. For them ten roubles was an enormous income. They had generally had actors living there, and she was famous among them for her good nature. That is why they had sent us to her. Living in her house, we breathed freely again.

There were once many kind people, and even unkind ones pretended to be good because that was the thing to do. Such pretense was the source of the hypocrisy and dishonesty so much exposed in the realist literature at the end of the last century. The unexpected result of this kind of critical writing was that kind people disappeared. Kindness is not, after all, an inborn quality—it has to be cultivated, and this only happens when it is in demand. For our generation, kindness was an old-fashioned, vanished quality, and its exponents were as extinct as the mammoth. Everything we have seen in our times—the dispossession of the kulaks, class warfare, the constant "unmasking" of people, the search for an ulterior motive behind every action—all this has taught us to be anything you like except kind.

Kindness and good nature had to be sought in remote places that were deaf to the call of the age. Only the inert had kept these qualities as they had come down from their ancestors. Everybody else had been affected by the inverted "humanism" of the times.

In the seamstress' house we lived quietly, like ordinary human beings, and we quite forgot that we had no place of our own. Later on, traveling in a car or a tram through the streets of some huge city or other, I often counted the windows as they flashed by, wondering why I could call none of them mine. I had grotesque dreams in which I saw enormous corridors, like covered streets, with doors leading off on either side. Now, I thought, the doors would open and I would be able to pick a room for myself. Sometimes I found dead relatives of mine inside, and this made me angry: Why are you living here, while I have to wander without a home? What Freud would dare to explain such dreams in terms of sexual repression, the Oedipus complex or similar monstrosities?

It has been said that Soviet citizens do not need to build houses for themselves because they have the right to demand a free apartment from the State. But whom does one demand it from? Even in my dreams I wondered about this, and always woke up before the blissful moment of receiving the piece of paper entitling you to move into an apartment and get your residence permit. In Voronezh I lived on the illusion that I still had my own hard-won place in Moscow, something quite unique in its way. But I no longer have such illusions and am familiar with the laws under which I have no right to anything. And how many of us are there like me? Please don't think that I'm an exception. Our name is legion.

Future generations will never understand what "living-space" means to us. Innumerable crimes have been committed for its sake, and people are so tied to it that to leave it would never occur to them. Who could ever leave his wonderful, precious twelve and a half square meters of living-space? No one would be so mad, and it is passed on to one's descendants like a family castle, a villa or an estate. Husbands and wives who loathe the sight of each other, mothers-in-law and sons-in-law, grown sons and daughters, former domestic servants who have managed to hang on to a cubby-hole next to the kitchen—all are wedded forever to their living-space and would never part with it. In marriage and in divorce the first thing that arises is the question of living-space. I have heard men described as perfect gentlemen for throwing over their wives but leaving them the living-space. I have also heard of eligible girls with apartments, and of bachelors who want nothing more. Some clever women have been known to put on old clothes and hire themselves out to clean student dormitories, in exchange for a corner to live in. Here they would stay, putting up for years with curses and threats of eviction. Even faculty members brave insults to live in such places. I too could at one time have done this, and sat cooped up until late at night, listening to the women students singing and dancing. Often there were not enough places for them, and they had to sleep two to a bunk.

Your permit to reside went with your accommodation and if you lost it you could never return to the city you had lived in. For many people their apartments turned out to be real traps. The clouds were already gathering, their friends and colleagues were being picked up one after another, or, as we used to say, the shells were falling nearer and nearer, but the possessors of permanent titles to apartments stayed put for the police to come and get them. As they waited, they deluded themselves with the hope that this cup might for some reason pass from them. In this way they clung to the wretched dumps they called "apartments," and if they were self-contained ones in new buildings, the only way out—to complete the resemblance to a trap—was the window, since there were no back stairs. I knew only one woman who, during the expulsion of former aristocrats from Leningrad, was sensible enough to pack her things and flee to the provinces, thus keeping her record clean and avoiding a great many misfortunes.

I too was saved from arrest by not having a home. The only time I had living-space of my own was in 1933, when, under pressure from

Bukharin, we were given our perch on the fifth floor of a building put up specially for writers. When M. was arrested a year later, we kept our right to the apartment, but, egged on by other writers living in the building, Mate Zalke (who was in charge of it) went personally to the MGB to ask permission to make room for a "real" Soviet writer by throwing out M.'s old relative—that is, my mother. But the "miracle" was still in operation and his request was turned down with a comment to the effect that the writers should not be more royalist than the king. The fact that we had been left in possession of the apartment gave me some hope that they might allow M. to go back to Moscow, but when it was needed, it was taken away and I was thrown out too, even though I did not count as an exile. If I had stayed there together with the literary general, my bones would long ago have moldered away in some common grave in a prison camp. After M.'s second arrest I kept on the move, and when they came to look for me in the room where we had last lived in Kalinin, they could not find me. That room I could not in any case have kept—it was in a private house and cost too much for me. So I was not caught in a trap, and because I was homeless they overlooked me. That is why I was able to survive and preserve M.'s poems.

And what would have happened if in the summer of 1937, after we left her house, some other tenant had moved in with the good seamstress and stopped paying her rent on getting a title to the room from the local Soviet? Would she have done the same as the rest of them and gone to denounce him to the secret police ("My tenant holds illegal meetings and carries on counter-revolutionary talk . . . as a householder I regard it as my duty . . .")? Or would she have meekly given up the little extra she got to feed her mother and son? All I know is that her little house was destroyed during the war, and that something very different has been put up in its place.

31

MONEY

At first we were materially better off in Voronezh than we had ever been before. Impressed by the "miracle," the State Publishing House gave us translation work. As my brother Evgeni put it, Moscow looked better after it burned down. I hastily translated some ghastly novel or other, and was immediately given a second contract. But in the winter of 1934–35 the persons responsible were evidently reprimanded for their kindness. I was summoned to Moscow for a talk about my "method of translation." The editor-in-chief was then Startsev. He spoke well of my methods, but after that the head of the translation section asked me to let him have the book back on the pretext that he had to see whether or not the novel should be abridged. I never saw the book (*Nest of Simple Folk*) again, and it soon came out in somebody else's translation. We were paid a little that was due to us under an old contract for a translation of Maupassant, and after that the flow of money from Moscow dried up.

In search of work M. wrote innumerable applications, and also kept going to the local branch of the Union of Writers. The question of giving him work had been "posed in principle," as they used to say in those days. This meant that the Union of Writers, as the organization to which M. belonged, had asked for instructions "from above" and was still waiting for them. Neither M. nor I could ever get work without a great deal of preliminary fuss and delay. Even as late as 1955 I was able to take up a job in Cheboksary only after Surkov had been somewhere to get authorization and then, in my presence, phoned the result to the Minister of Education. But in 1934 no organization would give work to an exile without instructions "from above." This was because heads of departments wanted to guard against being held responsible for having a dubious person on their staff—though in times of increased "vigilance" it was no good referring to permission or authorization "from above," since such instructions were never given in writing. It was always done by a nod of the head, or by a mumbled remark over the phone: "Well, all right" or, at best, "You decide, we don't mind." There was never any trace of this in the records, and officials often paid dearly for cluttering up their staff with "alien elements." We had been "alien elements" for so many years that we knew only too well how this mechanism worked. We saw how it evolved with the passage of time as the State's power over the individual became more and more elaborate. In the eight years since the Twentieth Congress things have changed radically—we are now living in a new era—but I am talking about the Stalin period and the various phases of the subjugation of literature as M. experienced them—it was essentially the same in other fields too, with only minor differences.

In 1922, when we returned from Georgia, all the literary monthlies still had M.'s name on their lists of potential contributors, but it became more and more difficult for him actually to publish anything. Typical in this respect was Voronski, who rejected everything. "What can I do?" complained the secretary, Sergei Antonovich Klychkov. "He says it's not topical." In 1923 M.'s name was removed from all the lists of contributors to the literary magazines. Since it happened in all of them simultaneously, this can scarcely have been a coincidence. That summer there must have been some kind of ideological conference at which the process of dividing writers into friend and foe had begun. In the winter of 1923–24 Bukharin, who was then editing the magazine *Prozhektor* [*Searchlight*] said to M.: "I cannot publish your verse—let me have some translations." It seems likely that the restriction applied at first only to magazines, since a book of verse (the *Second Book*) acquired by a publisher in 1922 actually appeared the following year, but two years later Narbut, who managed the Land and Factory Publishing House, said the same thing as Bukharin: "I can't publish you, but I can give you all the translating you like." By this time everybody was saying that M. had given up poetry for translation. M. was very upset when the *émigré* paper *Nakanune* [*On the Eve*]* echoed our press in putting this story about. Things were in general very difficult just then: "They will only let me translate," M. complained.

But even this was not plain sailing. Apart from the fact that there was a lot of competition, M. was not among those who were being "looked after" on special instructions, and from the second half of the twenties it became much harder to obtain translating work, so that his right to a livelihood was always being contested. Nothing came of his books for children either. Marshak made a terrible mess of *Balloons* and *The Tramcar*, and only the poverty-stricken private publishers, while they still existed, offered some kind of outlet. M. was able to print a few articles in the provinces (in Kiev) and in theatrical magazines. There was evidently not yet a total ban—it was rather a question of restrictions and "recommendations" to be more in step with the times. A new stage in the struggle for the "purity of the line" was opened in 1930 by Stalin's article in *Bolshevik* in which he called for a complete prohibition of unsuitable works. I was working at that time on the magazine *For a Communist Education*, and from snatches of conversation in the editor's office I realized that the sniping phase was over and we were now

* Published in Berlin, 1922–24, *Nakanune* was pro-Soviet and Moscow-financed.

in for a general offensive. M. still managed to get a few poems printed, but for publishing his "Journey to Armenia" in *Zvezda* [*Star*] one of the editors, Caesar Volpe, lost his job—he knew, incidentally, the risk he was taking. The screws were gradually being tightened. M. and Akhmatova were the first to feel the effects of Stalin's rule, but everybody else soon learned as well. Many found all the new restrictions to their advantage—these are the ones who even now would like to see a return to the past, and are still fighting to maintain their own previous positions and keep the old prohibitions in force.

During the period of M.'s exile there could be no question at all of his publishing any original work, and neither was he given translations any more. Even his name was no longer mentionable—during all those years it cropped up only once or twice in denunciatory articles. Now his name is no longer banned, but, from force of habit, people don't mention it, and in Kochetov's circles people are moved to fury by it. Not for nothing was Ehrenburg attacked mainly for the passages about M. and Akhmatova in his memoirs.

In the winter of 1937–38 there was no work of any kind to be had, and I was unable to get a job again until 1939, when it was announced that the wives of prisoners still had the right to work. But in periods of "vigilance" I was always thrown out. Since all work is in the hands of the State, the only thing one can do is "scream under the Kremlin walls."* Private means of subsistence scarcely existed. If you had your own house and plot of land, you could grow vegetables and keep a cow (but for hay you depended on the authorities); you could do dressmaking at home—until the tax inspector caught up with you; or you could take in typing, but before the war typewriters were very expensive. Finally, you could beg, but this was not easy because only the faithful servants of the regime had money to spare, and they were not the sort to compromise themselves by contact with outcasts.

Of all these means the one we chose was to "scream"—as long as it was possible. M. badgered the local branch of the Writers' Union in Voronezh, and I went to Moscow to talk with Union officials there—while they would still see me—such as Marchenko, Shcherbakov and other grandees. They wore inscrutable expressions and never answered any of my questions, but they nevertheless made some kind of inquiries "higher up." In the first winter after his exile, M.'s pension was

---

* Quoted from Akhmatova's "Requiem."

stopped. I tried to get it restored, pleading with Shcherbakov on the grounds that M.'s "services to Russian literature" could not be denied, and that it was therefore wrong to take the pension away. My eloquence was wasted on Shcherbakov, who replied: "What sort of services to Russian literature can there be if Mandelstam has been exiled for his works?" Like everybody else, I had lost all sense of normal legal standards, and I am still curious to know whether it is in order to deprive someone of his pension if he has been sentenced to exile without loss of civil rights.

I deliberately referred to Shcherbakov and his like as "grandees." Our officials were now even of a different physical type. Until the middle of the twenties we had been dealing with former members of the old revolutionary underground and their younger assistants of a similar type. They were brusque, utterly self-righteous, and often ill-mannered, but they loved to hold forth and argue. There was about them something of the seminarists and Pisarev. Gradually they were replaced by round-headed, fair-haired types in embroidered Ukrainian shirts who affected a cheerful familiarity, cracked jokes and liked to be taken for bluff, straightforward fellows. It was all completely put on. These were superseded in their turn by diplomats who weighed every word, never gave anything away or made any promises, but at the same time tried to create the impression that they were men of power and influence. One of the first functionaries of this kind was Shcherbakov. When I first came to see him, we were both silent for a few minutes. I wanted him to speak first, but it didn't work: he was very much the dignitary waiting for the humble petitioner to make her request. I raised the question of publishing M.'s work, though I knew this was quite hopeless. He replied that the only criterion for publication was the quality of an author's work, and since M. was not being printed, it could only mean that his work did not pass the test. The same thing, only with a less practiced inflection of the voice, was said to me by Marchenko. Only once did Shcherbakov betray any feeling. This was when he asked me what M. was writing about now, and I replied: "About the Kama River." He misheard this and half smiled: "About the guerrillas?" But the smile disappeared when I explained that it was not about the Civil War partisans. "What is he writing about the Kama for?" he asked. The idea seemed grotesque to him. The way his face had lit up for a moment suggested that they probably expected M. to compose hymns of praise and were surprised he was not doing so. On this step he decided only in 1937, but by then it was too late to help him.

In the end, M. and I did manage to break through the blank wall—thanks to our joint efforts, he was given work in the local theater as its "literary director." He had little idea of what he was supposed to do, and in practice it just meant gossiping with the actors, with whom he got on very well. We were also able to make a little money out of the local broadcasting station—anonymous work of this kind was permitted even to exiles, though only in relatively quiet periods, when the word "vigilance" was not constantly appearing in the newspapers. We worked on several broadcasts together: "Goethe as a Young Man," "Gulliver for Children." M. often wrote the program notes for concerts, notably for a performance of Gluck's *Orpheus and Eurydice*. He was very pleased when he walked along the street and heard his story of Eurydice coming over all the loudspeakers. It was at this time that he did his free versions of some Neapolitan songs for a contralto also living as an exile in Voronezh.

But even in this comparatively prosperous Voronezh period it was still difficult for us to get by. The theater paid 300 roubles a month, which just covered our rent (we paid between 200 and 300 for the various miserable rooms we lived in) and perhaps cigarettes as well. The radio also brought in between 200 and 300, and I sometimes made a little extra by advising the local newspaper on literary works submitted to them for publication. Altogether it was enough to keep us going in food. We lived mainly on cabbage soup and eggs. We could afford tea and butter, but canned fish was a rare luxury. Sometimes we let ourselves go and bought a bottle of Georgian wine. On top of everything, we also managed to feed Sergei Borisovich Rudakov—his wife sent him 50 roubles a month, but this was exactly what it cost him to rent the bunk in which he slept. This was during the year spent in the "agent's" house, when we had visitors nearly all the time—actors from the local theater were always coming to see us, or musicians on tour. Voronezh was one of the few provincial cities with their own symphony orchestras, and anyone on tour always passed through it. M. used to go not only to the concerts, but also to the rehearsals: he was fascinated by the fact that each conductor had a different way of working with the orchestra, and he wanted to write a piece about conductors, but nothing came of it—he never got around to it. When Leo Ginzburg and his namesake Grigori came to Voronezh on a concert tour, they spent a lot of time with us, and added variety to our meals by bringing with them cans of the fruit preserves they liked so much. Maria Veniaminovna Yudina went out of her way to give concerts in Voronezh so she could see M. and play for him. Once, when we happened to be away in the country, the singer Migai came to see us, and we were very sorry to miss him. Visits like these were great events in our life, and M., with his sociable nature, couldn't have lived without them.

Our relatively prosperous life came to an end in the autumn of 1936 after our return from a trip to Zadonsk. The local radio was abolished, as part of a move to centralize all broadcasting, the theater folded, and our newspaper work also dried up. Everything collapsed at once. Going over all the possible private means of making a livelihood, M. now decided we should try keeping a cow. But this dream faded when we realized that a cow wasn't much good without hay.

Hard as it was even during the days of relative comfort, our life in Voronezh was happier than any we had ever known. M. was very fond of the town itself. He liked everything connected with borderlands, and what interested him about Voronezh was that in Peter the Great's time it had been a frontier town—it was here that Peter had built his Azov flotilla. In Voronezh M. could still sense the free spirit of the borderlands, and he listened with fascination to the local speech, which was still Southern Russian, not Ukrainian—the dividing line between the two languages ran a little to the south of Voronezh. In the nearby village of Nikolskoye, M. wrote down the names of the streets— though they had been given new Soviet ones, the inhabitants still remembered the old ones. The people of the village were proud of their descent from outcasts and runaway convicts of Peter's time, and the streets were called after the different kinds of criminal: Strangler's Lane, Embezzler's Lane, Counterfeiter's Row, etc. The diary with M.'s notes of this period was confiscated during his second arrest, and I have now forgotten the old Russian terms which came so naturally to the people of Nikolskoye. They were sectarians of the kind known as "jumpers" and composed religious ballads of a traditional type about their unsuccessful attempts to leap up to heaven. Not long before we visited it, the village had been the scene of dramatic events. The sectarians had fixed a day on which they would take off for heaven, and, convinced that by next morning they would no longer be of this world, they gave away all their property to their earthbound neighbors. Coming to their senses when they fell to the ground, they rushed to recover their belongings, and a terrible fight broke out. The most recent ballad which we were able to get from them told about a "jumper" saying goodbye to his beloved beehive before giving it away. M. remembered the lines by heart and often recited them. The "jumper" in the ballad didn't want to fly up to heaven, and was happy enough on earth with his beehives, his house, his wife and children.

In winter Voronezh was like a vast field of ice, and one was always slipping—as Akhmatova says in her poem: "Gingerly I tread on glass. . . ." By this time not even the big cities always had their proper complement of janitors to clear away the snow with shovels and sprinkle sand on the sidewalks. M. was not worried by ice and wind, and at times he was entranced by the town. But as often as not he cursed it and longed to get away. What irked him was the feeling of being confined, as though he had been locked in a room. "By nature, I'm the sort who is always waiting for things," he said once, "and so they have to send me to Voronezh and make me wait for something here." And, true enough, our life there consisted of nothing but waiting—for money, for answers to all our letters and petitions, for a propitious nod from on high, for salvation. But, all the same, I have never known a man who lived so greedily for the passing hours as M. He seemed to have an almost physical sense of time, of the minutes which compose it. In this respect he was the exact opposite of Berdiayev, who says somewhere that he could never abide time and that all the anguish of waiting is longing for eternity. It seems to me that for any artist eternity is something tangibly present in every fleeting fraction of time, which he would gladly stop and thus make even more tangible. What causes anguish in an artist is not longing for eternity, but a temporary loss of his feeling that every second of time is, in its fullness and density, the equal of eternity itself. Anguish such as this naturally gives rise to concern with the future, and M. willy-nilly became "the sort who is always waiting for things." In Voronezh this side of M. developed just as much as his acute sense of the passing moment, and when anguish came upon him he wanted to rush off into the blue—but he couldn't because he was firmly tied to the spot. He was like a bird that could not stand its cage, and he was always collecting various documents in support of applications to go to Moscow for a few days—to have some glands removed (though he had never had trouble with them before) or to put his "literary affairs" in order (quite forgetting that he had no "literary affairs"). Of course he could not get permission to make the trip. In response to his sighs, Akhmatova and Pasternak even went to see Katanian to ask whether he could be transferred to another town. This request was also turned down. Katanian's office, always open to visitors, existed only for the purpose of receiving requests that were unfailingly turned down. So M. spent the whole of his three years in the Voronezh region, except for one visit beyond the boundary to Tambov, where he stayed very briefly in a rest home. He also made several journeys round the Voronezh area on assignments from the local newspaper, and once we were able to have a little vacation in Zadonsk. This was possible because Akhmatova had got 500 roubles from Pasternak for us, and when she added 500 of her own, we felt so rich that we stayed in Zadonsk for six weeks.

M.'s attempts to break loose ended in the summer of 1936 when we heard over the radio in Zadonsk about the trials then being prepared—an ominous sign that our life had entered a new phase. 1937 was approaching. By this time M. was very ill with something the doctors did not want or were unable to diagnose. He had bouts of what looked like angina pectoris. Although he had difficulty breathing, he went on with his work. Perhaps it was as well that he consumed himself like this—if he had been physically healthy, his later suffering would only have been more protracted.

It was a terrible road that stretched ahead of him, and, as we now know, the only possible deliverance was death. People of M.'s generation—and of mine, for that matter—no longer had anything to live for. He would not have lived to see even the comparatively good times since Stalin's death which Akhmatova and I regard as bliss. I realized this at the end of the forties and the beginning of the fifties, when most people who had returned from the camps after the end of their sentences (including many who had fought in the war) were sent back to them again. "M. did well to die straightaway," said Kazarnovski,* who met M. in a transit camp and then spent ten years in Kolyma. Could we ever have believed such a thing in Voronezh? We probably imagined that the worst was behind us, or, rather, like other doomed people, we tried not to peer into the future. We slowly prepared for death, lingering over every minute and relishing it, to keep the taste on our lips, because Voronezh was a miracle and only a miracle could have brought us there.

---

* A journalist whose evidence about Mandelstam's last days is discussed in the final chapters.

32
THE ORIGINS OF THE MIRACLE

In his letter to Stalin, Bukharin added a postscript saying he had been visited by Pasternak, who was upset by the arrest of Mandelstam. The purpose of this postscript was clear: it was Bukharin's way of indicating to Stalin what the effect of M.'s arrest had been on public opinion. It was always necessary to personify "public opinion" in this way. You were allowed to talk of one particular individual being upset, but it was unthinkable to mention the existence of dissatisfaction among a whole section of the community—say, the intelligentsia, or "literary circles." No group has the right to its own opinion about some event or other. In matters of this kind there are fine points of etiquette which nobody can appreciate unless he has been in our shoes. Bukharin knew how to present things in the right way, and it was the postscript at the end of his letter that explained why Stalin chose to telephone Pasternak and not someone else.

Their conversation took place at the end of July, when M.'s sentence had already been commuted, and Pasternak told a lot of people about it—Ehrenburg, for instance, who was in Moscow at the time and whom he went to see the same day. But for some reason he said not a word about it to anyone directly involved—that is, to me, my brother Evgeni, or Akhmatova. True, on the same day he did ring Evgeni, who already knew about the revision of the sentence, but only to assure him that everything would be all right. He said no more than this, and Evgeni, thinking his words were simply an expression of his optimism, attached no particular importance to them. I myself only learned about Stalin's call to Pasternak several months later when I came to Moscow from Voronezh a second time after being ill with typhus and dysentery. In casual conversation Shengeli asked me whether I had heard the story about Stalin's telephone call to Pasternak, and whether there was anything in it. Shengeli was convinced that it was just a figment of somebody's imagination if Pasternak himself had not told me anything about it. I decided, however, to go to the Volkhonka* and see Pasternak, since there is never smoke (and what smoke!) without fire. Shengeli's story was confirmed down to the last detail. As he told

---

* A street in Moscow.

me about the conversation, Pasternak reproduced everything said by Stalin and himself in direct speech. It was just the same as what Shengeli had told me—evidently Pasternak had told it to everybody in identical terms and the version going around Moscow was entirely accurate. This is how Pasternak told me the story:

Pasternak was called to the phone, having been told beforehand who wished to speak with him. He began by complaining that he couldn't hear at all well because he was speaking from a communal apartment and there were children making a noise in the corridor. The time had not yet come when such a complaint would have been taken as a request—to be granted by way of a miracle—for an immediate improvement in one's living conditions. It was simply that Pasternak began any telephone conversation with this complaint. Whenever he was talking on the phone to one of us, Akhmatova and I would quietly ask the other—whichever of us happened to be on the phone with him: "Has he stopped carrying on about the apartment yet?" He talked with Stalin just as he would have talked with any of us.

Stalin began by telling Pasternak that Mandelstam's case had been reviewed, and that everything would be all right. This was followed by a strange reproach: why hadn't Pasternak approached the writers' organizations, or him (Stalin), and why hadn't he tried to do something for Mandelstam: "If I were a poet and a poet friend of mine were in trouble, I would do anything to help him."

Pasternak's reply to this was: "The writers' organizations haven't bothered with cases like this since 1927, and if I hadn't tried to do something, you probably would never have heard about it." Pasternak went on to say something about the word "friend," trying to define more precisely the nature of his relations with M., which were not, of course, covered by the term "friendship." This digression was very much in Pasternak's style and had no relevance to the matter in hand. Stalin interrupted him: "But he's a genius, he's a genius, isn't he?" To this Pasternak replied: "But that's not the point." "What is it, then?" Stalin asked. Pasternak then said that he would like to meet him and have a talk. "About what?" "About life and death," Pasternak replied. Stalin hung up. Pasternak tried to get him back, but could only reach a secretary. Stalin did not come to the phone again. Pasternak asked the secretary whether he could talk about this conversation or whether he should keep quiet about it. To his surprise, he was told he could talk about it as much as he liked—there was no need at all to make a secret of it. Stalin clearly wanted it to have the widest possible repercussions. A miracle is only a miracle, after all, if people stand in wonder before it.

Just as I have not named the one person who copied down M.'s poem about Stalin, because I believe he had nothing to do with the denunciation and arrest of M., so there is one remark made by Pasternak in this conversation which I do not wish to quote since it could be held against him by people who do not know him. The remark in question was entirely innocent, but it had a slight touch of Pasternak's self-absorption and egocentrism. For those of us who knew him well, it just sounded faintly comic.

Everybody could now clearly see what miracles Stalin was capable of, and it was to Pasternak that the honor had fallen not only of spreading the good tidings all over Moscow, but also of hearing a sermon in connection with it. The aim of the miracle was thus achieved: attention was diverted from the victim to the miracle-worker. It was extraordinarily symptomatic of the period that, in discussing the miracle, nobody thought to ask why Stalin should have rebuked Pasternak for not trying to save a friend and fellow poet while at the same time he was calmly sending his own friends and comrades to their death. Even Pasternak had not thought about this aspect, and he winced slightly when I raised it with him. My contemporaries took Stalin's sermon on friendship between poets completely at its face value and were ecstatic about a ruler who had shown such warmth of spirit. But M. and I couldn't help thinking of Lominadze, who was recalled to Moscow for his execution while we were in Tiflis talking with him about the possibility of M. staying there to work in the archives. And apart from Lominadze, there were all the others whose heads had rolled by this time. There were already very many, but even now people still stubbornly continue to reckon only from 1937, when Stalin supposedly went to the bad all of a sudden and began to destroy everybody.

Pasternak himself was very unhappy about his talk with Stalin, and to many people, including me, he lamented his failure to follow it up with a meeting. He was no longer worried about M., since he had complete faith in Stalin's word that he would be all right. This made him feel his own failure all the more keenly. Like many other people in our country, Pasternak was morbidly curious about the recluse in the Kremlin. Personally, I think it was lucky for him that he did not meet Stalin, but at the time all this happened there was a good deal we did not yet understand—we still had much to learn. This was another extraordinary feature of the times: why were people so dazzled by absolute rulers who promised to organize heaven on earth, whatever it might cost? Nowadays it would never occur to anyone to doubt that in their confrontation with Stalin it was M. and Pasternak who came out on the side of right, displaying both moral authority and a proper sense of history. But at the time Pasternak was very upset by his "failure" and himself told me that for a long time afterward he could not even write poetry. It would have been quite understandable if Pasternak had wanted, as it were, to touch the stores of the era with his own hands, and, as we know, he subsequently did so. But for this he had no need of any meetings with our rulers. At that time, however, I believe that Pasternak still regarded Stalin as the embodiment of the age, of history and of the future, and that he simply longed to see this living wonder at close quarters.

Rumors are now being spread that Pasternak lost his nerve during the talk with Stalin and disowned M. Not long before his final illness I ran into him on the street and he told me about this story. I suggested we both make a written record of his conversation, but he didn't want to. Perhaps things had now taken such a turn for him that he no longer had any time for the past.

How can Pasternak possibly be accused of such a thing—particularly since Stalin started off by telling him he had already exercised mercy? According to the present rumors, Stalin asked Pasternak to vouch for M., but Pasternak supposedly refused to do so. Nothing of this kind happened, and the question of it never even arose.

When I gave M. an account of the whole business, he was entirely happy with the way Pasternak had handled things, particularly with his remark about the writers' organizations not having bothered with cases like this since 1927. "He never said a truer word," M. said with a laugh. The only thing that upset him was that the conversation had taken place at all. "Why has Pasternak been dragged into this? I have to get out of it myself—he has nothing to do with it." Another comment of M.'s was: "He [Pasternak] was quite right to say that whether I'm a genius or not is beside the point. . . . Why is Stalin so afraid of genius? It's like a superstition with him. He thinks we might put a spell on him, like shamans."* And yet another remark: "That poem of mine really must

---

* Shaman: Siberian witch doctor.

have made an impression, if he makes such a song and dance about commuting my sentence."

Incidentally, it's by no means certain how things might have ended if Pasternak had started praising M. to the skies as a genius—Stalin might have had M. killed off on the quiet, like Mikhoels, or at least have taken more drastic measures to see that his manuscripts were destroyed. I believe that they have survived only because of the constant attacks on M. as a "former poet" by his contemporaries in LEF and among the Symbolists.* As a result, the authorities felt that M. had been so discredited and was such a has-been that they did not bother to track down his manuscripts and stamp them out completely. All they did was to burn whatever came into their hands—this, they thought, was quite enough. If they had been led to think more highly of M.'s poetry, neither his work nor I would have survived. It would have been a case, as they say, of scattering our ashes to the winds.

The version of the telephone call from Stalin that has been told abroad is completely absurd. According to accounts published there, M. supposedly read his poem at a party in Pasternak's apartment, after which the poor host was "summoned to the Kremlin and given hell." Every word of this shows a total ignorance of our life—though one might well ask how any outsider could be expected to have enough imagination to picture the extent of our bondage! Nobody would have dared to breathe a word against Stalin, let alone read a poem like that "at a party." This is the sort of thing that only a provocateur would do, but even a provocateur would scarcely have dared to recite a poem against Stalin at a party. And then, nobody was ever summoned to the Kremlin for questioning. One was invited to the Kremlin for gala receptions and the ceremonial award of decorations. The place for interrogations was the Lubianka, but Pasternak was not asked to go there in connection with M. Indeed, Pasternak came to no harm at all as a consequence of his talk with Stalin, and it is not necessary to feel sorry for him because of this particular episode. One final point: it so happens that we never visited Pasternak at his home, and we saw him only when he came to see us from time to time. This arrangement suited us very well.

---

* For LEF and Symbolists, see page 426.

33

THE ANTIPODES

In certain respects M. and Pasternak were antipodes, but since antipodes are by definition located at opposite poles of the same sphere, it is possible to draw a line between them. In other words, they had common features and qualities that united them. Neither of them could ever have been the antipode of, say, Fedin, Oshanin or Blagoi.

There are two poems of M.'s which seem to be in the nature of rejoinders to Pasternak—one occasioned by some lines of Pasternak's, and the other by an unfinished conversation between them. First I will tell about the second poem—the one beginning "The apartment is quiet as paper." It was written in response to an almost casual remark by Pasternak. He had looked in to see how we were getting on in our new apartment in Furmanov Street. As he was leaving, he lingered for quite a time in the entrance, saying how wonderful it was: "Now you have an apartment, you'll be able to write poetry," he said as he finally went out.

"Did you hear what he said?" M. asked me. He was furious. He couldn't stand it when people blamed their inability to work on external circumstances, such as bad living conditions or lack of money. It was his profound conviction that nothing should prevent an artist from doing what he had to do, and, conversely, that material comfort was not in itself a stimulus to work—though he wasn't against comfort as such and would not himself have turned up his nose at it. At that time, as we saw all around us, there was furious competition among the writers for the good things of life, among which the greatest prize of all was an apartment. A little later country villas were also handed out "for services rendered." Pasternak's words touched M. to the quick: he cursed the apartment and said it should go to one of those it was intended for: "the worthy traitors, the portrait-painters," and all the other timeservers. This curse he pronounced on our apartment does not mean that he thought it better to be homeless—he was simply expressing his horror at the price one was expected to pay. We got nothing—apartments, villas or money—without paying the price.

In Pasternak's novel [*Dr. Zhivago*] there is also some concern with apartments, or, rather, with the writing table that a creative person supposedly needs for his work. Pasternak could not do without his writing table—he could only work with pen in hand. But M. composed his verse in his head, while walking around, and only needed to sit down briefly to copy out the result. Even in their manner of working they were antipodes. M. would scarcely have wanted to assert the poet's special claims to a writing table at a time when the whole nation was utterly deprived of basic needs.

The second poem connected with Pasternak is the one beginning "It's night outside. . . ." This is a reply to those lines of Pasternak where he says: "Rhyme is not the echoing of line-ends, but a cloak-room check, the ticket for a seat by the columns." This is a clear allusion to the main auditorium of the Moscow Conservatory, to which people like us were always admitted even if we didn't have tickets, and was thus symbolic of the privileged social position of the poet. In his reply M. renounced his "seat by the columns." In his attitude toward worldly goods and his refusal to come to terms with the age he lived in, M. was much closer to Tsvetayeva than to Pasternak. But with Tsvetayeva the rejection was more abstract, whereas for M. it was a head-on collision with something more precisely defined, the shape of which he knew fairly well, just as he knew the nature of his quarrel with it.

As early as 1927 I remember once saying to Pasternak: "Watch out, or they'll adopt you." He often reminded me of these words—for the last time thirty years later, after *Dr. Zhivago* had appeared. During our conversation in 1927—I was comparing him with M.—I said that he [Pasternak] was a domesticated creature of a familiar Moscow type, very much attached to the comforts of home and his dacha in the country. Thanks to this "Muscovite" quality, I continued, our literary bigwigs understood him very well and they would be glad to come to terms with him, but he was bound nevertheless to break with them—because they were set on a course he could never accept. I then said that M., on the other hand, was a nomad, a wanderer, whom the walls of Moscow houses could never hold. Later I realized that it was not quite like this, and that M. was deliberately being made into a nomad, whether he liked it or not. As for Pasternak, I was not trying to be a Cassandra—it was simply that I had come up against the facts of life a little earlier than he, just as the housekeeper in the Cherdyn hospital had seen many things before I had. In any case, I have noticed that sooner or later everybody's eyes are opened, even though many won't admit it. At one of our very last meetings Pasternak reminded me of how I had prophesied his break with his fellow writers.

In the cases of both Pasternak and M., destiny was hatched from character, like a butterfly from its chrysalis. Both were doomed to be rejected by the literary establishment, but whereas Pasternak, for a time at any rate, sought points of contact with it, M. always shied away. Seeking for a stable life, particularly in the material sense, Pasternak knew that the path to it lay through membership in the literary community, and he never shunned it or tried to leave it. Like his creator, Dr. Zhivago is a poet, but he becomes a literary outcast only because Pasternak had seen that his own break with the world of Soviet literature was inevitable.

As a young man Pasternak had given much thought to the question of what form of literature would assure him of a stable situation in life. In a letter to M. he wrote that he had once considered becoming an editor. Of course this was sheer fantasy on the part of the still unfledged Pasternak, but even in their fantasies he and M. were strikingly unlike each other. All his life M. refused to have anything to do with the literary profession as such—such things as translating, editing, going to meetings in Herzen House or making the sort of pronouncements expected of writers. None of this was for him. Pasternak was drawn to all these things, while M. was repelled by them. The world of literature treated them both accordingly, smiling on Pasternak (at least to begin with) and seeking, right at the start, to destroy M. Fadeyev once said to me, as he glanced through some of M.'s poems, "You know, Pasternak is not one of us either, but all the same he is a little closer to us and we can come to terms with him in some things." At that time Fadeyev was editor of *Krasnaya Nov* and M. was already under a ban. I had taken the poems to Fadeyev on behalf of M., who was ill. These were the poems which are now gathered in the "First Voronezh Notebook." Fadeyev paid no attention to the "Wolf" poem or any other of that cycle. His eye was caught only by one eight-line poem in which the twinkling stars in the night sky are compared to officials sitting up late writing their reports. Fadeyev noted that the word for "reports" (*rapportichki* in Russian) was spelled with two "p's." "Why is it with two 'p's'?" he asked, but then suddenly realized that it was a dig at RAPP.* He shook his head and handed the poems back to me with the words: "Things are easier with Pasternak—he only writes about nature." But, of course, it was not just a question of subject matter—the fact was that Pasternak

---

* The Russian Association of Proletarian Writers, of which Fadeyev was a leading member. See page 426.

had some points of contact with the traditional world of literature, and consequently with such things as RAPP, whereas M. had none whatsoever. Pasternak wanted to be friendly, while M. turned his back on them. There is no point in debating which of them was right, this is not the issue. But it is noteworthy that at the end of their lives both of them acted in ways quite at variance with the whole of their previous stands. While Pasternak, by writing *Dr. Zhivago* and publishing it abroad, put himself in open conflict with the Soviet literary world, M. was ready to seek a rapprochement with it—only, as it turned out, he had left it too late. In essence it was an attempt by M. to save himself when the noose had already been put around his neck, but the fact remains that it was made. What happened with Akhmatova was a little different—they got what they wanted by keeping her son Lev as a hostage. If it hadn't been for this, her "positive" verse would never have been written.*

In one thing Pasternak was consistent throughout his life: in his feelings about the intelligentsia, or rather those members of it for whom the Revolution meant the end of gracious living and the destruction of their peaceful mode of life. He virtually ignored the situation of the intelligentsia as a whole—university teachers, for instance, with their commonplace notions were not considered worthy of Zhivago's friendship. It was the destruction of the way of life of such intellectuals as Zhivago that concerned him, and he put the blame for it on the revolt of the ordinary people. Pasternak would have liked to see a protective wall between the intelligentsia and the people. Who is Zhivago's mysterious younger brother, Evgraf, the man of aristocratic appearance with the slanting Kirgiz eyes, who always arrives like a good genie with food supplies, money, advice, patronage and help? "The mystery of his power remained unexplained," says the author, but in fact his connection with the victorious revolutionaries and the new State is quite clear from the whole of the novel, and the help which he gives his brother is obviously one of those "miracles" which were wrought only by telephone calls to the right people, "transmission belts" and "commissions for assistance to scholars" of the kind set up on the advice of Gorki. Evgraf holds such a high position that he even promises to send his brother abroad, or have his exiled family brought back to Moscow. Pasternak knew very well how high up you had to be to do this kind of thing at the beginning of the thirties. If

* In 1952 Akhmatova wrote several poems in praise of Stalin.

Zhivago had not died, his brother would certainly have got him a "ticket for a seat by the columns." It was simply not in M.'s nature to bank like this on the State with its miracles. He understood early what to expect from the new State, and he placed no hopes in its patronage. He also believed that, "like a judge, the people judges," or, as he puts it in another line, "In years of desolation you rise, o sun, people, judge." I share this faith, and I know that, even when reduced to silence, the people still sits in judgment.

In his novel Pasternak describes the killing at the front by his troops of a Provisional Government commissar named Linde (in the novel he is called Gints). In Pasternak's eyes his death was retribution for the fact that he and his like had failed to keep the troops under control, as Cossack officers would have done, and had stirred up the ordinary people. M. knew Linde well—he had probably met him at the Sinanis'. To show what he thought about his death it is enough to quote the following lines: "To bless him, treading lightly, Russia will descend to farthest hell."

In his article on Hamlet, Pasternak wrote that the Prince's tragedy was not his lack of will, but the fact that in carrying out the act incumbent on him as a son, he would lose his birthright—that is, his "ticket for a seat by the columns." Moscow had belonged to Pasternak from the time of his birth. There was a moment when he might have felt he was ready to give it up, but the moment passed and he remained in possession of his heritage. Marina Tsvetayeva also came to Moscow as a rightful heiress, and was greeted as such, but she had no time for heritages of any kind, and as soon as she had found her own voice in poetry, she quickly turned her back on it. The reception given to the Acmeists—Akhmatova, Gumilev and M.—was quite different. They brought something with them that provoked blind fury in both literary camps: Viacheslav Ivanov and his entourage, as well as the Gorki circle, met them with hostility. (With Gumilev this didn't happen all at once, but only after his first book of Acmeist poems, *Alien Skies*.) For this reason the war against them was one of annihilation, and it was waged much more fiercely than against any other group of poets. M. always said that the Bolsheviks preserved only those who were passed on to them by the Symbolists—a favor certainly not shown to the Acmeists. In Soviet times the LEF group and the remnants of the Symbolists made common cause in their battle against the surviving Acmeists—Akhmatova and M. The campaign sometimes took on comic forms—

as, for example, in articles by Briusov in which he extolled the "Neo-Acmeist" school supposedly headed by M. and then proceeded to describe as his disciples the most compromising people he could think of. Even more grotesque were M.'s personal encounters with Briusov. Briusov once called M. into his office and lavished praise on his verse, while constantly quoting a Kiev poet called Makaveiski who was notorious for his use of dog Latin. Another time, during a meeting held to decide on food rations for writers and scholars, Briusov insisted that M. be given a ration of the second category, pretending he had confused him with a lawyer of the same name. Such tricks were very much in the style of the decade before the Revolution, and it must be said that Briusov never applied political discrimination—this was left to the younger people in LEF.

M. himself was very anxious to be recognized by the Symbolists and by LEF—in particular by Verkhovski and Kirsanov—but nothing came of his efforts. Both groups were adamant in their attitude toward him, and all M.'s friends teased him about his complete failure in this respect.

34

TWO VOICES

In Andrei Bely's definition, the term "sketch" could be applied very broadly to almost any literary composition which did not bear the mark of the social novel which he so detested, or any other kind of fiction. "In this sense," M. said, "my 'Conversation About Dante' is a sketch." Bely agreed.

We had met Bely in Koktebel in 1933. M. got on well enough with him, but Bely's wife evidently remembered some old articles of M.'s and was in no mood to let bygones be bygones. Perhaps she knew about M.'s negative attitude to anthroposophy and theosophy, and felt he must therefore be hostile to her. But the two men nevertheless met—albeit surreptitiously—and enjoyed talking with each other. M. was writing his "Conversation About Dante" at the time and read it out to Bely. Their talk was animated, and Bely kept referring to his study of Gogol, which he had not yet finished.

Vasilisa Shklovski has told me that no one else has ever impressed her as much as Bely, and I can well understand this. He seemed to radiate light, and I have never met anyone else who was so literally luminous. Whether this effect was produced by his eyes, or by the constant flow of his ideas, it is hard to say, but he charged everybody who came near him with a sort of intellectual electricity. His presence, the way he looked at you, and his voice stimulated the mind and quickened the pulse. My memory is of something disembodied, an electric charge, a thunderstorm incarnate, a miracle of some kind. At this time he was already nearing his end, and he collected pebbles and autumn leaves at Koktebel to make complicated patterns with them, as he strolled under his black umbrella along the beach with his small, clever and once beautiful wife, who despised everybody not initiated into her involved, anthroposophic world.

The Symbolists were great proselytizers and fishers of men. Like all of them, Bely too was always casting around with his nets. Once he buttonholed me and gave me a long account of the theory of verse put forward in his book *Symbolism*. M. told him with a laugh that we had all been brought up on this book, and that I in particular was a great reader of it. This was of course an exaggeration, but I did not protest, because Bely, whom we felt was extremely spoiled by the almost cult-like devotion around him, was suddenly very pleased at having me as one of his readers, and beamed all over his face. In those years he must already have been keenly aware of his loneliness and isolation, feeling rejected and unread. The fate of his readers and friends was very sad: he was always seeing them off into exile, or going to meet them on their return when they had served their sentences. He himself was spared, but everyone around him was swept away. Whenever they detained his wife, which happened several times, he stormed and shouted with rage. "Why do they arrest her and not me?" he complained to us that summer—not long before our meeting she had been kept at the Lubianka for several weeks. The very thought of all this enraged him and did much to shorten his life. The last straw, which finally embittered him, was Kamenev's preface to his book on Gogol. This showed that, whatever the twists and turns of inner Party politics, the one thing that would never be permitted was normal freedom of thought. Whatever else might happen, the idea of indoctrinating people and watching over their minds would remain the basic line. Here is the high road, they had told us, and we have marked it out for you, so why do you want to wander off on side roads? Why indulge your whims, if the only worthwhile tasks have already been set and their solution given beforehand? In all their different incarnations, our guardians were always sure they were right and never knew what it was to doubt. They always boldly claimed to know just by looking at a seed what its fruit would be, and from this it was but a step to decreeing the destruction of any seedling they thought was useless. And this they do all too thoroughly.

Bely was convinced that his ideas were very hard to understand, and hence his manner of speaking, which was the exact opposite of Pasternak's. He enveloped you as he spoke, gradually overwhelming, convincing and captivating you. His tone of voice was rather embarrassed and cajoling, as though he was unsure of his listener and dreaded that he might not be understood or properly heard—he felt the need to win your confidence and attention.

Pasternak, on the other hand, spoke and smiled at you as though bestowing a gift. He deafened you with the drone of his organ-like voice, in complete confidence that you were already prepared to take everything in. He neither sought to persuade, like Bely, nor argued like M., but boomed on jubilantly and confidently, allowing all to listen and admire. It was as though he was singing an aria, certain that the Moscow which had been his from childhood had provided an audience worthy of him, endowed with the requisite ear and intelligence and—above all—in love with his voice. He even, in fact, took some account of his audience and was very careful not to offend it. But the main point is that he needed only listeners, not partners in conversation—these he avoided. Bely needed material to stimulate new thought—people who in his presence would begin to grope for new ideas. I once asked M. which manner he himself preferred, and he said: "Bely's, of course." But it was not true. M. only liked to talk with people on a footing of equality. He was just as irritated by an audience as by disciples and admirers. He had an insatiable craving for the company of equals, but as the years went by, it became harder all the time to satisfy it. By a process of intellectual mimesis all thought, and the voices that gave it expression, were taking on protective coloring in our society.

35

THE PATH TO DESTRUCTION

The death of an artist is never a random event, but a last act of creation that seems to illuminate the whole of his life under a powerful ray of light. M. already understood this when, as a young man, he wrote an article about the death of Scriabin. Why are people surprised that poets are able to foretell their own fate with such insight and know beforehand the manner of their death? It is only natural, after all, that death, the moment of the end, should be a cardinal element—one to which all else is subordinate—in the structure of one's life. There is nothing determinist about this—it is rather to be seen as an expression of free will. M. steered his life with a strong hand toward the doom that awaited him, toward the commonest form of death, "herded with the herd," that we could all expect. In the winter of 1932–33, at a poetry reading given by M. on the premises of *Literary Gazette*, Markish suddenly understood this and said: "You are taking yourself by the hand and leading yourself to your execution." This was his interpretation of the poem: "I have led myself by the hand along the streets. . . ."

In his verse M. spoke all the time about his death like this, but nobody paid any attention, just as nobody listened to Mayakovski's talk about suicide. But, preparing for death, people nevertheless try at the last moment to put off the inevitable end. They close their eyes and pretend that all is not lost, perhaps looking for a new apartment, or buying themselves a good pair of shoes—anything not to see the pit already dug for them. This was how M. behaved after he had written his poem about Stalin.

The poem was written at the end of collectivization, between "Old Crimea" and "The Apartment." Had he some particular motive for writing it? There wer at least several, and perhaps a great many. Each of them had its part in what the interrogator was to call M.'s "provocation," or "act of terrorism," as he styled it at the beginning.

The major factor was no doubt a feeling that he could no longer be silent. The phrase "I cannot be silent" was often on the lips of our parents' generation. The same could not be said of ours. But there is always the drop that fills the cup to overflowing. By 1933 we had made great progress in our understanding of what was going on. Stalinism had shown its colors in one large-scale undertaking—the mass deportation of the peasants, and in the lesser one of bringing the writers to heel.

We spent the summer of that year in the Crimea, and it was then that M.'s poetry for the first time showed traces of how much he had been affected by collectivization and the terrible sight of the hungry, wraith-like peasants he had recently seen on the way through the Ukraine and the Kuban. In the first draft of the poem for which he was arrested, Stalin is called a "murderer and peasant-slayer." Everybody

at that moment thought and said as much—in whispers, of course—
and the poem was thus not in advance of its time, except from the point
of view of the ruling circles and their hangers-on.

The second most important factor in the writing of the poem was
M.'s awareness that his fate was sealed. It was too late now to hide "like
a cap in a sleeve." His other verse of the early thirties was by then being
passed from hand to hand. *Pravda* had already published a lengthy unsigned article in which M.'s "Journey to Armenia" was damned as the
"prose of a lackey." This was no longer a mere warning, but an indictment. Before it appeared, the editor-in-chief of the State Publishing
House for Literature, Chechanovski, had approached me with the
"advice" that it would be as well for M. to repudiate his "Journey to
Armenia"—otherwise, as he put it, "you will be sorry." All the warn-
ings, in the form either of threats or of advice, had already been given
(by Gronski and Gusev, for example), but M. ignored them. His end
was approaching.

I can remember nothing more terrible than the winter of 1933–34,
which we spent in our new apartment—the only one I have ever had
in my life. Through the wall we could hear Kirsanov playing his
Hawaiian guitar, the ventilation system wafted in the smell of cooking
from other writers' apartments and the stench of the insecticide they
used to kill the bedbugs. We had no money and nothing to eat, and
every evening there were hordes of visitors—half of them police
spies. Death might come to M. either quickly or in the form of a slow
process of attrition. M., an impatient man, hoped it would come
quickly. He preferred to die not at the hands of the writers' organizations who had initiated the process of his destruction, but rather at
those of the "punitive organs."

Like Akhmatova, M. did not believe in suicide in the ordinary
sense—even though everything was driving us to it: our loneliness,
isolation, and the times themselves, which were scarcely on our side.
Loneliness is not just the absence of friends and acquaintances—there
are always enough of these—it is rather life in a society which heed-
lessly, with blindfolded eyes, follows its fratricidal path, dragging
everybody with it. Not for nothing did M. call Akhmatova "Cassandra." Apart from a few poets like her, there were also some other people of an older generation who could see what was coming, but their
voices had died away. Even before the victory of the "new spirit" they
had spoken out about its ethics, its ideology, its intolerance and its

perverse notions of law. But these had been voices in the wilderness, and with every day that passed it clearly became more and more difficult to speak. How could you speak when your tongue had been cut out?

In choosing his manner of death, M. was counting on one remarkable feature of our leaders: their boundless, almost superstitious respect for poetry. "Why do you complain?" M. used to ask. "Poetry is respected only in this country—people are killed for it. There's no place where more people are killed for it."

Looking at the portraits of our leaders in store fronts, M. once said that he feared only people's hands. The "fingers . . . fat as grubs" in the Stalin poem are certainly an echo of Demian Bedny's trouble with Stalin (no wonder he was so frightened and advised Pasternak not to get mixed up in M.'s business). The adjective "thin-necked" was inspired by the sight of Molotov—M. had noticed his thin neck sticking out of his collar and the smallness of the head that crowned it. "Just like a tomcat," said M., pointing at his portrait.

The first people to hear the poem were horrified, and begged M. to forget it. For these particular people, its value was also lessened by the self-evident nature of the truth it contained. In more recent years it has been received with greater sympathy. Some people ask me how it was that M. could understand everything so well already in 1934, and wonder whether there is a mistake in the dating. These are people who accept the official story that everything was all right until the Yezhov terror, and that even that wasn't so bad—it was only after the war, when he was in his dotage, that the old man went out of his mind and made a mess of things. This may no longer hold water, but we continue to idealize the twenties and the beginning of the thirties. This is a stubborn legend. The old generation is dying out without having had its say, and there are now old men—including even former camp inmates—who go on talking about the glorious years of their youth as a golden age cut short only by their arrest. What will our grandchildren make of it if we all leave the scene in silence?

Among those who heard the Stalin poem, I noted three different views. Kuzin thought M. shouldn't have written it because it conflicted with his general attitude toward the Revolution. He accused M. of inconsistency: if he had accepted the Revolution, then he should put up with its leader and not complain. There is a kind of blockheaded logic about this, though I do not understand how Kuzin, who knew M.'s verse and prose by heart (though in his old age he forgot about this and even claimed in a letter to Morozov that he had never read "Journey to Armenia"), could not see the ambivalence and constant torment in M.'s work. People evidently find it hard to understand anything that is camouflaged, or even just slightly veiled. They need to have everything said straight out, and I think that is why M. wrote this poem in such plain language—he was tired of the deafness of his listeners who were always saying: "What beautiful verse, but there's nothing political about it! Why can't it be published?"

Ehrenburg does not like the poem, correctly regarding it as untypical of M.'s work because of this straightforward, uncomplicated quality.

But, whatever one may think of it as poetry, can one really regard it as incidental to the rest of his work, as a kind of freak, if it is the poem which brought him to his terrible end? It was, to my mind, a gesture, an act that flowed logically from the whole of his life and work. It is true, however, that it is peculiar in that he makes concessions to his readers he had never made before. He had never met them halfway or striven to be understood, regarding every listener or partner in conversation as his equal and therefore not trying to simplify things for him. But he was concerned to make his Stalin poem comprehensible and accessible to anybody. On the other hand, he did his best to make sure it could not serve as an instrument of crude political propaganda (as he even said to me, "That is none of my business"). But he did write the poem with a view to a much wider circle of readers than usual, though he knew, of course, that nobody would be able to read it at the time. I believe he did not want to die before stating in unambiguous terms what he thought about the things going on around us.

Pasternak was also hostile to the poem. He poured out his reproaches to me (this was when M. was already in Voronezh). Only one of these reproaches stands out in my memory: "How could he write a poem like that when he's a *Jew*?" I still do not see the logic of this, and at the time I offered to recite the poem to him again so he could tell me exactly what it was wrong for a Jew to say, but he refused with horror.

The reaction of those who first heard the poem was reminiscent of Herzen's story of his conversation with Shchepkin, who went to London to ask him to stop his activities because all the young people in Russia were being arrested for reading "The Bell." Fortunately, however, nobody suffered because he had heard M.'s poem. M., moreover, was not a political writer, nor was his role in society in any way like Herzen's. Though who is to say where the distinction lies? And to what extent is one obliged to protect one's fellow citizens? I am surprised that Shchepkin was so concerned about Herzen's young compatriots and wanted at all costs to shield and cloister them from the outside world. As for my own contemporaries, I cannot say that I would want to expose them to any hazards—let them live out their lives in peace and do the best they can in these hard times. It will all pass, God willing, and life will come into its own again. Why should I try to waken the sleeping if I believe that they will in any case wake up by themselves one day? I do not know whether I am right, but, like everybody else, I am infected by the spirit of passivity and submissiveness.

All I know for certain is that M.'s poem was ahead of its time, and that at the moment it was written people's minds were not ready for it. The regime was still winning supporters and one still heard the voices of true believers saying in all sincerity that the future belonged to them, and that their rule would last for a thousand years. The rest, who no doubt outnumbered the true believers, just sighed and whispered among themselves. Their voices went unheard because nobody had any need of them. The line "ten steps away no one hears our speeches" precisely defines the situation in those days. The "speeches" in question were regarded as something old and outmoded, echoes of a past that would never return. The true believers were not only sure of their own triumph, they also thought they were bringing happiness to the rest of mankind as well, and their view of the world had such a sweeping, unitary quality that it was very seductive. In the pre-revolutionary era there had already been this craving for an all-embracing idea which would explain everything in the world and bring about universal harmony at one go. That is why people so willingly closed their eyes and followed their leader, not allowing themselves to compare words with deeds, or to weigh the consequences of their actions. This explained the progressive loss of a sense of reality—which had to be regained before there could be any question of discovering what had been wrong with the theory in the first place. It will still be a long time before we are able to add up what this mistaken theory cost us, and hence to determine whether there was any truth in the line "the earth was worth ten heavens to us." But, having paid the price of ten heavens, did we really inherit the earth?

36

CAPITULATION

M. had a long period of silence—about five years between 1926 and 1930—when he wrote no verse (though he did write some prose during this time). The same thing happened for a time with Akhmatova, and with Pasternak it lasted a good ten years. "It must be something about the air," said Akhmatova—and there was indeed something in the air: the beginning, perhaps, of that general drowsiness which we still find so hard to shake off.

Was it just coincidence that these three active poets were stricken by dumbness for a time? Whatever the differences in their basic attitudes, the fact is that before they could find their voices again, all three had first to determine their places in the new world being created before their eyes—and this they could only do by learning from experience how it affected everybody else. The first to fall silent was M. This was probably because he was the one most acutely affected by the process of determining what his place was. The question of his relationship to the times was, for him, central to his life and poetry, and his character was such (to quote his own line: "In spirit he was not as the lilies") that he was incapable of glossing over rough edges—if anything, he tended to the opposite. When he stopped writing verse in the middle of the twenties, what was it in the air that stifled him and made him fall silent?*

Judging by externals, we have lived through not just one but several epochs. A historian can easily divide the last forty years into periods or stages which may seem not only different but incompatible with each

---

* *Author's Note:* It was at this time that M. began to suffer from heart trouble and shortness of breath. My brother, Evgeni Yakovlevich, always used to say it was not so much a physical as a "class" disease. This was borne out by the circumstances in which he had his first attack in the middle of the twenties. Marshak had come to see us and was telling M. at great length in his saccharine way what poetry was. He was laying down the official line, and, as usual, spoke with great feeling, carefully modulating his voice. He is a superb fisher of men, whether weak, susceptible ones or men of power. M. did not argue with him—he had nothing in common with Marshak. But suddenly he could stand it no longer and he heard a ringing in his ears that drowned out Marshak's orotund voice. This was his first bout of angina pectoris.

other. I am convinced, however, that each one logically followed from its predecessor. True, the top group was always changing, and with it even the physical appearance of Soviet functionaries (at one moment, for example, we suddenly noticed that dark ones had given way to fair ones—but these too were soon removed from office). After each major change, the whole style of life and leadership were modified, but there was nevertheless an element of sameness throughout these successive stages. These rulers of ours who claim that the prime mover of history is the economic basis have shown by the whole of their own practice that the real stuff of history is ideas. It is ideas that shape the minds of whole generations, winning adherents, imposing themselves on the consciousness, creating new forms of government and society, rising triumphantly—and then slowly dying away and disappearing. Viacheslav Ivanov once said in my presence—we visited him on our way through Baku in 1921—that he had fled from Moscow and sought seclusion in Baku because he had become convinced that "ideas have ceased to rule the world." What Dionysian cults did he understand by "ideas," this teacher and prophet of the pre-revolutionary decade, if he had failed to see, at the time of our conversation, what enormous territories and vast numbers of people had just been won over by an idea? The idea in question was that there is an irrefutable scientific truth by means of which, once they are possessed of it, people can foresee the future, change the course of history at will and make it rational. This religion—or science, as it was modestly called by its adepts— invests man with a god-like authority and has its own creed and ethic, as we have seen. In the twenties a good many people drew a parallel with the victory of Christianity, and thought this new religion would also last a thousand years. The more scrupulous developed the analogy further and mentioned the historical crimes of the Church, hastening to point out, however, that the essence of Christianity has not been changed by the Inquisition. All were agreed on the superiority of the new creed which promised heaven on earth instead of other-worldly rewards. But the most important thing for them was the end to all doubt and the possibility of absolute faith in the new, scientifically obtained truth.

"And suppose it isn't so? What if people take a different view in the future?" I once asked Averbakh with reference to a literary judgment he had just delivered about M. ("They say he has just returned from Armenia and published some bad verse.") I asked him how he could know this, and he replied that M. did not have the right "class approach." He then explained that there was no such thing as art or culture in the abstract, but only "bourgeois art" and "proletarian art"— nothing was absolute and all values were conditioned by class. He was not at all put out by the fact that his own class values were now regarded as absolutes: since the victory of the proletariat was the dawn of a new era which would last forever, the values attributed by Averbakh to the class whose servant he was constituted absolutes. He was genuinely surprised that I could cast doubt on his judgments, which, being based on the only scientific method, were infallible—anything he damned was damned forevermore. I told M. about this conversation, which had taken place in a tramcar. He was fascinated by the monolithic quality of Averbakh's faith in his own truth and the way he reveled in the peculiar elegance of his logical constructions. This was in 1930, when M. could afford to be merely fascinated by the workings of Averbakh's mind. By this time M. had recovered his own inner freedom and found his voice again—the twenties with their inhibitions and doubts had ended, so he could now listen with some detachment to "hempen speeches" and not take them too much to heart.

Averbakh was a very typical product of the first decade after the Revolution. This was how all the adepts of the new religion thought and talked—in other spheres as well. There was something very cocksure about them—they loved to talk down at you and shock you. They had taken it upon themselves to overthrow all the old idols—that is, to destroy the values of the past—and since the tide was flowing in their favor, nobody noticed how primitive their weapons were.

The cry "What did we fight for?" went up at the very beginning of the twenties, but immediately died down again. The nation had not yet been reduced to silence, but it was quiet enough as it looked forward to the life of ease promised by NEP. The intellectuals, meanwhile, set about a leisurely "revaluation of all values." This was the period of mass surrender when they all took the path marked out by the pre-revolutionary extremists and their post-revolutionary successors of the Averbakh type—though, needless to say, they tried to avoid the fanaticism and crudity of the vanguard. The capitulationists were led by men of about thirty who had been through the war, and the younger people followed them. In general, the people between thirty and forty were the most active age group in those days. Such members of the older generation as had survived stood silently on the sidelines. The basic premise behind the surrender was that the "old" had given way to the "new," and anybody clinging to the former would go to the wall. This view was rooted in the whole theory of progress and the determinism of the new religion. The proponents of surrender attacked all the old concepts just because they were old and had outlived their usefulness. For most of the neophytes, all values, truths and laws had been done away with—except for those which were needed at the moment and could conveniently be given a "class" label. Christian morality—including the ancient commandment "Thou shalt not kill"—was blithely identified with "bourgeois" morality. Everything was dismissed as a fiction. Freedom? There's no such thing and never was! Since art, and particularly literature, only carried out the orders of the ruling class, it followed that a writer should consciously put himself at the service of his new master. A number of terms such as "honor" and "conscience" went out of use at this time—concepts like these were easily discredited, now the right formula had been found.

It was characteristic of those years that all such concepts were treated as pure abstractions, divorced from the actual social and human framework which alone gave them substance. This made it all the easier to dismiss them out of hand: nothing was simpler, for example, than to show that nowhere in the world is there such a thing as absolute freedom of the press, and then to conclude that instead of making do with the wretched substitutes fobbed off on us by liberals, it was better to face up to the situation like a man and abandon all this hankering after "Freedom." Such arguments seemed plausible enough to minds not yet capable of making finer logical distinctions.

Psychological factors that worked in favor of capitulation were the fear of being left out in the cold, of not moving with the times, and the need for an all-embracing "organic world-view" (as it was called) which could be applied to all aspects of life. There was also the belief that the victory was final, and that the victors were here to stay for all eternity. But the main thing was that those who surrendered had nothing of their own to offer. This extraordinary emptiness was perhaps best expressed by Shklovski in his *Zoo,* that sorry book in which he tearfully implores the victors to take him under their wing. Whether this attitude was self-induced or whether it was a bitter reaction to the war and the trenches, the fact is that the desire to be looked after and protected like a child was enormously strong, and only those who shared it were regarded as being in step with the times.

Once, in the editorial office of Priboi,* M. refused to sign a collective letter from the writers to the Central Committee, on the grounds that "in literary matters they should appeal to us, not we to them." The letter was a petition on behalf of a certain critic who was being hounded by RAPP for allegedly having reviewed a novel by Liashko without reading it to the end. The writers were now asking the Central Committee to order an end to this persecution, and in support of their appeal they quoted the Central Committee's resolution on literature (1925)† in which the Party had called on the writers to end their squabbles and make common cause in their efforts to fulfill the Party's command.

As usual, there were a lot of people in the *Priboi* office, and they all crowded round M. They were genuinely puzzled by the reason he gave for his refusal to sign. His words seemed to them like a musty old rag pulled from some family chest of the past, a sign of how backward and out-of-touch he was. There can be no doubt of their sincerity. I remember the astonished look on Kaverin's face—it was he who was collecting the signatures. He thought M. was simply an old-fashioned eccentric who didn't understand the times he lived in. When M. and Akhmatova were still not much over thirty, they were quite seriously thought of as old people. As things turned out, however, they gradually came to seem younger in the eyes of others, as the views of those who had espoused the "new age" grew hopelessly obsolete.

The boy in the Hans Andersen story who said the king was naked did so neither too late nor too soon, but just at the right moment. Others had no doubt said it before him, but nobody paid any attention. M. also said many things too early—at a time when normal judgments seemed hopelessly out-of-date and doomed. There was no room for those who wouldn't sing in chorus with the rest—and it was indeed a powerful chorus that drowned out all other voices. There are now many people who would like to bring back the twenties and re-create the self-imposed unity of those days. Survivors from those times do their best to persuade the younger generation that this was an age in which everything—science, literature, the theater—flourished as never before, and that if everything had continued to develop on the lines then laid down, we should by now have attained the height of

---

* Leningrad publishing house for which Mandelstram did translations.
† See page 427.

perfection. Survivors of LEF, people who worked with Tairov, Meyerhold and Vakhtangov, former students and teachers of IFLI* and the Zubov Institute, former members of the Institute of Red Professors, old Marxists, not to mention the Formalists†—they would all like us to go back to that time when they were young men of thirty, so that we might once again set out on the road which they then opened up for us—this time without deviating from it. In other words, they deny responsibility for what happened later. But how can they? It was, after all, these people of the twenties who demolished the old values and invented the formulas which even now come in so handy to justify the unprecedented experiment undertaken by our young State: you can't make an omelet without breaking eggs. Every new killing was excused on the grounds that we were building a remarkable "new" world in which there would be no more violence, and that no sacrifice was too great for it. Nobody noticed that the end had begun to justify the means, and then, as always, gradually been lost sight of. It was the people of the twenties who first began to make a neat distinction between the sheep and the goats, between "us" and "them," between upholders of the "new" and those still mindful of the basic rules that governed human relations in the past.

The victors might well have been surprised at the ease of their victory, but they were so sure they were right, and so sure they were bringing happiness to mankind, that they only took it as their due and gradually increased their demands on those who had surrendered to them. This was shown by the speedy disappearance of the term "Fellow Traveler" and its replacement by the term "Non-Party Bolshevik." Eventually we had "the true son of the Motherland who ardently loves his People and unhesitatingly serves his Party and Government."

People's memories are such that they remember not actual events but only vague stories or legends about them. To establish the facts, one must shatter the myths, but this can only be done if one first points to the circles in which they have been created. This hankering after the idyllic twenties is the result of a legend created by people who were then in their thirties, and by their younger associates. But in reality it was the twenties in which all the foundations were laid for our future: the casuistical dialectic, the dismissal of older values, the longing for

* Institute of Philosophy and Literature.
† See page 427.

unanimity and self-abasement. It is true that those who shouted loudest were then the first to lose their lives—but not before they had prepared the ground for the future. In the twenties our "punitive organs" were still only gathering strength, but they were already in action. The thirty-year-old iconoclasts fervently preached their faith. At first coaxing, and later threatening, they led their hosts of followers into the coming era, during which all individual voices ceased to be heard.

We do not have—nor can we have—an institute for the study of public opinion, though there is no other way of gauging the undercurrents in people's mental processes. The part of such an institute was once played to some extent by the "punitive organs." In the twenties they even took soundings among the public to find out what it was thinking—for this purpose they had a special network of informers. Later on it was decided that public opinion must be the same as official opinion, and the role of these informers was reduced to reporting any cases in which there was a divergence—these were then systematically followed up by the appropriate action. After 1937 such "study" of public opinion (by now completely "rationalized") lost all significance because of the massive nature of the "preventive" terror.

But in the twenties we were still innocently playing with fire. No sooner had M. decided that everything would be all right ("What are you worrying for? They won't touch us, they won't kill us") than we got a foretaste of the future from the rosy-cheeked Vsevolod Rozhdestvenski, who came to see us in Tsarskoye after a brief spell of imprisonment. He said he wanted to warn us that his interrogator had been very interested in M., but he blankly refused to give any details: "I gave my word, and I was brought up as a child always to keep my word." M. threw this model child out, and when he had gone, it occurred to us that he must have been sent simply to give M. a fright and remind him that there was no escaping the all-seeing eye. This kind of thing was to happen frequently. In his "Conversation About Dante" M. mentions the interlocking of prison with the world outside and the fact that any ruler is only too happy if his subjects put the fear of God in each other with stories from jail. Vsevolod Rozhdestvenski carried out his assignment well enough, but he omits all reference to it in his memoirs. On the other hand, he has M. speak about poetry in a conventional Parnassian and Acmeist manner, attributing to him the sort of opinions and pronouncements which Soviet critics always put into the mouth of the "typical aesthete" of their imagination. Many other absurd utterances of this kind will no doubt be laid at M.'s door, and they should be judged in the light of his essays, which give a real sense of the sort of things he said in conversation and argument. His contemporaries were no match for him, and in their memoirs they will give a garbled version of his ideas, whether they intend to or not. Least of all is he understood by those who lived through the twenties as true believers, during those times when the noose was being pulled tighter and people worked on each other, preaching the new religion, destroying values and preparing the way for the future.

37
THE CHANGE OF VALUES

M. did not believe in the "new" millennium, but he had not come to the Revolution with empty hands. He was heavily weighed down by his Judaeo-Christian culture on the one hand, and on the other by his faith in social justice, the "fourth estate," Herzen, and Revolution as a way of deliverance and renewal. He was no longer reading Herzen after I came to know him, but this was undoubtedly one of the formative influences in his life. It shows in his work—in *The Noise of Time,* in the story of the lion cub which complains to the indifferent crowd about the splinter in its paw (the splinter later turned into the "pike's bone stuck in my Underwood"), in his horror of double talk, in his translations of Barbier, in his understanding of the role of art. "Poetry is power," he once said to Akhmatova in Voronezh, and she bowed her head on its slender neck. Banished, sick, penniless and hounded, they still would not give up their power. M. behaved like a man conscious of his power, and this only egged on those who wanted to destroy him. For them power was expressed in guns, agencies of repression, the distribution of everything—including fame—by coupons, the possibility of commissioning their portraits from any artist they chose. But M. stubbornly maintained that if they killed people for poetry, then they must fear and respect it—in other words, that it too was a power in the land.

It is hard to imagine anything worse than the equipment M. brought to the Revolution. It was easy to see in advance that he was doomed and would never find his place in the new world. It would have been a hopeless task to justify what was happening in the name of Herzen—

indeed, in the name of Herzen it could only be condemned. It is true that Herzen reserved the right to retreat into proud isolation ("*omnia mea mecum porto*"), but such a course was not for M. He could not bring himself to shun his fellow men, and he did not regard himself as someone standing above the crowd, but as part of it. Any self-exclusiveness was anathema to him—this was no doubt connected with his sense of belonging to the Judaeo-Christian tradition. Many of my contemporaries who accepted the Revolution went through a severe psychological crisis. They were trapped between a reality which could only be condemned and the need for a principle by which to justify it. Sometimes, in order to be able to vindicate it without qualms, they simply closed their eyes to what was going on, but when they opened them again, it was still there for them to see. Many of them had awaited the Revolution all their lives, but at the sight of what it meant in terms of everyday life, they were horrified and looked away. Then there were others who were frightened of their own fears and were terrified of not seeing the wood for the trees. Among these was M. Not realizing the extent to which he had believed in revolution, people who knew him less well had an oversimplified picture of his life and dismissed as insignificant a major component of his way of thinking. Without this "revolutionary" element he would not have been so concerned to understand the course of events, or to weigh them in the scales of his values. If he had simply turned his back on reality, it would have been easier to live and adjust. This was impossible for M.—he had to live the same life as his contemporaries right through to the logical end.

As one can see from the verse he wrote in the twenties, M. never doubted that a new era had begun with the victory of the Revolution: he says that "the fragile chronology of our era nears its end," and that of the old world only a sound remained, though the "source of the sound has gone." Then there is the image of the age as a wild animal with a broken backbone, looking round at its own footprints.* In all this verse he speaks either directly or obliquely about his own position in the new life ("a sick son of the age, with quicklime in his blood"), and in "The Slate Ode" he calls himself a "double-dealer with divided soul." Avowals such as these are scattered throughout this verse—never fully stated, they seem to break from him involuntarily and

---

* These quotations are from the poems "The Finder of a Horseshoe" (1923) and "The Age" (1923).

sometimes appear in the most unexpected context (for example: in a poem of 1922, at the end of an extended image about baking bread, he describes himself as "the drying crust of a loaf long since taken out"). M. never made things easy for his readers. To understand him, you have to know him.*

In the poetry of this period he prophesies the onset of dumbness ("human lips preserve the form of the last word they have uttered"— in "The Finder of a Horseshoe," 1923). It was in fact this line that Brik and Tarasenkov seized on as proof that M. had "written himself out"— they gave little thought to the real sense of the poem before pronouncing this judgment. For them all means were fair in the struggle. Brik had turned his apartment into a place where his colleagues in the Cheka (including Agranov) could meet with writers and sound out public opinion, simultaneously collecting information for their first dossiers. It was here that M. and Akhmatova were first branded as "internal émigrés"—a label which was to play an important part in their subsequent fate. Brik was almost the first to employ non-literary weapons in the literary controversies of the twenties, but I should like to point out the difference between him and other hatchet men of the type of Tarasenkov. Tarasenkov (M. once called him a "fallen angel") was a good-looking youth with a passionate interest in poetry who at once fell in with the Party's plans to turn literature into its handmaiden, and carefully collected manuscripts of all the poetry he so busily prevented from appearing in print. In this respect he was different from, say, Lelevich, who hated poetry as such because he considered it "bourgeois."

The position of Brik was completely different. With his usual

---

* *Author's Note:* In M.'s verse of the thirties there are sometimes completely open statements or deliberately camouflaged ones. In Voronezh we were once visited by an "adjutant" of the semi-military kind (one of those we now refer to as "art historians in uniform") and questioned about the sense of the line "wave follows wave, breaking the back of the one ahead." "Could that be about the Five Year Plans?" he asked. M. walked up and down the room and replied with a look of astonishment: "Is that what you think?" When the man had gone, I asked M. what to do when they inquired about the hidden meaning like this. "Look surprised," M. said. I didn't always see the hidden meaning, and M. never explained it to me, in case I should ever be interrogated in prison. Genuine astonishment might not save me, but at least it could make things easier. Feeblemindedness and ignorance were always a good recommendation, both for a prisoner and for a bureaucrat.

shrewdness he realized at the outset that the State would grant a monopoly to one or another of the literary movements that existed in those days, and he fought for this monopoly against numerous competitors. It was a fierce struggle and at one moment it looked as though he might win. A large number of supporters gathered around him, and he knew how to win younger people over with his charm. In Party circles he had powerful sponsors, particularly among Chekists with artistic and literary inclinations. He maneuvered with great dexterity and at considerable risk to himself, but the prize was won by Averbakh, who, with his RAPP, was a latecomer in the contest. Averbakh owed his victory to a view of literature derived from Pisarev—who had always been dear to the middle ranks of the intelligentsia. With the fall of RAPP there could no longer be any kind of literary struggle, but until then the different factions, each seeking to win the monopoly for itself, relied exclusively on political weapons. In sweeping Akhmatova and M. out of his path, Brik was not, however, concerned with the political effect of his denunciation—all he wanted was to take away their young readers, those ardent devotees of the "new." In this he was successful: for a long time Akhmatova and M. were isolated. The last of the Mohicans from LEF, who are now over sixty, continue to extol the twenties and shake their heads in wonderment at the young readers over whom they have lost all influence.

The twenties were perhaps the worst time in M.'s life. Neither before nor after—even though things became much more frightful—did he speak with such bitterness about his situation in the world. In his early verse, however full of youthful anguish, there is always anticipation of future triumphs and a sense of his own strength ("I feel the span of my wing"), but in the twenties he speaks all the time of his illness, inadequacy and sense of inferiority. By the end of this period he was almost confusing himself with Parnok, or making him out to be his double. One can see from his verse that he thought his illness and inadequacy were caused by his first doubts about the Revolution. In his poem "January 1, 1924" he asks: "Whom will you next kill? Whom will you next extol? What lie will you now invent?" He feels he is a "double-dealer" for trying to "join the broken vertebrae of two centuries" and for not being able to change his values.

M. was very cautious about the Revolution's demand for a change of values, though he did pay some lip-service to it. This took the form, in the first instance, of making clear what his relations with the "old world" had been. He wrote about this in *The Noise of Time, The Egyptian Stamp* and in the poem which begins: "With the world of Empire I was linked only as a child / fearing oysters and looking askance at the Lifeguards." Although this poem was written in 1931, it expresses more the mood of the early twenties. His most serious concession to the demand for a change of values was in the three or four literary articles he published in Kiev in 1926 (he was by this time completely barred from the Moscow press, but in the provincial press it was still possible to "get away" with things). One senses in these articles that he wanted to be heard at any cost, and that he was therefore making a timid effort to be accepted by admitting or approving certain things and yielding on others. He even, for instance, tried to find excuses for some of the so-called "Fellow Travelers," though he must have known that he could never travel the same road as they. In two articles in *Russian Art* (Kiev) there were critical remarks about Akhmatova which were also a concession to the times. A year previously, in an article in a Kharkov newspaper, M. had written about her roots in Russian prose, and even earlier, in an unpublished review written for *The Almanach of Muses* (1916), he had prophesied that "this poorly dressed but majestic woman" would one day be the pride of Russia. In 1937, under questioning by the Voronezh writers—they had forced him to give a lecture about Acmeism and expected him to "unmask" it—he said of Akhmatova and Gumilev: "I do not disown either the living or the dead." He said something similar to the Leningrad writers at a meeting there in the House of the Press. In other words, he always felt linked with these two, particularly with Akhmatova, and his attempted disavowal of them in 1922 was a concession to all the hue-and-cry about Acmeism, the allegations that it was outmoded and "bourgeois," etc. M. was then "alone on every road," and could not stand it. He really was in a state of confusion: it is not so simple to go against everybody and against the times. To some degree, as we stood at the crossroads, we all had the temptation to rush after everyone else, to join the crowd that knew where it was going. The power of the "general will" is enormous—to resist it is much harder than people think—and we are all marked by the times we live in. The logic of the times demanded that M. part company with Akhmatova, his only possible ally. It is no easier for two than for one to swim against the tide, and M. made this one attempt to cut himself off from her. But he very soon came to his senses. In 1927, when he was gathering his articles together as a book, he threw out one of the pieces that had appeared in *Russian Art* and removed his attack on Akhmatova from the other. He also discarded the articles in the Kiev newspaper and those in *Russia,* calling them "fortuitous" in his preface to the collection *On Poetry,* published in 1928. He regarded the period during which he wrote these articles (1922–26) as the worst in his life. It was a period of decline, and in repudiating it altogether, M. took no account of the many good and genuine things he wrote at that time—notably the passages in a number of articles where he attacks the general tendency toward stagnation.

His mood during this period of an attempted "change of values" is best seen from his attitude toward an article he had written on the death of Scriabin (1915) where he outlined his views on Christian art, giving expression to what he really believed (it was here that he spoke about the death of an artist being not the end, but a final creative act). The article was never published. It had originally been a lecture to some Petersburg society (perhaps the Religious and Philosophical Society) which held its meetings in a large private house.* M. used to go to the meetings of this society and evidently knew one of its organizers, Kablukov, an old man who was very kind to M. as a budding poet. (I recently bought a copy of M.'s first collection, *Stone* [1915], which belonged to Kablukov, and in which he had stuck various early poems by M. written in his own hand.) Kablukov took the manuscript of M.'s lecture on Scriabin away with him. While we were in the Caucasus in 1921, Kablukov died and all his papers went to the Petrograd Public Library. M. complained to me bitterly about the loss of this manuscript ("It's the most important thing I've written and now it's lost.... I'm just unlucky") and he was very pleased when a little later I found some pages of a rough draft in a trunk belonging to M.'s father. But his attitude to the article was by now ambivalent: he asked me to keep it, but in this period of doubt about his own values he was tempted to revise the views expressed in it. In the first drafts of *The Egyptian Stamp* there is a passage in which he makes fun of Parnok for reading a lecture in the "salon of Madame Perepletnik"—a clear allusion to his own lec-

---

* *Author's Note:* Once the notorious adventurer Savin came there, set up a table at the foot of the stairs and collected an entrance fee from everybody who came in. Later, at the meeting, he got up and made a long speech about the Russian Devil, who, he said, was distinguished from all others by his cunning, inventiveness and sense of humor.

ture about Scriabin. In the text as published, all that remains of this is the threat made to Parnok that one day he will be ejected from the smart salons of St. Petersburg (including Madame Perepletnik's) because as an upstart intellectual he has no business there and "the aristocrat's fur coat is not for him." M. was always coming back to this theme of the upstart intellectual in fashionable St. Petersburg—as a young man he probably had several encounters with various snobs who made it quite clear to him that he did not "belong." He was very upset by Makovski's account (which he read not long before his arrest) of how his mother came with him in 1908 (when he was eighteen) to the editorial offices of *Apollon*. They had come to show M.'s verse to Makovski, who makes out that M.'s mother behaved like the stupid wife of a Jewish tradesman. Evidently Makovski was trying to produce a cheap journalistic effect by contrasting the young genius with his vulgar family background. In fact, however, M.'s mother was a woman of considerable culture, a music teacher who gave her children a good education and brought M. up to love classical music. She could never have said the preposterous things that Makovski attributes to her. This is a good example of the kind of aristocratic superciliousness that prompted M. to declare himself a member of the "fourth estate" of intellectuals from the lower classes. In *The Egyptian Stamp* he made clear his attitude to the "world of Empire" and traced his own and Parnok's lineage back to the raznochintsi.* There is also something similar in "Conversation About Dante," where he describes how the urbane Virgil is always preventing the gauche and embarrassed Dante from making a fool of himself. But by the time he wrote this he had to contend with the new "world of Empire" that made the old one look woefully amateurish by comparison. This period of confusion about his values helped M. to define his place in the new world, and he once more— this time in verse—proclaimed himself an upstart intellectual ("Did those raznochintsi wear out the dried leather of their boots that I should now betray them?"—*Midnight in Moscow*, 1932). But what was left to a Soviet raznochinets except his handful of Judaeo-Christian culture? M. preserved it, together with the pages from his article on Scriabin. On the other hand, in the poem written in 1931 where he addresses Parnok's brother, Alexander Gertsovich, he tells him he might

---

* Russian intellectuals, particularly in the sixties of the nineteenth century, who were not of noble origin. The singular form is raznochinets.

as well give up ("There was a Jewish musician by the name of Alexander Gertsovich. . . . May as well give up now, what does it matter any more?").

His efforts to come to terms with the new era thus ended in failure—very much more was demanded of those who surrendered. At the same time he had something to say to the Revolution, as opposed to the new "world of Empire" in which we suddenly found ourselves. There was nobody left in our society who would have understood what he wanted to say. The chorus of true believers in the new religion and the new State used the language of revolution in their ritual observances, but they had no time for a new "upstart intellectual" with his doubts and hesitations. For the true believers and "Fellow Travelers" everything was quite clear already: "You have to understand where you're living! What do you expect?" M. heard on all sides. It was with them in mind that he chose to translate Barbier's "Pack of Hounds":

> They tear the flesh with claws—each must have his piece . . .
> That is the right of the kennel, the law of honor among hounds:
> Take home your share to your proud and jealous bitch
> who waits to see the steaming bone between her good mate's teeth
> and hear him shout as he throws it down:
> That is power—this is our part in these great days.

(The theme of the "good mate" was to crop up again in 1933, in the poem about the apartment: "Some worthy traitor . . . a good family man. . . .") He translated the Barbier poem in the summer of 1923, and his "oath of allegiance to the fourth estate" appeared the following winter—no wonder it was so coldly received by those on whom the distribution of worldly goods now depended.

Perhaps the reason he stopped writing verse in the mid-twenties was that in this period of confusion he was no longer certain of being right. His prose writings were an attempt to find his bearings again, to regain the ground under his feet so that he could say, "Here I stand and can do no other." Poetry came back to him when he once more knew that he was right and had taken the proper stand. In one of his early articles that appeared in *Apollon* in 1913, he had spoken about "the precious sense of poetic rightness." Obviously this sense was essential to M. if he was able to define it so confidently at the very beginning of his career as a poet (he was then only eighteen). In so far as he accepted the new reality, M. could not help but condemn his own doubts. Listening to the chorus of its supporters, he was bound to be sorely troubled by his isolation from it; attacked by the Symbolists, LEF, RAPP and all the other groups which unreservedly supported the new system, he could scarcely help feeling that he was indeed a "drying crust of a loaf long since taken out." Assailed by such doubts, he could not possibly feel certain of his own "rightness." True, there were always readers who stood up for him and swore by him, but M. was somehow, despite himself, repelled by them. I think he grew more and more unhappy with his readers at this time, as he looked on them too as "drying crusts" and believed that somewhere there must be some real "new people." In the early twenties he still failed to see how these "new people," so extrovert in appearance, were going through the classical metamorphosis—a process of turning into wood—that comes over those who lose their sense of values.

M.'s release came through his prose, this time his "Fourth Prose" (1931). This title was our private way of referring to it: it was literally his fourth piece of prose, but there was also an association with the "fourth estate" which so much preoccupied him, as well as with our "Fourth Rome."* It was this work which cleared the way for poetry again, restoring M.'s sense of his place in life and his "rightness." In it he spoke of our bloodstained land, cursed the official literature, tore off the literary "fur coat" he had momentarily donned and again stretched out his hand to the upstart intellectual, "the first Komsomol, Akaki Akakievich."† At a certain dangerous moment we destroyed the opening chapter, which dealt with our idea of socialism.

The "Fourth Prose" was based on the episode of the Eulenspiegel translation,‡ which, with all its ramifications, would have died down

---

* "Fourth Rome": a reference to the idea, proclaimed by the monk Philotheus in the seventeenth century, that Moscow was the Third Rome—"and a Fourth there shall not be."

† Akaki Akakievich, a down-trodden clerk, is the "fourth estate" anti-hero of Gogol's *Greatcoat* (1842).

‡ In 1928 Mandelstam was accused of plagiarism by a translator, A. G. Gornfeld, because his name had been omitted from his version of Charles de Coster's *La Légende d'Uylenspiegel* after it had been revised by Mandelstam. The fault for this omission lay with the State Publishing House, which had commissioned Mandelstam to revise Gornfeld's translation. The whole affair was blown up into a scandal by the press, but a savage attack on Mandelstam by David Zaslavski (see the note on Zaslavski in the Appendix) provoked a strong defense of him by a group of leading Soviet writers, including Pasternak, Zoshchenko, Fadeyev, Katayev, Averbakh and others, published as a collective letter to *Literary Gazette* in May 1929.

sooner if M. had not insisted on keeping it alive. It was this that really opened M.'s eyes to what was happening around us. As Bukharin had said, the atmosphere in Soviet institutions was indeed like that of a cesspool. During the Eulenspiegel affair we felt as though we were watching a film about literature at the service of the new regime, about the fantastic bureaucratic apparatus that had now grown up (we even had a talk with Shkiriatov), about the Soviet press with its Zaslavskis, about the Komsomol, in whose newspaper M. worked for a year after breaking with the writers' organizations, and so forth. The two years spent on this business were rewarded a hundred times over: the "sick son of the age" now realized that he was in fact healthy. When he started writing poetry again, there was no longer a trace of the "drying crust." M.'s was henceforth the voice of an outsider who knew he was alone and prized his isolation. M. had come of age and assumed the role of a witness. His spirit was no longer troubled. In the first phase of the campaign of destruction against him, right up to May 1934, the methods used had had nothing to do with either literature or politics, but had been quite simply a vendetta on the part of writers' organizations which enjoyed support "up above." "They cannot get at me as a poet," said M., "so they are snapping at my calves as a translator." Perhaps it was this attempt to belittle him that helped him to straighten up his shoulders. Strange to say, even in his case, it needed this personal experience to open his eyes completely. Soviet people prized their own blindness and were prepared to recognize the facts of life only if they were directly affected. Collectivization, the Yezhov terror and the post-war campaigns of mass repression helped very many to see the light. M. was one of the earliest to do so, though he was by no means the first.

M. always knew that his ideas were out of tune with the times and went "against the grain of the world," but after writing the "Fourth Prose" he was no longer worried about it. In his "Conversation About Dante" and in the poem "Canzona" (1931) he spoke of the special kind of sight with which birds of prey and the dead in Dante's *Divine Comedy* are endowed: they are unable to see things close to them, but they can make out objects at a great distance; blind to the present, they are able to see into the future. Here, as always, M.'s prose supplements and throws light on the poetry.

Poetry came back to him during our return journey from Armenia when we were held up in Tiflis. We still felt as though we were watching a film: while we were there, Lominadze met his end. In his last days this man showed real kindness to M. He had received a telegram from Gusev in the Central Committee with instructions to help M. find work in Tiflis, and he very much wanted to oblige, but at that moment he was summoned to Moscow and never returned. The papers were now suddenly full of denunciations of the "hostile faction of Lominadze and Syrtsov." That was our fate: anyone in the leadership whom M. was able to approach always perished. There was no place for a latter-day raznochinets in the new "world of Empire." Incidentally, right after the fall of Lominadze, whom M. had visited three or four times at the local Party headquarters, we noticed that we were being followed everywhere by someone in plain clothes. The local branch of the secret police had probably decided it would be as well to keep an eye on the mysterious person who had visited the fallen leader. We now realized that Tiflis was no place for us, and we hastily left for Moscow. When we told Gusev (who had sent M. to Lominadze) about how we had been followed, he listened with a stony face. Only Soviet officials could make their faces turn to stone like this. What it meant was: How was I to know that Lominadze was an enemy of the people, or what reasons the Georgian comrades had for putting you under surveillance? It was already not unusual for innocent people to be implicated in cases they had nothing to do with, and Gusev was taking no chances. We should have had exactly the same reception from Molotov—it was he who, at Bukharin's request, had instructed Gusev to organize our journey to Sukhumi and Armenia and make sure we were properly looked after. Wherever we went, Gusev sent instructions to the heads of the local Party organizations asking them to make arrangements for us. Among them was Lominadze, who was fated to perish at the moment he was instructed to help us. M. might well have been swept away with him, but this time he was spared—the case that could have been made against him in this connection was not made. We were lucky. But at the time we didn't realize it and made fun of Gusev's stony mask. After the Lominadze episode his protecting hand was withdrawn from us, but I cannot say that we were left, as in the fairy tale, with nothing more than a slab of clay—the journey to Armenia restored the gift of poetry to M., and a new period of his life began.

38

WORK

Only in 1930 did I first understand how poetry is made. Before this I had always seen it as the working of a miracle, the sudden appearance of something that had not been there before. In the beginning—from 1919 to 1926—I would not even know that M. was at work, and was always surprised when he became tense and broody, sometimes running outside into the street to escape from small talk. I soon came to know what the reason was, but I didn't really understand it. When his period of silence ended in 1930, I had more than enough opportunity to observe him at work.

In Voronezh I got a particularly clear impression of what it involved. Hopelessly uprooted and restricted as it was, our life there in rented rooms (if that is the right name for the squalid hovels we made our home in) meant that we were constantly alone together, and I was able to watch very closely as he went about his "sweet-voiced labor." As soon as M. had reached the stage of actually composing a poem, he did not need to hide from people because, as he said, once the work was in progress, nothing could stop it. Vasilisa Shklovski, with whom he was very friendly, tells how in 1921, when they were neighbors in the House of Arts in Leningrad, M. often wandered into her room to warm himself by the iron stove. Sometimes he lay on the divan and covered his head with a cushion so as not to hear the conversation going on in the crowded room. Whenever he got bored with his own company while "composing," he would come to see Vasilisa like this. His poem about the Angel Mary came to him in the Zoological Museum while we were sitting with the curator, Kuzin, and his friends, drinking a bottle of Georgian wine—one of them had smuggled it in, together with some food, in his academic-looking briefcase. Constantly disrupting the ritual of drinking the wine, M. kept getting up from the table and pacing quickly around Kuzin's vast office. As usual, he was composing the poem in his head, but I wrote it down to his dictation while we were still in the Museum. After he married me he became very lazy and always dictated his verse to me, instead of writing it down himself.

In Voronezh he had absolutely no privacy when he was working. In none of the places we rented was there so much as a passage or a kitchen to which he could escape if he wanted to be completely alone. This is not to say that things were much better in Moscow, but at least there was always somewhere I could go for an hour or so, leaving him alone to work. But in Voronezh there was nowhere to go, except out into the freezing streets—and it so happened that the winters were particularly hard during those three years. But all the same, whenever a poem was approaching its final stage of "ripeness," I used to take pity on poor M., who was like a caged animal, and did what I could—lying down on the bed, for instance, and pretending to sleep. Seeing this, M. sometimes urged me to sleep properly, or at least to turn my back on him.

In the last year in Voronezh, in the seamstress' house, our isolation was really complete. We scarcely left our room except to go to the nearby telephone exchange to phone my brother: he sent us the money—a hundred roubles each—that Vishnevski and Shklovski gave us every month during that winter. They were frightened to do it directly—everything in our life was by now a cause for fear. This money went to pay our rent, which came to exactly 200 roubles a month. We were no longer earning anything—neither in Moscow nor in Voronezh would anyone give us work now that "vigilance" was the order of the day. People turned away from us in the street and pretended not to recognize us. Only the actors departed from the general rule, coming up to us and smiling even in the main street. This is perhaps to be explained by the fact that the theaters were less affected than other Soviet institutions by the big purges now under way. The only people who came to see us at home were Natasha Shtempel and Fedia Marants, but both of them went out to work and could not easily find the time. Natasha told us that her mother had warned her of the possible consequences of coming to see us and she tried to hide where she was going. But then her mother had said to her: "I know where you're going. Why are you trying to keep it from me? I was only warning you, not telling you what to do. Why don't you invite them here?" After that we often went around to see Natasha, and her mother always put out everything she had on the table. She had long since separated from her husband, a former nobleman, and had supported her two children by teaching at first in the town's secondary school and then in the elementary school. Modest, intelligent, light-hearted and easy-going, she was the only person in Voronezh who admitted us to her home. All other doors were shut tight in our faces and double-bolted: we were pariahs, untouchables, in this socialist society.

Everything suggested that the end was near, and M. was trying to take full advantage of his remaining days. He was possessed by the feeling that he must hurry or he would be cut short and not allowed to say what he still wanted to say. Sometimes I begged him to rest, to go out for a walk or have a nap, but he dismissed the idea: there was so little time left, and he must hurry. . . .

The poems poured out of him, one after another. He worked on several at once, and he often asked me to take down at one sitting two or three which he had already completed in his head. I could not stop him: "You must understand that I shan't have time otherwise."

Of course, he was just taking a sober view of his approaching end, but I could not yet see it as clearly as he. He never spoke about it to me in so many words, but in letters to people in Moscow (where I went a couple of times during the winter to get money) he once or twice hinted at what was in store for us—but then immediately changed the subject in mid-sentence, as though he had been talking only about our usual difficulties. Perhaps he really was trying to put such thoughts out of his mind, but the greater likelihood is that he wanted to spare my feelings and not darken the last days of our life together.

He drove himself so hard during the whole of that year that he became even more painfully short of breath: his pulse was irregular and his lips were blue. He generally had his attacks of angina on the street, and in our last year in Voronezh he could no longer go out alone. Even at home he was calm only when I was there. We sat opposite each other and I watched his moving lips as he tried to make up for lost time and hastened to record his last words.

Each time I copied out a new poem, M. would count up the lines and decide how much he had "earned" at the highest current rates of payment. (He would not "settle" for less unless, as occasionally happened, he was very unhappy about a poem, in which case he agreed to a "reduced rate." It was reminiscent of Sologub, who used to sort his verse by quality and price it accordingly!) When we had thus added up his "earnings" for the day, we would go out to borrow money for our supper on the strength of them. We got money like this from some of the actors, the compositors at the local printing works, and sometimes from two professors we knew (one was a friend of Natasha, and the other was a literature specialist). We generally arranged to meet them in some deserted side street, where, like conspirators, we walked slowly past each other while they slipped us an envelope with their offering of money. If we had not managed to arrange to meet someone (it had to be done the day before), we would look in on the compositors. M. had got to know them in the summer of 1935 when we were living in the "agent's" house, which was next to the printing works and the offices of the local newspaper. M. used to go in to read them poems as he finished them—particularly if this was late at night when nobody else was awake. They were always very pleased to see him, though the younger ones would sometimes stagger him by spouting opinions straight out of *Literary Gazette*—to the indignation of the older ones. In the bad times that were now upon us, these same older ones listened silently as M. read his new poems and then talked to him for a while about this and that while one of their number went out to buy food for him. They were miserably paid and could hardly make ends meet themselves, but they felt that "you can't let a comrade down in times like these."

On the way to borrow money, we would go to the post office and send off some of M.'s poems to the literary magazines in Moscow. We only once got an answer—when we sent "The Unknown Soldier" to *Znamia* [*The Banner*] and got back a letter pointing out that wars may be just or unjust, and that pacifism as such cannot be approved. But to us even this stilted reply was very welcome: at least somebody had bothered to communicate with us!

The poem about the shadow which wanders among men, "warming itself with their wine and their skies," was sent, by way of an exception, not to Moscow but to Leningrad (probably to *Zvezda*). Among the copies of M.'s poems that now pass from hand to hand I sometimes find missing versions that must go back to these copies we sent to the literary magazines at that time. People working on the magazines in question must have purloined these forbidden poems, with the result that they found their way to readers.

The journalist Kazarnovski, who met M. in a transit camp after his second arrest, has told me that one of the accusations against M. was that he had circulated his verse (which was described by some utterly damning word) among the staffs of the literary magazines. Though what does it matter what he was accused of? When I was summoned to the Prosecutor's office in 1956 to be told that M. had been cleared of the charges brought against him after his second arrest, I actually saw the file on his case and the whole thing seemed to take up only two small sheets of paper. I should like to be able to read what is written there and, even more, to be able to publish it as it is, without commentary.

39

MOVING LIPS

In 1932 I was coming home one day from the offices of the newspaper *For a Communist Education* on Nikitski Street. At that time we were living on Tverskoi Boulevard. On my way I saw M. sitting on the front steps of a shabby house. His head was twisted around so that his chin almost touched his shoulder; he was twirling his walking stick with one hand and resting the other on one of the stone steps to keep his balance. The moment he saw me, he jumped up and we walked along together.

When he was "composing" he always had a great need of movement. He either paced the room (unfortunately we never had very much space for this) or he kept going outside to walk the streets. The day I came across him sitting on the steps, he had just stopped to rest, tired of walking around. He was then working on the second part of his "Verses About Russian Poetry." For M. poetry and walking were closely connected. In his "Conversation About Dante" he asks how many pairs of shoes Alighieri must have worn out while writing the *Divine Comedy*. The same theme occurs in his poems about Tiflis, of which he says that they "remember the worn splendor" of a visiting poet's shoes. This is not just about his poverty—the soles of his shoes were always worn—but about poetry, too.

I only once saw M. composing verse without moving around. This was in Kiev at my parents' home, where we spent Christmas in 1923; he sat motionless by the iron stove for several days, occasionally asking me or my sister, Anna, to write down the lines of his "January 1, 1924." The other time was in Voronezh at a period when he was terribly exhausted by his work and had lain down to rest. But a poem was still buzzing in his head and he could not rid himself of it—it was the one about the singer with the deep voice at the end of the "Second Voronezh Notebook." Not long before this he had heard Marian Anderson on the radio, and the previous day he had visited a singer who had been exiled from Leningrad—the same one for whom he did some free translations of Neapolitan songs, which she sang on the radio, where they both made a little money from time to time. We had rushed around to see her on learning that her husband, recently released after five years in a camp and allowed to come to Voronezh, had again been arrested. This was the first time we had heard of someone being immediately re-arrested like this, and we wondered what it could portend. The singer was lying in bed. People are always literally prostrated by this kind of misfortune. My mother, who as a doctor was mobilized after the Revolution to help with famine relief in the Volga region, told me that the peasants just lay quite still in their houses, even in parts where there was already something to eat and people were not totally exhausted by hunger. Emma, a teacher at the Chita Teachers' Training College, once told me how she had gone out to work on a kolkhoz with some of her students, and that all the kolkhozniks were lying down. It is the same with students in their hostels, and with office workers when they get home in the evening. We all do this. I have spent my whole life lying down.

The singer frantically made plans for the future—as often happens when we are overwhelmed by someone's death or arrest, by a summons to the secret police, or a similar calamity. Perhaps this kind of delirious talk about the future helps us to get over such incomprehensible things as the death of someone close, or his removal to one of our twentieth-century prisons. She kept telling us that her husband could not possibly have been sent back to a camp, since he had only just returned from there. They must be going to exile him, and that didn't really matter. Wherever he was sent, she would go after him. And she would carry on with her singing—she could always sing anywhere: it was just as easy in Ishim or Irgiz as it was in Leningrad or Voronezh. In whatever Siberian village they went to, she would sing and earn enough to buy flour and bake him bread.

Her husband was the victim of a general directive ordering the re-arrest of all those who had already been in prison. There was also an order at that time (or it may have been in the fifties, I don't remember) under which everybody who was sent to the camps must be kept in permanent exile after their release. The singer soon disappeared herself. She was sent somewhere—we never learned the details—either to sing or to fell timber.

M. told me that in his poem about the singer with the low voice there was a merging of two images: the woman from Leningrad and Marian Anderson. On the day he was composing this poem, I didn't realize he was working, because he was lying as quiet as a mouse. Restlessness was the first sign that he was working on something, and the second was the moving of his lips. In one poem he says that his lips can never be taken away from him, and that they will still move when he is dead and buried. This has indeed happened.

Since he works with his voice, a poet's lips are the tool of his trade, and in his poem about the flute player who "treads with his lips," M. is also speaking about his own whispering lips and the painful process of converting into words the sounds ringing in his ears.

The poem is actually about a flute player we knew. He was a German called Schwab and he was terribly frightened in case anything should happen to his only flute, which had been sent to him from Germany by an old comrade from the conservatory. We went to see him occasionally and he would take his flute out of its case and bring great comfort to M. by playing Bach or Schubert for him. He was loved by all the musicians who came to Voronezh on tour. Once, in the days when M. still had his job at the theater and he had finished his work for the day, we went into one of the balconies to listen to a symphony concert. From above we had a perfect view of the orchestra, and I suddenly saw that Schwab's place had been taken by another flutist. I bent over to M. and whispered to him. Despite hisses from the people around us, we went on whispering. "Could he have been arrested?" M. asked, and in the interval he went behind the scenes to find out. The assumption proved correct, as such assumptions always did—to the extent that we superstitiously feared to voice them in case this made them come true. Schwab, as we learned later, had been accused of espionage and sent to a camp for common criminals near Voronezh. He was already an old man and he ended his days there. M. kept wondering whether he had taken his flute with him or whether he had been afraid in case it should be stolen from him by the thieves there. Or if he had taken it, what did he play to his fellow prisoners? M.'s poem was inspired by the sound of Schwab's flute and his wretched fate, as well as by his own anxieties about "the beginning of dreadful deeds."

In the poem M. speaks of the flutist's lips "recalling" something. But is it only a flute player's lips that know beforehand what they have to say? The process of composing verse also involves the recollection of something that has never before been said, and the search for lost words is an attempt to remember what is still to be brought into being ("I have forgotten the word I wished to say, like a blind swallow it will return to the abode of shadows"). This requires great concentration, till whatever has been forgotten suddenly flashes into the mind. In the first stage the lips move soundlessly, then they begin to whisper and at last the inner music resolves itself into units of meaning: the recollection is developed like the image on a photographic plate.

M. hated all the hackneyed talk about form and content which was so much to the liking of the new "client," who wanted official ideas to be clothed in "beautiful" dress. Over this question he immediately had a row with the Armenian writers when, not realizing who* had launched it, he attacked the call to make literature "national in form and socialist in content." So even in Armenia we found ourselves isolated. M.'s feeling that form and content are absolutely indivisible evidently came to him from the process of working on his poetry, which was always born from a single impulse—the initial "ringing in the ears," before the formation of words, already embodied what is called "content." In "Conversation About Dante" M. likened "form" to a sponge—if a sponge is dry and contains nothing, then nothing can be squeezed out of it. The opposite approach is to think in terms of finding the "right form" for a subject matter conceived independently of it. M. damned this approach (also in "Conversation About Dante") and called its proponents "translators of ready-made meaning."

Ilia Ehrenburg once said to Slutski in my presence that M. spoiled his poems by making "phonetic modifications" in them. I never saw anything of the kind. If Ehrenburg was referring to variants of the same poem, he should have known that these are something radically different from "modified" versions. It is translators who introduce modifications, as they try to find the best way to express the ideas in the original. As for "phonetic" modifications, they can only serve decorative purposes. A variant consists either of superfluous material that has been trimmed away, or it is an "offshoot" that may be developed into a separate, self-contained entity. As the poet tries to dig down to the nugget of harmony in the recesses of his mind, he throws away all the spurious or unwanted matter under which it is hidden. Composing verse is hard, wearisome work that demands enormous inner exertion and concentration. When the work is in progress, nothing can stop the inner voice, which probably takes complete possession of the poet. This is why I cannot believe that Mayakovski was speaking the truth when he said that he had "stepped on the throat of his own song."†

---

* Stalin.
† In the poem written before his suicide.

How was he able to do this? From my own rather unusual experience as an observer of the poet at work, I would say that it is quite impossible for him to curb or silence himself by "stepping on the throat" of his own song.

The work of the poet, as a vehicle of world harmony, has a social character—that is, it is concerned with the doings of the poet's fellow men, among whom he lives and whose fate he shares. He does not speak "for them," but with them, nor does he set himself apart from them: otherwise he would not be a source of truth.

I was always struck by the absolute character of the urge to serve—with and among one's fellow men—as an instrument by which harmony reveals itself. In this sense it was impossible either to simulate or induce it artificially, and of course it is nothing but a misfortune for the poet himself. I can understand Shevchenko's lament—which M. appreciated only too well—about the way his poetry would not leave him alone, bringing him nothing but misery and not allowing him to pursue his craft as a painter, the one thing that gave him pleasure. The urge ceases to be felt only when the poet's material begins to run out—that is, when his contact with the world at large is broken and he no longer hears his fellow men or lives with them. There can be no poetry without such contact, which is the source of the poet's sense of "rightness." The urge dies together with the poet, though the movement of his lips is recorded for all time in the verse he leaves behind. Incidentally, how can people be so stupid as to say that poets are no good at reading their own verse? What do such people know about poetry? Poetry only really lives in the poet's own voice, which is preserved in his work forever.

In the period when I lived with Akhmatova, I was able to watch her at work as well, but she was much less "open" about it than M., and I was not always even aware that she was "composing." She was, in general, much more withdrawn and reserved than M. and I was always struck by her self-control as a woman—it was almost a kind of asceticism. She did not even allow her lips to move, as M. did so openly, but rather, I think, pressed them tighter as she composed her poems, and her mouth became set in an even sadder way. M. once said to me before I had met Akhmatova—and repeated to me many times afterward—that looking at these lips you could hear her voice, that her poetry was made of it and was inseparable from it. Her contemporaries—he continued—who had heard this voice were richer than future generations who would not be able to hear it. This voice of hers, with all the inflections it had in her youth and later years, and still possessed of the depth which so impressed M., has come out remarkably well on a tape-recording recently made by Nika. If this recording survives, it will confirm the truth of what I have written here.

M. was struck by several of Akhmatova's characteristic gestures and always asked me, after we had been with her, whether I had noticed how she had suddenly stretched her neck, tossed back her head and pursed her lips as though to say "no." He would show me what he meant and was always surprised that I didn't remember it as well as he. In variants of the "Wolf" poem I have found a reference to a mouth that seems to say "no," but here it belongs not to Akhmatova but to M. himself. The lifelong friendship between these two terribly ill-fated people was perhaps the only consolation for the bitter trials they both endured. In her old age Akhmatova has found a little serenity, and she knows how to make the best of it. But much of her verse remains unpublished, and the past can never be forgotten. If it were not for the ability to live in the present seemingly granted to all poets—or at least to these two—she would hardly be able to rejoice in her life as she does now.

40

BOOK AND NOTEBOOK

"You have a book in you," said Charents, listening to M.'s poems about Armenia. (This was in Tiflis—in Erivan he would not have dared to come to see us.) M. was very pleased by these words: "Perhaps he's right—I may really have a book in me." A few years later, at M.'s request, I took a sheaf of his Voronezh poems to Pasternak, who, after looking at them, suddenly spoke of the "miracle of a book in the making." With him, he said, it had happened only once in his life, when he wrote *My Sister Life*. I told M. about this conversation and asked: "So a collection of verse doesn't always make a book?" M. just laughed.

The way in which separate items in a lyrical sequence follow each other may be just as natural as the order of the lines in a single poem, but the outer signs of this are less clear. It is obvious in the case of a work whose unity is not in doubt, such as a narrative or epic poem, but the inner thread running through a series of lyrics is not so easily seen. Yet M.'s words about the poet's "stereometric instinct" (in "Conversation About Dante") are just as applicable to lyric poems gathered together as a "book."

The way in which a "book" comes about probably varies from poet to poet. Some write interlinked poems in their chronological sequence; others rearrange work written at different times (though in the same general period) to make a "book"—this was Pasternak's procedure, and Annenski's (in his *Trefoils*). M. belonged to the first type of poet: his poems came in groups, or in a single flow, until the initial impulse was spent. In order to put a book together, all he had to do was establish the right chronological order of the items. This does not, however, apply to *Tristia*, which was not put together by M. himself.

It is no easy matter to reconstruct the chronology of M.'s work— not only because many of his things bear no date, but also because even if they do, the date refers to the moment when the poem was written down, not to the beginning or the end of M.'s work on it. It seems to me, indeed, that one can pinpoint the precise genesis of a poem only if it is a matter of coldly calculated versification rather than true poetry. How could M. know beforehand what exactly would come out of the movement of his lips after he had begun to listen to the voice inside him, or at what moment he would begin to write it down? Another difficulty about dating is whether one should regard the beginning or the end of the actual work of composition as the crucial moment. This is all the more important in that work could be in progress on several poems at one time.

In a number of cases M. was not himself certain in what order to put the poems of a cycle—this was so, for instance, with the poems in the "Wolf" cycle, and those in the middle of the Second Voronezh Notebook. He didn't manage to make up his mind about this while he was still able to. I have often been asked about the origin of these "Notebooks." This was the name we used to refer to all the poems composed between 1930 and 1937 which we copied down in Voronezh in ordinary school exercise books (we were never able to get decent paper, and even these exercise books were hard to come by). The first group constituted what is now called the "First Voronezh Notebook," and then all the verse composed between 1930 and 1934, which had been confiscated during the search of our apartment, was copied down into a second notebook—M. himself looked on these two notebooks as distinct, evidently thinking of them as sections of a "book."

In the fall of 1936, when some more poems had accumulated, M. asked me to get a new exercise book, although there was still room in the old ones. Though there was practically no interval of time between the "Third Notebook" and the "Second," it is clear from the contents of the "Third" that it is a new departure—not a continuation of the impulse, by then exhausted, which had given rise to the poems in the "Second Notebook." If there were precise methods for analyzing poetry, one would be able to see exactly where one impulse ends and another begins—though even without this, one can see it clearly enough.

We always associate the word "book" with printing, and think of it in terms of format and typographical convenience, but such mechanical criteria do not apply to notebooks, whose beginning and end are determined only by the unity of the poetic impulse which gives birth to a given series of poems. In other words, a notebook is the same as a "book" in the sense in which the term was understood by Charents, Pasternak and M. himself. The only difference was that M. did not have to stick to some particular length or structure—often artificial—which is required for a published book. But the word "notebook" itself, as I have said, arose in our usage quite accidentally, owing to the fact that we were forced to write in school exercise books. It has the drawback of being too concrete in its meaning, as well as reminding one of Schumann's "Notebooks." The only thing in its favor is that it faithfully reflects the way in which we had been thrown back into a pre-Gutenberg era.

In his younger days M. had used the word "book" in the sense of "phase." In 1919 he thought he would be the author of one book only, but then he realized that there was a division between *Stone* and the poems that came to be known under the general title of *Tristia*. This title, incidentally, was given to the collection by Kuzmin, and the book itself is a miscellany of jumbled-up manuscripts taken to Berlin by the publisher without M.'s knowledge. His *Second Book* was garbled by censorship and M. gave it this name because he realized his mistake in thinking that he would write only one book. He was not quite certain where the boundary lay between the pre-revolutionary *Stone* and this second book with his poems about the war, his presentiment of revolution and the Revolution itself. The poems grouped together under the title "New Verse" (1930–35) reflect his consciousness of being an outcast, and the Voronezh "Notebooks" his exile and approaching doom. Under each of the poems I copied out for him in Voronezh, M. put the date and the letter "V." When I asked him why, he just said: "Just because." It was as though he was somehow branding these pages, but very few of them survived: 1937 was close at hand.

41

CYCLE

The word "phase" refers to stages in the growth of a person's outlook—his changing view of the world and his own work. *Tristia* consists of poems which came to M. as he was waiting for the Revolution and as he experienced it in the early days. The "New Verse" is what he wrote after he overcame his silence by writing "Fourth Prose." It is possible for there to be different "books" within the same phase: I believe, for instance, that "New Verse" and the "Voronezh Notebooks," though separate "books," comprise a single phase divided in two by M.'s arrest and exile. In the first there are two and in the second three sections called "notebooks." In other words, for M. a "book" represents a biographical period, while a "notebook" is a poetic division embracing material born of a single impulse.

A "cycle" is a smaller subdivision. In the first section ("Notebook") of the "New Verse," for instance, one can pick out the "Wolf" (or "convict") cycle and also the Armenian cycle—though the group entitled "Armenia" is actually more in the nature of a selection than a cycle. By this I mean that it resulted—as in many of M.'s earlier cycles—from a ruthless weeding-out process by which the more immature poems were discarded. The remaining ones were arranged not necessarily in the order in which they were written—thus breaking the sequence and obscuring the quality of a lyrical diary which is otherwise so typical of the Voronezh Notebooks.

These cycles are generally built around one particular "theme poem"—it is obvious, for example, that the matrix of the "convict" or "Wolf" cycle is the poem beginning "For the thundering prowess of future times. . . ." This kind of cycle—as opposed to those in which the items simply follow each other like links in a chain—resembled a cluster of shoots all sprouting from a main stem, and in these cases the poet's work was rather like a gardener's: training the viable shoots away from the stem and letting them develop independently. The common origin, however, was always visible in the repetition of certain key words or themes. In the "Wolf" cycle M. dwelt on his fear of succumbing to falsehood ("my mouth is twisted by lies"), the need to preserve his own voice ("Save my speech forever"), and there are echoes of the idea that so haunted him in Cherdyn: that he might be executed with an ax as in Peter's time.

The Russian fur coat (shuba) in the "Wolf" cycle is a recurring theme in M.'s work. It can symbolize a number of things: the Russian winter, a cozy, stable existence, social status (from which the raznochinets is debarred). It occurs in the first book of poems, *Stone* (where there are doorkeepers in fur coats), in the poem about Alexander Gertsovich and "I drink to officers' epaulettes" (where the fur coat stands for his supposed identification with the old regime). His first piece of prose was even called "Fur Coat," but it was lost by the publishing house run in Kiev by Rakovski's sister. In *The Noise of Time* there is the aristocratic fur coat which is not for the likes of Parnok and himself, and in "Fourth Prose," to signify his break with his fellow Soviet writers, he strips off his "literary fur coat" and stamps on it.

His ironical toast to the aristocrat's fur coat in "I drink to officers' epaulettes" goes back to a comic episode at the end of the twenties when a certain well-connected lady (who was later to perish) complained to Emma Gerstein that she had always thought M. was definitely "not one of us" because she could never forget how at the beginning of NEP he had strutted around Moscow in a magnificent fur coat. We could only gasp at this. We had bought this coat, which had belonged to an impoverished priest, in the market place in Kharkov. It was made of reddish, moth-eaten raccoon and was as long and ungainly as a cassock. The old priest had sold it to get money for bread, and M. had bought it on our way from the Caucasus to Moscow so he wouldn't die of cold in the north. This "aristocratic" fur coat was then given to Prishvin to use as a mattress when he was staying at a hostel on the Tverskoi Boulevard. One day his primus stove exploded and he used it to stifle the flames. The last bits of raccoon fur were scorched away, and M. never even had the satisfaction of actually stripping it from his shoulders and trampling on it, as he should have done: to wear a fur coat was above his station.

In the "Wolf" cycle, preparation for exile is also a dominant theme, hence the references to Siberian forests, bunks (of the labor-camp type) and peasant frame houses. By extension, wood becomes the main material of the whole cycle, and objects made of it are frequently referred to: "pine tree," "wooden pail," "pinewood coffin," "skittles," "splinters" (used by peasants for lighting their huts). Some of the words are less domestic and echo his fear of execution: "chopping block," "ax handle." . . . A characteristic epithet of this cycle is "rough"—a word appropriate to wooden surfaces.

Premonition of exile began before the "Wolf" poems, and it is expressed, for instance, in the line of another poem where chains for fastening doors were likened to a convict's fetters. Petersburg is compared to a coffin ("To sleep in Petersburg is to sleep in a coffin") from which the only escape is to the railroad station "where no one can seek us out." The theme here is his sense of having been cast out and rejected. In the poem "Preserve my speech . . ." (1931) he speaks of himself as an "unrecognized brother." I have read somewhere in Boudouin de Courtenay that "brother" was originally used not of blood kinship, but of acceptance by one's tribe. M. had not been accepted by the "tribe" of his fellow writers, he had been cast out of Soviet literature, and even the wretched priest's coat on his shoulders was held to bear witness to his bourgeois ideology.

42

THE LAST WINTER IN VORONEZH

In the summer of 1936, thanks to money given us by Akhmatova, Pasternak and my brother, Evgeni, we were able to get out of Voronezh and spend some time in the country. This was very important because of M.'s heart trouble, which was getting worse and worse. We decided to go to Zadonsk, on the upper reaches of the River Don, once famous for its monastery and the monk Tikhon. For six weeks we rested, thinking about nothing and enjoying life. But then we heard over the radio about the beginning of the terror. The announcer said that Kirov's murderers had been discovered and that trials were in preparation. After listening to this, we walked out silently onto the monastery road. There was nothing to talk about—everything was clear. That same day M. stuck his walking-stick into the imprints left by horses' hoofs on the roadway—it had been raining the day before and they were full of water. "Like memory," he said. These imprints turned up (as "thimbles made by hoofs") in verse written in the following January, when M.'s memory of the celebrated radio announcer's booming voice prompted him to undertake something for his own salvation.*

When we returned to Voronezh, we found that all doors were closed to us. Nobody wanted to talk with us or invite us to their homes or even recognize us—at least, not in public places. But some people still tried to help us on the quiet. The theater manager, for example, arranged for us to rent a room in the house of the seamstress who worked for the theater. Her house was on a hill above the river—an old, tumbledown wooden place that had sunk into the ground. From the plot of ground near the house one could see the far bank with a fringe of forest, and little boys tobogganed down the slope right to the water's edge. This view was always in front of our eyes, and M. often referred to it in his verse, sometimes cursing it but always nevertheless admiring it.

The little boys would ask him: "Are you a priest or a general, mister?" and to this M. always replied: "A little bit of both." As we soon found out, they thought he might be a general because he held himself so erect and "stuck his nose in the air"—that is, kept his head well back. Through Vadik, the landlady's son, M. took part in a bird auction† at which Vadik bought some birds. As M. said, boys have a particular feeling for birds—"Have you ever seen a girl with pigeons," he asked me, "or at a bird auction?" There were frequent mentions of wild birds in M.'s verse.

We realized that this winter, calamitous as it was, would be our last breathing-space, and we wanted to make the best of it. We could say with Klychkov, in the lines which M. loved to repeat: "Ahead is only torment, and torment is behind me / Sit with me a while, for God's sake, sit with me a while." This is why the "notebook" written in this last period is the most serene and life-affirming of them.

For any intellectual activity, a man has to tune himself up, like an instrument. Some people can no doubt do this as they go along, functioning without interruption, while others always have to tune them-

---

* The reference is to the abortive attempt to write an ode in praise of Stalin, described in the following chapter.
† Catching wild birds and selling them as songsters is still a widespread practice in Russia.

selves afresh each time they begin a new work. Like all poets whose work clearly divides into distinct phases, M. belonged to the second category, and at the beginning of each new cycle there is always a "key" poem which, like a tuning fork, strikes the required note for the rest. At the beginning of the "Second Notebook," this function is fulfilled by the poem about the "factory whistle of Soviet cities" which "whistles into the depths of the ages." When I asked him what he meant by "factory whistle" here, he said: "Perhaps I mean myself."

How could this man, living at bay in the isolation, emptiness and darkness to which we were consigned, think of himself as the "factory whistle of Soviet cities"? Virtually excluded from the life of the country, how could he imagine that his voice could sound forth in its cities? It can only be explained by that sense of being right without which it is impossible to be a poet. If one were to name the dominant theme in the whole of M.'s life and work, one might say that it was his insistence on the poet's dignity, his position in society and his right to make himself heard.

This is why, after the opening poem about the factory whistle, the "Second Notebook" contains this theme of the poet's self-assertion. In the atmosphere of increasing terror, it would have been impossible, if he had been guided by reason alone, for him to strike this note. But the point is that the theme came to him spontaneously, as a poetic subject always did—it was not something arrived at by a rational process. At first it appeared only in a muted form, disguised by references drawn from everyday life, such as the factory whistle.

The theme of the poet's situation also comes out in his poem about the goldfinch, or at least in the variant of it where he addresses the bird as his own likeness and orders it to live. In one of his early articles M. had told a story about a youthful poet who went from publisher to publisher trying to sell his literary wares which nobody had any use for. This youth is described by a Russian word almost identical in sound with "goldfinch," and since M. never forgot previous associations or images, he must have thought of this, and of the rejection of his own literary wares, as he wrote the poem on the goldfinch. Perhaps this is why he was so insistent in telling it to live.

The goldfinch was now kept in a cage, and not allowed out into the forest glades. "But," M. said to me once, "they cannot stop me moving about. I have just been on a secret trip to the Crimea." He was referring to the poem "Gaps in Round Bays" (February 1937), which is remarkable for its slow-motion effect ("a slow sail continued by a cloud. . . ."). We were always distressed at the way time flew by, and M. felt that only in the south did you have a tangible sense of present time.

"You've been on a trip to Tiflis as well," I said to him. "I was forced to make that journey," he replied. "I was dragged there by the Evil Spirit." By this he meant that his verses about Tiflis were a by-product of his attempt to write the ode to Stalin.

In another poem, written in January 1937, he writes of his "bright nostalgia" which will not let him leave the "young hills of Voronezh" for the "bright ones of Tuscany that belong to all mankind." Italy dwelt with us in the shape of M.'s volumes of Italian poetry and our illustrated books on architecture. M. would invite me to stroll in imagination with him round the Baptistery in Florence, and we got as much pleasure from this as we did from the view in front of the seamstress' house.

Then there was the changing of the seasons. "This is also a journey," M. said, "and they can't take it away from us." With his infinite love of life he was able to draw strength from things which other people, including me, only found oppressive: the autumn slush, for instance, or the bitter cold of winter. These were things that could not be "taken away"—the word he used to describe how his enforced residence in Voronezh had deprived him of all that he felt had formerly belonged to him: the south, journeys, trains, steamships . . .

When he started writing poems about stars, M. was upset—this was always a sign that his poetic impulse was coming to an end ("the tailor's material is running out"). He remembered how Gumilev used to say that stars had a different meaning for every poet. For M. they signified abandonment of the earth and hence a feeling that he had lost his bearings.

He was even more upset by the poem he wrote in May 1937 about the woman of Kiev—the second he had written during those months about a woman parted from her husband. Terrified as he was of our parting, he thought this was ominous. He was very often afraid of things that appeared like this in his poetry, and after he had read me a few lines from the first of these poems, he never mentioned them to me again. "Don't talk about them," he said, "or it may all happen." We also had a superstitious belief that anything referred to in his poetry was bound to disappear: after writing "The Patriarch," he lost the white-handled walking-stick mentioned in it. A traveling rug with which I used to cover him began to fall apart as soon as it appeared in the line "you will cover me with it, as with a military flag, when I die." Our apartment, for which I had fought so hard, did not long survive the poem he wrote about it, and our goldfinch was eaten by a cat.

43

THE ODE

A poet's understanding of reality comes to him together with his verse, which always contains some element of anticipation of the future. "They're all the same," Akhmatova once said to me in a matter-of-fact tone when I showed her a poem of M.'s which clearly demonstrated foreknowledge of the future: she knew his work only too well and was not surprised in the least.

In the "Second Voronezh Notebook" there is a cycle whose matrix is the "Ode to Stalin" which he forced himself to write in the winter of 1936–37. This "Ode" did not fulfill its purpose—to save his life—but it gave rise to a whole series of other poems which were not only unlike it but also flatly contradicted it. Rather like the uncoiling of a spring, they were a natural response to it.

The "Goldfinch" cycle, which immediately preceded it, had sprung from an intensified craving for life and an affirmation of it, but even here there is a foreboding of death ("I shall take my seat in the lilac sleigh"), of our parting and the horrors lurking ahead. We were witnessing "the beginning of dreadful deeds," and the future was approaching "grimly," like the dark thunderclouds which occur in his poem about the Voronezh region (December 1936). Finally, in early January 1937 there was the poem about the "deadness of the plains" over which comes slowly crawling "He of whom we shriek in our sleep / The Judas of peoples to come." At this moment he saw his choice with utmost clarity: either he could passively await his doom or he could make some attempt to save himself. The turning point came in the middle of January, and is expressed in the poem entitled "Yeast of the World" (the one where he refers to the imprints made by horses' hoofs). This marked the moment at which the "Goldfinch" cycle came to an end and a new one, triggered by the "Ode," began.

The man to whom the "Ode" was written so dominated our minds that one can find veiled references to him in the most unlikely contexts. These allusions are always betrayed by certain associations from which one can see M.'s train of thought. A poem written in December 1936, for instance, is about an idol living in the middle of a mountain and trying to remember the days when it still had human shape. In Russian there is a clear phonetic trail of association leading from "Kremlin" to "mountain" via the words *kremen* ("flint") and *kamen* ("stone"). There is also a dangerously suggestive use of the word "fat" in the line: "The fat of pearls drips from his neck." One immediately thinks of the "fat fingers" in M.'s first poem about Stalin. The line about the idol desperately trying to remember the time when it was human could have been inspired by Yakhontov's wife, Lilia, a Stalinist of the sentimental type, who told us during their visit to Voronezh how wonderful, brave and high-spirited Stalin had been as a young revolutionary.... Living as we did in Assyria, it was impossible not to think of the Assyrian.

By the window in the room we rented from the seamstress there was a square dining table which we used for everything under the sun. M. now took possession of it and laid out pencil and paper on it. He had never done anything like this before: paper and pencil were always needed only at the end of his work on a poem, to copy it out when it was already composed in his head. But for the sake of the "Ode" he changed all his habits, and while he was writing it we had to eat on the very edge of the table, or even on the window sill. Every morning he seated himself at the table and picked up the pencil, as a writer is supposed to: for all the world like Fedin, or someone of that kind. I would not even have been surprised if he had pronounced the ritual "Never a day without at least a line," but this, thank God, he didn't say. After sitting for half an hour or so in this posture of the real man of letters, he would suddenly jump up and begin to curse himself for his lack of skill: "Now, look at Aseyev—he's a real craftsman, he would just dash it off without a moment's thought." Then, calming down, he would stretch out on the bed and ask for tea. After that, he would get up to feed lumps of sugar to the neighbor's dog through the air vent at the top of the window—to do this he had to climb up on the table with the paper neatly laid out on it. Next he would begin to pace the room and, suddenly brightening, start mumbling to himself. This was a sign that he had not been able to stifle the real poetry inside him, and that it had now broken its bounds, overwhelming the Evil Spirit. His attempt to do violence to himself was meeting stubborn resistance, and the artificially conceived poem about Stalin simply became a matrix for the utterly different material seething inside him—real poetry which was antagonistic to the "Ode" and canceled it out. This cycle, generated by the "Ode," starts with "Yeast of the World" and continues to the end of the "Second Voronezh Notebook."

The main outward sign of the relationship between the "Ode" and the series of poems which burst from M.'s lips in opposition to it is a phonetic one involving the syllable *os*, which appears in a number of unrelated words such as "wasp" *(osa)* and "axle" *(os)*. A key poem dated February 8, 1937, for example, begins:

> Armed with the sight of narrow wasps [*os*]
> Sucking the axis [*os*] of the earth . . .

But much more important than this phonetic link between the "Ode" and the rest of the cycle is the way in which details in the "Ode" are contradicted or given a different interpretation in the "free" poems. In the "Ode," for example, an artist, with tears in his eyes, draws a portrait of the Leader. But the poem of February 8 quoted above has the line "I do not draw and I do not sing." M. himself was astonished at this admission which had burst from him quite spontaneously, and commented to me: "Look what the trouble with me is: it seems I don't draw. . . ."

A mention of Aeschylus and Prometheus in the "Ode" led on in the "free" poems to the theme of tragedy and martyrdom (in the poem dated January 19–February 14). The theme of martyrdom also comes into the poem on Rembrandt (February 8), which speaks, by implication, of a Calvary devoid of grandeur (the museum in Voronezh, which we visited constantly, had a small painting of Golgotha by Rembrandt and some Greek vases—all that remained of the treasures of Dorpat University).

The Caucasus, naturally mentioned in the "Ode" as Stalin's birthplace, occurs again in the reference to Tiflis as the place which remembers not the Great Leader but the poor poet with his worn shoes (the poem of February 7–11), and in the mention of Mount Elbrus* as a measure of the people's need for bread and poetry.

In the opening poem of the cycle ("Yeast of the World" and its

---

* The highest mountain in the Caucasus.

variants) there is even a direct complaint that the "Ode" is at cross-purposes with the rest:

> I'm bored: my direct work
> babbles obliquely
> crossed and mocked by another that has dislocated its axle.*

Poetry is the "yeast of the world," a "sweet-voiced labor" which is "blameless." M. declares that he is a poet when his "mind is not deceitful" and his work is "selfless":

> a selfless song is its own praise,
> a comfort to friends, and pitch to enemies.

The enemy who had been installed in our Moscow apartment, the writer with the rank of general, copied out all of M.'s verse on his typewriter. Since very few people had typewriters in those days and he offered to do this as a "favor," it was impossible to refuse—and in any case he would have obtained the poems somehow, even if it had meant stealing them from under my pillow. Just as a little warning to us he underlined the words "selfless song" in red pencil. When the archives are one day thrown open, it will be interesting to see his report on this poem.

In the poems of this cycle M. also exalted man ("Do not compare: the living are incomparable") and gave rein to his love of life for the last time. He lamented his failing eyesight, which had once been "sharper than a whetted scythe" but had not had time to pick out each of the "lonely multitude of stars" (the last poem in the cycle, dated February 8–9). He summed up his life and work in the last three lines of the poem dated February 12:

> And I have accompanied the universe's rapture
> As muted organ pipes
> Accompany a woman's voice.

Speaking of himself, he used here the "inexorable past tense"—to borrow his own expression from "Conversation About Dante." A few more

---

* The syllable *os* occurs four times here.

months were to pass, and he would say to Akhmatova: "I am ready for death." She later used this phrase in her "Poem Without a Hero," which also has a dedication dated December 27, 1938—the date of M.'s death.

But perhaps the high point of the cycle is contained in the following lines, which are the proud words of a man condemned to death, yet still clinging to life:

> Unhappy is he who, as by his own shadow,
> is frightened by the barking of dogs and mowed
>   down by the wind
> and wretched is he who, half-alive himself,
> begs a shadow for alms.*

The word "shadow" here referred to the man from whom everybody "begged alms"—and a shadow is what he eventually proved to be. Struggling for breath, frightened by everything but afraid of no one, crushed and condemned, the bearded poet thus defied once more, in his last days, the dictator whose power was greater than any the world had ever known.

People who had voices were subjected to the vilest of tortures: their tongues were cut out and with the stump that remained they were forced to glorify the tyrant. The desire to live is insuperable, and people accepted even this, if they could thereby prolong their physical existence. But those who survived at this price were as dead as those who perished. There is no point in mentioning names, but it is safe to say that among all those who continued to play the role of writers in those years, none have come forth as witnesses. They can never overcome their state of confusion, or say anything with the stumps of their tongues. Yet there were many among them who in different circumstances would have found their way in life and said what they had to say.

To be sure, M. also, at the very last moment, did what was required of him and wrote a hymn of praise to Stalin, but the "Ode" did not achieve its purpose of saving his life. It is possible, though, that without it I should not have survived either—their first impulse was to destroy me, too, but it was counted in a widow's favor if her husband had

---

* From the poem beginning "I am not yet dead, I am not yet alone" (January 1937).

made his submission even though it wasn't accepted. M. knew this. By surviving I was able to save his poetry, which would otherwise have come down only in the garbled copies circulating in 1937.

The prayer "May this cup pass from me" can only be understood if you know what it is to wait for the slow, inevitable approach of death. It is far harder to wait for a bullet in the back of the neck than to be stricken down unawares. We waited for the end during the whole of our last year in Voronezh, and then yet another year, moving from place to place to place in the Moscow region.

To write an ode to Stalin it was necessary to get in tune, like a musical instrument, by deliberately giving way to the general hypnosis and putting oneself under the spell of the liturgy which in those days blotted out all human voices. Without this, a real poet could never compose such a thing: he would never have had that kind of ready facility. M. thus spent the beginning of 1937 conducting a grotesque experiment on himself. Working himself up into the state needed to write the "Ode," he was in effect deliberately upsetting the balance of his own mind. "I now realize that it was an illness," he said later to Akhmatova.

"Why is it that when I think of *him*, I see heads, mounds of heads?" M. said to me once. "What is he doing with all those heads?"

When we left Voronezh, M. asked Natasha to destroy the "Ode." Many people now advise me not to speak of it at all, as though it had never existed. But I cannot agree to this, because the truth would then be incomplete: leading a double life was an absolute fact of our age, and nobody was exempt. The only difference was that while others wrote their odes in their apartments and country villas and were rewarded for them, M. wrote his with a rope around his neck. Akhmatova did the same, as they drew the noose tighter around the neck of her son. Who can blame either her or M.?

44

GOLDEN RULES

At the beginning of January 1937, just after M. had written his poem "Smile, angry lamb," he was visited by a youth, a real guttersnipe, who sat down in front of us and announced that "writers must collaborate with their readers." This was a familiar tune: he wanted M. to give him his new verse so he could make copies of it. This is what he had been sent for, but he had been badly briefed and was too confused and tongue-tied to explain what he needed.

We are all very long-suffering people and we have one golden rule: if they start badgering you, never resist—just do what they want, whether it is voting in "elections," signing some public appeal or other, or buying State bonds.* When you are talking with a police spy, always answer all his questions, so that he can duly report to his superiors, otherwise you will "never hear the end of it"—and they'll get what they want anyway. The main thing in these situations is to get rid, as politely as possible, of the person sent to badger you. M. also observed this rule, but on this occasion he was so angry that, to use Akhmatova's expression, he "burst his banks." Against the general background of our isolation from the outside world, visitors of this type were utterly unbearable. M. lost patience with our uninvited guest and told him to leave. Later he laughed at himself for being so fastidious and expecting them to send agents who really knew their stuff! But when the next one appeared and turned out, though a little older, to be just as ill-suited for the job, M. no longer thought it funny and—to use Akhmatova's expression—"had an epileptic fit."

It was not done to expose police spies. The agency which sent them would not put up with any attempt to discredit its operations and sooner or later wreaked vengeance on people who did so. Even now, many people who have been in prisons or camps prefer to keep quiet about their "godfathers"†—they know that to be indiscreet about such things is asking for trouble. In those years people were even more careful. The rare exceptions only proved the rule. Everybody knew, for instance, that Marietta Shaginian never allowed any police spy to come near her. If one tried to, she made a terrible fuss, not caring who heard her. In 1934 she created a scene in my presence, and I thought I could see what her game was. We had come out of the State Publishing House together and she started asking me about life in Voronezh—this was in the early days of M.'s exile there, when nobody was yet afraid of

---

* Under Stalin, all Soviet citizens were obliged to buy State bonds, "volunteering" at factory and office meetings to subscribe a month's salary. It was a kind of recurrent capital levy.

† Officers of the secret police charged with the surveillance of prisoners.

being seen with us because the story of Stalin's conversation with Pasternak had spread far and wide. Suddenly the poet B. came running after us—he also wanted to inquire about M. But Marietta rounded on him fiercely. "I have friends in the Central Committee," she shouted, "and I will not put up with police spies." I tried to stop her, saying that I knew B. well. But she wouldn't listen to reason, and I had the suspicion that the whole scene had been deliberately contrived by her: she attacked completely decent people in the hope of frightening off real police spies, whom she would not of course have dared to treat in this way. But, as I say, Marietta was an exception, and for the most part the informers who surrounded us had a completely free hand and became more and more brazen.

The Voronezh police spy—the one sent to replace the guttersnipe thrown out by M.—dropped in on us without warning any time he liked. The door in the seamstress' house was never closed because her son Vadik—the young bird-fancier who bought goldfinches and bullfinches at auctions—was always running in and out. The new police spy would appear so unexpectedly in the doorway that we were always caught unawares with manuscripts lying all over the table. Without taking his coat off, he would sit down at the table and start going through everything. He made comments such as "Why are there so many couplets here?" or "I can't make out a thing in this handwriting—hers [that is, mine] is much better." M. would snatch the sheets of paper from him and angrily tear them to pieces. Later we had to reconstruct whatever it was from memory—which only made us even more furious.

"Why do you come in working hours?" M. asked him. The man was posing as a factory worker of some kind—a fitter or a lathe operator. He replied that he had got off work, or that he was on the night shift. "So they let you leave the factory whenever you like?" we asked. But it was all like water off a duck's back, and he just said the first thing that came into his head, not even trying to be plausible. Every time M. threw him out, he said: "That's the end, he won't turn up again." He just couldn't believe that the man would have the impudence to come back after being so thoroughly exposed. But it was a vain hope: two or three days later we would have to go through the same business all over again. He wasn't such a fool as to tell his superiors that he had failed— an agent who has been exposed is scarcely worth his salt.

M. was working on the poem about begging alms from a shadow

when he suddenly decided to ring the GPU and ask for an interview with the Commandant. Most unusually, his request was granted. The normal thing would have been for him to be told to write out his complaint and leave it in the special box at the GPU office—this is how we are used to communicating with our authorities: by dropping petitions in boxes. I learned about this move of M.'s only after the interview had been arranged, and I went with him to the GPU building (always known in any Soviet city as "the Big House"). After his bout of heart trouble in the summer of 1936, M. never went out alone. He would not have gone out to phone the GPU without me if the telephone exchange had not been very close to our house. Natasha Shtempel later told me that while they had been out walking together M. had gone to phone the GPU to find out whether the interview was going to be granted. He had asked her not to tell me anything about it—he knew I would be against it and argue that, apart from being futile, it was wrong to draw attention to oneself.

After a brief exchange of words in the GPU guardroom, we were given passes for both of us—they knew that M. was sick and couldn't go out unaccompanied. We were received by the Deputy Commandant, who looked like an ordinary Red Army officer. Men of this type are often found in the higher secret-police posts. M. was convinced that people like this were employed specially for relations with the outside world—so that, seeing their broad, open faces, nobody would guess what went on "inside." The one who received us was shortly afterward transferred to the film industry, where, according to Shklovski, he was quite easy to get along with. The same was probably true of Furmanov's younger brother, who had a similar career—the film world is swarming with such people. There are also a great many of them in the universities and institutes, where they work in the faculties of literature, philosophy, economics and so forth. They are always gladly given places on the pretext of what is known as "staff consolidation." I have the impression that as a matter of deliberate policy great numbers of young people are given their early training by the secret police before being let out into the world at large—where they never forget their alma mater. Among them there were some perfectly decent kids who in a drunken state would tell you amusing tales about their service with the "organs" (as the secret police is often called). I knew one such splendid fellow when I taught at the Chuvash Teachers' Training College. He was writing a dissertation about the "material base" of the

Chuvash kolkhozes and complained that it was a subject of which no one could make head or tail. He told me he had gone to work for the "organs" as soon as he left school. He had done so in search of "adventure," but his first job had been to stand for hours, come fair weather or foul, in front of the house where a certain old man lived, with orders to take note of any visitors. But the devil of it was that nobody ever came to see the old man and he never came out himself—the only sign of life he gave was to pull back the curtain and peep out occasionally. My young acquaintance even wondered sometimes whether the old man hadn't been instructed to keep an eye on *him*—making sure he didn't sneak off to have a beer while on duty. His job was the same as that of the "tails" I have already mentioned whom we saw loitering in front of Akhmatova's house—only they had a more cheerful time, because she at least had fairly frequent visitors! The old man, incidentally, had been described to my young colleague as a former Menshevik.

People of this type, sent to work in colleges and institutes by the "organs," were regarded with tolerance by their colleagues. It is said that they were never used as informers—which makes good sense, since they were less suited for the part than certain ladies or young gentlemen with an intellectual or upper-class background who could more easily gain one's confidence. Moreover, these people appointed on the grounds of "staff consolidation" were not frightened of losing their jobs and were therefore less likely to take part in departmental intrigues aimed at getting rid of rivals.

The Voronezh Commandant saw us in a vast office with lots of doors—just like the office of M.'s interrogator in Moscow. He asked what M. had come to see him about, and he looked at us with unconcealed curiosity—perhaps the reason he had broken with custom and decided to receive us was a desire to have a look at this odd bird sitting in his cage. Even men like him had their human weaknesses. But I do not think that M. could have made much of an impression on this Soviet general—he must have had a very different image of what a writer was. Haggard, with sunken cheeks and bloodless lips, M. indeed looked "half alive" (as he said of himself in the poem about the shadow) next to the burly, clean-shaven and pink-cheeked Commandant, who, though a trifle portly, was still in very good trim.

M. said that he had come on two matters. The first was: How was he to earn enough money to keep himself alive? Exiles were not given work anywhere—anybody who was rash enough to offer a job to some-one like M. would be dismissed himself for "lack of vigilance." There was no such thing as a labor exchange, so how could he exercise his constitutional right to work? At the moment all doors were closed to him, but while he had still at least been able to gain access to people, he had managed to talk with someone in the Regional Party Commit-tee about the question of finding work. Here they had said to him: "You will have to start all over again: get a job as a watchman or as a cloak-room attendant and show what you're capable of." But this was hypocrisy—nobody would even give him a job as an attendant for the same reason: fear that they might be accused of "lack of vigilance." In any case, if an intellectual took a menial job like that, it would be re-garded as a political demonstration. No organization, beginning with the Union of Writers, would take any responsibility for him, and there was no question of any of them finding work for him. Evidently, as M. told the Commandant, the only organization which had any responsi-bility for him was the GPU. Since people sent to the camps were given work, M. asked whether the same did not apply to exiles.

The Commandant replied that the "organs" could not concern themselves with finding work for people: not only would that be "too much of a burden," but it was also unnecessary, since exiles were free to take any job they liked and, "as is well known, there is no unem-ployment in our country." "And what are you doing at the moment?" he asked. M. replied that, not having any regular paid work, he was study-ing the Spanish language and literature, in particular the work of a poet, Jewish by origin, who spent many years in the cellars of the In-quisition and every day composed a sonnet in his head. When he was released, he wrote down all his sonnets, but he was soon imprisoned again and this time put on a chain. It was not known whether he con-tinued to compose poetry or not. Perhaps, M. suggested, it might be possible to organize a Spanish study group in the local GPU club and put him in charge of it? I can't be sure, but I think that by this time we had heard rumors of the arrest of the Leningrad Spanish scholars, and this was probably why M. mentioned his Spanish studies to the Com-mandant rather than anything else. The Commandant was quite taken aback by M.'s proposal for a Spanish study group and replied that "our fellows" would scarcely be interested in learning Spanish. I doubt whether he got the point about the Inquisition, and imagine that he was simply puzzled by the eccentric character sitting in front of him.

"And why don't your relatives or friends help you?" he asked suddenly. M. replied that he had no relatives, and that his friends now pretended not to know him and did not answer his letters—"for reasons you understand," he added.

"We don't prevent anybody meeting exiles," said the Commandant with a genial laugh, and asked M. what the other thing was he wanted to discuss.

The second question concerned M.'s verse. M. suggested that in future it might be better for him to mail the Commandant all his new verse—"so you don't have to waste your men's time," he explained. As he told me later, it had been on the tip of his tongue to use the Commandant's own word for his colleagues and say: "Why should your *fellows* have to waste their time coming to get my verse?" But luckily he refrained from this extremely patronizing turn of phrase.

The Commandant became more and more genial. He assured M. that his organization was not at all interested in his verse, only in counter-revolutionary activity. "Write just what you like," he said, but he at once went on to ask: "Why did you write that poem that got you into trouble? Upset by collectivization, were you?" In Party circles it was now customary to speak of the mass deportation of the kulaks as past history and to say that it had been carried out so vigorously because it was essential, but that some unstable citizens had been upset by the excesses which had admittedly taken place. M. mumbled an evasive reply to this question.

During our conversation the Commandant's phone rang and we heard him say to the person at the other end: "Yes, yes. . . . That's slander. . . . Send it along, we'll attend to it." We realized that somebody's fate was being decided, that a warrant was being issued as the result of a denunciation: So-and-so said such and such. This was quite enough for someone to disappear for good. Whatever we said—things that anywhere else but this country might seem quite ordinary—could be produced in evidence against us. After talking with friends, we often joked as we left: "Today we've said enough to get ten years."

We parted from the Commandant in a perfectly amicable way. I asked M.: "Why all this tomfoolery?" "So that he knows what's what," M. replied. "But they know in any case," I wailed with my usual female logic. But I was not able to spoil M.'s mood, and for several days he went around cheerfully, remembering the details of the conversation. In one thing he had certainly been successful: the police spies vanished into thin air, and for the rest of our stay in Voronezh we were never troubled by any of them again. And what in fact had been the point of them? All M.'s verse came into the hands of the "organs" anyway—admittedly not in Voronezh, but in Moscow, through the vigilant Kostyrev and the editorial offices of the literary magazines.

The only question is: Why did the Commandant remove his police spies instead of accusing M. of "slander" and issuing a warrant for his arrest? Is it possible that the original order to "isolate but preserve" M. was still in force? Or it may be that since M. was "in the charge of Moscow," the Voronezh branch of the secret police attached their agents to us simply out of excess of zeal—just to show their mettle. A third possibility is that the Commandant was actually displaying a certain liberalism. This did sometimes happen—even secret-police officials were human, and some of them were tired of killing. The only really strange thing is that all this was done by people, the most ordinary sort of people: "people like you and me, with eyes hollowed out in skulls, / with as much right to judge as you." How can we understand or explain it? And what is the point of it all?

45

"HOPE"

M.'s three-year term of exile was supposed to end in the middle of May 1937, but we did not attach too much significance to this. We knew only too well that the length of your sentence was a matter of chance rather than of law—they could always add to it or shorten it, depending on how your luck ran. Experienced exiles, such as the ones we had met in Cherdyn, were always pleased if they were given a few more years without any formal proceedings. Otherwise it meant going through the ordeal of a new arrest and interrogation, after which you would be exiled to a new, unfamiliar place. Nobody knows better than an exile or a camp inmate how important it is to stay as long as possible in one place. This is the basic condition of survival, because it means you make friends with people who will help you to come through, and you acquire a few pitiful belongings—in other words, you strike some kind of roots and spend less of your strength on the struggle to stay alive. But this is true not only of exiles: moving to a new place is an intolerable ordeal for anybody in our conditions. No wonder people hang on so grimly to their "living-space." Only an incorrigible vagabond like M., who hated the very idea of being tied to one place, could dream of moving. A change could only bring trouble. But M. was tired of Voronezh.

In April I went to Moscow, but found myself confronted by a blank wall which it was quite impossible to breach. However, to keep M.'s spirits up I wrote to him in Voronezh to say that we should soon be moving, now that his sentence was almost over. M. did not react to my words of encouragement, but my mother took them seriously and went to look after M. in Voronezh for a while so that I could again visit Moscow in search of new hope.

Why, at the dawn of the new era, at the very beginning of the fratricidal twentieth century, was I given the name Nadezhda ["Hope"]? All I now heard from our friends and acquaintances was: "Not a hope!"—not a hope that anybody would help us, or give us work, or read letters from us, or shake us by the hand. By now everybody was too used to thinking of us as doomed. But one cannot live without hope and, however often our hopes were disappointed, we could only go on trying. The head of the local branch of the MGB had generously explained to us that we would not be able to stay in Voronezh unless we got some kind of private help. Since there was no hope of that, we had nothing to look forward to but the prospect of moving to some other place.

On May 16, 1937, we went up to the same window in the MGB office through which three years previously M. had handed over his travel warrant from Cherdyn and had ever since conducted all his business with the State. This was where all exiles had to come to "report"— some once a month, others every three days. There were so many of us, small fry caught in the toils of the State, that there had always been a long line at this window. We did not realize that these crowds of waiting people had been the outward sign that the good times described by Akhmatova as "vegetarian" were still with us. Everything is relative— we were soon to read in the newspapers that under Yagoda the forced-labor camps had been run like "health resorts." The press unleashed a flood of abuse against Yagoda, accusing him of being soft on all the scum in the camps and in exile. "Who would have thought that we have been in the hands of humanists!" we said to each other.

By the middle of May 1937 the line at the MGB window had

dwindled to a dozen or so gloomy and shabbily dressed intellectuals. "Everybody's left Voronezh," M. whispered to me. Despite our isolation, we at once understood the reason: nearly all the old exiles had been re-arrested and no new ones were being sent. The "vegetarian" phase was over. People were no longer being banished, as we had been. From prison one now went either to a forced-labor camp or to the other world. A privileged few were kept in prison. The wives and children of prisoners were no longer sent into enforced residence away from the big cities, but were now also interned in special camps. There were even special institutions for small children, who were seen as potential avengers for their fathers. In 1956 Surkov said to me: "There must have been some case against Gumilev*—if you had a father like that and he was shot! He must have wanted to get revenge for him." It was curious that Surkov should have said this to me, of all people: he was so steeped in Stalin's Caucasian mentality that he thought only men might want to take vengeance.

Until 1937 all such potential avengers had merely been banished and one saw them standing in line in provincial MGB offices, waiting to "report." When we first arrived in Voronezh we saw there the son of Stoletov, who wandered the streets, alone and half out of his mind, complaining that his father had turned out to be a "wrecker." In 1937 the son of a man who had been shot would not have been sent to Voronezh, but would have been put straight behind barbed wire, and no complaints about his father would have been of any avail. Incidentally, neither M. nor I nor anybody else thought Stoletov's son really meant it—but there were sons who sincerely cursed their executed fathers. After M.'s death, when I lived for a time on the outskirts of Kalinin, I met there a few wives who for some reason had been banished rather than sent to camps. They had also sent here a boy of fourteen who was distantly related to Stalin. He was being looked after by an aunt who lived nearby—also in exile—and his former governess. For days the boy went on raving against his father and mother as renegades, traitors to the working class and enemies of the people. He used a formula which had been instilled in him during his very careful upbringing: "Stalin is my father and I do not need another one," and he kept referring to the hero of all the Soviet schoolbooks, Pavlik Morozov, who had managed to denounce his parents in time. He was tor-

---

* Lev Gumilev, the son of Akhmatova and Nikolai Gumilev.

mented by the thought that he had lost the chance of becoming a second Pavlik by likewise exposing the criminal activity of his parents. His aunt and governess were forced to listen in silence—they knew what the boy would do if they dared breathe a word. The fact that he was allowed to live in Kalinin as an exile was only an exception that proved the rule. By 1937 no more exiles were being sent to Voronezh.

Without any hope or expectations, we stood for half an hour in the much diminished line. "What surprise will they have for us now?" M. whispered as we came up to the window. He gave his name and asked whether they had anything for him now that his term of exile had just come to an end. He was handed a piece of paper. For a moment he couldn't make out what was written on it, then he gasped and said to the clerk behind the window: "Does that mean I can go where I please?" The clerk snapped something back at him—they always snapped at us, they had no other way of talking—from which we gathered that M. was free again. A kind of electric shock went through the people glumly waiting behind us. They began to shuffle and whisper. They suddenly saw a faint gleam of hope: if one had been released, perhaps the same could happen to others as well?

It took us a few days to wind up our affairs in Voronezh. Despite the poverty of our existence, we had accumulated some possessions: buckets, a frying pan, a flatiron (M. wrote to Benedikt Livshits about how well I ironed his shirts), a cooker, a lamp, a kerosene stove, a mattress, jars, plates and a few saucepans. We had bought all this in the market and it had cost us a lot of money: every purchase was an event. But it would have cost us even more to take it all with us—cab drivers and porters would have ruined us, if that word meant anything in our situation. Some of the things we sold, and others we gave away. What use would we have for buckets in Moscow, where we would get water simply by turning a faucet? We had no doubt that we should be going back to Moscow: if M. had not been given an additional sentence at such a difficult time, it could only mean he was being allowed back to the capital. It suddenly appeared significant to us that for some reason we had been able to keep possession of our Moscow apartment during these three years. Other writers in the building, tired of living only in one room, had often asked to be given more space at our expense and had tried to get my mother to show them what was available in the apartment. She would never let them inside and gave them a lecture on the doorstep about how writers should behave toward an exiled colleague under the traditional code of the old intelligentsia. We did not worry about Kostyrev, who had been given one of our rooms right at the beginning: he had been vouched for by Stavski himself, and, still believing in his elementary good faith as a representative of the Writers' Union, we assumed that the room would be vacated the moment we needed it back. We also recalled Stalin's remark in his telephone conversation with Pasternak: "Mandelstam will be all right." But we completely forgot the warning Vinaver had given us. We had also forgotten where we were living.

A few days later we were sitting on a pile of our belongings at the Voronezh railroad station. My mother and I had brought just enough money from Moscow to buy tickets for all three of us. There was nobody to see us off. Fedia was at work, and Natasha, who was a teacher, was giving lessons at that time of day. M. was always composing comic doggerel about her ("If God knew that Natasha was a pedagogue, he would say: Take this pedagogue away, for the sake of God"). The evening before, we had drunk a bottle of wine with her and M. would just not let her go home, though she complained that her mother would be worried. About this, too, he made up some lines:

> "Where've you been?" asks Mother dear,
> "Eating and drinking, I do declare,"
> And black as night she sniffs the smell of
> Wine and onion in the air.

We left in good spirits, full of the rosiest hopes, quite forgetting how insidious and delusive is the one whose name I bear....

46
"One Extra Day"

We opened the door of our apartment with our own key and were pleasantly surprised to find it empty. On the table there was a brief note from Kostyrev saying he had moved out to a dacha with his wife and child. He had left nothing at all to remind us he had ever lived here and sat copying out M.'s verse, listening in as I talked with my mother, brother, or the few friends who had still dared to come and see me on my trips from Voronezh. We had no idea why Kostyrev had decided to clear out. It was certainly not from tact. We could only regard it as a good sign—it must mean that all restrictions on M. had really been lifted.

The absence of Kostyrev and the reality of the familiar walls and belongings—beds, curtains, shelves with a handful of books on them—suddenly blotted out the whole memory of Cherdyn and Voronezh. We had the illusion that this was a real home to which we had returned after a time of incomprehensible and needless wandering. The process of rejoining past and present took no more than a second—the intervening period that had been forced on us from outside and not freely chosen, suddenly faded away. Thanks to his ability to live for the moment, M. easily passed, without looking back, from one part of his life to another—as one can see from his poetry with its clear division into different phases. Hence, when he entered our apartment, his three-year exile at once ceased to have any reality for him, and the business of fitting together the two parts of his life was achieved straightaway, on the spot, without any preliminaries.

Sometimes the two parts of one's life come together again like this, but sometimes the opposite happens—as when we were setting off for Cherdyn. Now, back in Moscow, we felt as though we had never been away. It is a common enough experience, known, for instance, to prisoners returning from the camps—as long as they have a home to return to. But enormous numbers of them have been away so many years that when they come back they find nothing: their wives have been sent away, their parents are dead, and their children have disappeared or grown up as strangers. Such people have to begin life all over again, piecing it together from whatever may be left to them. Sometimes, after many years of forced labor, they can reconstruct their lives, even if they have no home or family, by returning to their former profession. Although I escaped the camps myself, I know what it is to go through this process of remaking one's life. It means that you can become yourself again and throw off the mask which you have been forced to wear for so long. Many of us were only able to survive on condition that we concealed our true nature and pretended to be like those around us. It was essential not to betray one's past. A deported kulak, for instance, could save himself only by taking up manual labor and forgetting about the land. Twenty years went by between the time of M.'s death and the moment when I was able to take from their hiding place all the poems I had managed to save and put them openly on the table (or, rather, the suitcase which served me as a table). During all those years I had to pretend to be someone else, wearing, as it were, an iron mask. I could not tell a soul that I was only waiting secretly for the moment when I could again become myself and say openly what I had been waiting for, and what I had been keeping all these years.

If the severed parts of my life were to come together in 1956, there could be no question of it in 1937: the trend of the times was not toward mending broken lives, and on that day when we came back to Moscow we were the victims of an optical illusion, a pure hallucination. But, thanks to this hallucination, M. was granted his "one extra day."*

In our sort of life everybody gladly falls for illusions or seeks some belief that gives a sense of reality. If the life around you is illusory, you take refuge in illusory activity, entering illusory relations with others, embarking on illusory love affairs—you must have something to hang on to. Once, long before his first arrest, M. had said to me as we waited at a tram stop: "We think that everything is going along as it should, and that life continues—but that is only because the trams are running." Our empty apartment with its bookshelves was an even greater invitation to delude ourselves than the sight of our overcrowded tramcars. We also cheered each other with reminders of what Stalin, or Stavski, had said—as though we didn't know that such promises were the most terrible illusions of all. But we tried to close our eyes to this—anything to maintain our sense of false security. Instead of sitting down to consider our position soberly, which would only have meant upsetting ourselves with gloomy thoughts, we deposited all our things in the middle of the room and went off to the small gallery in Kropotkin Street to see "the French."

In Voronezh M. had often said to me: "If I ever get back, the first thing I shall do is go and see the French." Maria Veniaminovna Yudina had noted how much he missed the French painters. Whenever she came to Voronezh, he would ask her about them, even while she was playing to him. She once sent him an album put out by the gallery, but the reproductions were very bad, and they only whetted his appetite. Now, without changing after the journey, pausing only to drink some tea, he went straight to the gallery. He also talked of going to see Tysh-

* Quoted from the end of Mandelstam's "Journey to Armenia."

ler: "I must have a good look at everything while there is still time." He had appreciated Tyshler very early, when he had seen the series of drawings at the first OSZ* exhibition. Later, after he had joined me in Yalta, he said: "You still don't know what this Tyshler of yours is capable of." The last time he went to see him and look at his paintings was just before the end, in March 1938.

47

THE "BESSARABIAN CARRIAGE"

The first person to come and see us was Akhmatova. This was on the morning of the day we arrived. She had timed her own arrival in Moscow to coincide with ours. I lay on a mattress in the kitchen with a fearful headache while M. paced rapidly round the tiny "sanctuary," as we called it, and recited to Akhmatova. He was giving her an account of what he had written in Voronezh (the Second and Third Notebooks)—from the early days of their friendship, they had always told each other of every line they wrote. In return Akhmatova read him the poem she had written about him in Voronezh. It ends with the lines:

> But in the room of the banished poet
> Fear and the Muse stand watch by turn
> and the night falls
> without the hope of dawn.

It was quite true that while Akhmatova had been visiting us, we had all been overcome by a sudden paroxysm of wild and senseless terror. It had happened in the evening as we were sitting in the room we rented from the "agent" (the one who threatened to roast mice on our grill). As often happened in the provinces, the electricity had been cut off, and we had lit an oil lamp. Suddenly the door opened and in came Leonov, the biologist from Tashkent, together with another man. Though this happened without any warning at all, there was no reason for us to be frightened—we knew Leonov had a father in Voronezh and

---

* Obshchestvo Stankovoi Zhivopisi (Society of Easel Painting), founded by Yuri Annenkov and David Sternberg in 1921.

that he often came to see him. He was a kind of Russian dervish who was always a little drunk, but we trusted him absolutely. He had first been brought to us by Kuzin, and often turned up out of the blue to see us before going back to the university in Tashkent—he worked there together with Polivanov, who had given him a taste for philology and poetry. So why were we so startled at his coming in like that? Whenever we met with Akhmatova, we felt a little conspiratorial and were easily frightened. And then, like all Soviet citizens, we were afraid of unexpected visitors, cars stopping outside the house, and the sound of elevators at night. At the time of Akhmatova's visit, fear was not yet "standing watch" and only occasionally clutched us by the throat. In Moscow, on the other hand, during those days when we were under the

---

Poem by Anna Akhmatova
written after her visit to Mandelstam in Voronezh (1936)

VORONEZH

And the town stands locked in ice:
A paperweight of trees, walls, snow.
Gingerly I tread on glass;
the painted sleighs skid in their tracks.
Peter's statue in the square points to
crows and poplars, and a verdigris dome
washed clean, seeded with the sun's dust.
Here the earth still shakes from the old battle
where the Tartars were beaten to their knees.
Let the poplars raise their chalices
for a sky-shattering toast,
like thousands of wedding-guests drinking
in jubilation at a feast.
But in the room of the banished poet
Fear and the Muse stand watch by turn,
and the night falls,
without the hope of dawn.[1]

Translated by Stanley Kunitz and Max Hayward

---

[1] The last four lines have been omitted in the Soviet edition of Akhmatova's verse.

spell of our illusions, we had no fears at all. Improbable as it may seem, we fell into an inexplicable state of calm and believed for some reason that our life was at last secure.

My memory of those days in Moscow is strangely fragmented—I can recall very vividly several moments, like stills from a film, but in between there are gaps which I can no longer reconstruct. One such "still," which also features Akhmatova, was the time when we waited endlessly for Khardzhiev to arrive at the apartment. He had promised to come and bring some wine with him, but he was intolerably late, as only Muscovites can be—particularly in those days when nobody had watches and the trams and buses ran very erratically. Akhmatova decided not to wait for him any longer, and set off back to where she was staying—with Tolstaya on the Prechistenka. She had to go back all the way on foot—it was the rush hour and she could not get on a tram, but the moment she arrived she was called to the telephone. It was M. ordering her to return to our apartment again: Khardzhiev had come after all. She immediately started out, like Phoebus Apollo in the anthology of mock-classical verse that M. had made up together with Gumilev, Georgi Ivanov and Lozinski in their carefree younger days: "Phoebus in his golden carriage rolls across the sky. / Tomorrow he'll come back again in the same old way."

We had been sitting in our large room (which we had now dubbed the "Kostyrev room"), but when Akhmatova came back, we moved to the narrow passage which we preferred. We had partitioned it with a cupboard and put in a small table and a mattress on a wooden frame with castors—in our cramped conditions we had soon learned to do without proper beds. The mattress was usually placed lengthwise, but for fear of bedbugs we had put it crosswise, with the head against the wall. There was only a narrow gap at the other end through which one could get to the large window, always kept wide open. While I busied myself in the kitchen, the three of them sat talking on the mattress.

"Look at our Bessarabian carriage," M. said as I came in, "and the impoverished lady of the manor with her steward. . . . I am just the Jew."

When he was with Akhmatova, one could always see that their relations went back to the madcap days of their youth. Whenever they met, they both became young again and made each other laugh with words from their private vocabulary. Some of these went back to certain episodes. For instance, when Akhmatova was posing for Altman's portrait of her, M. occasionally looked in, and one day they told him how

Altman's neighbor, also an artist and an Italian by origin, had come in, heard them laughing, and used a macaronic form of the Russian word for "laughter" which they found very funny. This was the word by which Akhmatova and M. described the fits of giggling that came over them whenever they met.

The scene on the "Bessarabian carriage" was the last with Akhmatova. She probably went back to Leningrad to have things out with Punin—she had been on bad terms with him for a long time and I can't remember when it was she first told me how difficult she found life with him. In Moscow she had also been to have a talk with Garshin, and this had brought on her final break with Punin. After she left, her place on the mattress was taken by Yakhontov, who brought his girl friend Lilia along with him. Lilia could easily have been taken for a Bessarabian "lady of the manor," but she would not have been amused by the comparison. She earnestly tried to re-educate M. in a spirit of sentimental Stalinism (there was such a thing!). In her opinion, a writer who did not devote himself to Stalin's service was finished. Who would read such a writer? He would be barred from literature and forever consigned to oblivion. Lilia had no doubt whatsoever that Stalin was the savior of mankind. She also wanted, incidentally, to write a letter to Stalin saying he ought to help M. to mend his ways, and that the best way to achieve this would be to let him publish his verse. This kind of thing later came to be known as "Gaponism."* Lilia was very well read in Party literature because she had to write sketches for Yakhontov. Every day she turned out some new story about the miracles performed by the Leader. Yakhontov didn't share her views, but said nothing, preferring to joke and act funny little scenes for us. One of his best turns was an imitation of his own father, a large, fat, perspiring man—in Czarist times he had been an official and was always terrified of his superiors (Lilia's commentary on this was: "All officials were cowards in Czarist times"). Sometimes Yakhontov recited Lermontov's "Prophet," manipulating his walking-stick like a puppet—an imaginary crowd would timidly part before it and it went up to Lilia and bowed, while Yakhontov recited the line: "He is poor and naked," pointing at M. as he did so. Yakhontov was himself by no means rich, but if we had no money difficulties during those days, it was because of him.

Before we left for Voronezh, Lilia had offered some of her books on

---

* See the note on Gapon in the Appendix.

Marxism to M. for his edification, but Yakhontov had said: "There's no point: it's utterly useless," and instead gave his Bible to M.—I still have it. Yakhontov was also hard to re-educate.

Akhmatova knows the Old Testament very well and is very fond of discussing fine points of interpretation with Amusin, whom I introduced to her. M., on the other hand, was rather afraid of the Old Testament God and his awesome, totalitarian power. He used to say (and I later found the same idea in Berdiayev) that, with its doctrine of the Trinity, Christianity had overcome the undivided power of the Jewish God. Undivided power was, of course, something of which we were very afraid.

48

THE ILLUSION

The knowledge of what an illusion is first came to us in the autumn of 1933, when we were still settling down in the only apartment we ever had, in the street once called Nashchokin but later renamed Furmanov in honor of our neighbor there.

Once a man with a rucksack knocked on our door and asked for M.'s brother Alexander. He had an improbably feudal-sounding name with several components (of which one was Dobropalovy), but he preferred to be known by his nickname, "Bublik." I wanted to send him away to my brother-in-law's apartment—I was already tired of people begging to be put up for the night because they couldn't get into a hotel—but M.'s father, who was staying with us at the time, interceded for him. He said he remembered him as a neat, rosy-cheeked schoolboy from the days when he had attended the same classical grammar school as Alexander. "And now look what he's come to!" said M.'s father, almost crying. M. pushed me aside and asked Bublik to come in. To set our minds at rest, he told us that he had been in prison only on ordinary criminal charges, so we needn't worry: there was no suggestion at all of the dreaded Article 58. In those years M. was impressed by the fact that in the West the police were armed with nightsticks, and when he happened to mention this, Bublik just smiled: "If only you knew what they do to criminals here!" In fact we had heard some rumors about what was done to prisoners—and not only criminals—already in the twenties.

Bublik was an incorrigibly cheerful soul and he kept running off to meet some comrades with whom he was hoping to go to the far north, where, he said, there were "many of our kind"—which meant it would be easier to settle down there. While he lived with us, he helped us with the housekeeping and ran errands for M. M. often sent him with a note to the State Publishing House so that Bublik could collect installments on the money which was then being advanced to M. for a collected edition of his work. This collection never actually appeared, because M. refused to exclude "Journey to Armenia," some of his verse and a great many articles. The edition wouldn't have come off in any case: Bukharin no longer had any influence and at some stage it would have been "killed." Even so, it was good tactics to try to reach a compromise whereby *something* might be published. The fact that nothing of M.'s was appearing at all made it possible for our officials to spread the story that M. had stopped writing verse in the twenties and now spent his time drinking in the Moscow taverns. Many people believed this—particularly in the West, where the absence of publications is taken to mean that an author is no longer writing. How could we possibly explain that things were different with us? But poetry is a law to itself: it is impossible to bury it alive and even a powerful propaganda machinery such as ours cannot prevent it from living on. "I am easy in my mind now," Akhmatova said to me in the sixties. "We have seen how durable poetry is."

Bublik would bring the money in a briefcase and make me count it: the only reward he would accept for all the waiting in line at the cashier's was to buy himself a sandwich out of the money. M. now looked on him as indispensable, particularly when it turned out that he was a first-rate Latin scholar.

Everybody who came to see M. had his own particular line of talk. Kuzin and the other biologists talked about genetics, the Bergsonian élan vital and Aristotle's entelechy. M. was quite happy to listen to them. With Kuzin he often went to concerts—they both had an excellent knowledge of music and could reproduce (M. by whistling, Kuzin by singing them) the most complicated scores. Margulis, whom I have already mentioned, was also a musical companion for M. His wife, Iza Khantsyn, teaches in the Conservatory. She often recalls how M. listened to music and how she played for him on her visits to Moscow—at that time she lived mainly in Leningrad while her husband combed Moscow in search of work. M. used to say that Margulis was his substitute for a printing press: hungry for verse, he always begged to be given the latest new poem, which he would then circulate in manuscript form. This was the beginning of the era of the circulation of literature in this way—though it was not made easier by the fact that whenever a poet's apartment was searched by the police they confiscated both his manuscripts and his books.

Another visitor in those days was Chechanovski, with whom I worked at the beginning of the thirties on the magazine *For a Communist Education.* Chechanovski was a Marxist, and the main point of our inviting him was to give M. a chance of arguing with him. The concept of "development," he told us, was equivalent to "progress" and could not be "taken away from us by Mandelstam." It was he who was entrusted with the mission of suggesting to M. that he disavow his "Journey to Armenia." Whether he was spying on us, I do not know. Probably not. In any case, it is not very important, since M. never read the poem on Stalin to him—though he said many other things every evening which were quite enough to get him arrested.

We also used to see Nilender, a Greek and Hebrew scholar. A former naval officer, he now worked in the Public Library and generally came around midnight, bringing a packet of tea with him, just in case we had run out by then. He was translating Sophocles and talked all the time about the "golden section." Finally, during that year we saw something of Vygotski, the author of *Language and Thought,* a very intelligent psychologist (though somewhat hampered by the rationalism of the time), and on the street we sometimes ran into Stolpner, the translator of Hegel, who tried to convince M. that he did not think in words.

Bublik now took his place among these learned men. With his superb classical education, he was a great help to M., and together they delighted in reading Ovid's poems, which for M. were a portent of the future, while for Bublik they evidently spoke of the pleasures of exile already behind him.

Bublik stayed with us for several weeks and was very glad of this unexpected breathing-space. He lost his sallow convict's complexion and began to look like a Latin teacher in a provincial grammar school in the old days. But his comrades were urging that it was time to leave for the north, and his fear of the police also prompted him to get out of Moscow. It so happened that M.'s father had to go to Leningrad, and we asked Bublik to accompany him for that part of his journey. He agreed and helped the old man to pack all his stuff in his comically old-fashioned suitcase. He asked us for a kettle ("so we can get hot water at the stations") and an old blanket ("so we don't have to waste money hiring one on the train"). He carefully tied the kettle to the handle of the suitcase ("so it won't get lost").

The next day we had an indignant cable from M.'s father: Bublik had abandoned him on the platform in Leningrad and disappeared together with the suitcase. The old man was utterly mortified and demanded that the criminal be tracked down by the police and brought to trial. For this M. would have had to write a full statement and then to go to the police and demand action on the strength of his status as a writer. He did not do this, needless to say. What he couldn't understand was why Bublik had been tempted by his father's suitcase with the kettle tied to the handle, but had shown no interest in the considerable sums of money M. had asked him to bring from the State Publishing House. We were very grateful to Bublik for having behaved with such noble forbearance, and with what was left of the money from the publishing house we bought M.'s father some new clothes. But for a long time he swore and cursed, reproaching himself for having insisted that we let "that vagrant" into the house. He was not even mollified by a package from Bublik in which he returned all the old man's papers, including his memoirs about his travels—he had been writing them in German, in his abominable handwriting, and was always asking M. to read them and get them published.

It was Bublik who explained to us what is meant by the word "illusion." On that first evening, when M. and his father had insisted he stay, I was not feeling very well and went to bed early, doing my best to show what an unwelcome guest he was. Women, as is well known, dislike upsets of this kind and are quick to assume their role as guardians of domestic order—even if there's no longer any such thing. Bublik understood this and decided to make his own bed for the night. He spread several sheets of newspaper in the kitchen and called in M. "Osip Emilievich," he said, "do you know what an illusion is? Here you have one!" and with a broad gesture he pointed at the newspapers. M. could not stand the idea of his sleeping on them, and he pulled the only mattress we had out from under me. I generously added cushions and sheets and the same torn blanket that later disappeared together with the suitcase.

The whole of our apartment with its bookcase—indeed, our life in general—was an illusion of normal existence. Burying our heads in our pillows, we tried to believe that we were peacefully asleep.

49

THE READER OF ONE BOOK

In his youth M. always carefully weighed his words—it was only later that he tended toward levity. In 1919, when he was still very young, he once told me that there was no need at all to have a lot of books, and that it was best to read one book all one's life. "Do you mean the Bible?" I asked. "Why not?" he replied. I thought of the splendid graybeards of the East who read the Koran throughout their lives—perhaps they are the only representatives left of that ancient tribe who read a single book—but I could scarcely picture my light-hearted companion as one of them. "Well, I didn't mean I will, of course," he admitted, "but all the same . . ."

M. did not achieve his own ideal—such single-minded devotion is impossible in the twentieth century—but this remark he made to me in 1919 was not accidental. There are people whose every word flows from a general, integrated view of the world, and perhaps this is always true of poets, even though they vary in the range and depth of their understanding. Perhaps it is this that drives them to express themselves and serves also as the measure of their authenticity. There are, after all, people who write verse as readily as poets, and though there is always something obviously lacking in such verse, it is not easy to define. For this reason it is naïve to talk about poets not being recognized by their contemporaries. A real poet is always recognized immediately—by his enemies as well as by his well-wishers. It seems inevitable that a poet should arouse enmity. At the end of his life this happened even to Pasternak, who for so long and with such skill—the same skill with which he charmed all who met him—had avoided provoking the blind fury of the philistines. Perhaps people are angered by the poet's sense of his own rightness, by the categorical nature of his judgments ("The bluntness of our speech is no mere children's bogey," as M. said in one poem), which in turn derives from the "wholeness" of his vision. Every poet is a "disturber of sense"—that is, instead of repeating the ready-made opinions current in his time, he extracts new sense from his own understanding of the world. People who are content with generally received formulas are inevitably outraged by a new idea when it comes to them in its raw state, still unrefined, with all its rough edges. Isn't this what M. had in mind when he spoke of poetry as "raw material," saying that it was incomparably "rougher" than ordinary everyday speech? People shy away from this raw material and ask in what way the poet is better than they, or they accuse him of arrogance and a desire to lay down the law. This was the spirit in which Akhmatova, Mandelstam and Pasternak were hounded—and Mayakovski, too, until he was made into a State poet. For a long time after he was dead, people also talked in this vein of Gumilev. This is how it always is—though the captives of ready-made formulas easily forget what they were saying a week ago if they are ordered to adopt a new set of opinions. Luckily, however, poets also have their friends, and it is they who matter in the long run.

In what he said about reading only one book, M. was condemning something he loathed—namely, the mechanical absorption of incompatible things, the impaired sense of discrimination which he described in his "Fourth Prose" as "omni-tolerance" ("Look what has happened to Mother Philology—once so full-blooded . . . and now so omni-tolerant").

The first time I heard M. denounce the omnivorous approach was in 1919, in Kiev, when he criticized Briusov for his poems about different historical epochs, comparing them to gaudy Chinese lanterns. If such a comparison sprang to mind, M. concluded, it meant that Briusov was really lukewarm about everything, and that he looked at history as an idle spectator. I don't remember his exact words, but this was the sense of what he said. Later on, he and Akhmatova used to dismiss this kind of stuff as "the story of the nations down the ages." M. always knew, or at least tried to know, whether he should say "yes" or "no" to something. All his views gravitated to one pole or the other, and to this extent he was a kind of dualist, believing in the ancient doctrine of good and evil as the twin foundations of existence. Poets can never be indifferent to good and evil, and they can never say that all that exists is rational.

M.'s acutely discriminating mind very much affected the choice of what he read. In his notebooks and in "Journey to Armenia" he has something to say about the "demon of reading" in a culture that "plays havoc" with our minds. When they read, people immerse themselves in a world of make-believe, and, anxious to remember it all, they fall under the spell of the printed word. M. never tried to commit what he read to memory, but rather to check it against his own experience, always testing it in the light of his own basic idea—the one which must underlie any real personality. It is reading of the passive type which has always made it possible to propagate predigested ideas, to instill into the popular mind slick, commonplace notions. Reading of this kind does not stimulate thought, but has an effect similar to hypnosis— though it must be said that the modern age has even more powerful means for dominating people's minds.

M. always referred to reading as an "activity"—and for him it was indeed mainly the active exercise of his powers of discrimination. Some books he just glanced through, others he read with real interest (for instance, Joyce and Hemingway), but on a quite different level from all this there was his reading of really formative books with which he entered, as it were, into lasting contact and which left their mark on some part of his life, or the whole of it. The coming of a new book into his life was like a first encounter with someone destined to be a friend. His line: "I was awakened by friendship, as by a shot" refers not only to his meeting with Kuzin, but also—to a far greater degree— to his "meeting" at the same time with the German poets, of whom he wrote: "Tell me, friends, in what Valhalla did we crack nuts together, what freedom did we share, what milestones did you leave for me?" M. had known these poets before: Goethe, Hölderlin, Mörike, and the Romantics—but he had only read them, which wasn't the same as a real "meeting."

The "meeting" with them took place in Armenia—and this was not by accident. M.'s journey to Armenia, which he had looked forward to so eagerly (in "Fourth Prose" he tells of an earlier, unsuccessful attempt to get there), awoke his latent interest in what I would now loosely describe as "Naturphilosophie"—and would once have referred to even less accurately as "philosophy of culture." It took the form of lively curiosity about a small country, an outpost of Christianity in the East, which for centuries had withstood the onslaught of Islam. Perhaps in our age of crisis for the Christian consciousness M. was attracted by Armenia's steadfastness. Georgia, which history had treated much more kindly, did not have the same appeal. Our small hotel room in Erivan was soon full of books on Armenia: Strzigovski, the Armenian chronicles, Moses of Chorene, and much more. The general description of the country that impressed M. most of all was the one by Shopen, an official under Alexander I. He couldn't help comparing Shopen's keen interest in the country with the indifference of the many embittered and querulous visiting Soviet officials we saw in the hotel.

It was Armenia that took M. back to Goethe, Herder and the other German poets. If his meeting with the young biologist Kuzin—whose enthusiasm for literature and philosophy was somewhat in the Bursche tradition—had taken place in Moscow, it might have made little impact, but in Armenia he and M. hit it off at once. They first got talking in the courtyard of a mosque, where they drank Persian tea served in small glasses, and they were still talking when M. brought him back to the hotel. M. was interested in what he had to say about the application of biology to the things that concerned him, such as the perennial question as to how new forms arise. Even before he met Kuzin, M. had once written that the study of poetry would only become a science when it was approached in the same spirit as biology. This idea may well have been an echo of a theory of linguistics popular in the first decade of the century, which stressed its links with the social sciences and biology.

Kuzin was very fond of Goethe, which was also most relevant to M.'s concerns at the moment. Later on, in Moscow, when M. "met" Dante, his friendship with Kuzin and the other biologists in his circle was reduced to a mere acquaintanceship over an occasional glass of wine. M. immediately decided that nobody was more important than Dante, and regarded him as an inseparable companion ever afterward—even twice taking him to prison with him. Anticipating his arrest—as I have already said, everybody we knew did this as a matter of course—M. obtained an edition of the *Divine Comedy* in small format and always had it with him in his pocket, just in case he was arrested not at home but in the street. You could be arrested anywhere—sometimes they came for you at your place of work, and sometimes you were lured out to another place on a false pretext and no one ever heard of you again. One friend of mine used to complain that he found it difficult to lug around the heavy bag with all the things he would need in a forced-labor camp. In the end, however, he was arrested at home and so much lost his head that he forgot to take his bag with him. When M. went to Samatikha (the place where he was arrested the second time), he left his pocket Dante in Moscow and took another, rather more bulky edition. I do not know whether he managed to keep it until he reached the transit camp at Vtoraya Rechka, near Vladivostok, where he died. I somehow doubt it: in the camps under Yezhov and Stalin, nobody could give any thought to books.

It so happens that by sheer coincidence Akhmatova started reading Dante at the same time as M. When he learned this, she recited to him a passage she had learned by heart: "*Donna m'apparve nello manto verto*," and M. was moved almost to tears at hearing these lines read in her voice, which he loved so much.

Both M. and Akhmatova had the astonishing ability of somehow bridging time and space when they read the work of dead poets. By its very nature, such reading is usually anachronistic, but with them it meant entering into personal relations with the poet in question: it was a kind of conversation with someone long since departed. From the way in which he greeted his favorite poets of antiquity in the *Inferno*, M. suspected that Dante also had this ability. In his article "On the Nature of Words" he mentions Bergson's search for links between things of the same kind that are separated only by time—in the same way, he thought, one can look for friends and allies across the barriers of both time and space. This would probably have been understood by Keats, who wanted to meet all his friends, living and dead, in a tavern.

Akhmatova, in resurrecting figures from the past, was always interested in the way they lived and their relations with others. I remember how she made Shelley come alive for me—this was, as it were, her first experiment of this kind. Next began her period of communion with Pushkin. With the thoroughness of a detective or a jealous woman, she ferreted out everything about the people around him, probing their psychological motives and turning every woman he had ever so much as smiled at inside out like a glove. Akhmatova took no such burning personal interest in any living person. She could not, incidentally, stand the wives of other writers, particularly those of poets. I will never understand why she made an exception of me, but the fact is that she did—though she was unable to explain it herself. In this respect M. was the opposite of Akhmatova and almost never took any interest in the personal life of dead poets, though, despite his apparent absent-mindedness, he was extraordinarily observant and knew a great deal more about our living friends than I did. Sometimes I didn't believe him, but he always turned out to be right. But he showed no interest whatsoever in Natalia Goncharova, Paletika or Anna Grigorievna Dostoevski. Knowing his lack of curiosity about such matters, Akhmatova never raised them with him. As regards living people, he would never be drawn by her and thought people should behave as they wished. His conversation with her was always about the work of their favorite poets ("Do you remember this line?" "Did you notice that wonderful bit?") and they often read them aloud together, pointing out the passages they liked best, sharing their finds with each other. During M.'s last years they were much taken by Dante and other Italians, and—as always—by the Russian poets.

I find it more difficult to say which books influenced M. most in his earlier years. When he came to Kiev in 1919 he had Florenski's *Pillar and Affirmation of the Truth* with him—he was evidently struck by the pages about doubt, since he sometimes talked on the same lines, without, however, mentioning Florenski as his source. As a schoolboy he certainly read Herzen, and in his adolescence he was interested for a time in Vladimir Soloviev, who meant more to him (as a philosopher, not as a poet) than people imagine. The fact that Soloviev's name is never mentioned in M.'s articles has a very simple explanation: most of them were written for publication in Soviet times, when no editor would have passed a single word about Soloviev unless it was abusive. Nevertheless, there are traces of Soloviev's influence scattered throughout M.'s writings: one sees it in his Christianity (which was of a Solovievian kind), in his methods of arguing, in many recurring ideas, and even in certain individual words and expressions. For instance, in his poem to Bely, the line about "crowds of people, events, impressions" is a direct echo of Soloviev's phrase about "crowds of ideas" that occurs somewhere in his philosophical writings. M. also mentioned him in conversation and obviously had a high regard for him. When we stayed in the CEKUBU rest home on the former Trubetskoi estate where Soloviev died, M. was struck by the indifference to his memory with which Soviet scholars sat writing articles, reading newspapers or listening to the radio in the same blue study where Soloviev had once worked. At the time I knew nothing of Soloviev myself, and M. was quite indignant: "You're a barbarian, like them." For M. these professors were nothing but a horde of barbarians invading the holy places of Russian culture.

Whenever we went to these rest homes he scarcely talked with anybody and kept very much to himself. Once, in Bolshevo, he was pestered by some ladies concerned with literary and philosophical studies. They asked him to read his verse to them and assured him that they looked on him as "our poet." He told them that his verse was totally incompatible with the sort of scholarship they went in for and that they had no need to try and appease him by pretending to be so catholic in their tastes! M. let himself go like this very often—

in editorial offices, at meetings (closed ones, of course) and in private conversation—and as a result people were always saying how "impossible" he was. In fact, it was simply that he was uncompromising: what a pity this was not a quality that could be doled out to others—he had enough of it for a dozen writers. He was particularly uncompromising in his attitude toward our academic intelligentsia: "They've all sold out." At the end of the twenties and in the thirties our authorities, making no concessions to "egalitarianism," started to raise the living standard of those who had proved their usefulness. The resulting differentiation was very noticeable, and everybody was concerned to keep the material benefits he had worked so hard to earn—particularly now that the wretched poverty of the first post-revolutionary years was a thing of the past. Nobody wanted to go through that again, and a thin layer of privileged people gradually came into being—with "packets,"* country villas, and cars. They realized only later how precarious it all was: in the period of the great purges they found they could be stripped of everything in a flash, and without any explanation. But in the meantime those who had been granted a share of the cake eagerly did everything demanded of them. Once, in Voronezh, M. showed me a newspaper with a statement by Academician Bakh concerning the publication of the *Short Course*.† "Just look what he writes: 'The *Short Course* is a turning point in my life.' " "He probably only signed it," I suggested—people were generally presented with such "statements" and asked to put their signature to them. "That makes it even worse," said M.

But what, objectively speaking, could Academician Bakh have done? Could he have revised the text a little, so that his name would not appear under an obviously official document? I doubt it. Or should he have thrown out the journalist who came to collect his signature? Can one expect people to behave like this, knowing what the consequences will be? I do not think so, and I do not know how to answer these questions. The distinguishing feature of terror is that everybody is completely paralyzed and doesn't dare resist in any way.

---

* Cash emoluments secretly given to officials in addition to their regular salaries.
† *The History of the C.P.S.U.* [Communist Party of the Soviet Union]: *Short Course* was published in 1938, and until Stalin's death it was the basis of all political indoctrination. At first Stalin was proclaimed to be the author only of Chapter 4 (on Dialectical Materialism), but in the post-war years he was credited with having written the whole of it.

But a question one may ask now is: Was there a moment in our life when the intelligentsia could have held out for its independence? There probably was, but, already badly shaken and disunited before the Revolution, it was unable to defend itself during the period when it was made to surrender and change its values. Perhaps we are now witnessing an attempt to regain the values which were then abandoned. It is a slow, groping and arduous process. Whether it will be possible to preserve them during the new ordeals that face us, I shall never know.

50

TIKHONOV

Nikolai Tikhonov, the poet, always talked in loud, self-confident tones. He had great charm and, with his beguiling ways, was good at winning people over. His literary debut was greeted with joy by all those who spoke of him in such glowing terms as a man of the new generation, a wonderful story-teller—and every inch a soldier to boot. Even now many people are still captivated by him, not realizing what he later became. He was first brought to see us by Nikolai Chukovski, and M. took a liking to both of them. "See what a kind person Kornei Chukovski's son is," he said. About Tikhonov he said: "He's all right—though I have the feeling he's the sort who might come into your compartment in a train and say 'Let's see your papers, citizens!' " M. pronounced the phrase in the way it was spoken by the commanders of grain-requisition units during the Civil War when they came through trains looking for black-marketeers. Even so, M. also fell under Tikhonov's spell—but not for long. We saw Tikhonov in his true colors earlier than other people. I particularly remember the passionate conviction in his voice as he said to us: "Mandelstam will not live in Leningrad. We will not give him a room." This was after our return from Armenia, when we had nowhere to live and M. had asked the writers' organization to let him have a vacant room in the Leningrad House of Writers. When Tikhonov refused this in such extraordinary terms, I asked him whether M. would have to obtain the permission of the writers' organization to live in Leningrad in a privately rented room. He stubbornly repeated his previous statement: "Mandelstam will not live in

Leningrad." I tried to find out whether he was saying this on his own initiative or on somebody else's instructions, but I could not get any sense out of him. If it was on instructions, it was difficult to account for the depth of feeling in his voice. Whatever the truth of the matter, it boded no good, and we returned to Moscow. What Tikhonov was trying to convey by his tone of voice was more or less as follows: "We all behave in the way expected of us, and who does Mandelstam think he is to carry on like this, not caring a damn for anybody, and then come and ask us for work and a place to live! He flouts all the rules, and we have to answer for him." From his own point of view, Tikhonov was quite right. In the eyes of someone so totally devoted to the regime M. was an anomaly, a harmful emanation of the past, a person for whom there was no room in a literature where places were allotted by higher authority.

By this time we had already gained some insight into Tikhonov. Not long before our conversation about a room and the right to live in Leningrad, we happened to meet him as he was coming out of the editorial offices of *Zvezda* with his pockets full of manuscripts that he had been asked to advise on. He patted his pockets and said: "Just like at the front . . ." We knew that Tikhonov was dominated by his memories of the Civil War, but we failed to see what connection there could be between his bulging pockets and the front line. He explained that there was now a "war" going on in literature and it appeared that he was applying himself to his very modest literary activities with all the dash which had once distinguished him as a soldier. All he had to do to feel he was fulfilling his revolutionary duty was to "kill" half a dozen hack novels, of the kind with which any editor's desk is always cluttered, and simultaneously expose their ideological shortcomings. Wasn't that war? Moreover, it was war without the usual risks, and he didn't have to go out marauding to furnish his apartment with the modest attributes of Soviet comfort. What was wrong with that?

"Just like at the front" was Tikhonov's favorite saying, but we occasionally heard him use other triumphant war-cries. Once I had to go and see him in Moscow—it happened to be April 23, 1932, the day that RAPP fell, as we had learned from the newspapers in the morning. Tikhonov was staying in Herzen House—where we were living at the time—but he was in the "aristocratic" wing, with Pavlenko. The fall of RAPP had come as a complete surprise to everyone. I found Tikhonov and Pavlenko sitting over a bottle of wine, drinking toasts to "victory."

"Down with RAPP and all its works!" Tikhonov was shouting, resourceful as ever. Pavlenko, who was a much cleverer man (and a much more terrifying one), said nothing.

"But," I said to Tikhonov, "I thought you were a friend of Averbakh." It was Pavlenko, not Tikhonov, who replied to this: "The war in literature has entered a new phase."

When we were in Voronezh, M. sent Tikhonov his poem about Kashchei* and the Tomcat, hoping for some reason that he might be prompted by the lines about gold and precious stones to send some money to a penniless fellow poet in exile. Tikhonov immediately cabled that he would do everything he could. This was the last we were to hear from him. Evidently there was nothing he could do. I reminded him (through Surkov) of this cable at the beginning of the sixties, when the Poets' Library† was desperately looking for someone to write a preface to a volume of M.'s poetry which had been scheduled by the editors. One after another, the people approached had refused to write it—nobody wanted to assume any part of the responsibility for "resurrecting" Mandelstam. If Tikhonov had agreed to write it, the book would probably have come out a long time ago—it was then a propitious moment, just before the publication of Solzhenitsyn's *One Day in the Life of Ivan Denisovich*. Tikhonov would have been the ideal person to write the preface—the mere fact of his agreeing to would have protected the volume from attacks on it. Such attacks can be fatal right up to the moment of publication. Surkov tried to persuade him to do it, and reminded him of his cable promising to "do everything." But Tikhonov refused outright. "He has turned into a Chinese idol," I said to Surkov, who did not demur.

It is difficult to dismiss entirely the "young Kolia," the youth with the expansive gestures, as we had once known him. "Tikhonov and Lugovskoi," Akhmatova once said to me, "have never done a thing to help anyone, but, all the same, they are a little better than the rest." She also told me how in 1937 she had run into Tikhonov in Leningrad and they had walked along one of the embankments for half an hour or so. Tikhonov kept complaining about how terrible the times were: "He said what we were all saying"—this is the reason Akhmatova still has a soft spot for him. But she was also struck by the way he said it. When

---

* A figure in Russian folklore.
† Famous series of poetry editions, founded by Maxim Gorki.

she came home, she could not remember a single word of what he had actually said about the terror: everything had been so skillfully camouflaged that even in talking with Akhmatova he had managed not to compromise himself. All he did was to complain in general terms, without saying a word out of place: no one could say that he wasn't highly disciplined! I do not think he can be put in the same category as Lugovskoi, who was a completely different type—he had been scared stiff at the front, never involved himself in the "literary war," and when he was drunk he could say all kinds of odd things. Tikhonov, on the other hand, has always been true to himself and the cause he serves. The last of the Mohicans will come to his funeral to pay military honors to this literary warrior who never forgot that the magazine *Zvezda* was also part of the front line.

They say that Tikhonov's wife used to make toys out of papier-mâché. Tikhonov himself is a papier-mâché figure—scarcely a good repository for values of any kind. I doubt whether he had any to change when he first appeared on the scene at the beginning of the twenties as one of the best representatives of the "new era."

51

THE BOOKCASE

More than a quarter of a century ago, during the May Day celebrations of 1938, I returned to Moscow from Samatikha, a rest home near Murom, where M. had been arrested. In the hope of helping him to survive while his fate was decided, I took a few books from our bookcase, sold them in a secondhand bookstore and spent the proceeds on the first and only food package I was able to buy for him. It was returned "because of the death of the addressee." I had always wanted to preserve some of these books which had once helped us create the illusion of an untroubled existence. Apart from this, they also reflected M.'s interests in the thirties. At the time, in order to keep a record of them, I compiled a rough list of all the books I had sold and gave it to Khardzhiev. It was, of course, incomplete: given my state of mind, it could hardly be otherwise. The remainder of the books (that is, those the secondhand bookstore wouldn't take) are now with my brother, Evgeni—I still have no place to put them myself.

We began to buy books when I got my job in the editorial office of *For a Communist Education,* where every month I was given a free "voucher for the acquisition of books"—this was by way of encouraging us to improve our minds. "Get something fundamental," Chechanovski said to me, handing me my first voucher. He particularly recommended the six-volume edition of Lenin and the collected edition of Stalin that was just beginning to come out then. All my friends already had the "classics of Marxism-Leninism" on their bookshelves—they were by now a standard feature of any intellectual's apartment. Our mentors were very insistent about this. Stalin genuinely believed that if the intellectuals read all these works properly, they would at once be convinced by their irresistible logic and give up all their idealistic preconceptions. Marxist literature has never been in such demand as it was then. The pink-cheeked Chekist who treated us to hard candy from a tin box during the search of our apartment in 1934 was quite taken aback by the absence of Marxist literature in our bookcase. "But where do you keep your Marxist classics?" he asked me. M. overheard him and whispered to me: "This is the first time he's arrested anybody who doesn't have Marx."

In general, we had no "standard editions" or sets of collected works—though such things were always being urged on us. Benedikt Livshitz did, indeed, succeed in persuading M. to buy a Larousse in several volumes, saying that it was "quite essential for a translator." This was in the mid-twenties, when M. had no option but to try and make his living by translating. These fat volumes of Larousse lay untouched, still tied together with string, until they were eventually sold back to the secondhand bookstore after M. had failed to become a translator. Apart from his indifference to standard editions of the classics, he had no interest at all in collecting books. He had no need of "rare editions," nor was he ever concerned to have a complete set of anything. All he needed were those books with which he had already established his own intimate relationship. There were other books he may have valued but was easily able to do without. For instance, he let Katayev take away his copy of Pasternak's *My Sister Life* shortly after it had appeared. "What I need I can remember—he needs it more than I do," M. explained.

M. was rarely enthusiastic about my finds in the bookstores. Once I brought along in triumph a copy of Ivanov's *Cor Ardens* which I had found in a pile of secondhand rubbish, but M. was quite indifferent to it: "Why the same things again?" (This was at a time when I was trying to restore items lost from my own bookcase.) This was something belonging to a past phase, and M. did not want to return to it. On the other hand, he was very pleased with a volume of Bürger—"You always know what I want." (But this was untrue—apart from Bürger, he turned down all my offerings!)

Among the books we had in the thirties there were no twentieth-century poets except Annenski, the two Acmeists, Gumilev and Akhmatova, and a few miscellaneous things. M. had gone through the poetry of the twentieth century in 1922 when two young men who wanted to try their luck as private publishers asked him to compile an anthology of Russian verse from the Symbolists "to the present day." It started with Konevskoi and Dobroliubov and ended with Boris Lapin. As usual, M. looked for the particularly felicitous lines: Dobroliubov's "speaking eagles," Balmont's "Song of an Arab Whose Name is Naught," Komarovski's "On the squares the only word is *daki*," Borodayevski's "Swifts" and Lozina-Lozinski's "Chess-players." He very much liked two or three poems by Boris Lapin: one about "stars in the windows of the Cheka," and another beginning: "As though nibbling the fingers of asters, Tril-Tral kissed the flowers." The great stumbling-block was Briusov. M. could find nothing suitable, but it was impossible to leave him out. He looked much bigger to us in those days than he does now—proportions are always distorted in close-up. Briusov had to be well represented in the volume, and M. was driven frantic as he read him in search of something appropriate. " 'Hot as a flame you must be, and sharp as a sword'—what does *that* mean?" he asked with exasperation. And when he came to the poem in which Dante's cheeks are singed by the flames of hell, he rushed to the two publishers, saying he would have to give up. To make matters worse, they were always bringing him piles of new things by Briusov. But they both were very well-behaved boys, and after a little argument they would put the stuff back in their pockets and keep it for their own private delectation. M. often remembered them in later years—they seemed like angels to him compared with any Soviet editor. The anthology was eventually forbidden by the censor because M. had not included any of the "proletarian" poets who were already being sponsored by the State. Their names are now totally forgotten, and I do not remember which ones it was proposed to include. The censor also insisted on the removal of a great many poems he condemned as "bourgeois and alien from a class point of view." All that remains from this work are a few page proofs. Of all the things commissioned from M., it was the one he thought made the most sense—it is a good idea for a young poet to put together his own anthology of verse in his native language.

"What does it mean?" was M.'s usual question about verse that irritated him. This was what he once asked about Mayakovski's celebrated line: "Our god is speed, our heart—a drum." I had always liked this jingle until I began to ponder its meaning. But on the whole M. thought well of Mayakovski and told me how they had once made friends in Petersburg, only to be dragged apart because it was "not done" for poets of rival schools to associate with each other. There is a photograph from this period showing M. with Mayakovski, Livshitz and Kornei Chukovski. It was published in some magazine or other with the intention of showing what cretins were now trying to pass themselves off as writers. It should be said, by the way, that the new attitude toward poetry which made itself felt so clearly by the beginning of the First World War, or by the time of the Revolution, and the fact that people began to read it again, was something for which we have to thank the Symbolists and the enormous work they did in re-educating the public taste. I was born at the beginning of the century and hence belong to the generation schooled by them. It was in the circles dominated by them—and they grew all the time—that Tolstoi and particularly Dostoevski were seen in a new light, Pushkin was first properly studied, Baratynski, Tiutchev, Fet and many others were revived. The Russian realist tradition, with its emphasis on "social" themes, was losing its following among the public, but it was still firmly entrenched in the literary establishment. It was these people who made war on everything done by the Symbolists and the cultural revival which explained their success—though the persons of the Symbolists themselves were already immune to attack even from this quarter. For a long time it appeared as though the tradition of the "Silver Age," as it is called, had been completely stamped out. But at the moment there are some faint gleams of it again. What will become of them? And where are we headed now, I wonder?

In the thirties M. showed no further interest in the twentieth-century Russian poets, and kept mainly the nineteenth-century ones on his shelves. He liked first editions of a poet's work. This does not contradict what I said about his lack of interest in collecting rare volumes—it was simply that a first edition always betrays the head of the poet himself and gives the best idea of how he appraised, selected and arranged his own work. We had such first editions of Derzhavin, Yazykov, Zhukovski, Baratynski, Fet, Polonski and others. Reading the nineteenth-century poets, M. was, as usual, on the look-out for things that struck him as particularly successful. He liked Mei's "Woman of Pompei," Sluchevski's "Yaroslavna" and "Execution in Geneva" (where the lines about the old woman sound almost like Annenski) and Polezhayev's poem about the gypsy woman. I have forgotten what he liked in Apollon Grigoriev, whom he also had in a first edition acquired by chance (perhaps it was "Hymns," which appeared in only fifty copies). He liked a large number of Fet's poems, among them "The Snake." In these preferences he was no doubt subconsciously influenced by the tastes of his first teacher, Vladimir Vasilievich Gippius, about whom he talks in *The Noise of Time*. Akhmatova's favorite line from Fet was: "He who made this rose's whorls / wished to drive me mad." They were always exchanging the lines they liked best, making a gift of them to each other. With Maikov it was the same as with Briusov—M. could find nothing to his taste. The corner of the bookcase reserved for the Russian poets was being constantly added to, but there would never be a publisher for M.'s anthology of them.

The second-largest section in the bookcase was devoted to the Italians: apart from Dante, M. also had Ariosto, Tasso, Petrarch—both in the original and in German prose translations. At first, before he had made himself at home in Italian, M. sometimes turned to these and other translations. The only Russian translation he had any regard for was one published in the late 1900's (Gorbov's, I think). He could not stand verse translations—it was all too rare that they were successful enough to become part of literature (as Gnedich's have). All these editions of the Italian classics were very modest, with a bare minimum of learned notes (e.g., the Oxford edition of 1904). Of course, we would have bought newer editions, but even now it is impossible to get hold of them. Of the Italian prose writers I remember Vasari, Boccaccio and Vico—but there were probably others as well.

There were also quite a lot of Latin poets: Ovid, Horace, Tibullus, Catullus. . . . We nearly always bought them with German translations—the Germans are better at this than the French.

M. had taken up the Germans again in Armenia, and in the thirties he bought a great many of them: Goethe, the Romantics, Bürger,

Lenau, Eichendorff and both Kleists. He also acquired Klopstock (because—as he said—"he sounds like an organ"), Herder and others. Then, he had Mörike and Hölderlin and also one or two of the poets who wrote in Middle High German. He had far fewer French poets. From earlier days he had kept Chénier, Barbier and the perennial Villon. In the thirties he again bought Verlaine, Baudelaire and Rimbaud. In his youth he had once tried to translate Mallarmé—on the advice of Annenski, who said translating was good practice—but nothing came of it. M. told me that Mallarmé was not serious and also that Gumilev and Georgi Ivanov used to make fun of one line of his translation which sounded ambiguous in Russian.

M. had brought with him from Leningrad all the books in Old French from his student days—he had needed them in 1922 when some translations of Old French epics were commissioned from him. Sasha Morozov has recently discovered these versions in some archive or other: the eleventh-century "Lament of St. Alexis" and "Aliscans" (of the Guillaume d'Orange cycle). Both are free translations, and M. has brought out something in them that speaks of his own destiny: in the "Lament of St. Alexis" it is the vow of poverty, and in "Aliscans" he appears to be making a solemn oath never to hide in order to save his own life.

M. was always extremely careless with manuscripts and never kept anything ("it will be kept by those who need it") and trusted to archives and editors. He gave his only copy of these translations from the Old French to the magazine *Rossia* and didn't allow me to make a copy. But, apart from his usual carelessness, there was another reason here: he was afraid of these poems, just as he was of those couplets in which he speaks of a woman's coming doom. He hid from verse like this, never mentioning it or keeping it at home: it was just like a child closing its eyes and thinking it cannot be seen, or a bird hiding its head under its wing. There was nothing all that prophetic about this work—how could our future have worked out otherwise, given the world in which we lived? The only piece of good fortune is that I was somehow able to survive and preserve M.'s work, and that Akhmatova too managed to hold out. Isn't that miracle enough?

As regards other Russian books, M. eagerly bought the work of thinkers, such as Chaadayev and the Slavophiles. On the other hand, he clearly had no time for German philosophy. Once he bought a volume of Kant, sniffed at it and said: "Nadia, this isn't for us," and threw it behind the other books, out of harm's way. But he felt very close to the Russians. We often heard stories about how Berdiayev had matured in emigration, and M. was always asking about him and trying to get his books, but this became more and more difficult—and dangerous—all the time. We lived cut off like this from the modern world, with nothing but dry crusts for our sustenance. All we had was the past, and we lived off it as best we could.

In the short period from 1930 to his arrest in 1934, M. did a lot of work on Old Russian literature. He bought the various editions of the *Chronicles*, the *Song of Igor's Campaign* (which he had always loved very much and knew by heart), some early prose tales (povesti) and also Russian and Slavic songs as gathered by Kireyevski, Rybnikov and others. He eagerly snatched up everything Old Russian—and was as familiar with Avvakum as with the unfortunate princess who was married off to the brother of the Czar's bride. He also had Kliuchevski on his shelves—including early works, such as *Tales of Foreigners*—and the historical archives which have been published here on a fairly large scale: documents relating to the Pugachev uprising, the records of the interrogation of the Decembrists and of the members of the "People's Will." Akhmatova also had a brief period of interest in the latter kind of material—during the Yezhov terror she read scarcely anything but *Exile and Forced Labor*.[*] I must say that the Tenishev school[†] gave an excellent grounding in Old Russian language and literature, and, teaching in Soviet teacher-training colleges, I often thought how catastrophic the destruction of the old secondary-school system had been. I doubt whether M. or I would ever have been able to get through a Soviet school—if we had, we would certainly not have equipped ourselves for life with the straightforward and unforced learning given us by the prerevolutionary Russian grammar school.

Later interests represented in M.'s bookcase were the Armenian chronicles (he managed to buy a secondhand copy of Moses of Chorene among other things) and biology: he was lucky enough to be able to buy Linnaeus, Buffon, Pallas and Lamarck, as well as Darwin (*The Voyage of the Beagle*) and some of the philosophers, such as Driesch, who take biology as their starting point.

Despite his interest in the philosophy of culture and biology, M.

---

[*] *Ssylka i katorga*, a periodical on Czarist political prisoners, closed down in 1935.
[†] The Tenishev Commercial School, in St. Petersburg, attended by Mandelstam.

could not stomach Hegel (any more than Kant), and his enthusiasm for Marx had not outlasted his school years. Just before his arrest in 1934 he had declined Engels' *Dialectic of Nature* when it was offered to him as a gift by Lezhnev, the former editor of *Rossia*, to which M. had once contributed. Lezhnev was astonished by M.'s nerve in refusing it. It was Lezhnev who had asked M. to write *The Noise of Time* for *Rossia*, but then turned it down after reading it—he had expected a totally different kind of childhood story, such as he himself was later to write. His was the story of a Jewish boy from the shtetl who discovers Marxism. He was lucky with his book. At first nobody wanted to publish it—though it was probably no worse then others of its kind—but then it was read and approved by Stalin. Stalin even tried to phone Lezhnev to tell him, but Lezhnev was not at home at the moment Stalin called. When he learned what had happened, Lezhnev sat by his phone for a whole week, hoping that Stalin might ring back. But miracles, as we know, are not repeated. A week later he was informed that there would be no further telephone call, but that orders had been given for his book to be published (it was already being printed), that he had been made a member of the Party on Stalin's personal recommendation and appointed editor of *Pravda's* literary section. In this way Lezhnev, hitherto a nobody who could always be trampled underfoot as a former private publisher, was suddenly raised to the greatest heights and almost went crazy from joy and emotion. Of all the Haroun al Rashid miracles, this, incidentally, turned out to be the most enduring: Lezhnev kept his *Pravda* post, or an equivalent one, right up to his death.

On hearing all this, Lezhnev at last left his telephone and rushed off to the barber—his beard had grown considerably during the week of waiting. Next he called on us to present us with *The Dialectic of Nature* and to tell us about the great change that Marxism had brought into his life. None of this had ever entered his head in the days when he was editor of *Rossia*. From what he said, it appeared that he had read some newly discovered works by Engels, notably *The Dialectic of Nature,* and seen the light. He had even gone into a bookshop just now and bought a copy for us, because he hoped it would help M. to see the light as well. Lezhnev was an exceptionally sincere and well-meaning person. I was even a little envious of him at that moment—a genuine conversion to the true faith, which suddenly puts an end to all your troubles and at the same time starts bringing in a regular income, must be a remarkably agreeable thing.

M. padded around the room in his slippers, whistling to himself and occasionally glancing at Lezhnev as the book was urged on him. He was trying to turn it down as gracefully as possible, but Lezhnev kept insisting, and finally M. said, pointing at me: "No, she has read it and says I shouldn't." Lezhnev just gasped: How could anybody entrust his choice of reading on such crucial ideological questions to his wife? "Why not?" M. said. "She knows better than me, she always knows what I should read." Lezhnev departed in a huff, and when we ran into each other years later in Tashkent—we were both evacuated there during the war—he just cut me dead. He probably regarded me as M.'s evil genius—though, to give him his due, he does not seem to have denounced me to the authorities. I do not know how he behaved on *Pravda*—probably like the rest of them—but to me he always seemed a decent and honest person. I am even prepared to believe that his eyes really were opened by reading *The Dialectic of Nature*—it was just about his level.

By hiding behind my back M. had fended off Lezhnev's gift, so we had no Marxist literature on our shelves. Incidentally, long before Lezhnev had offered him *The Dialectic of Nature*, it had been shown to M. by his biologist friends, who complained about how much it complicated their lives. As regards the fact that Lezhnev didn't shave for a whole week while waiting for Stalin to call back—there is nothing surprising about it: any Soviet citizen would have done the same, even at the risk of losing his job for absenteeism.

But if we had no Marxist literature, we had a few art books, and some illustrated works about architecture, including Rodin on French Gothic. In 1937 someone sent us several books put out by museums in Italy. M. was overjoyed, but his pleasure was spoiled by Kostyrev, who told him to beware of any contact with imperialist countries because they were all spies there: "They must have had a purpose in sending you these things!"

On the bottom shelf M. kept the books from his childhood days: Pushkin, Lermontov, Gogol, the *Iliad*—they are described in *The Noise of Time* and happened to have been saved by M.'s father. Most of them later perished in Kalinin when I was fleeing from the Germans. The way we have scurried to and fro in the twentieth century, trapped between Hitler and Stalin!

There were many more books I cannot remember: Winckelmann, for example, a magnificent Rosary, and a great deal else besides. The secondhand book dealers knew how to tempt us. They once offered M. a very amusing *Danse Macabre*, but it was too expensive and we couldn't buy it. "Very well," said the old bookseller, "it will go to Leonov—he takes everything over fifty roubles." I have never met Leonov and do not know whether this piece of gossip was true—it must remain on the conscience of those who launched it.

52

OUR LITERATURE

In the forties the Marxism-Leninism study room of the Tashkent University was looked after by a little old woman with close-cropped hair who walked with a crutch. The story was that she had been knocked down by a berserk cyclist and that the doctors had had to amputate her leg because of gangrene—though Alisa Usov swore that it had been done on purpose because everybody was fed up with her. The old woman once did me a great service, and I cannot believe Alisa's malicious explanation.

After her accident the old woman, who had been a member of the Party since 1905 and until recently a high official, had little choice but to find this niche for herself in the university. Nobody took her very seriously, but they were rather afraid of her all the same. She had as much idea of what was going on around her as a blind puppy, but, faithful to the sacred traditions of the past, she was always prepared to make a fuss whenever she thought it was necessary. It was difficult to imagine how she had survived during the Yezhov terror—probably she was simply overlooked because she spent that year in the hospital—though if they had remembered her, they would not have hesitated to come into the ward to arrest her. There were such cases. Once when I was standing in line at the Butyrki jail with other people whose names began with M, a woman who had the same name as I told me that her husband, an old man of seventy (could he have been the lawyer Mandelstam?), had been arrested in the Botkin hospital, where he was being treated for heart trouble. As for our one-legged old woman, she was such an anachronism, with her Party membership going back so far, that she was in all probability simply forgotten during that fateful time.

I was preparing for my doctor's degree in philosophy (for which I had to do an exam) and sitting in the Marxism study room at a table piled with books. They were all required reading for the written examination, and I was quickly going through them. The old lady came into the room and could scarcely believe her eyes: somebody sitting there reading in the original the literature that had played such an enormous part in her life! She no doubt thought back to her youth in the underground and the thrill that went through her when she first opened the hallowed *Das Kapital.*

"Ah, if only all the graduate students read the way you do!" she said. "The only thing they ever want from me is the Dictionary."*

I was embarrassed by the undeserved compliment: I was myself not innocent of using the Dictionary in preparing for exams.

"No, no," she continued, "you don't know them. All they use are their lecture notes and the Dictionary, nothing else." She let me take out all the books I had in front of me and went around to see all my examiners, telling them how good I was: "You don't know what the young are like. They want it all cut and dried, in case they trip up and fail the exam. We older people are not used to this. But I told them how you are reading—not like their other graduate students." What she said about the other students was her most effective argument. Afraid of antagonizing the difficult old lady, my examiners hesitated to fail me, though it would have been the easiest thing in the world: I had not mastered the art of bandying question-and-answer, like a tennis ball, with the lecturers, and I was quite capable of mixing up the Party Congresses. Furthermore, there was already whispering in the corridors that I was not to be trusted and should be examined as strictly as possible. Admittedly, this was not in obedience to instructions "from above"—it was rather "initiative from below" on the part of the young instructors who didn't want to pass me, thus admitting an outsider into the privileged caste of persons qualified to teach in the universities and entitled to be paid accordingly. It has to be said that they had an excellent flair: they could unerringly spot an "outsider," however much he avoided their gaze. In a word, the old woman saved me—and she knew what she was doing. She knew how hard it was for a helpless person to keep afloat among these younger people with all their intrigues and jealousies. Apart from this, she must have felt instinctively that we had something in common—the fact that in those years nobody was read-

---

* I.e., the standard Soviet *Philosophical Dictionary,* a compendium of potted ideology.

ing either my literature or hers. Both had gone out of use, and we both hoped that they would come back again. We both believed that our respective values were indestructible—though mine had now gone "underground," while the underground literature she had read in her youth had been canonized by the new State. Both her literature and mine had lost its readers.

About twenty years have gone by since then. The old woman must be long since dead, but we still have others who think the same way—people of the twenties who stubbornly hope that the young will come to their senses and seek the answer to all questions in the dialectical ABC of those days. They hope that this ABC was abandoned only because it was replaced by the "Fourth Chapter."* There are also younger people, still under sixty, who dream of a restoration of the "Fourth Chapter" and of everything that went with it. They are fairly isolated, but they find comfort in the doctrine of thesis, antithesis and synthesis. They hope they may last out till a new "synthesis" which will allow them to come into their own again with a vengeance. Then, finally, there are some young people who remember the glorious days of their now retired fathers. "The aim does not justify the means," a student once said in a class I was teaching. "I think it does," he was primly contradicted by a pretty girl student who lived in a good apartment and enjoyed all the amenities that a provincial town can provide for a privileged citizen: clinics, rest homes and exclusive stores. The father of this girl had been retired after the Twentieth Congress and had chosen to settle in the town where I was then teaching. She was the only student in my class who knew her own mind. She was the only one, for instance, who had read Solzhenitsyn, and she vigorously denounced the publication of such things. The old woman who looked after the Marxist literature was upset because research students didn't read *Das Kapital,* but this girl was interested only in the "Fourth Chapter" and the maintenance of "order." Both hoped for a restoration of the past.

For my part, knowing that permanent ideas are formed in youth and are rarely revised in later life, I can only watch with hope and bated breath as more and more people read poetry—and the "Fourth Prose." Between people like myself and those who stand on the other side, there is a clear division: we are thesis and antithesis. I do not expect to see a synthesis, but I would love to know whom the future belongs to.

---

* The chapter on Dialectical Materialism in Stalin's *Short Course.*

53

ITALY

To the question: "What is Acmeism?" M. once replied: "Nostalgia for world culture." This was said in the thirties, either in the Press House in Leningrad or at the lecture he gave to the Voronezh branch of the Union of Writers—on the same occasion when he also declared that he would disown neither the living nor the dead. Shortly after this he wrote: "And bright nostalgia does not let me leave the still young Voronezh hills for those of all mankind so bright in Tuscany."

Perhaps these lines give a better idea than anything else of his attitude toward Italy and the Mediterranean. I happen to have seen a note by Gleb Struve in which he wonders whether M. ever visited Italy and lists all the "Italian themes," as he calls them, in M.'s verse. M. in fact went to Italy twice, in the days when he was a student at Heidelberg and the Sorbonne. But these long trips, short and superficial (they only lasted a few weeks), left him with a feeling of frustration. ("It's as though I'd never been there," he said once.) But this is not important. The main thing is what Italy, the land "for all mankind," or, rather, the Mediterranean as a whole, meant to M. In a youthful article about Chaadayev he wrote: "One cannot launch a new history—the idea is altogether unthinkable—there would not be the continuity and tradition. Tradition cannot be contrived or learned. In its absence one has, at the best, not history but 'progress'—the mechanical movement of a clock hand, not the sacred succession of interlinked events." These words refer to Chaadayev, but the idea behind them was certainly close to M.'s own way of thinking as well. The Mediterranean was for him a holy land where history had begun, and which by a process of continuity had given Christian culture to the world. I do not quite understand a gibe of M.'s in "Journey to Armenia" which so much upset all the Marxists such as Chechanovski: "A plant is an event, an occurrence, an arrow, not a boring 'development' with a beard." For him, the concept of "development" was evidently firmly associated with the positivists—Comte, Stuart Mill and others, read and revered by people of his mother's generation, who had prepared the way for Marxism. At any event, M. distinguished between two types of phenomena—one, as it were, positive and the other negative. Positive phenomena included such things as thunderstorms, events, precipitation of crystals—these were words that M. applied to history, art and even the formation of human character. "Negative" were all varieties of mechanical movement: the motion of a clock's hands, "development," progress. To these one could add the progression of images on a cinema screen which in "Conversation About Dante" he compared to the "metamorphosis of a tapeworm." This was a dig at the specious glitter of the then fashionable Eisenstein with his mechanical splendors. Motion of this kind was tantamount, in M.'s view, to immobility, to Buddhism as understood by Vladimir Soloviev, to the "movement of Barbarian carts." This is why he described the Moscow of his day as "Buddhist" in the line: "I have returned, or rather been returned against my will to Buddhist Moscow." During the conversations that we were always having about the new life and the coming millennium of uninterrupted progress, M. always got furious and began to argue. In all such talk he suspected the old "Slav dream of halting history." I do not know to what extent M. retained any faith in the purposefulness of the historical process—it has not been easy in the first half of the twentieth century—but he certainly did not see its purpose in the attainment of universal happiness. His attitude here was the same as toward personal happiness ("Why do you think you should be happy?"). The concept of happiness for all seemed to him the most bourgeois thing in the whole intellectual baggage inherited from the nineteenth century.

Another thing that constantly provoked argument was the question of continuity, which he sought everywhere—in history, culture and art. Here, too, he found the analogy with a clock's hands useful: a clock is wound up and movement begins from nothing, but an "event" is inconceivable without continuity.

M. was distinguished by a rather comic and childish literalmindedness: once he had found this analogy between a clock hand and "drab infinity," he took a dislike to clocks and watches, always refusing to have one. "What do I need a watch for?" he used to say. "I can always tell the time without one." As is generally the case with townspeople (and he was one to the marrow of his bones), his sense of time was indeed quite remarkable and he was never wrong by more than a few minutes. The only sort of clock he would tolerate in the apartment, when I insisted very much, was a Swiss clock—the pendulum, the weight at the end of a chain and the picture on its face made the idea of a mechanical timepiece more bearable. He also thought it was something that went with a kitchen—his favorite room in any apartment, though we never had a proper one of our own. He was also fond of hourglasses and wanted to buy one for our bathroom—but we had a bathroom for such a short time before his arrest that we never got around to doing this. In a poem he wrote for children he refers to the hands of a clock, but they are compared to a pair of mustaches running around a plate—there are faces as flat as plates.

M. had no dislike at all for machines—he was interested in them, liked the way they worked, and was always glad to talk with engineers—though he was unhappy that none of them read him. In those years young technologists were attracted to LEF—in so far as they had any interest in literature at all. Some of them read Pasternak, who came to them via LEF. Today the situation is different and, moreover, the technologists are no longer felt to be the spokesmen of their age, or the ones most in touch with modern life. The more intelligent among them are even a little embarrassed at having become technocrats. The myth about the greatness of industry and its decisive role in history, about "historical necessity" and the idea of a superstructure totally dependent on the "basis," have now almost faded away. The era of social determinism seems, indeed, to be coming to an end, but it has left behind another myth about the supposed incompatibility between "civilization" and "culture." How can anyone say that the sickness of our culture is due only to the fact that we now have more sophisticated tools than a hundred years ago?

Blok already spoke about "civilization" overlaying true "culture" and compared our era to that of the fall of Rome. In Blok's view, our individualistic civilization, devoid of "wholeness," had collapsed together with humanism and its ethical values. It would be replaced by barbaric masses, untouched by "civilization," who had preserved the "spirit of music" and would bring a new culture with them. It is interesting that Blok saw these masses as Germanic and Slavic—as though he could already foresee fascism in 1918. Blok's idea was similar to Spengler's. Despite his nominal Christianity and his belief in the "spirit of music," Blok remained in essence a positivist: for him personality was a mark not of Christian culture but only of humanism (the same applied to ethical values and humane behavior). M. was not for a moment taken in by Spengler's theories. After reading *The Decline of the West,* he said to me quite casually that Spengler's analogies are in all probability not applicable to Christian culture. M. never shared the feeling of the approaching end of the world that was one of the main sources of Blok's pessimism. By "culture," M. understood the idea underlying the historical process, and he thought of history as a testing-ground for both good and evil.

His conviction that culture, like grace, is bestowed by a process of continuity led M. to see the Mediterranean as a "holy land." This explains the constant references to Rome and Italy in his verse. Rome is man's place in the universe, and his every footstep there resounds like a deed. M. also included the Crimea and the Caucasus in the Mediterranean world. In his poem about Ariosto he gave expression to his dream of uniting them: "Into one broad and brotherly blue we shall merge your azure and our Black sea."

"The land by which the first people learned" was the only part of the world to which M. felt drawn to go on pilgrimage. With all his love of travel, he flatly turned down chances to make trips to the central Asian or far eastern parts of the country. He was attracted only by the Crimea and the Caucasus. The ancient link between these areas (particularly Armenia) with Greece and Rome seemed to him a token of the unity of world (or, rather, European) culture. Most of the Soviet writers who traveled to the borderlands—something that was very popular—chose the Muslim areas. M. thought this preference for the Muslim world was not accidental—the people of our times were less suited by Christianity with its doctrine of free will and the inherent value of the person than by Islam with its determinism, the submerging of the individual in the army of the faithful, and the formalized design of an architecture which made man feel insignificant.

M., to whom the Muslim world was alien ("and with shame and pain she turned away from the bearded cities of the East"), was more concerned with the outward signs of Hellenic and Christian tradition. He fell in love with Feodosia in the Crimea not only for its unusual landscape, but also because of its name, the remains of its Genoese fortress, and for its port with the Mediterranean ships. M. once said to Khardzhiev that he regarded himself as the last Christian-Hellenic poet in Russia. The word "last" in that remark was the only time he ever betrayed any fear that culture itself might be coming to an end. . . . I think he would have liked to be buried in the Crimea, not in the land of his exile, near Vladivostok.

One can understand very well why poetry returned to him in the Caucasus. Somewhere he says that he could work when he felt the "quivering of Colchis"* in his breast—that is, when he felt he was in communion with the world of culture and history. Only in such conditions could his "selfless song" come to him. He tried very hard and for a long time to get to Armenia, preferring it—probably as a Christian outpost in the East—even to Georgia, though he often spoke of the importance of Georgia in Russian poetry.

Like all the good things in our life, the trip to Armenia was eventually arranged by Bukharin. He had first tried to send us there at the end of the twenties, when the Armenian People's Commissar for Education was Mravian. He had invited M. to Erivan University to give a course of lectures and a seminar. Nothing came of this—partly because of Mravian's sudden death, and partly because M. was terrified to death at the thought of giving lectures. He had never imagined himself in the role of a teacher, and he was aware that he had no systematic knowledge. When he was asked in 1931 by Bukharin's secretary Korotkova (the "squirrel" of the "Fourth Prose") where we wanted to go and M. said: "To Armenia," she sighed and, looking earnestly at him, replied: "Still to Armenia? Well, it must be serious, then." M. had good reason to write about Korotkova in "Fourth Prose"—she was kind and attentive in a way not characteristic of our institutions. By way of contrast I remember the "secretary of inhuman beauty" in some dramatic fragments written by Akhmatova but then destroyed in a fit of terror (which was all too well justified). The secretary portrayed by Akhmatova keeps repeating a phrase which we heard all the time wherever we went: "There are many of you and only one of me." This phrase summed up the style of the era as seen at the level of the humblest official.

The editor of the American collection of M.'s work, Filippov, with the usual perspicacity of editors, says that M. went to Armenia to get away from the Five Year Plans. This is cheap political speculation. In the borderlands industrialization was far more hectic than in the central areas, and in any case M. had nothing at all against it. Why should he have been put out by the planned organization of the economy? As if that mattered! What mattered was that, as M. saw them, by virtue of their links between the Black Sea and the Mediterranean, the Crimea, Georgia and Armenia were part of world culture. But the measure of all things was Italy. It was not for nothing that he chose Dante as the

---

* Colchis: ancient Greek name for the Caucasus.

starting point for a discussion of his own poetics: for M., Dante was the source of all European poetry, and the measure of poetic "rightness." In the notes he made for "Conversation About Dante" there are several references to the "Italian inoculation" received by the Russian poets. These notes did not get into the final text, probably because M. did not like to be too open in revealing the process by which he arrived at his ideas. In the Kremlin cathedrals he was struck by their Italian quality ("the five-headed Moscow cathedrals with their Italian and Russian soul" and "the gentle Assumption—Florence in Moscow"). While looking at Rublev's "Trinity," he remarked that Rublev must have known some Italian artists—which was what distinguished him from the other ikon painters of his day. In the short narrative about Goethe's life which he did for the radio in Voronezh, M. selected episodes he thought were characteristic of the life of any poet, and he ended it by talking about Goethe's Italian journey—this kind of pilgrimage to the holy places of European culture seemed to him an essential and crucial event in the life of any artist.

Why then, dissatisfied as he was by his trips to Italy as a student, did M. let slip a chance to go abroad in the twenties? Bukharin, still all-powerful, had given him a note of recommendation, and so had Voronski. With these he could have had a passport for the asking. But they lay untouched in my trunk right until the house search in 1934, when they were taken away, together with the manuscripts of M.'s poems, and presumably added to his file in the Lubianka.

In my younger days I did not always fully understand the connection between M.'s actions and what he wrote. At the moment much is clearer to me than it was in those days when he was alive and all our time and thoughts were taken up by daily squabbles, mutual banter and argument. I have now found the reason for his renunciation of a second journey to Europe in his article on Chaadayev, where he writes that Chaadayev, having visited the West, "the historical world," nevertheless returned to Russia. The fact that he found his way home again was very much to his credit in M.'s eyes. With the same naïve and stubborn consistency because of which he refused to have a watch, he thought of Chaadayev's return to Russia and himself decided to renounce the chance of revisiting Europe. M. always gave literal application to his ideas, but, fearing that I might make fun of him, he did not always reveal his train of thought to me. But I understood well enough that the key to his behavior was to be found in his verse and prose, or, rather, that some things in his writings had the force of vows for him.

Such was the vow of poverty in the "Lament of St. Alexis," the promise to continue the struggle, however dangerous and difficult, in "Aliscans," and the renunciation of Europe in the article about Chaadayev. This article was written in his early youth, but his view of the world had already formed, and he was true to the vows he took then until his death.

54

THE SOCIAL STRUCTURE

At the beginning of the thirties M. once said to me: "You know, if ever there was a golden age, it was the nineteenth century. Only we didn't know."

We really didn't know and understand many things—and we paid a heavy price for our ignorance. Why do people always have to pay so dearly for their attempts to build the perfect society? Recently I heard someone say: "It is well known that everybody who has ever tried to make people happy only brought total disaster on them." This was said by a young man who does not want to see any changes now, in case they only bring new misfortune on him and others. There are large numbers of people like him nowadays—among the more or less well-off, needless to say. They are mostly young specialists and scientists whose services are needed by the State. They live in inherited apartments of two (or even three or four) rooms, or they can expect to get one from the organization in which they work. They are horrified at what their fathers have wrought, but they are even more horrified by the thought of change. Their ideal is to pass their lives quietly working at their computers, not bothering their heads about the purpose or result, and devoting their free time to whatever gives them pleasure: reading, women, music, or vacationing by the Black Sea. Victor Shklovski put it well when he was moving into his new apartment. "Now," he said to the other lucky persons who had been allotted space in the same building, "we must pray God there won't be a revolution." He could not have said a truer word: they had achieved the height of good fortune and wanted nothing more than to make the best of it. All they needed was just a little peace to enjoy it, just a little peace. This is something we have never had.

The young specialist opposed to change couldn't have expressed himself better: it is quite true that the pursuit of happiness can lead to disaster. I was recently struck by an admission from an elderly and very experienced man of a quite different kind who in his day was an active fighter for the "new order" (but not in this country, which is why he still feels responsible for what happened): "Once in our lives we wanted to make people happy, and we shall never forgive ourselves." But I think he too will be able to forgive himself and will not renounce the material rewards due to him for the services he has rendered. In the meantime the "masses," about whom so much nonsense has been written (by Blok, for instance, with his idea that they are untouched by "civilization" and embody the "spirit of music"), are concerned only to try and eke out their wages and get through life as best they can. Some of them spend what little money they have on their homes, or on clothing and footwear; others are more interested in drink. How do they get the money to stupefy themselves with vodka? I remember one of my neighbors in Pskov, a house painter and former partisan who is still a die-hard Stalinist. Every day he came home swearing obscenely and shouting in the corridor of our communal apartment about how good things had been under Stalin. Then his wife would drag him off to the room where they lived with their two children, but we could still hear his drunken praise of Stalin: "He gave me an apartment, he gave me a medal, he gave me my self-respect. . . . You know who I mean. . . . He lowered the prices. . . ." On holidays they were visited by the wife's sisters and their husbands. They sat together staidly reminiscing about collectivization, during which the women had managed to get away from their farm in good time and find work as domestic servants. The house painter's wife had been the most enterprising of them—during the war with Finland she had worked in an MGB canteen at the front line, and she still talked about "those wicked Finns." They drank to Stalin's memory and kept saying how much better off they had been in his day, whereas now there was nothing but shortages. . . . The house painter's wife helped me with my housework all winter and then in the spring, from force of habit, reported to the police that her neighbor, the woman from whom I rented my room, had an unregistered tenant. Later she wept bitterly and asked my forgiveness, and went to the church to pray for her sins. She is part of the formidable past that we are now gradually living down. The only change such people might want is to go back to their younger days—they pine for the time when life was reduced to a few such simple formulas as "Thanks to Comrade

Stalin for our happy life." Now they even have the "spirit of music" too—no home is complete without a television set. As to the "happy life" bestowed on us, nobody feels sorry about that.

I suppose it was at the beginning of the twentieth century that people decided the time had come to create a perfect, ideal society which would really ensure universal well-being and happiness. This notion grew out of nineteenth-century humanism and democracy, which, paradoxically, could only hamper the creation of a new order based on social justice. The nineteenth century was therefore denounced as an age of rhetoric, compromise and basic instability, and people now looked for salvation in a rigid order and authoritarian discipline. At the end of the last century and the beginning of this, people craved for an "organic" system and a unitary idea to embrace the whole of their thinking and behavior. Free thought—the favorite child of humanism—only undermined authority and had to be sacrificed to new ideals. A rationalist program of social change demanded blind faith and obedience to authority. The enthusiasm for the resulting dictatorship was quite genuine—a dictator is strong only if he can rely on followers who blindly believe in him. Such followers cannot be bought—that would be too simple—but once they exist, there are always plenty of venal people ready to swell their ranks, especially if they have no choice. But every grand idea eventually goes into a decline. Once this has happened, all that remains is inertia—with young people afraid of change, weary middle-aged ones craving for peace, a handful of old men horrified at what they have done, and countless petty myrmidons repeating by rote the phrases they were taught in their youth.

M. never renounced humanism and its values, but he had come a long way if even he could say that the nineteenth century was a "golden age." Like all his contemporaries, he had taken stock of the last century's legacy and drawn up his own balance sheet. I think that a great part in the formation of M.'s ideas was played by his personal experience as an artist—which, like the mystic's, powerfully affects one's view of the world. M. also sought harmony in social life, and the integration of the parts with the whole. This was consistent with his view of culture as the underlying idea which imposes order on the historical process and defines its structure. The nineteenth century repelled him by the poverty, not to say wretchedness, of its social structure—as he says in some of his articles. In the Western democracies, of which

Herzen spoke so scornfully, M. did not see the harmony and grandeur he wanted. He wanted a society with a clearly defined structure, a "Jacob's ladder," as he put it in his article on Chaadayev and in *The Noise of Time*. He sensed the presence of such a "Jacob's ladder" in the organization of the Catholic church and in Marxism—he was simultaneously interested in both as a schoolboy. He wrote about this in *The Noise of Time* and in a letter from Paris to his teacher, V. V. Gippius, in the days when he was a student there after finishing the Tenishev school. In both Catholicism and Marxism he felt the presence of a unifying idea that bound the whole structure together. I remember him saying to me in 1919 that he suspected the best form of social organization would be something like a theocracy. For this reason he was not frightened by the idea of authority, even when it was translated into dictatorial power. The only thing that worried him in those days, perhaps, was the Party organization. "The Party is an inverted church," he said. What he meant by this was that it had the church's hierarchical subordination to authority, but without God. The comparison with the Jesuits was not yet so obvious in those days.

The new order only began to make itself felt after the Civil War. Engels once pointed out that the industry producing lethal weapons is always the most advanced. This is borne out by its whole history, from the invention of gunpowder to the splitting of the atom in our times. Similarly, the most "advanced" sector of the State apparatus—the one that best expresses its essence—is that concerned with killing people in the name of "society." M.'s first encounter with the new State was his visit to Dzerzhinski to plead for his brother when he was arrested in 1922. This meeting gave him much food for thought about the relative value of the "social structure" and the human personality. The new structure was then only beginning to take shape, but it already promised to be of unprecedented grandeur—something that would dwarf the Egyptian pyramids. And it could not be denied that it had unity of design. M.'s youthful dream of harmony seemed to be coming about, but as an artist M. never lost his sense of reality, and the grand scale of the socialist State structure frightened rather than dazzled him. His apprehensions are reflected in his poem "The Age," where he harks back to the past and asks how he might "join the vertebrae of two centuries"; and in his article "Humanism and the Modern World" he says the measure of the social structure is man, but that there are eras in which this is lost sight of, when people "say they have no time for man, and that he is to be used like bricks or cement as something to be built *from,* not *for.*" As examples of social structures hostile to man he mentions Assyria and Ancient Egypt: "Assyrian slaves swarmed like chickens at the feet of the gigantic king; warriors embodying the might of a state hostile to man killed shackled pygmies with their long spears; the Egyptian builders treated the mass of human beings as material which had to be provided in the necessary quantity." Though our new age thus reminded M. of Egypt and Assyria, he still hoped that the monumental character of the State system would be mitigated by humanism.

Among the photographs of M. that have been preserved, there is one showing him as a young man in a sweater with an earnest, preoccupied look on his face. This was taken in 1922 when he first understood the Assyrian nature of our new order. Then there is another one that shows him as an old man with a beard. The interval between these two photographs was only ten years, but in 1932 M. already knew the fate of his youthful dreams about a social structure based on authority, free of the faults bequeathed by the nineteenth century. By this time he had already written his lines about the Assyrian king:

> He has taken away the air I breathe:
> The Assyrian holds my heart in his hand.

He was one of the first to look back to the nineteenth century as a "golden age," though he knew that the new ideas had grown from seed nurtured then.

At the very end of his life M. spoke once more of the ill-fated "social structure," and at the same time spoke mockingly of himself:

> Adorned by choicest meat of dogs
> the Egyptian State of shame
> thrusting puny pyramids aloft
> richly endowed its dead. . . .
> Next to all the Gothic, impishly spitting
> on all his spider's rights
> a brazen scholar, a thieving angel
> he lived, the incomparable François Villon.

Perhaps we really are Assyrians. Is this why we can look on with such indifference at mass reprisals against slaves, captives, hostages and heretics? Whenever something like this happens, we say to each other:

"It's on such a mass scale, what can one do?" We have a peculiar respect for massive campaigns, for measures or orders carried out on a mass scale. The Assyrian kings could be good or bad, but who was to stay their hand, whether they gave a sign for the slaughter of prisoners or graciously permitted the court architect to build himself a palace?

And what difference is there between those prisoners destroyed on the orders of Assyrian kings and the "masses" which now inspire us with such awe, always appearing whenever an "iron" social order is established? Yet in their everyday working lives, people remain true to their individual selves. I have always been struck by the fact that in the closed world of a hospital, factory or theater, people live in their own completely human lives, not becoming mechanized or turning into "masses."

55

"NE TREBA"

"It turns out we are part of the superstructure," M. said to me in 1922, after our return from Georgia. Not long before, M. had written about the separation of culture from the State, but the Civil War had ended, and the young builders of the new State had begun—for the time being in theory only—to put everything in its proper place. It was then that culture was assigned to the superstructure, and the consequences were not slow in making themselves felt. Klychkov, an outlandish but most gentle creature, a gypsy with bright dark-blue eyes, told M. with embarrassment about a conversation he had had with Voronski: "He has made up his mind and he wouldn't budge. 'We don't need it,' is what he said." Voronski, like other editors, refused to publish M. The superstructure is supposed to reinforce the basis, but M.'s verse was not suitable for this purpose.

The formula "We don't need it" sounded even more grotesque in Ukrainian. In 1923 M. went to the Arts Department in Kiev to ask for permission to hold a reading of his poetry. An official in an embroidered Ukrainian shirt refused it. When we asked why, he said tonelessly: "*Ne treba.*" From then on, M. and I adopted the phrase as a standard saying. As for Ukrainian embroidered shirts, as I have mentioned before, they became fashionable in the middle twenties, replacing the Russian kosovorotka and becoming almost the equivalent of a uniform for officials of the Central Committee and the People's Commissariats.

Complete order was established in the "superstructure" in 1930 when Stalin published his famous letter in *Bolshevik,* saying nothing should be published that was at variance with the official point of view. This, in effect, robbed censorship of all significance. The much-abused censorship is really a sign of *relative* freedom of the press: it forbids things that are directed against the existing order, but, however stupid it is, it cannot destroy literature. But the editorial apparatus that served Stalin worked much more purposefully—it rejected everything that did not explicitly meet the State's wishes. In the editorial offices of *For a Communist Education,* where I was working at the moment Stalin's article appeared, all the manuscripts were rechecked in great panic and we went through huge piles of them, cutting mercilessly. This was called "reorganization in the light of Comrade Stalin's remarks." I brought home a copy of *Bolshevik* with Stalin's letter and showed it to M., who commented: "*Ne treba* again, but this time good and proper." He was right. The letter was a crucial turning point in the building up of the "superstructure." Even now it has not been forgotten by the upholders of Stalin's tradition as they try to prevent the publication of such writers as Mandelstam, Zabolotski, Pasternak and Tsvetayeva. The "*ne treba*" argument still rings in our ears today.

Sergei Klychkov was our neighbor for many years in Herzen House and then in Furmanov Street, and we were always very friendly with him. The third part of M.'s "Verses About Russian Poetry" is dedicated to him—this after Klychkov had commented on the line about freaks playing cards for no stakes: "That's about you and me," he said to M. Neither of them in fact played cards, and the stakes they were playing for were higher than in any gambling game.

Klychkov was dismissed from his work as an editor very early. He was too much of a peasant to make a good official and worry about the purity of the "superstructure." He made his living by translating some infinitely long epic poem. In the evenings he put on his spectacles (one of the arms was broken off and he used a piece of string instead) and read an encyclopedia, just as a self-taught cobbler reads his Bible. He once paid me the nicest compliment that a woman could hear: "Nadia," he said, "you are a very clever woman, and a very silly little girl." This was because I had read Luppol M.'s epigram about him.

M. very much admired Klychkov's cycle of poems on the theme of being an outcast, and he often read passages from them, imitating Klychkov's northern accent. All these poems were taken away by the police when Klychkov's apartment was searched —he did not have time to hide them—and they have disappeared, like everything else that was taken to the Lubianka. Klychkov himself disappeared with them. His wife was told he had been given ten years "without the right of correspondence." It was some time before we learned that this meant he had been shot. It is said that he stood up to his interrogator with great courage and independence. With those eyes of his he must have infuriated his inquisitors. In those days the secret police did not bother much about formal trials for people they had decided were guilty, and they sometimes simply shot them out of hand during the interrogation. It is said that this is what happened to Klychkov.

After Klychkov's death Moscow seemed a much poorer place. He was a great friend of Pavel Vasiliev, whom he called his "evil genius" because Pavel used to take him on womanizing and drinking expeditions. The girls working in the *Krasnaya Nov* office once inadvertently published some verse of Klychkov's under M.'s name. Both of them had to go and tell the girls off and get the fee transferred to Klychkov. It never occurred to them that there might one day be a problem about the authorship of this poem, and they didn't insist on a correction being published because the girls thought they might be fired if their superiors found out. As a result, this verse of Klychkov's has now appeared as the last item in the American edition of M.'s poetry. I would like to tell the editors about this mistake, but how can one reach them?

In the days when Klychkov's and Vasiliev's fate was being decided, M. and I were waiting for a train at the Savelovo station and happened to buy a newspaper in which it was announced that the death penalty was being abolished, but that the maximum length of prison sentences was being increased to twenty years. M.'s first reaction was one of joy—he had always been horrified by executions—but then it struck him how little it meant. "The number of people they must be killing, if they have to abolish the death penalty!" he said. In 1937 we clearly understood that whether a prisoner was marked down for physical destruction or not depended only on the principle *treba* or *ne treba*. . . .

56

THE EARTH AND ITS CONCERNS

A woman who has come back after many years in the forced-labor camps tells me that she and her companions in misfortune always found comfort in the poetry which, luckily, she knew by heart and was able to recite to them. They were particularly moved by some lines M. wrote as a young man: "But I love this poor earth, because I have not seen another. . . ."

Our way of life kept us firmly rooted to the ground, and was not conducive to the search for transcendental truths. Whenever I talked of suicide, M. used to say: "Why hurry? The end is the same everywhere, and here they even hasten it for you." Death was so much more real, and so much simpler than life, that we all involuntarily tried to prolong our earthly existence, even if only for a brief moment—just in case the next day brought some relief! In war, in the camps and during periods of terror, people think much less about death (let alone about suicide) than when they are living normal lives. Whenever at some point on earth mortal terror and the pressure of utterly insoluble problems are present in a particularly intense form, general questions about the nature of being recede into the background. How could we stand in awe before the forces of nature and the eternal laws of existence if terror of a mundane kind was felt so tangibly in everyday life? In a strange way, despite the horror of it, this also gave a certain richness to our lives. Who knows what happiness is? Perhaps it is better to talk in more concrete terms of the fullness or intensity of existence, and in this sense there may have been something more deeply satisfying in our desperate clinging to life than in what people generally strive for. I always remember my conversation about happiness with Vishnevski's widow, Sonia. We were trying to draw the balance sheet of everything that had happened to us. How different our lives had been! Sonia summed up: "Mine has been so happy, and yours has been so unhappy." Poor, stupid Sonia! Her husband had an illusion of power: other writers tried to keep in with him because he controlled certain funds and he was able to make the Government's wishes known to his cronies. He had access to the Central Committee and was several times received by Stalin. He drank no less than Fadeyev, greedily breathed in the heady air of State, and permitted himself no more than token expression of fronde—suggesting, for instance, that James Joyce be published, and sending money to exiles (first to a naval officer banished to Tashkent, and then—through my brother—to us in Voronezh). He had a car and a villa in the country which was rather meanly taken away from Sonia after his death. Until her own death, she remained faithful to him, and was angry with Khrushchev for cutting royalty payments to a writer's heirs by half. Many stories were told about Sonia, but she was not a bad sort, and nobody could really hold it against her when she went around shouting that her husband had been killed by saboteurs in the Kremlin hospital. In fact she was very lucky that he died in good time, without managing to transfer his assets to one of Sonia's rivals—that none of them succeeded in snatching it all from her hands was certainly fortunate for her, and in this sense she was entitled to describe her life as "happy."

I also would have been glad, if not of "happiness," at least of a little well-being (as M. put it in one of his poems, "Oh, how much dearer to her the creak of rowlocks, a boat's deck broad as a bosom, a flock of sheep")—a peaceful life with its ordinary despairs, its thoughts about the certainty of death and the vanity of earthly things. None of this was granted to us, and perhaps this is what M. meant when he told his interrogator that with the Revolution he had lost his sense of awe.

For M., Acmeism was not only "nostalgia for world culture," but also an affirmation of life on earth and social concern. With his integral view of the world, one could see how every one of his judgments was part of his understanding of things in general. This was not, of course, an elaborate philosophical system, but what he called in one of his articles "the world-view of the artist." T., a wonderful artist, once said to me: "A man sits and carves a piece of wood, and out of it comes God." And about Pasternak he asked: "Why did he have to change his religion? What does he need intermediaries for when he has his art?" Just as mystical experience gives rise to a religious view of the world, so the working experience of an artist defines his view of the material and spiritual world around him. It is probably this experience as an artist that explains why M.'s view about poetry, the role of the poet in society and the "merging of the intellectual and the moral" in an integrated culture (as well as in each of its individual representatives) never underwent any substantial changes, so that throughout his life he was able to stand by what he wrote in his early articles for *Apollon*. Despite its division into distinct periods, his poetry also reflects the unity of his views and "world-sense" throughout his life, and in this it often echoes his prose, even that of the earliest days. His prose thus serves as a commentary on his poetry.

Until his last days M. remained true to the earth and its concerns, and he hoped for his reward "only here on earth, not in heaven," though he feared he would not live to see it. "If only we live long enough," he used to say to me. In one of his last poems, already preparing for death, he wrote:

> under Purgatory's ephemeral sky
> we often forget that
> the happy heaven above
> is but the boundless house in which we live our lives.

Reading *Self-Knowledge* by Berdiayev—one of our best modern thinkers—I couldn't help being struck by the great difference between him and M. in their attitudes toward life and earthly existence. Perhaps this was because one was an artist, while the other was concerned with abstract thought. Furthermore, Berdiayev was inwardly tied to the Symbolists, and though he had his disagreements with them and was even to a certain extent disillusioned with them, he had never broken with them. For M., on the other hand, the revolt against Symbolism was crucial for the whole of his life and art.

For Berdiayev "life is a daily round of cares," and though he was receptive to "the poetry of life and beauty," he thought life was "dominated by prose and ugliness." Berdiayev's idea of beauty is the direct opposite of what I have always found in the poets and artists who rejected Symbolism: they do not look down on ordinary everyday life—on the contrary, it is a source of beauty for them, whether they are poets or painters. The Symbolists—such as Viacheslav Ivanov and Briusov—assumed the role of high priests standing above everyday life, and for them beauty was something apart from it. By returning to earth, the generation that followed them considerably enlarged its horizon, and for it the world was no longer divided into ugly prose and sublime poetry. In this connection I think of Akhmatova, who knew "from what trash poetry, quite unashamed, can grow," and of Pasternak with his passionate defense of the "daily round" in *Dr. Zhivago*. For M. there was absolutely no problem here: he did not, like Berdiayev and the Symbolists, seek to escape into some realm of pure spirit from the earthly confines of our everyday here and now. In his essay "The Morning of Acmeism" he tried to give a poetic justification for remaining attached to earth with its three dimensions: "The earth is not an encumbrance or an unfortunate accident, but a God-given palace." This is followed by a polemical passage about people who, like Berdiayev, cannot wait to get to a better world and regard life on earth as being literally God-forsaken. In the same essay, which was a kind of manifesto, he asked: "What would you think of a guest who, while living at the expense of his host and enjoying his hospitality, actually despises him in his heart of hearts and thinks only of ways to outsmart him?" "Outsmart" here means to escape from time and three-dimensional space. To M., as a self-styled Acmeist, three-dimensional space and life on earth were essential because he wanted to do his duty by his "host"—he felt that he was here to build, which can only be done in three dimensions. This explains his attitude toward the world of things. In his view, this world was not hostile to the poet or—as he put it—the builder, because things are there to be built from. Stone—the title of M.'s first published collection of poems—is a building material which "seems to crave for another mode of being" and longs to find its place in "a vaulted nave" and thus joyfully interact with others of its kind. M. never talked of "creating" things, only of "building" them. As a young man he already thought of himself as a builder: "From a sullen dead weight I shall one day make something of beauty." He was therefore not repelled by matter, but was very conscious of its "dead weight" as something that predisposed it to be used in building. Berdiayev often speaks of man's higher destiny and his creative powers—but he does not define the nature of this creativity. This is probably because he lacked the artist's sense of things and words as inert matter to be used in building. Berdiayev's experience was that of the mystic and it took him to the limit of the world of things. The artist's intuition is similar to the mystic's, but it reveals the Creator through his creation, God through man. It seems to me that this way of perception is justified by Soloviev's (and Berdiayev's) doctrine of "God-manhood." Isn't this also why every true artist has the sense of his own "rightness" about which M. spoke?

However much he tried to overcome it, Berdiayev felt contempt for the "man in the street." In this, too, he had common ground with the Symbolists—perhaps they got it from Nietzsche, who had such an influence on them. Berdiayev complains that "we live in a middle-class age" which is antagonistic to the appearance of "strong personalities." Yet Berdiayev himself wanted to be self-effacing. He hated, he says, to "draw attention to his own significance and intellectual superiority." Reading this, I thought of Pushkin's line: "And among all the lowly of the world, perhaps the lowliest is he"—words which were completely misunderstood by the whole Veresayev crowd. All Pushkin was trying to convey was the simple sense of being at one with his fellow men, of being flesh of their flesh—though perhaps not quite as well made as others.... It seems to me that this feeling of being the same as everybody else (and even perhaps of envy at not being quite as well formed) is an essential feature of the poet. In his early article "On the Reader" M. has the following to say about the difference between literature and poetry: "The man of letters as opposed to the poet always addresses himself to a specific audience, to his living contemporaries ... the content of his writing is decanted into them by virtue of the physical law of unequal levels—which means that the man of letters must be 'above' his contemporaries, 'superior' to the society in which he lives. Literature in this sense is essentially didactic.... Poetry is quite different: the poet is linked only with readers sent his way by Providence and he does not have to be superior to his age, or to the people he lives among." M. sincerely believed that he was no better than others, or even not as good ("I walk with bearded peasants, a passerby"). The Symbolists thought of themselves as teachers with a cultural mission—hence the way in which they set themselves above the crowd and the attraction they felt for strong personalities. Even Blok was not free of a sense of his own exclusiveness—though it alternated with the other feeling, natural for any poet, of a common bond with the street, with ordinary people. Berdiayev, being a philosopher rather than an artist, naturally felt superior to the crowd, and in his aristocratic inclinations and liking for strong personalities he was only yielding to the spirit of his times.

M. did not approve of attacks on the "middle class" and its values. If anything, he respected the middle classes—which is why he once described Herzen, who was always attacking them, as an "aristocrat." He was particularly dismayed by the constant attacks on the middle class and bourgeois values in this country. "What don't they like about the middle class?" he said once. "They are the most stable section of the community and everything rests on them." (The only members of the middle class he could not stand were literary ladies who kept salons—and their successors in Soviet times. He could not tolerate their pretentiousness, and the dislike was mutual.) In "Journey to Armenia" there is a passage which at first sight looks like an attack on the middle class, but M. was referring here to our neighbors in the old merchant quarter of Moscow—these were not people who had once enjoyed a stable, bourgeois existence, but a sullen, backward mob who were only too happy to accept a new form of slavery.

In this respect M. agreed with Berdiayev's remark that the First World War had given birth to a new generation that hated freedom and had a taste for authority and force. But Berdiayev was wrong in thinking that this was a consequence of "an age of democracy"—the last few decades of our history have been anti-democratic in the extreme, and it is particularly in this country that the results have been felt most acutely. The love of dictators, which has been the curse of the first half of the twentieth century, is a complete denial of democracy, and Berdiayev, as an émigré, failed to see how ordinary people were ground underfoot, and he was blind to the growth of the secret police's contempt for human rights. Furthermore, it wasn't a question of just one dictator—anybody who had the slightest power, down to the humblest police official or doorkeeper, was also a dictator. We had not previously understood what a temptation power can be. Not everybody wants to be a Napoleon, but people cling desperately to what little power they have and will do their best to get all they can out of it. There has never been such a proliferation of petty tyrants, and our country is still swarming with them. It is only now that they seem to be on the way out at last—people have had their fill of this game.

Like the Symbolists, Berdiayev does not recognize communal morality or the "hereditary principle" because it is not compatible with freedom. Here his idea of freedom comes close to the license that undermined the pre-revolutionary intelligentsia. Culture, after all, is not something generated by the upper layer of society at any given time, but an element passed down from generation to generation—a product of the continuity without which life would break up in chaos. What is thus handed down in the community often seems unbearably set in a conventional form, but it cannot be all that terrible if it has enabled the human race to survive. The threat to the human race comes not from its communal morality, but from the extravagant innovations of its more volatile elements. M. defined the poet as one who "disturbs meaning." What he had in mind, however, was not rebellion against inherited order, but rejection of the commonplace image and the hackneyed phrase by which meaning is obscured. This was another way of appealing for an art that faithfully recorded life and living events, as opposed to all that was deathlike. It was perhaps in the same sense that he spoke of "culture-as-convention"—in art this evidently referred to the repetition of things already spent and played out, but nevertheless eagerly accepted by people who want no truck with "disturbers of meaning."

Berdiayev's main preoccupation was with freedom, and it was a problem he wrestled with all his life. But for M. there was no problem here, since it probably did not occur to him that there can be people devoid of inner freedom. He evidently thought that freedom was inherent in man as such. In the social sphere Berdiayev was concerned to establish the primacy of personality over society, but for M. it was rather a question of assuring the place of personality *in* society—just as he fought for the poet's place in society. In other words, he accepted the idea of society, taking it for granted as the highest form of human organization.

Comic as it may seem, even in their attitudes toward women the difference between Berdiayev and M. was that between Symbolist and Acmeist. For the Symbolists, women were "Beautiful Ladies" (as in Blok's poems), high priestesses or, as Akhmatova and I called them, "bearers of myrrh." When I was young there were very many of them, and they were unbelievably pretentious with their grand views about their role as female acolytes. They perpetrated the most fearful nonsense—as witness E.R.'s notes to the *Autobiography*,* where snakes suddenly grow claws, the women have the faces of snakes and the men are fancied to have cloaks and swords. All these women—and relations with them—were quite out of the ordinary. With us things were much simpler.

Berdiayev had no time for the pleasures of life. Although M. did not seek happiness, he described everything he valued in terms of pleasure and play: "Thanks to the wonderful bounty of Christianity, the whole of our two-thousand-year-old culture is the setting of the world free for play, for spiritual pleasure, for the free imitation of Christ." And elsewhere: "Words are sheer pleasure, a cure for anguish."

* Eugenie Rapp, Berdiayev's sister-in-law, supplied footnotes to Berdiayev's autobiography.

I would have liked to describe M.'s attitude toward words, but it is beyond my power. All I can say is that he was aware that words have an "inner form," and that he did not confuse words, as units of meaning, with symbols. He was cool toward Gumilev's famous poem about words, but never told me why. Probably he did not share Gumilev's view of numbers either. Incidentally, he was always concerned about the number of lines and verses in a poem, or the number of chapters in a piece of prose. He was angry when I said I was surprised he thought this important. My lack of understanding struck him as nihilism and ignorance. It was not for nothing, he said, that some numbers—three and seven, for example—had magic significance for people: numbers were also part of our culture, a gift which had been handed down to us.

In Voronezh M. began to compose poems of seven, nine, ten and eleven lines. Seven- and nine-line stanzas also began to appear as parts of longer poems. He had a feeling that some new form was coming to him: "Just think what they mean, these fourteen-line groups. And there must be some significance in these seven- and nine-line stanzas. They keep cropping up all the time." There was no mysticism about this, it was seen simply as an index of harmony.

Everything I have said about the contrast between Berdiayev and M. applies only to those features of Berdiayev which he shared with the Symbolists. He was by no means identified with them as a philosopher, but some of his views on matters of taste bore the marks of his time. All of us are subject to the influences of our day, and although Berdiayev, like M., used to say he had never been anybody's contemporary, he nevertheless lived in his time. Yet it was Berdiayev who pointed out the main thing about the Symbolists: namely, that they ignored social and ethical questions. It was because of this that M. revolted against the "omnivorousness" of Briusov, against the haphazard way in which they arrived at their values. In everything except matters of taste Berdiayev had overcome the influence of the Symbolists, but he could not quite escape the seductive charm of these great fishers of men.

It is a shame that, though he tried very hard, M. was never able to get hold of Berdiayev's books, so I do not know what he would have made of him. Unfortunately, we were completely cut off from what the world outside was thinking. This is one of the worst misfortunes that can befall a man.

57

ARCHIVE AND VOICE

"An artist's feeling for the world is a tool, like a mason's mallet, and his only tangible product is the work itself," M. wrote in "The Morning of Acmeism."

Some of M.'s poetry and prose is lost, but most of it has been preserved. How this happened is the story of my battle with the forces of destruction, with everything that conspired to sweep me away, together with the poor scraps of paper I managed to keep.

When they are young, people do not bother to keep their papers. How can a young man imagine that his scribblings may one day be thought of value? Though perhaps it's not a bad thing that early verse gets lost—this can be a kind of weeding out which an artist should undertake in any case.

M. arrived in Kiev with a wicker basket that his mother had used to keep her sewing in—it was all he had left of his mother's things. It had a large lock on it, and M. told me it contained his mother's letters and some of his own writings—he couldn't remember exactly what. From Kiev M. went to the Crimea with his brother Alexander. Here Alexander got into a card game with some soldiers and gambled away his brother's shirts. While M. was gone for a moment, the soldiers broke the lock on the wicker basket and used all the paper inside to make cigarettes. M. very much valued his mother's letters and was angry with his brother. About his own papers he was less concerned—he remembered everything in them.

During the first few years that M. and I lived together, nothing was ever written down. He put together his *Second Book* from memory, dictating to me the poems he wanted to include, or jotting them down himself. He then looked them over, kept some and threw others away. Before that he had given a pile of rough drafts to Petropolis.* They were taken abroad and published there as the *Tristia* collection. In those days we never stopped to think that a man might die and his memory with him. Furthermore, M. always thought that anything he

---

* Russian publishing house in Berlin.

gave to editors was bound to be preserved. He had no idea of the slap-dash way in which our editorial offices work.

My mother had given me some very nice suitcases and a trunk plastered with foreign hotel labels. We gave the suitcases to a shoemaker to make shoes for us out of the stout yellow leather. In those days they were a luxury. The only use I could find for the trunk was to put papers in it—not realizing that I was in effect using it as an archive.

When M.'s father fell ill, we had to go to Leningrad. The old man could not go back to his wretched lodgings after leaving the hospital, so we took him to M.'s younger brother, Evgeni. While I was packing his things I came across another trunk, just like mine, only a little larger, and also covered with labels. It appeared that M. had once bought it in Munich so as to look like a proper tourist—trunks of this kind were very popular before the First World War. M.'s father had put all his ledgers in it, together with piles of worthless paper money from the times of Nicholas II and Kerenski. At the bottom I found a pile of manuscripts: fragments of early verse and some pages of the lecture on Scriabin. We took these manuscripts and the trunk back to Moscow with us.

This was the beginning of M.'s archive. Everything was thrown into it: rough drafts of poems, letters and essays. M. didn't seem to mind this system, and the pile grew and grew. The only things that did not find their way into the trunk were minor pieces of work such as translations, newspaper articles and notes on manuscripts and books—mostly foreign—sent to him by publishing houses for his opinion. All these notes have been lost by Lengiz,* apart from one or two that got into the trunk by accident. He needed his newspaper articles when he was putting together a book of his essays, and my brother Evgeni and I went to the library to copy them out as published—no doubt with censorship cuts. For some reason the manuscripts of *The Noise of Time* didn't get into the trunk—perhaps because we only began our "archive" after it was written.

The turning point in M.'s attitude toward his papers came with our experience over the "Fourth Prose"—this was a kind of warning signal that it was time to take greater care of them. The second warning was M.'s arrest in 1934.

When we left for Armenia, I did not want to take the only copy of

---

* Leningrad State Publishing House.

"Fourth Prose." Although the climate was very good at the moment, M. could still have got into hot water because of it. We had to find a trust-worthy person to leave it with. This was the first time we had left a manuscript with somebody else. Or, rather, the second—in 1919, in the Crimea, M. had written two poems which he did not want to keep on his person, so he gave them to a friend, a certain Lenia L. In 1922 I saw this man in Moscow and he said he still had the poems. But then he dis-appeared, and I doubt whether they will ever be found. It was this that first made me appreciate the need to keep things in several copies and in different places. We gave "Fourth Prose" to a number of people for safekeeping, and I copied it out so many times that I remember it word for word.

When M. returned from Armenia and began to write verse in great quantity, he was immediately made to feel what an outcast he was. I re-member particularly one conversation in the Leningrad offices of *Izvestia*. A member of the staff, who appeared to be friendly, read through M.'s poem "I have returned to my native city" and said: "Do you know what happens after you write a poem like this? Three men come for you . . . in uniform." We knew this, of course, but at that mo-ment the authorities were in no hurry to act. This particular poem was quickly passed around from hand to hand, though in a fairly narrow circle of people. M. thought this was a good way of preserving his work: "People will keep it for me." But I felt it was not enough, and time has proved me right. I began to make copies and hide them in var-ious places. Generally I put them in hiding-places at home, but some copies I handed to other people. During the search of our apartment in 1934 the police agents failed to find poems I had sewn into cushions or stuck inside saucepans and shoes. When we arrived in Voronezh, I removed the poem about Ariosto from a cushion in which it had been hidden.

Voronezh marked a new stage in our handling of manuscripts. The idyllic era of cushions was at an end—and I remembered all too vividly how the feathers had flown from Jewish cushions during Denikin's pogroms in Kiev. M.'s memory was not as good as it had been, and with human life getting cheaper all the time, it was in any case no longer a safe repository for his work. It was also becoming harder to find people willing to keep things for us. During the whole of our three years in Voronezh, I made copies of everything and distrib-uted them to such people as I could find, but apart from my brother

Evgeni (who in any case kept nothing at his own home) I had nobody I could rely on to take them. Not, that is, until Sergei Borisovich Rudakov turned up.

Rudakov, the son of a Czarist general, had been expelled from Leningrad together with other people of aristocratic origin. His father and elder brothers had been shot at the beginning of the Revolution. He had been brought up by his sisters and had a normal Soviet childhood—he became a member of the Pioneers, distinguished himself in school and even got through the university. He was looking forward to a decent career when suddenly he was struck by the disaster of expulsion from Leningrad. Like many people who had lost their parents, he was anxious to get into step with the times, and he even had a theory that one should only write books that stood a chance of being published. He himself wrote elegant verse (a little under the influence of Tsvetayeva) which was popular at the time. He had chosen Voronezh as his place of exile in order to be near M. He first came there while I was in Moscow looking for translation work, and he spent about a month with M. all alone before I returned. When M. came to meet me at the station he told me that Rudakov had appeared, that he was going to write a book about poetry, and what a splendid fellow he was. After his illness M. had probably lost confidence in himself and needed a friendly listener for his new verse.

Rudakov did not try to find a proper place to live in Voronezh. He kept hoping that his wife might use her contacts with some top Soviet generals (who later perished in 1937) to get permission for him to return to Leningrad. He had a bunk in a room which he shared with a young worker called Tosha, but he came to us for all his meals. This was a relatively good period for us when we had earnings from translation, the local theater and the radio, and it was no hardship for us to feed the poor fellow. While I was in Moscow he had carefully collected all the drafts of "Black Earth," which M. was composing then, and after my return, when M. and I began trying to remember the poems confiscated during the house search, Rudakov copied them all into a notebook for us. Overnight he recopied them on drafting paper, in a rather comic copperplate hand with curlicues, and brought them along to us in the morning. He despised my spidery handwriting and complete lack of concern for the appearance of manuscripts. He thought, for instance, that it was scandalous to write with ordinary ink, and insisted on using India ink. (He also drew silhouettes in India ink, and the result was no worse than those done by street artists.) He showed me his beautifully executed copies of M.'s poems and said: "This is what they'll keep in the archives, not the messy things you and Osip Emilievich do." We only smiled, and tried not to hurt his feelings.

We often warned Rudakov that he would do himself no good by coming to see us, but he replied with such a string of noble phrases that we could only gasp. Perhaps for this reason we were so tolerant of certain unpleasant things about him. He was, for example, very arrogant and was always being very rude to our other constant visitor, Kaletski—also a Leningrader and a pupil of all our friends, such as Eikhenbaum and Tynianov. Though he was a modest and shy young man, Kaletski sometimes said things nobody else would have dared to at that time. Once, for instance, he talked to M. about the inefficiency of all the Soviet institutions with which we had any contact, the way they had deteriorated under the dead hand of bureaucracy. And suppose, he continued, the army was just the same? What would happen if there was a war? Rudakov remembered what he had been taught in school and said: "I believe in the Party." Kaletski blushed with embarrassment and replied softly: "I believe in the people." He looked very puny next to the tall, handsome Rudakov, but he had much more inner strength. Rudakov sneeringly called him a "quantum," explaining that this was the smallest unit of energy.

Another disagreeable feature of Rudakov was his constant grumbling. In Russia, he kept complaining, people of talent had always been ground down by life, and he would never be able to write his book. M. could not stand this kind of talk: "Why aren't you writing now?" he asked. "If someone has anything to say, he will always manage to say it." This made Rudakov lose his temper and, asking how he could work without money or a proper place to live, he would storm out, banging the door behind him. But in an hour or so he would come back, as though nothing had happened.

Rudakov had a strong didactic streak in him—he liked to tell me how to copy out M.'s verse, and M. how he should write it. He greeted every new poem with some theory or other from his still unwritten book, as though to ask why he hadn't been consulted beforehand. I could see that he often got on M.'s nerves, and would have liked to throw him out, but M. wouldn't let me ("How will he eat without us?") and everything went on as before. Even so, both he and Kaletski were some comfort to us. While they were in Voronezh we were not totally isolated—as we were after their return to Leningrad at the beginning of 1936. We would have been quite alone if it had not been for Natasha Shtempel, who started coming to see us then. While we were living in the "agent's" apartment, Rudakov had to go to the hospital with scarlet fever and met some girls there, but he was desperately anxious that we shouldn't get to know. One of them was Natasha, and before leaving Voronezh he made her swear she would never visit us, but, fortunately for us, she didn't keep this promise.

Altogether, Rudakov was a very strange type—and we should have known better than to get on such close terms with him. I gave him original copies of all M.'s most important work, and Akhmatova let him have the whole of Gumilev's archive, delivering it to him on a sledge.

During the war, after being wounded, Rudakov was posted to a draft office in Moscow. When one of his relatives came and pleaded to be exempted from military service because he was a Tolstoyan, Rudakov granted his request. For this he was arrested and sent to a penal battalion, where he was soon killed. Our manuscripts were left with his widow, but she did not return them to us. In 1953, meeting Akhmatova at a concert, she said that everything was intact, but six months later she told Emma Gerstein that she had been arrested herself and everything had been confiscated. Soon she was telling yet a third version: that she had been arrested and her mother had burned everything. What the truth of the matter is we just haven't been able to find out. All we know is that she has sold some of Gumilev's manuscripts—not directly, but through middlemen. Akhmatova is furious about it all, but there is nothing she can do. Once we got the widow to come and see Akhmatova on the pretext of trying to publish an essay by her late husband, but it was impossible to get any sense out of her. Khardzhiev had a little more luck—he was able to persuade her to let him copy out everything he needed from Rudakov's letters. But Khardzhiev is a man of great charm and good looks who can get anything he likes. However, in Rudakov's letters—which he wrote every day, carefully keeping numbered copies for posterity—there was nothing of special interest for us. The poor boy was obviously a psychopath. The letters were full of ravings about how the whole of poetry had been present in M.'s room—I've forgotten whether he said "world poetry" or Russian poetry, but he was referring to M., himself and a volume of Vaginov which M. had in his room. He also wrote about how he taught M. to write poetry and explained everything to him, and expressed his horror that all the praise would go to M. and he would get no credit. He compared M. to Derzhavin—sometimes like a god and sometimes like a worm. In one of the letters he spoke of himself as M.'s heir, alleging that M. had said to him: "You are my heir, do what you see fit with my verse." I am quoting all this from memory, since I have only seen the copies made by Khardzhiev. Reading them, Akhmatova and I understood that the theft of our archives had been part of a deliberate plan on Rudakov's part, and that his widow was only carrying out his will by refusing to return them to us. The selling of original manuscripts—which is very profitable—was being done not only for mercenary reasons, but also in fulfillment of Rudakov's maniac schemes. One wonders what would have happened if I had died much earlier. It is possible that Rudakov would have claimed all M.'s work as his own—though this would not have been easy, since many of the poems were circulating under the name of their rightful author. A similar attempt at plagiarism on the part of Seva Bagritski only ended in a scandal when his mother published M.'s "Goldfinch" poem as a work of her son's. Things would have been even worse if I had listened to Rudakov when he tried to persuade me (through Emma Gerstein, with whom he had become friendly) to hand over all M.'s papers to him. The reason he gave was that it was important for all the papers to be in one place. But Khardzhiev and I argued that, on the contrary, it was safer to disperse them. As a result of handing them to Rudakov, I have lost several poems altogether—nearly all the Voronezh rough drafts and many copies of *Tristia* in M.'s own hand.

M. seemed to foresee the fate of his archive in the passage in "Conversation About Dante" where he writes: "Whether first drafts are preserved or not depends on a struggle of opposing forces—to get them through safely one must take account of winds blowing in the wrong direction."

In this whole Rudakov episode I blame not the poor fool himself, whatever he may have been aiming at, but rather those responsible for creating this "happy life" of ours. If we lived like human beings rather than as hunted animals, Rudakov would have come to our house like any other visitor, and it would probably never have occurred to him to purloin M.'s papers and declare himself M.'s heir—any more than his widow would have carried on her trade in Gumilev's letters to Akhmatova.

Rudakov was one of the most important figures in the story of M.'s archives, but there were others too. Some of the episodes would have been worthy of a film script. For instance, when the Germans were approaching Voronezh, Natasha rescued M.'s letters to me by putting them all in an old tin tea caddy and taking them with her as she left the burning city on foot. Then there was Nina, who destroyed a copy of some verse by M. during the days when her mother-in-law was expecting to be arrested for a second time, and her friend Edik, who boasted about having saved the copies I gave him (though it was not too difficult for him, since he lived in the house of his father-in-law, a high police official who, as I have already mentioned, committed suicide in Tashkent after Stalin's death). All I could do was deposit copies with as many different people as possible and hope that some would survive. My only helper in this was my brother, and our main concern was never to leave the basic collection of M.'s papers too long in any one place. I used to carry around a heap of first drafts of M.'s prose pieces in my suitcase, and I always interleaved them with notes I had made on linguistics for my dissertation—I hoped that this would mislead any semiliterate police agents who might rummage in my belongings. Papers occasionally disappeared—as they do sometimes even now, though probably for a different reason. Not long ago a whole file marked "materials for a biography" disappeared from my room—I still have copies of these notes, but I have no idea where the originals have gone to. Earlier I mentioned an edition of *Stone* originally owned by Kablukov. I bought it (for 200 roubles) on account of the variants Kablukov had written in it, and also because of four loose pages written in M.'s own hand—two of these have now vanished. I have also lost a letter to me from Pasternak in which he wrote that the only people in contemporary Soviet literature—this was right after the war—who interested him were Simonov and Tvardovski, because he would like to understand the mechanism by which reputations are created. I imagine that this letter, as well as the two pages written in M.'s hand, were taken by lovers of literature and will not get lost. Be that as it may, I have now stopped keeping anything at home (if where I live can be called a home!) and I again worry constantly about where things have the best chance of surviving.

Despite everything, I have managed to save a good deal of M.'s work, though whether it will ever be published here is another matter—there is still no sign of it. I have had to give up one method of preserving his work—namely, committing it to memory. Until 1956 I could remember everything by heart—both prose and verse. In order not to forget it, I had to repeat a little to myself each day. I did this while I thought I still had a good while to go on living. But time is getting on now.

There are many women like me who for years have spent sleepless nights repeating the words of their dead husbands over and over again. As another example I should like to mention a woman whose name I cannot give because she is still alive. In 1937 there were daily newspaper attacks on her husband, a very high official. He sat at home waiting to be arrested and not daring to go out—the house was surrounded by police agents. At night he wrote a long letter to the Central Committee which his wife memorized. After he was shot, she spent twenty years in prisons and labor camps. When she returned at last, she wrote out the letter and took it to the Central Committee, where I can only hope it has not disappeared forever.

No recordings of M.'s voice have survived. The collection of recordings (including some of M. and Gumilev) made by Sergei Ignatievich Bernstein was destroyed after he was expelled from the Zubov Institute for "formalism."* This was during a period when the remains of dead people were being scattered to the winds. I have managed to keep such photographs as there were—there were not very many—in the same way as the manuscripts, but I never had any control over the recordings of his voice. I well remember M.'s voice and the way he read, but it was inimitable and lives on only in my ears. If people could hear his voice, they would understand what he meant by "interpretative reading"—that is, using the text as a conductor uses a score. This could never be properly conveyed by some form of phonetic notation showing where he paused or raised his voice. His treatment of vowel quantity and the timbre of his voice could not be indicated. And what memory could ever preserve all the inflections of a voice that fell silent a quarter of a century ago? Yet something of his voice is preserved in the very structure of his verse, and now, when the years of silence are coming to an end, thousands of youngsters have caught the intonation of M.'s poetry and, unknown to themselves, reproduce it when they recite him. Nothing can be completely scattered to the winds.

Fortunately, this poetry still has not been seized on by actors, pro-

* See page 427.

fessional reciters and schoolteachers. I once happened to hear the brazen voice of a woman announcer on Radio Liberty.* She was reading M.'s "I drink to officers' epaulettes. . . ." This innocuous humorous poem has always been exploited here by such people as Nikulin to cast cheap political aspersions on M., and now, lo and behold, it was being used in the same way by a foreign radio! The woman was reading it in the same odious tone of voice, full of "meaning," as our radio announcers. She must have learned it from them. Sickened and depressed, I switched off.

58

OLD AND NEW

On one of the first few days after our return from Voronezh, we were given a ride around Moscow by Valentin Katayev in the brand-new car he had just brought back with him from America. He looked at M. fondly and said: "I know what you need: a fixed place of residence." That evening he took us to the new apartment building for writers with the labradorite entry hall which so impressed those who remembered the hardships of the Revolution and the Civil War. In Katayev's new apartment everything was new—including his wife and child and the furniture. "I like modern stuff," he said, screwing up his eyes. But Fedin, who lived on the floor below, went in for mahogany and his apartment was crammed with it. The writers had gone wild at having so much money for the first time in their lives. Shklovski had been given a new apartment three floors above Katayev. The floor on which they put you depended on your standing as a writer. Vishnevski had insisted on moving into the apartment allotted to Ehrenburg (who was abroad) because he considered it unbecoming for someone holding his position in the Union of Writers to live right at the top, under the roof. But the official reason he gave was that he was frightened of heights.

Walking around Shklovski's apartment, Katayev asked him: "But where do you keep your suits?" Shklovski still had the same old wife, the same children, and only one pair of trousers—or two at the most. But he had already ordered a suit for himself—the first in his life. It was

---

* An émigré station based in Munich.

no longer done to go around in shabby clothes, and you had to look respectable to visit editorial offices or a film studio. The leather jackets and Komsomol blouses of the twenties had completely gone out of style and you were expected to dress in conventional fashion. At the end of the last war, prizes were promised to teachers who could manage to get decent dresses for themselves.

Katayev treated us to Spanish wine and fresh oranges—which were now on sale again for the first time since the Revolution. Everything was just like old times! Except that in the old days there were no refrigerators, such as the electric one Katayev had brought with him from America: the little chunks of ice floating in our wine were the last word of modern luxury. Nikulin came in with his new wife, who had just borne him twins. Katayev was quite astonished that such a promiscuous pair could have children. I remembered something that Nikulin had said a long time before, but it no longer seemed so funny: "None of us is a Dostoyevski—all we need is money." He drank Spanish wine and held forth about the Spanish dialects—he had just been to Spain to take a look at the Civil War.

At the time we left Moscow for exile, the writers had not yet become a privileged caste, but now they were putting down roots and figuring out ways of keeping their privileges. Katayev revealed his own plan when he told us: "Nowadays one must write like Walter Scott." This was not the easiest way—it required hard work and talent.

The inhabitants of this building with the labradorite entrance understood the meaning of 1937 better than we did, because they saw both sides of what it entailed. It was like Doomsday, with some being trampled underfoot by demons, and others having their praises sung. Those who had tasted the delights of heaven had no wish to be cast down into the pit. Who can blame them? The decision taken at family councils and in discussion with friends was, therefore, that the only way of dealing with the situation which arose in 1937 was to adapt to it. "Valentin is devoted to Stalin," said Katayev's new wife, Esther, who knew from life in her parents' home what it was to be an outcast. And Katayev himself, chastened by earlier experiences, had long since gone around saying: "I don't want any trouble. The main thing is not to upset the powers-that-be."

"Who remembers Mandelstam nowadays?" Katayev asked us ruefully. "My brother and I always mention him when we talk to the younger people, but that's about all." M. was not offended to be told this, since it was quite true that he had been forgotten—though it was certainly not true that Katayev and his brother would ever dare mention him in conversation with strangers.

The new Moscow was now being built up and adopting the ways of the world—people were opening their first bank accounts, buying furniture and writing novels. Everybody could hope for speedy advancement because every day somebody was plucked from their midst and had to be replaced. Of course, everybody was also a candidate for prison and death, but during the day they did not think about it, giving full rein to their fears only at night. The people who fell by the wayside were immediately forgotten, and their wives—if they had been lucky enough to hang on to part of the accommodation shared with their arrested husbands—found that the doors of all "decent" apartments were now firmly slammed in their faces. Actually, by now few wives survived the arrest of their husbands—in 1937 whole families were being wiped out.

M. thought rather well of Katayev and said that he had a "real bandit's charm." We had first got to know him in Kharkov in 1922. In those days he was a ragamuffin with intelligent, lively eyes and had already been in serious trouble (which he managed to get out of). He was on his way to Moscow, which he intended to take by storm. He later used to come and see us there and tell us jokes he had heard in Mylnikov Street, the old Bohemian quarter of Odessa. Many of these stories we were later to read in *The Twelve Chairs*—Valentin had made a present of them to his brother, who came to Moscow from Odessa to get a job as a detective, but on his elder brother's advice became a writer instead.

Toward the end of the twenties, after their early successes, all the prose writers I knew in my youth—with the exception of Tynianov and Zoshchenko—began to churn out fiction in a rather sordid way. In the case of Katayev, thanks to his special blend of talent and cynicism, it was particularly blatant. Right at the end of the twenties I remember going somewhere in a taxi with him. We hadn't seen him for a very long time, because we had been living in Leningrad and the Crimea. The meeting was very friendly, and, sitting on the jump seat in the taxi, he talked incessantly. I had never before heard the like of some of the things he said. He reproached M. for not producing enough or getting his stuff published in large editions: "Suppose you die, what will your collected works be like? How many pages will they make? It won't be enough to send to the binders! Every writer should have twelve volumes with gilt edges." All this had a very familiar ring, not of the "new" era, but of something much older. Everything Katayev wrote could have come out in the fiction supplement to the pre-Revolutionary magazine *Niva*. His wife played the part of the bourgeois housewife and he was the perfect family despot who stamped his foot at the cook for burning the roast. As a boy he had been through too many terrors and suffered too much hunger, and now he wanted peace and stability, money and women—and the trust of his superiors. For a long time I could not tell when he was just joking and when he was revealing the ugly side of himself under the mask. "They're all the same," M. said to me, "but this one is clever."

I once met Katayev during the war, when I was living as an evacuee in Tashkent. He was very happy because somewhere near Aralsk he had seen a camel and it reminded him of M.: "He held his head back, just like Osip Emilievich." The sight had reminded Katayev of his youth and inspired him to write a poem. This was the whole difference between Katayev and the others—they would not have risked such unwise associations. Fedin, for example, would scarcely have been moved to write verse on seeing a camel that reminded him of Mandelstam. Of all the writers who were allowed to survive and live in comfort, only Katayev did not lose his love of poetry and feeling for literature. Otherwise M. could not have borne to drink Spanish wine with him in Moscow in June 1937. As he showed us out, Katayev said to M.: "Osip Emilievich, perhaps they'll let you settle down and become a good citizen at last. It's high time."

In the period when people were being "rehabilitated" after the Twentieth Congress, Katayev kept wanting to publish some of M.'s verse in *Yunost* [*Youth*], but he was too worried about angering the authorities. Unlike others, however, he did at least entertain the thought.

What would have become of Katayev if he hadn't been obliged to "write like Walter Scott"? He is a very talented man, with a lively intelligence and a quick wit, who belongs to the most enlightened wing of the present-day best-selling Soviet writers.

That summer we really wanted nothing more than to settle down and become "good citizens." We made all kinds of plans for the future—thinking how nice it would be, for instance, to get another apartment in a building with an elevator, so we wouldn't have to walk up to the fifth floor. But we figured there was no hurry about this—let Stavski first keep his promise to move Kostyrev out of our present apartment.

M. had a violent argument with my brother Evgeni on a question which seemed most important to us just then: should he take translating work or not? Evgeni said it was absolutely essential for him to do this kind of work for the time being, "and if you can't stand it, then Nadia must take it on." M. replied that he couldn't bear it himself and hated to see me doing it. The argument was decided for us by Luppol, the editor-in-chief of Goslit,* who said that, as long as it depended on him, Mandelstam would never be given a single line of translation or any other kind of work to do. Luppol was soon arrested and disappeared for good, but nothing changed when his job was taken over by somebody else. People come and go, but "decisions of principle" remain. The one affecting M. is still in force, and there seems to be no power on earth that can change it.

At the time Luppol's decision did not bring us to our senses—we still hoped that everything would somehow come out all right. Narbut had gone, so had Margulis, Klychkov and many others. M. kept muttering Gumilev's line: "Woe, woe, fear, the snare and the pit," but then he would again look on the bright side and tell me that everything would be all right. "Why are you moaning?" he would ask. "Live while you can, and then we'll see. It just can't go on like this!" For many years this phrase had been the only source of optimism: "It can't go on like this. . . ."

Reading the Bible, Akhmatova discovered that the words of Gumilev's poem are taken almost literally from the prophet Isaiah: "Fear, and the pit, and the snare, are upon thee, O inhabitant of the earth."

59

A "Convicted Person"

"Do firemen die?" M. had once been asked by his young niece Tatka. He had later echoed her by asking: "Do the rich die?"—in Voronezh it occurred to him that money and comfort increase one's chances of living longer. "Do people have to register in Moscow as well?" he asked, when I reminded him that it was time we got our residence permits. It so happened that Kostyrev came back at that moment for a couple of days, and this made M. realize that there was no time to

---

* State Publishing House for literature.

waste. He went down to the house committee office, but came back almost at once and asked for my papers. It turned out that after I had returned to Voronezh after a visit to Moscow earlier in the year, Kostyrev had got them to cancel my permit to live in the city: this was his way of preparing for our homecoming. Until then I had counted officially as a Moscow resident, while in Voronezh I had the status of a "visitor." The house committee did not know I had last renewed my papers in Voronezh, but I had managed to get away with this. Kostyrev had obtained a residence permit as occupant of a room in our apartment, and his temporary permit had now been made permanent even though he had not been here the required length of time—as they told us in the house committee office, the rule had been waived in his case. The building was a co-operative, and we had paid a large sum of money for our apartment. In law we were the owners of it, and theoretically nobody could be registered for residence in it without our permission. The authorities were now having trouble with co-operatives, because the families of arrested people referred to their legal rights in an attempt to stay put and prevent new tenants being moved in with them. A new law was in preparation to abolish these "rights." So far there had only been talk about it in high quarters and it was not actually passed until the end of 1938, but in this country they don't wait until laws are passed before putting them into effect! The fact that Kostyrev had been registered for residence in our apartment showed that he was being encouraged to take over the whole place, and this was a bad sign. But for some reason M. was not at all upset. He had become a fatalist of the Soviet type: "Everything will be all right if they want it that way. If they don't, there's nothing we can do about it." This fatalism began to affect me as well. Not long before, he had said to me: "You will return to Moscow if they let me back. They won't let you back alone." Now, a quarter of a century later, they have indeed allowed me to reside in Moscow again—although M. himself is still not "allowed back," if one doesn't count the publication of a few of his poems in the magazine *Moskva*.

Kostyrev was only a cog in a complex mechanism. He was a faceless person—the sort you would never notice on the street or in a bus, but he looked like many others of the same kind. In an earlier historical period he would have worn a pea-green overcoat,* but in our day such people rise to greater heights, and he became both a writer and a gen-

---

* Such coats were worn by police spies in Czarist times.

eral. Having settled in our apartment, he spent all his time at the type-writer, writing his stories about the Soviet Far East—and copying out M.'s verse. Once, as he was typing one of M.'s Crimean poems, he said to me: "Osip Emilievich only likes the Crimea because he's never been to the Far East." In his view, it was important for every writer to visit the Far East. This was said at a time when endless prison trains were going east to Vladivostok, and Kolyma was being converted into a vast penal colony—as we all knew perfectly well. Anybody to whom the secret police had attached someone of Kostyrev's rank had every prospect of seeing the Far East. But at the moment we were worried more about getting a residence permit than about Kolyma.

The district militia refused us the permit with unusual speed. They said we could try the Central militia station on Petrovka. "If they refuse," M. said, "we'll go back to Voronezh." We even phoned our old landlady there to ask her to keep our room for us, just in case. At the Petrovka station they also refused to give us the permit and explained why: M. could not be allowed back in Moscow because he had been a "convicted person." Nowadays, I am told, a past conviction no longer counts against someone if his sentence did not exceed five years and he has not been specifically deprived of his civic rights by the court, but in those days, and until recently, not only ex-prisoners but their families as well were marked for life by the fact of having been convicted. I have often had to fill in forms with a question about whether I or any close relative has ever been convicted of an offense. To cover up such unpleasant facts, people were always inventing new life stories for themselves. Whether children should mention that their father had died in prison or in a camp was a constant theme of family discussions. For several years I have been free of the stigma of M.'s conviction, but the literary stigma is still there.

At the Petrovka station we first learned all the implications of M.'s status as a "convicted person." "Where are you going now?" asked the militia official as he handed M. a slip of paper rejecting his application for a permit: he was supposed to enter our next place of residence in our file. "Back to Voronezh," M. replied. "Very well," said the official, "but you won't get registered there either." We now discovered that while as an exile M. had been barred from only twelve towns, as a "convicted person" he was banned from over seventy, and for life at that!

"And what would have happened if I had stayed in Voronezh?" M. asked. The official explained that because "we still have deficiencies in our work" M. might have been overlooked for a while, but he would sooner or later have been expelled. This sort of thing no longer surprises us: we are now familiar enough with the residence permit as a high barrier which only the most agile can clear. Nobody can just go and settle in the town of his choice (unless he has been sent there to work), and there is no question of a residence permit at all without identity papers—which means that vast categories of people—such as collective farmers—cannot move at all. Not everybody realizes, even now, what a great privilege it is to have identity papers. But in 1937 we were learning for the first time about this "progress," as M. called it.

When we came home, M. said to me: "Why don't you try to register without me? You are not a convicted person."

This was the first and only occasion on which he ever suggested we act as separate persons. And—in the hope of saving our apartment—I agreed to try my luck, just this once.

But I, too, was refused a permit. I went up to one of the high-ranking militia officials sitting at desks in the main hall of the Petrovka station and demanded an explanation. "Convicted person," said the official. "I have no conviction," I said indignantly. "What do you mean," the man said, and started looking through my papers. "Here we are: 'Osip Mandelstam, convicted person—'" "That's a man," I interrupted, "but I am a woman—Nadezhda." He conceded this point, but then flew into a fury: "He's your husband, though, isn't he?" He got up and banged his fist on the table: "Have you ever heard of Article 58?" He shouted something else as well, but I fled in terror, even though I knew perfectly well that his anger was feigned, that he was just following his instructions in refusing me a permit and simply had no answers to my tiresome questions. We all unfailingly carried out our instructions, and if anybody argued with us, all we could do was shout at them. We were fortunate if the nature of our instructions was relatively innocent—such as refusing medical certificates to people who needed them, cutting off grants to students, or assigning them, on graduation, to work in uncongenial places. Others had instructions that required them to arrest and deport people, beat them with their fists, and so forth. It was simply a question of your profession. I should not have been frightened if it had been simply a case of a bad-tempered militiaman shouting at me, but I knew that the State was speaking out of his mouth. Ever since then I have not been able to enter a militia station without trembling—particularly since my troubles with them are not over and my right to live where I do remains precarious.

When I left the militia station, M. was waiting for me on the street. We went back to the apartment that was no longer our home.

60

CHANCE

The fact that I was not able to register as a Moscow resident and thus keep the apartment in Furmanov Street meant that my fate was not subsequently bound up with M.'s. Wandering from place to place, and never having a home of my own, my connection with him was less conspicuous than it would have been if I had continued to live in Moscow. Everywhere I went, I was of course followed by my police file, but since I remained "in charge of Moscow," I could not be seriously harmed by denunciations of me in the various small towns where I lived. In some ways I owe my survival to Kostyrev for getting us out of the Moscow apartment. If I had stayed there, other writers in the building—either because they wanted the space, or for higher "reasons of State"—would certainly have brought me to the attention of the authorities.

I was saved by chance. Our lives were ruled by chance, but it more commonly led to death than to survival. After M.'s second arrest I often heard about such cases as I stood in line, waiting for hours on end to hand over money for him, or trying to get information in the Prosecutor's Office. I shall never forget the woman whose son had been arrested by chance, instead of a person of the same name who lived next door and happened to be out when the secret police came to pick him up. Though it meant moving mountains, the woman had managed to get through to some official and prove that her son had been arrested by mistake. An order had gone out for his release, but she was now told that her son was dead, having been killed in some quite improbable accident.

On hearing this in the Prosecutor's Office, the woman screamed and sobbed. The Prosecutor himself came out of his cubby-hole and shouted at her in the same mock-angry way in which the militia official had shouted at me. His purpose was to make her understand that he could not be expected to do his work properly unless he had peace and quiet. The duty of the Prosecutor was to give information about the length and nature of a person's sentence, not to notify relatives of his death. This woman must have had extraordinary persistence if she had managed to get them to tell her of her son's fate; such things were learned either by chance or not at all.

Other people from the line gathered around the Prosecutor and the howling woman, but she got no sympathy from them. "What's the use of crying?" asked one long-suffering woman who was also trying to find out about her son. "That won't bring him back to life, and she's only holding us up." The disturber of the peace was removed and order was restored.

Soviet citizens have a peculiar respect for Government offices. If the woman had loudly lamented her son's death at home, nobody would have thought anything of it, but to do so in a Government office was offensive to people's sense of order. We all have amazing powers of self-control—we were quite capable of coming to work with a smile on our face after a night in which our home had been searched or a member of the family arrested. We were always expected to smile. This was dictated by the instinct of self-preservation, concern for our family and friends, and our peculiarly Soviet code of behavior. During the second arrest of her son, Akhmatova infringed this code by screaming out loud in the presence of those who came to take him away. Apart from this one "lapse," however, she kept herself so well in hand that she even earned Surkov's approval: "Anna Andreyevna has struck it out so well all these years. . . ." What choice had she, with a hostage in jail? Was it just coincidence that practically none of us broke the rules of Soviet etiquette? M., for example, didn't observe them at all. He had no self-control—he joked, shouted, hammered on closed doors, raged and fumed, and never ceased to express astonishment at what was going on around us.

My self-control and discipline have now weakened to the point that I am writing these pages—although we have been told to be discriminating in the way we talk about the past. The only approved way is to show that, however bad things may have been for you, you neverthe-less remain faithful to the idea of Communism, always able to distinguish the truly important—our ultimate objective—from minor factors—such as your own ruined life. Nobody worries about the inherent absurdity of this approach—it even seems to have been suggested by people who have spent half their lives in the camps, to approving nods from those who sent them there in the first place. I have only once had a personal encounter with someone who shared this point of view. This was a chance companion in a train on which I was traveling from Pskov to Moscow—otherwise I should never have met the man, given the insuperable social barriers that stand between me and people of his type. I had been seen off at the station by a group of friends who were all pleased and excited about news we had heard the day before—namely, that Tvardovski had at last got permission to publish Solzhenitsyn's story* in *Novy Mir.*

"Who is this Solzhenitsyn?" asked the man sitting next to me in the compartment. One look at his frowning face was enough to tell me that the only possible link between us would be like that of connecting retorts in which the liquid can never reach the same level in both halves.

I told him about Solzhenitsyn and he gave his judgment: he should not be published. "Did you read the story 'The Rough Diamond'?" he asked me. "We could have done without that, too, but at least it had educational values."

In reply I said something about the need to tell the truth about the past.

To this he said: "You should realize that it was all a historical necessity."

"Why a necessity?" I objected. "We're now being told it was all a historical accident due to Stalin's bad character."

"You look like an educated person, yet you don't seem to have read your Marx properly," he said. "You must have forgotten what he says about accidents—they also happen by necessity, but people aren't aware of it." What he meant was that if it hadn't been Stalin, somebody else would have sent all those people to the camps.

My companion wore a military tunic without epaulettes, and he had the puffy, sallow face of someone who had spent all his life behind a desk and suffered from insomnia.

Listening to me talking with my friends at the station, he had also caught the name of Pasternak. He now gave me his view of the *Dr. Zhivago* affair with professional forthrightness: it had been a case of gross negligence on somebody's part. "How could they have allowed him to send it abroad like that? What a blunder!" He had not himself read Pasternak and had no intention of doing so. "Who reads him? I keep up with literature—I have to—but I'd never heard of him."

One Day in the Life of Ivan Denisovich, published in November 1962.

I said I bet he'd never heard of Tiutchev or Baratynski either.

He took out a notebook. "Who did you say? I must find out about them."

At first he told me he was a retired doctor (though he looked a little young to be on a pension) and was now helping the militia with juvenile delinquents. "Why have you given up medicine?" I asked. "I just had to," he replied. It appeared that he had practiced medicine only in the distant past. For most of his career he had done work that brought him into contact with both supporters and enemies of the Stalin regime—he claimed to know the opinions of both. "Where did you meet people who talked against it?" I asked, but he gave no reply. After his retirement he had settled in Tallin, where he had to live "in connection with my work." He had been given a three-room apartment there for himself, his wife and his younger son. "I have never heard of doctors getting a three-room apartment for a family of that size," I said. "It can happen," he replied curtly.

At this point he began to tell me, as a teacher, about his family problems. His two eldest children were all right and he was in fact just on his way to visit them. His daughter had married a regional Party secretary, and his son was also a Party official. But the younger son, who was born after the war, was no good at all. He was an idler who wanted to give up school and go to work in a factory. "How can he be an idler if he wants to work?" I asked. It appeared that he simply didn't want to live at home with his father because of things his friends had told him. Moreover, he was having a bad influence on his mother, who was also beginning to play up. "It's all because he's had too easy a time—the older ones grew up during the war and know what it means to suffer hardship. The young one's had everything that money can buy—all the oranges and chocolate he wanted. And now look at him. I should never have had him." He was unable to tell me what it would be like after the achievement of "full Communism" when all children will supposedly have everything they need. Did that mean they would all get out of control? Evidently his son's friends knew something of his father's past activities.

It was quite clear to me that I was talking to a "relic of Stalin's empire." Was it accidental that his son had revolted against him and that he was so much opposed to anyone probing into the past and scrutinizing the "historical necessity" which he had served with such zeal? Solzhenitsyn's story is like a touchstone: you can judge what a man's past (or his family's) has been like by the way he reacts to it. The past weighs heavily on us and we still have to make sense of it. It is difficult for us to confront it because so many people were implicated, either directly or indirectly, in what happened—or at least silently acquiesced in it. It is perfectly clear what people such as my chance traveling companion would like: they are simply waiting for the moment when they can give their blessing to a new generation of like-minded but more sophisticated heirs to Stalin's empire.

People who were silent or closed their eyes to what was happening also try to make excuses for the past. They generally accuse me of subjectivism, saying that I see only one side of the picture and ignore all the other things: the building up of industry, Meyerhold's stage productions, the Cheliuskin expedition and so forth. None of this, to my mind, absolves us from our duty to make sense of what happened. We have lived through a severe crisis of nineteenth-century humanism during which all its ethical values collapsed because they were founded only on man's needs and desires, his longing for personal happiness. The twentieth century has also shown us that evil has an enormous urge to self-destruction. It inevitably ends in total folly and suicide. Unfortunately, as we now understand, in destroying itself, evil may destroy all life on earth as well. However much we shout about these elementary truths, they will only be heeded by people who themselves want no more of evil. None of this, after all, is new: everything is always repeated, though on an ever greater scale. Luckily, I shall not see what the future holds in store.

61

THE ELECTRICIAN

"We shouldn't give up yet," M. said the next morning and went to the Union of Writers to see Stavski. But Stavski wouldn't see him, letting it be known through his secretary that he couldn't receive him for at least a week because he was frantically busy. From the Union of Writers M. went to the Literary Fund,* but on the stairway there he had a

---

* This is administratively separate from the Union of Writers and is supposed to give material aid to writers: loans, medical care, vacations, etc.

slight heart attack. He was brought home in an ambulance and told he must rest for the time being. This suited him very well—if he could manage to stay here until he got an interview with Stavski, he thought there was a good chance of obtaining a residence permit. What he didn't realize was that people like Stavski, and all the other intermediaries between us and the authorities, always say they are too busy and cannot spare a moment. It was exactly the same in 1959 when I was again thrown out of Moscow (for the last time) and Surkov told me that he just couldn't find a second to speak with his colleagues about me. Admittedly, on this occasion I was faced only with the prospect of having nowhere to live—it was not a matter of life and death, as it would have been in Stalin's time.

M. was in a fairly good mood as he lay resting on the "Bessarabian carriage." Every day he was visited by a doctor from the Literary Fund, and after ten days they arranged for him to be seen by a specialist, Professor Razumova, a woman with an intelligent face who had sketches by Nesterov on the walls of her office. We were surprised how readily she wrote out a certificate saying M. needed further rest in bed and a general check-up. Of course she had no reason to know what our legal situation was, but after all our tribulations in Cherdyn and Voronezh we were much struck by the way in which she and the other Literary Fund doctors treated us—it was just like the attitude of intellectuals to exiles in pre-revolutionary Russia.

At this point M. became obsessed with the idea of cheating fate and staying on in Moscow at any price—as the only city where we had a roof over our heads and could lead some sort of life. He was encouraged by the way the Literary Fund had helped him, sent doctors to him and inquired after his health. What was the explanation? It could have been that one of the officials there was sympathetic to M., or they may simply have taken fright when he had his attack and didn't want to be accused of failing to give him help in time. Both things were quite possible. Whatever it was, there was no doubt of the Literary Fund's desire to help, and in our conditions this was quite astounding.

Kostyrev suddenly arrived in the apartment, nosed around a little, banged all the doors, and then went out, telling my mother he would be staying in Moscow for a few days. He soon came back and left the door into our room open—we were sitting with Rudakov (who was passing through Moscow on his way to the Crimea) in the passage, blocked off by a cupboard, where we had put the "Bessarabian" bed.

We thought Kostyrev just wanted to eavesdrop, but it turned out that he was waiting for a visitor. When the visitor arrived he brought him into our room, where we were sitting behind the cupboard. The man appeared to be an electrician and we heard him tell Kostyrev that the wiring needed fixing. It struck me as odd that Kostyrev should bother about such household matters. M. was quite alarmed and I thought for a moment that his hallucinations had returned—before I could stop him he went straight up to the electrician and said: "Stop pretending and tell us what you want! Have you come for me?" "What's he saying!" I whispered to Rudakov, convinced that M. was delirious again. But, to my astonishment, the "electrician" seemed to think it was all quite normal. After a further exchange of words, he and M. showed each other their papers, and then the "electrician" asked M. to go with him to the militia station. I felt both horror and relief—horror at the thought of his being arrested and sent to a camp, and relief that he was not suffering from delusions again.

The man took M. off to the militia station and Rudakov ran after them. But they did not get as far as the station—on the way M. had another attack. He was again brought home in an ambulance and carried upstairs in a chair borrowed from Kolychev's apartment on the ground floor. While a doctor attended to M., the "electrician" waited in the room. When M. was a little rested, he showed all his medical certificates to our strange visitor, who asked to be given the one with a triangular stamp which had been signed by Razumova. Taking it with him, he went to Kostyrev's room to make a telephone call. Having got his instructions, he came back and said to M.: "Stay where you are for now." Then he left us.

M. stayed in bed for several days. Every day, in the morning and evening, the "electrician" or one of his colleagues—always in civilian clothing—looked in on us. During the day M. was able to joke about it ("All the trouble they're having with me!") and consoled himself with the thought that if he hadn't exposed the "electrician" they would have come to pick him up at night. He was not so cheerful at night. Once I woke up and saw him standing at the foot of the bed with his head thrown back and his hands spread wide. "What is it?" I asked. He pointed at the wide-open window. "Isn't it time? Let's do it, while we're still together." "Not yet," I said, and he didn't argue. I am not sure I was right. We should both have been spared so much torment.

The next morning we endured the visit of the "electrician," who was now promising to send his "own doctor," but before he came again in the evening we slipped out of the house and went to Yakhontov's apartment, where we stayed the night. In the morning I came back to our place to get our things ready to leave, but Kostyrev insisted on taking me around to the militia station. "Where is Mandelstam?" they asked me. "He's gone away." "Where?" "I don't know." They then said we must clear out of Moscow within twenty-four hours.

For his pains Kostyrev was rewarded with our apartment. His widow and daughter still live there. I would like his daughter to read this, but the children of such parents do not read books—unless they also work in the literary section of the Lubianka and have to by way of duty. In that case it is probably better that she doesn't see this manuscript.

We stayed with Yakhontov for three days and spent the whole time consulting maps of the Moscow region. At last we settled on Kimry. It was easy to get to from the Savelovo railroad station near the Moscow suburb of Maryina Roshcha, where the Yakhontovs lived. Another attractive feature was that it was on the Volga—if one must live in a small provincial town, then better it should be on a river. We did not go back to our apartment on Furmanov Street—M.'s brother Alexander and my brother Evgeni volunteered to bring our things to the station. To say goodbye to my mother, who was still in the apartment, we called her down into the street. She was quite startled when M. went up to her with outstretched hand and said: "Hello, my illegal mother-in-law."

It was the beginning of June when we left Moscow.

It must be said that the militia had shown unusual humanity and tender-heartedness by allowing a sick man to stay on illegally in Moscow until he was well enough to travel. They are not generally so considerate, and they would have been quite within their rights to insist that we leave immediately.

62

IN THE COUNTRY

"Rather early for us to come out to the country this year," said M. after we had taken refuge from the Moscow militia in the small village of Savelovo on the high bank of the Volga opposite Kimry. It was set in sparse woodland, and in the market there the peasants sold berries, as well as milk and buckwheat for making kasha. There was a tearoom where we could go and read the local newspaper, which had the comic name *The Invalid's Echo.* The tearoom was lit by a smoky kerosene lamp, whereas at home we had only candles. It was very difficult for M. to read by this kind of light because of the bad state of his eyes. We have all ruined our eyesight through having to sit by kerosene lamps all our lives. In fact, however, we had brought very few books with us, since we did not expect to settle here. This was only a temporary halt which we needed to have a rest and take stock of our situation.

Savelovo is a village with two or three streets. All the houses looked well-built and were made of wood with old-fashioned fretwork window-frames and gates. Not far away was the village of Kalyazin, which would shortly be submerged in the waters of the artificial lake then being made. It would have been possible to get one of the excellent frame houses from Kalyazin and set up house in Savelovo if only we had had the money to buy one.

The inhabitants of Savelovo worked mainly at the nearby factory, but they got a livelihood from the river by catching fish and selling it on the black market. It also provided them with fuel for the winter—on summer nights they used boathooks to pull in logs as they were floated down from the lumber camps on the upper reaches of the river. In those days the Volga still fed those who lived on its banks, but now a stop has been put to this as well, and the rivers are no longer a source of livelihood.

We preferred to remain in Savelovo—which was the last station on the railroad—rather than cross over to Kimry, a shabby little town on the other side of the river. This would have made it more difficult for us to make day trips into Moscow. The railroad was a kind of lifeline for us. As our friend G.M. told us—she had been through the prisons and camps and knew what it was to be a "convicted person"—it didn't matter what god-forsaken place you settled in as long as you could hear the whistles of passing trains.

The forbidden city of Moscow was like a magnet. People of our status were allowed to reside only at points just over a hundred kilometers away, and all the places within reach of the railroads in this belt around the city were crammed with former prisoners and exiles.

Particularly popular was the small town of Alexandrov, because it was possible to get to Moscow and back in one day by changing to the electric train at Zagorsk. This meant a journey of three hours instead of four or four and a half on other lines into Moscow. After a day in Moscow, where one would go to get some money to live on, or to make the rounds of officials in connection with one's case, it was advisable to return by the last train to the place where you were registered.

In 1937, when people who had been in trouble were re-arrested on a mass scale, the secret police found it very convenient to have their victims all gathered together at these focal points just beyond the hundred-kilometer perimeter around Moscow. It was much easier than tracking them down individually. Whole towns could be cleared out at one fell swoop. Since these operations were carried out according to plans for which "production quotas" were set, the police agents involved were no doubt well rewarded for their self-sacrificing efforts in reaching their targets. Every time these small towns were emptied in this way, they would at once begin to fill up again with new ex-prisoners who in due course were all picked up in their turn.

People found it hard to believe that small places like Alexandrov could serve as traps. It never occurred to them that whole categories were being systematically wiped out. Everybody believed that he was the object of individual proceedings, and the stories about "bewitched places" (i.e., where you were more likely to be arrested) were dismissed as old wives' tales. We had already been warned in Moscow about a great round-up going on in Alexandrov, but we hadn't believed it. The only reason we didn't go there was that M. feared this "crazed borough," as he called it in one of his poems. "We couldn't find a worse place," he said. Furthermore, we heard that it was monstrously expensive to rent rooms there.

In Savelovo there were no former prisoners or exiles apart from us and a few common criminals who had come here to weather the storm of the current mass arrests. They were not a target of the great round-up, but they could always be thrown in for good measure if there was any danger of the "production quota" not being met. We got talking with one of these criminals in the tearoom and he gave us a very clear explanation of why Savelovo was preferable to Alexandrov or Kolomna: "If the mob all gathers in one place, they can be skimmed off like cream." He was wiser than all those gullible people sentenced under Article 58—many of them had been to a university in the old days and were firmly persuaded that nobody could be called to account twice for the same crime. And since they were not aware of having done anything wrong, they kept hoping they would be cleared ("It can't go on like this") but instead found themselves being taken away in the "Black Maria."

Between the years 1948 and 1953 I was again to witness one of these round-ups of former prisoners and exiles. It was in a sense a minor drama, without the mass graves and tortures so typical of our age. I was living at that time in Ulianovsk (Lenin's birthplace) and saw how it was swept clean of everybody who had previous convictions. Some of them were picked up straightaway, but others first had their residence permits canceled and were thus forced to move out somewhere beyond the hundred-kilometer radius. The most popular small town to which they went was Melikez. Among them was a violinist I knew who had once been a member of the Party and of the Association of Proletarian Musicians (RAMP), where he had dabbled in musical politics together with Briusov's sister. In 1937 he was sent to a camp and, after serving a sentence of eight or ten years, went to live in Ulianovsk at the end of the forties. Almost out of his mind with joy, and thinking the worst was now over—how many of us fell for this illusion!—he decided to start a new life. His previous wife and children having "disowned" him, he married a nice colleague of mine in Ulianovsk and got a job in the music school there. They had a son who was soon reaching for his father's violin, and his happy father was dreaming of making a violinist of him. He was always telling me that there was no greater happiness than to live for art, and he quoted the Marxist classics to this effect. Suddenly, when his little son was three years old, he was summoned to the militia station and told that his permit to reside in Ulianovsk had been rescinded, and that he must leave the city within twenty-four hours. I happened to visit him and his wife that same day, and I could see at once from their faces what had been done to them. From then on I was the only person they could confide in— such things had to be kept secret, otherwise the whole family was liable to suffer.

That same night the violinst left for Melikez, where he managed to rent a corner of a room and start making a little money by giving violin and piano lessons. But very soon they began arresting former camp inmates there, too. In small towns such news spread very quickly, since landladies could never resist telling their neighbors about the arrest of a lodger. These arrests meant that the local authorities had been ordered to clear the town of all "suspicious elements" that had gathered there. Everybody now rushed to leave the town, and the station was crowded with "refugees." My violinist friend managed to get out in time, and for the next two and a half years, right up to the death of Stalin, he kept permanently on the move, going up and down the Volga from one small town to another. In some places, already packed with refugees, he was not able to find a corner to live in, or the police refused to register him. Sometimes he managed to get a job teaching music in a local school, but wherever he went he always had to leave in a hurry the moment he heard they had started picking people up. In the course of these wanderings he sometimes passed through Ulianovsk and went to see his wife. But he could only do this at dead of night—if he had shown his face on the street in the daytime, the neighbors would have reported him immediately. He got very thin, developed a bad cough and constantly trembled with fear. After these visits he would set off once more with his violin to begin all over again in some new town. He once even went up to Moscow to complain to the Arts Committee, where he was still remembered, that the music schools were hiring people without any education while he, with all his qualifications, was unable to get work. They promised to help, but there were soon arrests in the small town where he was hoping to get a permanent job, and he had to flee as usual, without learning whether or not the Moscow officials had kept their promise.

After Stalin's death he was allowed, as an invalid, to return to his wife in Ulianovsk. He died at home, but he was never able to teach his son to play the violin—he didn't dare go near the boy for fear of infecting him with the TB he had caught while roaming the country to save his life.

Yet this violinst was comparatively lucky. His wife had been able to stay where she was and had not been dismissed from her work (this was because she had concealed their marriage, which had in any case not been officially registered); he managed to escape arrest thanks to his experience in recognizing the danger signals in time, and he was not Jewish—Jews were the most exposed at that period. His violin gave him the means of earning his daily bread—no more than this, but it kept him alive. He also had the advantage that musicians suffered less than members of other professions. Even so, it was only his tremendous stamina that saved him. Almost anybody else in his place would have waited to be picked up in Melikez on the principle that "you can't hide from them." His only reason for making such an effort to save himself was to be able to come home to die—even this is a great luxury in our conditions.

Looking at the fortunate violinist, I always wondered what would have happened to M.—who was about the same age—if he had survived and returned from the camps. If we had been able to foresee all the alternatives, we would not have missed that last chance of a "normal" death offered by the open window of our apartment in Furmanov Street.

Voronezh was a miracle, and it was a miracle that brought us there. But such things happened only once.

63

ORDEAL BY FEAR

When I used to read about the French Revolution as a child, I often wondered whether it was possible to survive during a reign of terror. I now know beyond doubt that it is impossible. Anybody who breathes the air of terror is doomed, even if nominally he manages to save his life. Everybody is a victim—not only those who die, but also all the killers, ideologists, accomplices and sycophants who close their eyes or wash their hands—even if they are secretly consumed with remorse at night. Every section of the population has been through the terrible sickness caused by terror, and none has so far recovered, or become fit again for normal civic life. It is an illness that is passed on to the next generation, so that the sons pay for the sins of the fathers and perhaps only the grandchildren begin to get over it—or at least it takes on a different form with them.

Who was it who dared say that we have no "lost generation" here? The fact that he could utter such a monstrous untruth is also a consequence of terror. One generation after another was "lost" here, but it was a completely different process from what may have happened in the West. Here people just tried to go on working, struggling to maintain themselves, hoping for salvation, and thinking only about their immediate concerns. In such times your daily round is like a drug. The more you have to do, the better. If you can immerse yourself in your work, the years fly by more quickly, leaving only a gray blur in the memory. Among the people of my generation, only a very few have kept clear minds and memories. In M.'s generation, everybody was stricken by a kind of sclerosis at an early stage.

True as this is, however, I never cease to marvel at our hardiness. After Stalin's death my brother Evgeni said to me: "We still do not realize what we have been through." Not long ago, as I was traveling in an overcrowded bus, an old woman pushed up against me and I found my arm was bearing the whole weight of her body. "That must be killing you," she said suddenly. "No," I replied, "we're as tough as the devil." "As tough as the devil?" she said, and laughed. Somebody nearby also laughingly repeated the phrase, and soon the whole bus was saying it after us. But then the bus stopped and everybody started to push toward the exit, jostling each other in the usual way. The little moment of good humor was over.

In the period of the Yezhov terror—the mass arrests came in waves of varying intensity—there must sometimes have been no more room in the jails, and to those of us still free it looked as though the highest wave had passed and the terror was abating. After each show trial, people sighed, "Well, it's all over at last." What they meant was: Thank God, it looks as though I've escaped. But then there would be a new wave, and the same people would rush to heap abuse on the "enemies of the people." There was nothing people wouldn't say about the victims in order to save themselves. "Stalin doesn't have to cut heads off," said M., "they fly off by themselves like dandelions." I think he said this after reading an article by Kossior and then learning that he had been arrested nevertheless.

In the summer of 1937 we lived in the country like vacationers—as M. said, "It's always easier in the summer." We went into Moscow fairly often, and we even visited friends at their dachas in other parts of the country around about. We went, for instance, to see Pasternak at Peredelkino.* He told us he thought his wife was baking a cake down in the kitchen. He went to tell her of our arrival, but came back looking glum: she clearly wanted to have nothing to do with us. A few years later, when I had returned from Tashkent and tried to telephone Pasternak, she answered the phone and said: "Please don't come out here to Peredelkino." After that I never tried to call him again, but whenever he ran into me on Lavrushinski Street, near the house where I lived for a long time with Vasilisa Shklovski, he would come up to see me in the apart-

* A writers' colony in the country near Moscow.

ment. He was also the only person to come and see me on hearing of M.'s death.

On that last visit that M. and I made to Pasternak in Peredelkino, he came to see us off at the station and we spent a long time talking on the platform, missing train after train. Pasternak was still obsessed by Stalin and complained that he could not write poetry any more because he had not been able to get a personal meeting with him as a result of their famous telephone conversation. M. smiled sympathetically, but I felt nothing but dismay. After the war it appears that Pasternak rid himself of this obsession—at least he never mentioned it again in conversation with me. As regards his novel, *Dr. Zhivago,* the idea must have come to him well before the war—every time we met him he told us he was writing a prose work "about us all." As one can see from the novel itself, the basic idea may have changed in the course of the years, but it was a time in which people were always frantically changing their minds, never sure who was right.

During the years of the terror Shklovski had no illusions, but he always hoped that the arrests reflected mainly a "settling of accounts" within the ruling group. For instance, when Koltsov was arrested, he said it did not affect us, but he was terribly upset whenever real intellectuals were picked up. He was anxious to survive so that one day he could be a "witness." But by the time the Stalin era was over, we had all grown old and lost the keenness of vision one needs to be a witness. This is what happened to Shklovski.

Lev Bruni, when we went to see him at this time, shoved some money into M.'s pocket and said: "Who needs this cursed regime?" Marietta Shaginian pretended that she hadn't heard anything about arrests: "Who are they arresting? What for? Why are the wretched intellectuals making such a fuss because half a dozen people have been arrested for conspiracy?" Her own daughter shouted into her ear about the Tretiakov family, but, taking refuge in her deafness, she affected not to hear.

Adalis was scared to let us stay the night, which was natural enough, but then she put on a silly act of trying to persuade us to go and spend the night at our old apartment in Furmanov Street: "I'll come along with you, and if the militia trouble you, I'll explain everything to them—I promise I will." People were quite beside themselves and said the first thing that came into their heads, in sheer self-defense. The ordeal by fear is the most terrible there is, and people never recover from it.

We had nothing to live on and we had to go and beg from our friends. We spent part of the summer on money given us by Katayev, his brother (Evgeni Petrov) and Mikhoels. Mikhoels embraced M. and vied with Markish in trying to console him. Yakhontov gave us money all the time, until he went away.

Every time we came into Moscow for the day, M. went to the Union of Writers, trying to get an interview with Stavski, but Stavski wouldn't see him and sent him instead to his deputy, Lakhuti.

Lakhuti did his best to arrange something for M. He even sent him on commission from the Union of Writers to the White Sea Canal, begging him to write a poem about it. This is the poem that Akhmatova empowered me to burn. It would not, incidentally, have satisfied those who commissioned it: M. was only able to turn out something on the landscape.

64

COW OR POETRY READING?

Like everybody else, we tried to devise ways of saving ourselves. It is only in the East that people voluntarily throw themselves into the flames, but we still thought of ourselves as Europeans. Both M. and I had different plans—all they had in common was their absolute unfeasibility.

My plan was summed up by the word "cow." In our country, where all means of earning a livelihood are in the hands of the State, there are only two ways of maintaining a private existence: begging, or keeping a cow. We had tried begging, but found it unbearable. Everybody shies away from beggars and nobody wants to give alms, particularly as all they have comes to them by courtesy of the State. There had been a time when the ordinary people in Russia always took pity on prisoners and convicts, and the intelligentsia regarded it as a duty to support anyone persecuted for political reasons. All this disappeared together with "abstract humanism." Apart from this, people were frightened of us—we were not only beggars, we were also lepers. Everybody was afraid of everybody else: not even the "safest" person was immune— they could even come at night for someone who had just published an article in *Pravda* denouncing the "enemies of the people." Every arrest was followed by a chain reaction of others—the relatives and friends of the arrested man, as well as those whose telephone numbers were scribbled in his notebook, or in whose company he had celebrated the New Year. . . . People were frightened of every meeting and of every conversation, but they gave a particularly wide berth to people like us who had already been touched by the plague. And we ourselves felt that we were spreading the infection and wanted nothing more than to hide away and not see anybody.

This was why I dreamed of a cow. Thanks to the vagaries of our economic system, a family could support itself for many years by keeping a cow. Millions lived in wretched huts, feeding themselves from the products of their tiny plots of land (on which they grew potatoes, cabbage, cucumbers, beets, turnips and onions) and their cow. Some of the milk had to be sold to buy hay, but there was always enough left over to add a little richness to the cabbage soup. A cow gives people some independence and, without over-exerting themselves, they can earn a little extra to buy bread. The State is still in a quandary about this relic of the old world: if people are allowed to buy hay to feed their cow, then they do only the very minimum of work on the kolkhoz; if, on the other hand, you take their cows away, they will die of hunger. The result is that the cow is alternately forbidden and then permitted again. But the number of cows is gradually decreasing, because the peasant women no longer have the strength to fight for them.

A cow would have saved us, and I was sure I would be able to learn how to milk it. We would have merged with the background somewhere, living very obscurely and never leaving our house. But to buy a house and cow you needed money—even now I wouldn't be able to afford them. Peasant women came to us in Savelovo, offering us their frame houses for a song, and nothing could have been more tempting. But to settle in the countryside you need to have been born there and inherit a hut with a leaking roof and a broken fence from some old peasant woman. Perhaps in capitalist countries there might be people eccentric enough to give an exiled poet the money to buy himself a peasant hut and a cow, but there could be no question of it here. To do so would have been regarded as a crime, and the benefactors themselves would speedily have ended up in a labor camp.

M. was not keen on my plan. Apart from the fact that we had no money to bring it about, the idea itself did not appeal to him. "Nothing ever comes of such schemes," he said. His plan was the reverse of mine—instead of merging with the background, he wanted to attract attention to himself. He believed that if only he could induce the Union of Writers to arrange a public reading of his poetry, then it would be impossible to refuse him work. He still harbored the illusion that you could win people over with poetry. This was something he had felt in his youth, when he once said to me that nobody could deny him anything if he wrote verse. It was probably quite true—things had been good for him in those days, his friends valued and protected him. But it was of course meaningless to apply those standards to the Moscow of 1937. Moscow no longer had faith in anything, and the order of the day was: every man for himself. Moscow now had no time for any civilized values, let alone for poetry. We knew this well enough, but M. was restless by nature and could not just sit waiting on events. Moreover, an outcast could live only if he kept on the move—M. was not to be given a moment's respite until his death.

Lakhuti seized on the idea of a poetry reading, which he too thought might save M. I know nothing at all of Lakhuti, except that he was friendly and kind to us. In the brutal atmosphere of those days, his friendliness seemed like a miracle. Neither he nor Stavski could decide the question of a reading without consulting higher authority. While this matter of State was being considered "up above," we waited in Savelovo, occasionally coming in to Moscow and going to the Union to see whether there was any progress. On one of these visits M. had a conversation with Surkov in the corridor, and when he came out, he found 300 roubles in his pocket. Surkov must have put them there without M. noticing. Not everybody would have risked such a thing— the consequences could have been very unpleasant. In any final estimate of Surkov, one should not forget this gift of money to M. It was rather like the onion which, in Russian tradition, the sinner must hang on to if he wants the Virgin to pull him into heaven at the last moment.

For a long time there was no word about the poetry reading, but then suddenly M.'s brother Evgeni had a phone call from the Union and was asked to inform M. urgently that it had been fixed for the next evening. Cables were very unreliable and, rather than take chances, Evgeni rushed to the station and caught the last train out to Savelovo. At that moment he too no doubt thought that M. might be saved by a poetry reading.

The next day we traveled to Moscow and went to the Union of Writers at the stated time. The secretaries were still there, but nobody knew anything about a poetry reading—they had only heard some vague rumor, but couldn't remember exactly what. All the rooms it could have been held in were locked, and there were no posters announcing it.

It only remained to find out whether anybody had received a circular about it. Shklovski told us that nothing had been sent to him, but he advised us to ring one of the poets—invitations were generally sent around only to members of the relevant section. We happened to have Aseyev's telephone number and M. phoned him to ask whether he had received a notice. After a moment or two M. turned pale and hung up: Aseyev said that he had heard something vaguely, but that he couldn't talk just now because he was about to leave for the Bolshoi Theater to see *The Snow Maiden*. . . . M. didn't have the heart to try anybody else.

We were never able to unravel the mystery of the poetry reading. Somebody had certainly rung Evgeni from the Union of Writers, but we never discovered who. It might have been the personnel department (always closely connected with the secret police) which had not bothered to inform the secretaries and given them no instructions—it was they who usually attended to the practical arrangements for such things. But why would the personnel department have been involved? The thought crossed our minds that it had all been a trap designed to lure M. from Savelovo for the purpose of arresting him in Moscow, but that nothing had come of it because somebody had forgotten to get top-level clearance—perhaps from Stalin himself. Since Stalin had been personally interested in M.'s case, this may well have been so. Otherwise M. might have been picked up in a way which had now become common practice for the overworked secret police—instead of going to arrest people in their homes, they lured them on some pretext to a convenient place from which they could be sent straight to the Lubianka. There were many stories about such cases. But there was no point in speculating about it, so we returned to Savelovo and pretended to be vacationers again.

Both our plans for salvation thus collapsed—M.'s suddenly, and mine more gradually. Such dreams offered no way out.

It was quite natural that Aseyev should have mentioned *The Snow Maiden*, rather than some other opera, as his excuse for not being able to talk: the poetic faction to which he belonged had once shown a weakness for pre-Christian Russia. But we omitted to inquire what was being performed that evening at the Bolshoi Theater and whether, indeed, it had not already been closed for the summer. I am told that in his old age Aseyev was lonely and isolated. He explained his isolation by saying that he had lost his standing because of his fight against the "cult of personality." Friends of Kochetov write articles to say that even he (Kochetov) fought against the "cult of personality." It now seems there were no Stalinists at all, only brave fighters against the "cult of personality." I can testify that nobody I knew fought—all they did was to lie low. This was the most that people with a conscience could do—and even that required real courage.

65
THE OLD FRIEND

The fiasco over the poetry reading did not break M.'s will. "We'll have to wait until the fall now," he said. It was already July and Moscow was empty, so we no longer hatched plans of salvation but thought only of how we could hold out till the fall. "We must change our profession—we are beggars now," M. declared, and he proposed we make a trip to Leningrad.

It was noteworthy that in this last year M. and I no longer conversed as we had always done earlier, when I had often remembered things he said and the exact words he used. Now we exchanged inarticulate phrases or short interjections ("I'm tired . . . must lie down . . . can't go on . . . must do something . . . Lord, who will they arrest next? . . .")

When life becomes absolutely intolerable, you begin to think the horror will never end. In Kiev during the bombardment I understood that even the unbearable can come to an end, but I was not yet fully aware that it often does so only at death. As regards the Stalinist terror, we always knew that it might wax or wane, but that it might end—this we could never imagine. What reason was there for it to end? Everybody seemed intent on his daily round and went smilingly about the business of carrying out his instructions. It was essential to smile—if you didn't, it meant you were afraid or discontented. This nobody could afford to admit—if you were afraid, then you must have a bad conscience. Everybody who worked for the State—and in this country even the humblest stall-keeper is a bureaucrat—had to strut around wearing a cheerful expression, as though to say: "What's going on is no concern of mine, I have very important work to do, and I'm terribly busy. I am trying to do my best for the State, so do not get in my way. My conscience is clear—if what's-his-name has been arrested, there must be good reason." The mask was taken off only at home, and then not always—even from your children you had to conceal how horror-struck you were; otherwise, God save you, they might let something slip in school. . . . Some people had adapted to the terror so well that they knew how to profit from it—there was nothing out of the ordinary about denouncing a neighbor to get his apartment or his job. But while wearing your smiling mask, it was important not to laugh—this could look suspicious to the neighbors and make them think you were in-dulging in sacrilegious mockery. We have lost the capacity to be spon-taneously cheerful, and it will never come back to us.

When we arrived in Leningrad, we went straight to see Lozinski, who was living in an isolated dacha near Luga. He immediately gave us 500 roubles so we could return to Savelovo and pay the rent for our room there till the end of the summer. There had never been any sta-bility about money and prices. On a free market the rise and fall of prices is governed by natural trends, but we could never make sense of the constant fluctuation of prices in our planned economy, where prices were always being raised or lowered in a seemingly arbitrary fashion. It was therefore difficult to say what the worth of these 500 roubles was, but there was still a certain magic in denominations of hundreds or thousands, and when Lozinski gave us 500 roubles we no longer felt like ordinary beggars, but like very superior ones who col-lected their alms wholesale instead of stretching out their hands for kopecks.

We had dinner with Lozinski, who played the fool and joked. Both M. and he laughed as in the old days at the Poets' Guild. Then M. read his poems for a long time. Afterward Lozinski saw us back to the sta-tion. The road at first went through woodland, but when we came to streets where there were people about, we did not want him to come any further in case somebody saw him with two suspicious strangers. The worst would have been to run into someone from the Union of Writers who knew M. by sight. We did not want to compromise Lozin-ski and left him at the edge of the woods.

Born in the nineties of the last century, Akhmatova, Lozinski and M. found that in the thirties they already constituted the oldest gener-ation of the intelligentsia—their elders had perished, emigrated or completely faded out of the picture. These three were therefore looked upon as ancients, while some of the Fellow Travelers like Kaverin, Fedin and Tikhonov, who were actually only a few years younger, were regarded as mere striplings. Babel stood apart from the rest, and was not thought of as being either young or old. As though to confirm the public attitude toward them, both Lozinski and M. aged very early. In 1929, when M. was working for the *Moscow Komsomol* newspaper on Tverskaya Street, the doorman there once said to me, as I was looking for him: "The old man has gone to the buffet." He was still not forty at the time, but his heart was already giving him trouble. Ehrenburg, incidentally, is wrong when he says that M. was short in height—he was in fact taller than Ehrenburg, and though I myself am of medium height, I scarcely came up to his ears, even when I wore high heels. Neither was M. as frail as Ehrenburg makes him out to be. He was in fact quite broad-shouldered. Ehrenburg remembered him as he was in the Crimea when he was starving, and he was also aiming at a journalistic effect by describing him as a puny, delicate Jewish type like Ashkenazi*—so weak and helpless, and look what they did to him! But M. was not like Ashkenazi at all—he was much more robust.

M.'s heart succumbed to the impossible demands made on it by our life and his own unruly temperament. Lozinski, on the other hand, was stricken by a mysterious kind of elephantiasis—it was like something Biblical and seemed out of place in Leningrad. His fingers, tongue and lips had swollen to twice their normal size. I had first seen him in the middle of the twenties, when he came to see us on Morskaya Street. He seemed to sense the approach of his illness already, and he was saying that after the Revolution everything had become difficult and people tired from the slightest exertion—talking, walking or just meeting someone. Lozinski, like M., had already tasted prison by this time, and he was one of those who always kept a bag packed in case of arrest. He was picked up several times—once because some of his students at a seminar on translation had given each other nicknames. Nicknames made the Cheka unhappy and put thoughts of conspiracy into their heads. The whole seminar was clapped in jail. Fortunately, Lozinski's wife had a good contact in Moscow, and whenever her husband was arrested, she at once rushed to her protector. The same thing was true of Zhirmunski's wife and it was only owing to this good fortune—the

* Vladimir Ashkenazi, the Soviet pianist, now resident in the West.

protecting hand of someone in Moscow—that both got off so lightly in those days. Both Lozinski and Zhirmunski seemed marked men from the beginning, and everybody was pleased to see Lozinski's name in the list of the first writers ever to receive Soviet decorations. He was quite out of place in this company, and it soon turned out that in any case such decorations were no guarantee—you were simply stripped of them on your arrest. But Lozinski was lucky and died of his own terrible and improbable disease.

We all emerged shaken and sick from the first years of the Revolution. At the beginning it was the women who were affected most, but in the long run they were the tougher and the more likely to survive. The men seemed stronger and withstood the first shocks, but then their hearts gave out and very few lived to be seventy. Those spared by war and prison were carried away by heart attacks or the sort of fantastic diseases from which Lozinski and Tynianov suffered. Nobody here will ever believe that cancer is not connected with the shocks to which we are constantly exposed. We have seen too many cases in which someone has been publicly hounded and threatened, only to hear shortly afterward that he has cancer. The statistics keep talking about the rise in the average life expectancy, but this must be due to the high proportion of women—we are certainly as tough as the devil!

66

TANIA, THE NON-PARTY BOLSHEVIK

M.'s brother, Evgeni Emilievich, lived with his family on Siverskaya Street. After leaving Lozinski, we went there only because M. wanted to see his father. He had no dealings with his brother, who had given up medicine to become a kind of literary agent on the fringe of the writers' organizations—he collected royalties for playwrights and did similar profitable jobs for the Literary Fund. Now, in his old age, he has switched to the film industry. He never helped M. and was always demanding that we take their father off his hands. He harped on this theme every time we met, and kept writing to us about it—even when we were in Voronezh and Savelovo. M. wrote to him several times from

Voronezh and, knowing that Evgeni would destroy these letters, made copies of them. In them he denounced Evgeni's attitude toward himself, and asked him never to remind people that he was his brother. Until 1956 Evgeni did not have to be asked to keep quiet about this fact, and he was always very rude to anybody who inquired about me. In recent years, however, he has come to respect M.'s memory, and has even tried to resume contact with me. Once he even came to see me out of the blue, and urged me to go and visit him. He is a man of mercenary instincts who has achieved everything he wanted in life: comfort, money, a car and a movie camera to amuse himself with in his spare time. In our cruel life, such people are not businessmen in the ordinary sense, but simply "get by" in a way which is never very pretty.

Another reason M. had for visiting him on this occasion was that he wanted to see his niece Tatka. This was Evgeni's daughter by his first marriage to the sister of Sarra Lebedeva. Later Tatka got TB during the blockade of Leningrad and died young. She was a wonderful little girl, completely unlike her father. She had been brought up by her maternal grandmother, the splendid old Maria Nikolayevna Darmolatova, in whose apartment Evgeni Emilievich still lives. After M.'s arrest, her grandmother arranged for me to meet her secretly at her mother's apartment—her father had forbidden her to see me. She complained to me that her father had burned a manuscript copy of M.'s poetry which she had acquired with great difficulty from some young literary enthusiasts. At that time there were still very few copies in circulation and they were always confiscated during house searches.

By the time the war began, Tatka was a student at the literature faculty of Leningrad University and was about to marry a young man who wrote poetry and revered the memory of M. He was killed in the first battles of the war, and Tatka trudged around starving Leningrad trying to get news of him. Tatka had a very hard time at home. Her father was always quarreling with her grandmother, exposing her as a "reactionary" in the manner of a militant young Komsomol. As for her stepmother, Tatka had nothing at all in common with her. I was constantly amazed that a girl who had grown up in such hard times and in such a difficult family had managed to withstand all the blandishments of the "new era" and preserve the best traditions of the Russian intelligentsia—forgotten, spurned and superseded by the higher reason of the "new" morality as it was.

Tatka's stepmother, Tania Grigoriev, the daughter of a chemistry teacher in one of the best and most progressive pre-revolutionary grammar schools, had grown up in an ultra-intellectual family of the kind that remained true to the style of the sixties and worshipped Belinski and Dobroliubov. She was proud of this family tradition and looked down on Tatka's grandmother because of her aristocratic origins. In appearance, too, Tania was the very image of a pre-revolutionary radical woman student—she had the clever face, the smooth nondescript hair done into a bun, and wore the dowdy dress once typical of the most "progressive" schoolmarms. She had a soft voice and a witty tongue. She was very proud of the fact that she knew the names of all the trees, grasses and birds, because her father used to take his daughters on long country hikes so they could study the fauna of their native country. She contrasted this with what she considered to be the thoroughly undemocratic upbringing that Tatka was getting from her grandmother, and she made fun of the girl for not being able to tell one bush or tree from another in winter. Tatka's decision to study literature at the university aroused Tania's scorn: she had no time at all for any profession which was "not useful to the people" or, as she put it in her more up-to-date terminology, "to the collective farms." So that the girl should not get the wrong ideas about religion from her grandmother, Tania took her to see the atheist museum in St. Isaac's Cathedral. During one of these visits there was a scene—Tatka refused to accept the museum's interpretation of a certain passage in the Gospels. Told that she must trust the collective wisdom of all the progressive people who had exposed the humbug of the priests and not be so uppish, she burst into tears. According to the museum, the Gospels called on people to bow down before Mammon, but the girl was too intelligent to believe this. M. and I happened to be staying in Leningrad at the time, and Tatka secretly came to see M. to ask him who was right—her grandmother or her father and stepmother. Her attachment to M. probably went back to this occasion.

From her father Tania had inherited some excellent contacts with the Party leaders. When he died at the beginning of the Revolution, she and her sister Natasha were taken care of by Yenukidze, whom they always called "Red Abel." This was either an old Party nickname or the joking way he was referred to in the Grigoriev household. When Yenukidze was arrested in 1937, Tania took it in the spirit of the times, and her comment to me was: "He must have done something—people are so corrupted by power." By this time she had no need of her former protectors and had even outgrown them—after all, as she pointed out, they had not been able to keep abreast of the times and follow Stalin in his efforts to carry through all the essential revolutionary changes of which her father had dreamed! This was Tania's explanation for the arrest of all the old Bolsheviks, and she fervently supported every "mass campaign"—whether it was collectivization, the expulsion of the former aristocrats from Leningrad, or the great purge of 1937.

Tania always had the last word on questions of ideology, and she ruled the household firmly, never raising her soft voice. She was probably just the same at work—though I never had a chance of observing her there, I knew the type only too well from my own experience. The only thing that upset Tania was Tatka's obstinacy. The girl had learned to keep her own counsel and there was no power on earth that could force her to say a single word in approval of Tania's opinions. The first major clash between them had been at the time of the expulsion of the former aristocrats, among whom was a girl next door, a playmate of Tatka's called Olga Chichagov. Tania said there was no place for aristocrats in the City of Lenin and that it was silly to shed tears over the banishment of the Chichagovs. Tatka said nothing, nor did she comment when her stepmother went on to say it was a crime to let aristocrats occupy living-space needed by the workers, and that she furthermore failed to understand what a girl brought up by herself and Evgeni Emilievich could possibly have in common with the young lady next door! Tatka listened to all this in silence—and then went to see Olga off at the station. Tania accused Tatka's grandmother of connivance.

This drama was soon followed by a farce, when Tania and her sisters were summoned before the commission charged with clearing aristocrats out of Leningrad. The commission was guided in its work by an old directory of the city in which their father, Grigoriev, was listed as a "personal nobleman."* The fact that he was not a hereditary aristocrat was of no concern to the commission—they were interested only in reaching their target figure, and there turned out to be too few real aristocrats, or at least they were hard to find. . . . The sisters were only rescued by "Red Abel," who had not yet lost his influence, or at any rate still had enough power to intervene in a small matter like this.

* A non-hereditary status automatically awarded for certain types of public service under the Czars.

"Justice has triumphed!" was how Tania put it when we met shortly afterward in Moscow.

"Why did your father allow himself to be listed as a 'personal nobleman'?" I asked. "You only had to give half a rouble as a bribe not to have that entered in documents."

"My father didn't give bribes, on principle," Tania replied coldly.

Maria Nikolayevna and I couldn't help winking at each other: neither of us could suppress the slightly malicious thought that Grigoriev, inveterate "progressive" though he was, had not been averse to styling himself a "nobleman" and had made use of his right to do so as a university graduate.

We knew beforehand what sort of reception we should get at Siverskaya Street and were relieved to find that Evgeni Emilievich was not at home. He arrived only late at night, and in the morning we had our usual battle with him over M.'s father. He demanded that we take the old man away because he was an intolerable burden for the whole family and was dragging them all down with him. M. didn't argue with his brother. Since he was an early riser, he had already done what he had come here to do—that is, see his father and Tatka. As soon as Evgeni Emilievich started talking about the old man, we said goodbye and started to leave. Only then did Tania ask why we had come to Leningrad. When we explained as best we could, she was astonished and said: "I don't understand why two grown people cannot find a way of earning their living." When I pointed out that all means of livelihood were in the hands of the State and hence unavailable to those considered "unworthy," Tania spoke scathingly of "panic" and "tales invented by the intelligentsia." Like Marietta Shaginian, she was deaf to all talk of the mass arrests now taking place. When I mentioned the case of Yenukidze to her, she made the comment I have already quoted. There was something quite inflexible about her which made one think of the august forerunners she might have modeled herself on: the women of Sparta, the mother of the Gracchi, or the women terrorists of the "People's Will." As we left, I said, "If your Bolsheviks turned into Fascists overnight, you wouldn't even notice." She said this could never happen.

This was M.'s last meeting with his father and with Tatka. As for Tania, he was just amused by her. "What do you expect? She's a non-Party Bolshevik," he said. This term was coming into usage at the time and everybody holding a good job was referred to in this way—and behaved accordingly. People like Tania were swiftly promoted in their work right up to the highest levels at which "non-Party Bolsheviks" were allowed to serve. They constituted the so-called "democratic intelligentsia" which Stalin had now said should be given every support in Soviet institutions. They looked remarkably similar to the self-sacrificing radicals of pre-revolutionary times—except that now they were needed by the State and were considered the mainstay of a good family life.

I met Tania again more than twenty years later when she and Evgeni Emilievich came to see me at the Shklovskis'. Needless to say, I asked her how she had reacted to the Twentieth Congress. Before she could say anything, Evgeni Emilievich answered for her. According to him, she had been very upset at first and wanted to know "why all this fuss about past history?" When Khrushchev visited Leningrad, she couldn't bear to look at him—he had passed her car in his on the Nevski Prospekt and, "would you believe it, she turned her head away!" Soon, however, Tania had changed her tune and admitted that there had been "excesses" and then, of course, there was the dialectic. . . .

In 1938, choosing a moment when Tania and Evgeni Emilievich were not at home, I went to see M.'s father just before his death. He was overjoyed to see me. He believed that M. and I might save him from his poverty, loneliness and the terrible disease of which he was dying. I could not bring myself to tell him of M.'s arrest. Shortly after this, Evgeni Emilievich took him to hospital, where he died of cancer. The doctors sent a cable to the second son in Moscow, but he arrived only in time for the funeral. The hospital staff told him that nobody had come to see the old man and he had died alone. I couldn't help remembering Tania's story about how her grandmother had died when she and her sisters were children—the old woman had gone off to her room as quiet as a mouse and died without any fuss, not wanting to upset her granddaughters. Tania was always repeating this story, and Maria Nikolayevna assured me that she did so for the benefit of M.'s father and herself. Both of them in fact died without causing any trouble to Tania and Evgeni Emilievich—the old man in the hospital during the summer, while Tania was at the dacha, and Maria Nikolayevna during the blockade. Tatka also died in a hospital—in Vologda, where she came after the blockade had been broken and a road out of the city was opened up. Her aunt, Sarra Lebedeva, was with her when she died. The day before her death, Tania came and took away her clothes—at that time everybody lived by bartering things for bread, and Tania thought it perfectly all right to exchange Tatka's poor rags for bread for herself and her son. This seems rational enough, but, as Sarra Lebedeva told me, it meant there was nothing to bury Tatka in.

People can be reduced to such straits that they are stripped of all the protective layers that hypocritical society has devised to hide the essence beneath. But the distinctive thing about us was that we never removed the smiling masks with which we confronted the world. I have often known people to make a good career because of their urbane intellectual appearance and suave speech. I remember, for instance, the director of the Ulianovsk Teachers' Training College, who in 1953 gleefully conducted the purge of Jewish members of the staff.* During a special faculty meeting under his chairmanship which had been called to expel me, I could not take my eyes off his face. He looked extraordinarily like Chekhov, and, as if to heighten the resemblance, he wore not the usual kind of glasses, but a pince-nez in a thin gold frame. The play of his features and the soft modulations of his voice were unforgettable—there's no point in trying to describe them, as people would think me guilty of overstatement.

I was the first of a series of people who were going to be expelled. The instructions to start this purge had taken some time to filter down to the provinces, and by the time they reached Ulianovsk it was too late: a few days after the meeting in the college we heard the news of the Leader's death. I went to memorial meetings at which people actually sobbed. As a woman messenger employed by the College said to me, "We managed all right, nobody ever touched us ... but what's going to happen now?" The director carried on with the purge interrupted by Stalin's death—he hadn't managed to finish it off in good time because each case had to be considered separately. He expelled twenty-six people—not only Jews, but some suspiciously intellectual staff members from other ethnic groups as well—before he was himself dismissed while hounding Professor Lubishchev, a biologist who had once spoken up against Lysenko. He was transferred to another college, where he is highly regarded because of his bland manner and Chekhovian appearance. This man is a real lover of pogroms, and with his deceptive appearance he was made for the times in which we live. Such skill at mimicry was much prized, and no end of gullible people were taken in by sophisticated mannerisms and smooth talk.

* The "exposure" of the "Doctors' Plot" led to a widespread purge of Jews in the last months before Stalin's death. (See note on page 116.)

67

POETRY LOVERS

During our two days in Leningrad we stayed overnight at Akhmatova's place, where everybody did their best to cheer M. up. They even called in Andronikov, then still in the bloom of youth, to show off his party tricks to M. In the evening we sat at the table, drinking toasts and talking. We all knew what we were about to go through, but nobody wanted to cast a shadow on the few moments left to us. Akhmatova seemed at ease and in high spirits, her husband Punin was quite boisterous and laughed a good deal—but I noticed that his left cheek and eyelid twitched more than ever.

The next day we went to see Stenich, the man whom Blok called a "Russian dandy." Among the Soviet writers he had the reputation of a cynic, but that may have been because they were so afraid of his sharp tongue. Like Andronikov, Stenich also liked to put on little acts for his friends, but his were very different. In the mid-twenties his star turn had been to talk about how much he feared and loved his superiors—so much so that he liked nothing more than to help the director of Gosizdat* on with his coat. This was rather coldly received by his fellow writers, who preferred to dismiss Stenich as a cynic reveling in his own servility rather than recognize themselves in the portrait he held up to them.

Stenich had begun by writing verse. In Kiev in 1919 he had run a kind of literary night club (called The Junk Room) in which he recited his rhymed burlesques. Many people still remembered his lines on "The Council of People's Commissars in Session," which had a genuine satirical bite, unlike the usual stuff turned out to order on topical themes. He soon stopped writing poetry himself, but he retained a great love for it. He might have become a brilliant essayist or critic, but the times were not auspicious, and he was now simply a kind of man-about-town who frittered away his time in gossip. He also did a few translations which were regarded as models of the art of prose translation. He was a man with a great feeling for language and literature and an acute sense of the modern age—this he managed to convey in his translations of American writers.

* The State Publishing House.

He greeted M. with embraces. When M. told him what we had come for, Stenich sighed and said that most of the writers were away just now, though some were out at their dachas. This made it more difficult to raise money for us. But his wife, Liuba, was more encouraging, and said she would go out to Sestroretsk. After lunch she put on a stylish hat and set off. Stenich insisted we stay until her return. Several people looked in on us there, including Akhmatova and Volpe—the same Volpe who had been dismissed as editor of *Zvezda* for publishing M.'s "Journey to Armenia," including the final part about King Shapukh who was granted "one extra day" by the Assyrian. This ending had been forbidden by the censorship. For us, this short time with Stenich was like King Shapukh's "one extra day."

Liuba returned with her booty: a little money and some clothing. Among the other things were two pairs of trousers, one very large and the other exactly M.'s size. We took the very large pair back to Savelovo and gave them to the criminal we had got to know—the one who had said that in such places as Alexandrov people of his kind were "skimmed off like cream." M. was never able to keep a second pair of trousers—there was always somebody whose need was even greater. At that time Shklovski also belonged to the category of people who possessed only one pair of trousers, and his son Nikita could expect no better from life. His mother once asked Nikita what he would do if a good fairy granted him one wish. Without a moment's hesitation he replied: "Get trousers for all my friends." In our conditions a man was better judged by his readiness to give a pair of trousers to a less fortunate friend than by his words—let alone by his articles, novels, or stories. From my observations, Soviet writers are a thick-skinned lot, but in the presence of Liuba Stenich it was not easy to refuse to help an exiled fellow writer.

The day we spent with Stenich seemed calm and peaceful, but reality kept breaking in. Stenich was friendly with the wife of Diki, and both she and her husband had been arrested. Stenich was now waiting his turn, and was worried about how Liuba would get on when she was left alone. In the evening the phone rang, but when Liuba picked up the receiver there was no sound at the other end. She burst into tears—we all knew that the police often checked in this way whether you were home before coming for you. However, nothing happened that evening, and Stenich was not arrested until the following winter. As we said goodbye on the landing, he pointed to the doors of the other apartments and told us when and in what circumstances their occupants had been taken away by the police. He was the only person on two floors who was still at liberty—if it could be called liberty. "Now it's my turn," he said. The next time we came to Leningrad, Stenich had been arrested, and when we went to see Lozinski, he was very frightened. "Do you know what happened to your Amphitryon?" he asked. He thought that Stenich had been picked up because of the day we had spent with him, and we had to leave Lozinski at once, before we even had time to ask him for more money.

I think he exaggerated the extent to which our secret police went in for ordinary detective work. They were not in the least bit interested in *real* facts—all they wanted were lists of people to arrest, and these they got from their network of informers and the volunteers who brought them denunciations. To meet their quotas, all they needed were names of people, not details about their comings and goings. During interrogations they always, as a matter of routine, collected "evidence" against people whom they had no intention of arresting—just in case it was ever needed. I have heard of a woman who heroically went through torture rather than give "evidence" against Molotov! Spasski was asked for evidence against Liuba Ehrenburg, whom he had never even met. He managed to send word about this from the forced-labor camp, and Liuba was warned—apparently Akhmatova passed on the message to her. Liuba could not believe it: "What Spasski? I don't know him." She was still naïve in those days, but later she understood everything.

In the torture chambers of the Lubianka they were constantly adding to the dossiers of Ehrenburg, Sholokhov, Alexei Tolstoi, and others whom they had no intention of touching. Dozens, if not hundreds of people were sent to camps on a charge of being involved in a "conspiracy" headed by Tikhonov and Fadeyev! Among them was Spasski. Wild inventions and monstrous accusations had become an end in themselves, and officials of the secret police applied all their ingenuity to them, as though reveling in the total arbitrariness of their power. Their basic principle was just what Furmanov had told us at the end of the twenties: "Give us a man, and we'll make a case." On the day we had spent at Stenich's apartment, his name was almost certainly already on a list of persons due to be arrested—his telephone number would have been found in Diki's address book, and no further information about him was needed.

The principles and aims of mass terror have nothing in common with ordinary police work or with security. The only purpose of terror is intimidation. To plunge the whole country into a state of chronic fear, the number of victims must be raised to astronomical levels, and on every floor of every building there must always be several apartments from which the tenants have suddenly been taken away. The remaining inhabitants will be model citizens for the rest of their lives—this will be true for every street and every city through which the broom has swept. The only essential thing for those who rule by terror is not to overlook the new generations growing up without faith in their elders, and to keep on repeating the process in systematic fashion. Stalin ruled for a long time and saw to it that the waves of terror recurred from time to time, always on an even greater scale than before. But the champions of terror invariably leave one thing out of account—namely, that they can't kill everyone, and among their cowed, half-demented subjects there are always witnesses who survive to tell the tale.

On the first of our two visits to Leningrad we went out to see Zoshchenko in Sestroretsk (or it may have been Razliv). Zoshchenko had a weak heart and beautiful eyes. *Pravda* had commissioned a story from him and he had written something about the wife of the poet Kornilov, who was refused work and turned away from every door as though she were the wife of an arrested man. The story wasn't printed, of course, but in those years only Zoshchenko would have dared to do anything so provocative. It is amazing he got away with it—though it must immediately have gone down on the "account" which he later had to pay.

On that first trip we went to the station from Akhmatova's apartment and were seen off by her as well as the Steniches. Since we were catching the last train, we left the house after midnight—"the light-blue midnight" of Akhmatova's poem in which she says that Leningrad seemed to her

> not a European city with the first prize for beauty
> but a terrible exile to Eniseisk, a stopping place on the way
> to Chita, to Ishim, to waterless Irgiz and famous Atabasar,
> to the town of Svobodny and the plague-ridden stench of
> prison bunks,
> so it seemed to me on this light-blue night—this city, glorified
> by the first of our poets, and by you and me.*

---

* These lines have not been previously published.

Is there any wonder that this was how the city looked to us then? We all felt the same way—and that's what the city was: a transit station to exile, except that the places Akhmatova mentions were by that time comparatively well settled and they had almost stopped sending people there.

Liuba Stenich has told me one detail of that night which I had forgotten: at the station M. hung something on a potted palm there and said: "An Arab wandering in the desert . . ."

The first visit gave us enough to live on for three months. When we came again in the spring just before leaving for Samatikha, we were less successful. In the morning we went to see Akhmatova, and she read to M. the poem quoted above. This was his last meeting with her. We were to have seen her later in the day at Lozinski's, but since we had to leave him almost at once, we were not there when she arrived. We were not able to stay overnight, and all we could do was say goodbye to her on the telephone.

After leaving Lozinski we stood outside on the street for a long time, wondering where to go next. We decided it would have to be Marshak.

Samuil Yakovlevich Marshak greeted us in such a crooning voice that M. couldn't bring himself to ask for money. Instead, they started talking about literature and M. read a few of his Voronezh poems. Marshak sighed—he didn't like the poems: "They give no idea of the people you meet, or what you talk about. Now, when Pushkin was in exile . . ." "What does he expect?" M. whispered to me and we took our leave. The next writer we went to see was out, and we waited on the street until he got back. But he said he had no money—he had spent everything on the dacha he was building. Apart from Selvinski, he was the only one to refuse help when asked, and I do not wish to name him because I believe his refusal was a momentary lapse—he was a decent man, a lover of poetry and one of the last of those who secretly remained true to the spirit of the old intelligentsia. It was only such people we could approach for help, but this man lost his head for a moment and behaved like a member of the Union of Writers.

In the very last days before we left for Samatikha M. said to me: "We ought to go and ask Paustovski for money." Since we didn't even know him, I was surprised, but M. assured me he was bound to help. Recently I told this to Paustovski, and he was very much upset. "Why didn't you come to see me?" he asked. "We didn't have time before M. was arrested," I explained. He was relieved. "If Osip Emilievich had come to me, I would have turned out all my pockets," he said and laughed his dry laugh. I do not doubt that he would have done just that: he was also a typical member of the "secret intelligentsia"—and no longer hides it, now there is no need to.

I recently heard that one of our literary officials has been going around asking what sort of fellow this Mandelstam was who was always borrowing money but never returned it. He obviously doesn't like M. It is possible that in his irresponsible youth M. didn't always pay back his debts, but the official wasn't even born then. As regards what happened in the Stalin period, the word "borrow" doesn't apply. It was a case of undisguised begging—which was forced on M. by the State and the life which our press constantly described as "happy." Beggary was not the worst thing about it, either.

68

ECLIPSE

"Who needs this cursed regime?" Lev Bruni had said as he gave M. the money to pay his fare to Maly Yaroslavets. In the autumn it began to seem advisable to move from Savelovo, and we again started studying the map of the Moscow region. Lev recommended Maly Yaroslavets, where he had had a small wooden house built for the wife and children of his brother Nikolai. Nikolai was a former priest who had become an aircraft designer and was then sent to a camp. In 1937 he had been given a second sentence for a "crime committed in the camp"—a standard formula in those days. In other words, he had been re-sentenced without being allowed out even for a single moment. His wife, Nadia, after being expelled from Moscow, had been living for several years with her children in Maly Yaroslavets. They lived on the produce of a small vegetable garden—Lev had not been able to afford to buy a cow for them. Apart from his brother's children, he had to feed his own large family as well. He probably didn't have too much to eat himself in the days before the war, when the staple food was potatoes, and after the war he died of malnutrition. This was something that happened to "secret intellectuals." Everybody was very fond of Lev. Despite all the trials visited upon him by fate, he managed not only to remain a human being, but also to live some kind of life—most of us didn't live in any real sense, but existed from day to day, waiting anxiously for something until the time came to die.

In autumn it gets dark very early, and apart from the railroad station, there was no lighting at all in Maly Yaroslavets. We walked up the streets, which were slippery from mud, and we saw not a single street lamp or lighted window—nor were there any passers-by. Once or twice we had to knock on windows to ask the way, and each time a fear-contorted face peered out. But when we simply asked the way, the faces were at once transformed and wreathed in smiles, and we were given very detailed instructions with extraordinary friendliness. When we at last arrived at Nadia Bruni's and we told her what had happened when we knocked on windows, she explained that there had been more and more arrests in recent weeks, not only of exiles, but of local people too. As a result, everybody was just sitting at home, waiting with bated breath. During the Civil War, people did not have lights in their windows for fear of attracting the attention of all the freebooters then roaming the country. In the towns occupied by the Germans, people also sat without lights. In 1937, however, it made no difference, since people were picked up not at random, but on individual warrants. All the same, everybody went to bed early, to avoid putting the lights on. Perhaps it was the most primitive animal instinct—better sit in the darkness of your burrow than in the light. I know the feeling very well myself—whenever a car stops outside the house, you want to switch off the light.

We were so horrified by the darkened town that after spending the night at Nadia Bruni's we fled back to Moscow the next morning. We didn't follow Lev's advice because we would have needed the strength of mind of the meek and gentle Nadia Bruni to stand the terror that lay like a pall over the town. It was the same throughout the whole country, of course, but in the villages and small towns it was generally less overpowering.

The next person we consulted was Babel. I do not think he ever lived in any of the apartment buildings reserved for writers, but always managed to find peculiar places of his own. With great difficulty we tracked him down in a strange house that must formerly have been a private villa. I have a vague recollection that there were foreigners living in this house, and that Babel rented rooms from them on the second floor. But perhaps he just said so to astonish us—he was very fond of startling people like this. At that time foreigners were avoided like the plague—you could lose your head for the slightest contact with them. Who in his right mind would have lived in the same house as foreigners? I still remember my astonishment, and still cannot understand it. Whenever we saw Babel he gave us something to be surprised about.

We told him our troubles, and during the whole of our long conversation he listened with remarkable intentness. Everything about Babel gave an impression of all-consuming curiosity—the way he held his head, his mouth and chin, and particularly his eyes. It is not often that one sees such undisguised curiosity in the eyes of a grownup. I had the feeling that Babel's main driving force was the unbridled curiosity with which he scrutinized life and people.

With his usual ability to size things up, he was quick to decide on the best course for us. "Go out to Kalinin," he said, "Erdman is there—his old women just love him." This was Babel's cryptic way of saying that all Erdman's female admirers would never have allowed him to settle in a bad place. He also thought we might be able to get some help from them—in finding a room there, for instance. But Babel, as it turned out, had exaggerated Erdman's hold over his "old women"—when we went to Kalinin, we found that none of them lived out there with him, and that he had to come into Moscow to see them.

Babel volunteered to get the money for our fare the next day, and we then started talking about other things. He told us he now spent all his time meeting militiamen and drinking with them. The previous evening he had been drinking with one of the chief militiamen of Moscow, who in his drunken state had declared that "he who lives by the sword shall perish by the sword." The chiefs of the militia, he said, were disappearing one after another and "today you're all right, but you don't know where you'll be tomorrow."

The word "militia" was of course a euphemism. We knew that Babel was really talking about Chekists. M. asked him why he was so drawn to "militiamen": was it a desire to see what it was like in the exclusive store where the merchandise was death? Did he just want to touch it with his fingers? "No," Babel replied, "I don't want to touch it with my fingers—I just like to have a sniff and see what it smells like."

It was known that among the "militiamen" Babel visited was Yezhov himself. After the arrest of Babel, Katayev and Shklovski said he had visited Yezhov because he was so frightened, but that it hadn't saved him—Beria had had him arrested precisely on this account. I am convinced that Babel went to see Yezhov not out of cowardice but out of sheer curiosity—just to have a sniff and see what it smelled like.

The question "What will happen to us tomorrow?" was the chief topic of all our conversations. Babel, with his storyteller's gift, put it into the mouth of his "militiamen." M. was generally silent about it—he knew too well what awaited him. Only once did he blurt out something when we happened to run into Shervinski on the street. He was no friend of ours, but M. suddenly told him it couldn't go on like this—"I am right in front of their noses all the time and they must have no idea what to do with me—in other words, they will soon have to pick me up." Shervinski listened to this brief outburst and said nothing at all. After M.'s death I sometimes met him, but he never mentioned it to me. I should not be surprised if he had forgotten—there was so much unpleasantness in our lives that this was the only thing to do.

69

A SCENE FROM LIFE

Babel was not the only one who knew Yezhov—we too had once made his acquaintance. This had happened in the 1930's when M. and I were staying in a Government villa in Sukhumi. The Yezhov we met then was remarkably like his later portraits and photographs—especially the one where he appears with a broad smile at the moment when Stalin is shaking his hand to congratulate him on some Government award. The Sukhumi Yezhov also had his famous limp, and I remember Podvoiski, who liked to lecture people about the qualities of a true Bolshevik, scolding me for my laziness and telling me to follow the example of "our Yezhov" who danced the gopak despite his lame leg. But there were many Yezhovs and I still find it difficult to believe that the man we saw in Sukhumi was the legendary People's Commissar at the dawn of his brief but dazzling career. It is hard to credit that we sat at the same table, eating, drinking and exchanging small talk with this man who was to be one of the great killers of our time, and who totally exposed—not in theory but in practice—all the assumptions on which our "humanism" rested.

The Sukhumi Yezhov was a modest and rather agreeable person. He was not yet used to being driven about in an automobile and did not therefore regard it as an exclusive privilege to which no ordinary mortal could lay claim. We sometimes asked him to give us a lift into town, and he never refused. At the Government villa, automobiles were a burning issue—cars from the Abkhaz Council of People's Commissars were always sweeping up the hill to the front entrance, and the children of Central Committee officials staying in the villa chased away the grubby brats of the service personnel, proudly taking their places in the driver's seat as though entitled to do so by right of birth. On one occasion M. called this expulsion scene to the attention of Yezhov's wife and another Central Committee lady. The two women told the children of their colleagues to make room for the servants' children and let them sit in the car as well. They were very much upset to see the children departing from the democratic principles of their fathers and told us they were sent to the same school as other children and were dressed no better than the others, so that they wouldn't "lose touch with the people." These children were now preparing themselves to rule the people, but many of them were to meet a different fate.

In the morning Yezhov got up before everybody else to cut roses for the young woman student of literature and friend of Bagritski with whom he was flirting. After him came Podvoiski—to get roses for Yezhov's wife. This was an act of pure chivalry—so the other inhabitants of the villa said—since Podvoiski was a model family man and never flirted with any wives except his own. The rest of the ladies, who had no one to pay court to them, came down to get their own roses, and discussed Podvoiski's gallant behavior as they did so.

Yezhov's wife (her name was Tonia, I think) spent her time lying in a deck chair on the terrace opposite the villa. If she was upset by her husband's conduct, she gave no sign of it—Stalin had not yet begun to insist on the need for a healthy family life. "Where is your comrade?" she asked me whenever she saw me alone. At first I didn't realize that she was referring to M. In these circles they still stuck to the usage of their days in the revolutionary underground, and a husband was primarily a comrade. Tonia was reading *Das Kapital* and softly recapitulated it to herself as she went along. She was angry with the vivacious and intelligent wife of Kossior for going out on horseback with a young and rather brash musician who was collecting Abkhaz folk music. "We all know Kossior," said Tonia, "he is a comrade of ours, but who is this fellow? He could be a spy, for all we know!" Everybody denounced Lakoba's irresponsibility in putting someone who was "not one of us" in such an important villa. Probably the presence of anybody who was not a member of the Party gave rise to similar protests, and I even heard some talk about the need to centralize the whole process of allotting places in Party rest homes, but Lakoba didn't give a damn for any of them: the villa belonged to the Abkhaz Council of People's Commissars—that is, virtually to him.

Next to us in a small room on the third floor was a Central Committee member of the older generation, a clever Latvian. He kept himself very much apart from the others, and talked only with M. We were taken aback by the note of alarm which we often detected in what he said. M. had already written his "Fourth Prose," and we knew that the outlook for literature was bad, but the Latvian was not concerned with literature—he was simply a high-ranking Party official. He had not been accused of any "deviations" and it was difficult to see why he was so apprehensive and kept harping on the question of what would happen tomorrow. I know nothing of his fate, but he must certainly have taken part in the "Congress of Victors"* and it is not difficult to guess what must have become of him—we are all wise after the event.

In the evenings Lakoba used to come up to play billiards and gossip with the guests in the dining room. This villa with its select visitors was the only place he could come to relax and talk. Once he brought us a bear cub that had been presented to him by the mountain people. Podvoiski kept it in his room, but then Yezhov took it back to Moscow and put it in the zoo. Lakoba was a good storyteller. He told us, for instance, about an ancestor of his who had gone all the way to Petersburg on foot to invite his blood enemy (it was Prince Shervashidze, I think) to come and partake of a feast in Sukhumi. The Prince decided this was the end of their blood feud and accepted the invitation. His imprudence cost him his life. M. was very much impressed by this story of Lakoba's and he thought there was some hidden meaning in it. We were told that by 1937 Lakoba was no longer alive. He had supposedly been buried with full honors in some Abkhaz equivalent of the Kremlin wall, but Stalin, angry with the dead man for some reason, had ordered his remains to be disinterred and destroyed. If this is true, one can only be glad for Lakoba's sake that he died in good time.

It was Lakoba who had put us in this Government villa so that we could rest before setting out on our Armenian journey—we had arrived with a note from the Central Committee requesting him to

---

* The Party Congress of 1934, many of whose participants perished in the terror three years later.

arrange this. Other writers there were Bezymenski and Kazin, both of whom felt completely at home. The same could not be said for us.

On the day of Mayakovski's death we were working in the garden with a proud and elegant Georgian, a specialist in radio. The guests had all gathered in the dining room for their evening's entertainment—they generally sang songs and danced Yezhov's favorite dance, the gopak. Our companion said: "Georgian People's Commissars would not dance on the day on which a Georgian national poet had died." M. nodded to me and said: "Go and tell that to Yezhov." I went into the dining room and passed on the Georgian's words to Yezhov, who was in very high spirits already. The dancing ceased, but I don't think anybody apart from Yezhov knew the reason. A few years before this, M. had rebuked Vyshinski for laughing and talking loudly while a young poet was reading his verse. This happened in the CEKUBU rest home.

We could not stand sanatoria and rest homes, but went to them very occasionally if there was nowhere else to go. They always smelled of death, for some reason.

70

THE SUICIDE

Who foresaw the disastrous consequences of abandoning humanism in the name of some overriding aim? Who knew what calamities we were calling down on our heads by adopting the principle that "everything is permitted"? Only a handful of intellectuals—but nobody listened to them. Now they are accused of "abstract humanism," but in the twenties everybody mercilessly heaped scorn on them. The standard epithets for them were "puny" and "spineless," and the word "intellectual" itself was always given a pejorative ending (*intelligentishka*). They were constantly caricatured in the press, and the thirty-year-old partisans of the "new era" would have nothing to do with them. The prime task was to hold them up to ridicule in literature, and Ilf and Petrov obliged by writing their savage lampoon on "spineless intellectuals" in *The Twelve Chairs*. The figures in question seem very dated now, and it would not occur to anyone at the present day to see a "typical" intellectual in the pitiful half-wit who pesters the wife who has left him. Reading this immortal work today, one has difficulty figuring out the point of the satire and whom exactly they are making fun of. Something similar has happened with a much more profound work, Erdman's play *The Suicide,* which Gorki found so impressive and Meyerhold wanted to produce. As originally conceived, the play was to feature a crowd of wretched intellectuals in repulsive masks surrounding a man who is about to commit suicide, and whom they want to exploit for their own purposes—as a way of calling attention to the difficulties of their existence, the hopelessness resulting from their inability to find a place in the new life. But a healthy instinct for life wins out in the end, and the man marked down for suicide—despite the farewell banquet and all the liberal speeches in his honor—decides not to die after all and thumbs his nose at the chorus of masked intellectuals who are egging him on.

Erdman, a real artist, couldn't help introducing genuinely tragic undertones into the polyphonic scenes with the masked intellectuals (who were always then referred to as petit-bourgeois grumblers). Nowadays, when nobody hesitates to say quite openly how unbearable our life is, the complaints of the masks in Erdman's play sound not like the whining of "spineless intellectuals," but like a tragic chorus of martyred ghosts. The hero's refusal to kill himself also takes on a different meaning now: life is hideous and intolerable, but one must go on living nevertheless, because life is life. . . . Did Erdman intend this implication, or was his aim much simpler? I do not know, but I believe that, with all its anti-intellectualism, there is an undercurrent of humanity in the play. It is really about why some of us decided to go on living even though everything was pushing us to suicide.

Erdman himself chose to fall silent—anything just to stay alive. In Kalinin he lived in a poky little hole of a room with a bunk to sleep on and a small table. When we came to see him, he was lying on the bunk—the only alternative was to sit on the only chair. He got up, shook himself and took us to the outskirts of the town where there were sometimes rooms to let in privately owned wooden houses. He came to see us quite frequently, but never with his co-author and antipode, Misha Volpin. He evidently visited us only on days when Misha was away in Moscow.

Erdman, as we know, first got into trouble for his fables, which Kachalov was irresponsible enough to recite at an evening in the Kremlin—that is, to the same sort of people as those we had stayed with in the Government villa in Sukhumi, where the companion of

Kossior's wife had immediately been suspected of being a spy. That same evening they were all arrested for their little joke and exiled— Misha Volpin was actually sent to a forced-labor camp, since it appeared that the secret police had old scores to settle with him, going back to his youth. They say that Erdman signed the letters he wrote home to his mother "Mamin-Sibiriak";* and that, as a parting shot, he wrote the following fable before being sent into exile:

> Once the GPU came by
> and grabbed old Aesop by the ass.
> The moral of this tale is clear—
> No more fables needed here.

This summed up Erdman's recipe for survival, and we heard no more of his fables and jokes—he lapsed into silence. Unlike M., who to the end defended his right to his "moving lips," Erdman sealed his tight. Very occasionally he would put his head close to mine and tell me the plot of a new play he had just thought of but would never write. I have already mentioned one of the unwritten plays: about the way people switch from official jargon to natural speech.

When I came to tell him of M.'s arrest, Erdman mumbled something that sounded like: "If they're picking up such people . . ." and got up to show me out.

During the war, when we lived in evacuation in Tashkent, two people in uniform came to see my brother. One was Erdman, the other was Volpin, who talked incessantly about poetry and kept on saying that it should be "interesting." He found Mayakovski and Yesenin "interesting," but not Akhmatova. Volpin was a product of LEF and knew what he liked. Erdman just sat and drank, without saying a word. Later they went up to see Akhmatova, who lived in the balakhana above my brother.

I still occasionally meet Erdman and Volpin at Akhmatova's. Erdman says: "Pleased to see you" and then goes on drinking, without another word, leaving all the talking to Volpin. They work together and seem to be perfectly all right nowadays.

One summer while he was living out in Tarusa, Garin was com-

---

* A minor novelist of the end of the nineteenth century whose name can be punningly interpreted to mean "Mummy's Siberian."

plaining about the modern theater and saying how awful everything was. In the evenings there were arguments about which was worse: literature, the theater, painting or music. Everybody present spoke up for his own particular field of interest, insisting that it came first in terms of its degradation. On one of these evenings Garin read Erdman's *Suicide,* this play that never got on the stage, and it now sounded very different in my ears. "I'll tell you," the author seemed to be saying, "why you didn't jump out of the window and went on living. . . ."

In the meantime, attacks on the intellectuals still go on. This is a legacy from the twenties, and it's time a stop were put to it.

Many people will be offended at what I have said in passing about *The Twelve Chairs.* I have always found it very funny and am still astonished at the boldness of the authors in the episode where they describe how Ostap Bender and the other crooks from Odessa join a group of Soviet writers in a specially reserved coach on the newly opened Turksib railroad and, mingling with them during the journey, are in no way distinguishable from them. But I find nothing funny about the description of the intellectuals living together in their dilapidated house—no wonder they had gone completely to seed and were being deserted by such of their womenfolk as still had any market value. It is all too easy to poke fun at people who have had the life crushed out of them.

71

REBIRTH

I must admit to being an incorrigible optimist. Like those who believed at the beginning of this century that life *had* to be better than in the nineteenth century, I am now convinced that we will soon witness a complete resurgence of humane values. I mean this not only in respect to social justice, but also in cultural life and in everything else. Far from being shaken in my optimism by the bitter experience of the first half of this incredible century, I am encouraged to believe that all we have been through will have served to turn people against the idea, so tempting at first sight, that the end justifies the means and "everything is permitted." M. taught me to believe that history is a practical testing-ground for the ways of good and evil. We have tested the ways of evil.

Will any of us want to revert to them? Isn't it true that the voices among us speaking of conscience and good are growing stronger? I feel that we are at the threshold of new days, and I think I detect signs of a new attitude. They are few and far between—indeed, almost imperceptible—but they are nevertheless there.

Alas, my faith and optimism are shared by almost nobody: people who know the difference between good and evil are more inclined to expect new misfortunes and new crimes. I realize the possibility of a return to the past, but I still think the general outlook is bright. We have seen the triumph of evil after the values of humanism have been vilified and trampled on. The reason these values succumbed was probably that they were based on nothing except boundless confidence in the human intellect. I think we may now find a better foundation for them, if only because of the lessons we have drawn from our experience. We can see the mistakes and crimes of the past, and the seductive delusions of former times have lost their glamour. Russia once saved the Christian culture of Europe from the Tatars, and in the past fifty years, by taking the brunt on herself, she has saved Europe again—this time from rationalism and all the will to evil that goes with it. The sacrifice in human life was enormous. How can I believe it was all in vain?

I have a certain acquaintance who, though still quite young, is both wise and gloomy beyond his years. The poet he likes best is Blok, because of his frantic presentiment of the end of Russian culture. This admirer of Blok looks down on me for wearing rose-tinted spectacles at my age. He believes that Blok's prediction came true, that our culture has really perished and we are buried under its ruins. This young pessimist fails to notice the changes that have come about since we first met. He came to see me straight after the Twentieth Congress, when people were asking in bewilderment: "Why have they told us all this?" Some would rather not have heard such disagreeable things; others, about to become members of the ruling class, were upset because their task had suddenly been made somewhat more difficult; then there were those who shook their heads sadly at the thought that the old ways of making a career would not work any more and they would have to think of something new.

This was the period known as the "thaw," when some people really believed that they would be granted permission to speak their minds. This hope was not fulfilled, but everybody knows that this is not what matters. What matters is the change in each individual and his way of thinking. The very need for permission from above is a hangover from the past, with its belief in authority and fear of punishment. People trembled with terror at every word of command. This terror could return, but it would mean sending several million people to the camps. If this were to happen now, they would all scream—and so would their families, friends and neighbors. That is something to be reckoned with.

My young friend first came to see me while I was living in the filthy barracks that served as a dormitory for the teachers of the Cheboksary Teachers' Training College. The stench was overpowering, and the air was thick with soot from the kerosene lamps. It was as cold in my room as it was outside: a plank in the wall on the second floor had slipped, and threatened to fall on the heads of the children playing down below. The wind that blew freely into my room brought the smell of melting snow. My visitor explained that he was an admirer of M. and had been dying to come and see me. He had come quite out of the blue—without any letters of introduction from mutual friends to give me an idea of what sort of person he was. But his whole bearing, and particularly the look in his eyes, inspired confidence.

I asked him to sit down and told him something I would not normally have said to a casual visitor: "When somebody comes and tells me how much he likes Mandelstam," I said, "I know that he is an informer. He has either been sent, or has come on his own initiative so that he can later submit a nice little report. This has been going on for twenty years now. Nobody else ever talks about Mandelstam with me—literary people who used to read his poetry never mention him in conversation with me. I am telling this to you because you make a good impression on me. I trust you. But even with you I cannot talk about Mandelstam and his poetry. Now you understand why."

He went away, but a couple of years later I heard about him again from some mutual friends and I invited him to come and see me. Bewildered by our first encounter, he was obviously reluctant to visit me a second time, but everything was soon forgotten. I do not know whether he ever realized what profound trust I had shown him at our first meeting by speaking to him as I did.

Several years have gone by since then, and I no longer mind talking with anyone who asks me about M.—they are mostly people of the younger generation, though sometimes even the older ones now bring the subject up. Nowadays we talk about a great many things that used to be so taboo that most people in my circle did not even dare think about them. At present, however, we no longer wonder whether something is "forbidden" or not—we have just stopped bothering and forgotten that kind of thing. But that is not all.

In the twenties, young people of education willingly gathered information for the authorities and the secret police, and thought they were doing so for "the good of the Revolution," for the sake of the mysterious majority which was supposedly interested in the defense and the consolidation of the regime. From the thirties, and right up to Stalin's death, they continued to do the same, except that their motivation had changed—they now acted to benefit themselves, in the hope of reward, or out of fear. They took copies of M.'s verse to the police, or denounced colleagues in the hope of getting their own writings published, or of being promoted in their work. Others did this kind of thing out of sheer terror—not to be arrested or destroyed themselves. They were very easily intimidated, and eagerly seized on any small favors offered to them. At the same time they were always assured that nothing about their activities would ever leak out or become public knowledge. This promise has been kept and the people concerned can calmly live out their days, enjoying the modest privileges their activities have earned them.

But people asked to do such work nowadays no longer have faith in any guarantees. There can be no return to the past for this new generation, which is by no means as terrified and submissive as earlier ones. These young people can never be persuaded, moreover, that their fathers were justified in their actions, nor do they believe that "everything is permitted." This does not, of course, mean that there are no longer any informers, but the percentage is much lower. Earlier I could expect the worst of any young man, not to mention corrupt members of my own generation, but it would now be rather a fluke if a scoundrel wormed his way into my circle of acquaintances—and even then he might hesitate to do anything really despicable, because in the new state of affairs it would not be to his advantage and everybody would turn their backs on him.

Among the new intelligentsia now growing up in front of our eyes, nobody blithely repeats old sayings like "You can't swim against the tide" or "You can't make an omelet without breaking eggs." In other words, the values we thought had been abolished forever are being restored, and they must be taken account of, even by people who could quite well do without them. This has come as a surprise both to those who never gave up these values and to those who tried to bury them once and for all. Somehow or other they lived on underground, taking refuge in all those hushed homes with their dimmed lights. Now they are on the move and gathering force. The initiative in their destruction belonged to the intelligentsia of the twenties, which, as a result, ceased to be itself and turned into something different. At the present day we are witnessing the reverse process. It is astonishingly slow, and we are impatient. How can we be patient after all we have gone through?

Nobody can define the intelligentsia or say how it differs from the educated classes. It is a historical term that was first used in Russia and then spread to the West. The intelligentsia has a number of distinctive features, but they don't add up to a neat definition. The history of the intelligentsia is obscured by the fact that the word is often applied to people who do not belong to it by right. How can one use it to refer to technocrats or bureaucrats, even if they have university diplomas, or, for that matter, even if they write novels and epic poems? During the period of capitulation, the real intelligentsia was mocked, and its name was appropriated by those who surrendered.

What, then, is the intelligentsia? If you take any one of its features, you will find it is shared with some other section of the community: a certain degree of education, the ability to think critically and the sense of concern that goes with it, freedom of thought, conscience, humanism . . . All these are especially important just now, because we have seen how their disappearance means the end of the intelligentsia itself: at the least attempt to change the values it embodies, it will itself lose its character and go under—as happened in this country. But it is not only the intelligentsia that preserves values—the ordinary people kept them alive even during the darkest times, when the so-called cultural elite was repudiating them. It may be that the intelligentsia is simply not very stable and that its values are correspondingly volatile. There is also a tendency to self-destructiveness. The people who made the Revolution and were active in the twenties sprang from an intelligentsia which had given up one set of values in favor of others regarded as supreme. The result was a plunge into self-destruction. What does someone like Tikhonov or Fedin have in common with a real Russian intellectual? Nothing—except perhaps their spectacles and false teeth. But the younger people now appearing on the scene—some of them still in their teens—are a very different matter; you can see immediately that they are true intellectuals, though it is very hard to define the qualities involved. The Danish linguist Jespersen, tired of hearing arguments about how to define parts of speech, once jokingly remarked that ordinary people can always tell a verb from a noun, just as a dog can tell bread from clay. But the main thing is: these young intellectuals have appeared and the process is now irreversible—it cannot be stopped even by the physical destruction which the representatives of the past would love to visit on them. Nowadays the persecution of one intellectual only creates dozens more. We saw this during the Brodski affair.

The Russian intelligentsia has one feature which is probably not known in the West. Among the teachers of modern languages I encountered during all my years in provincial colleges, I only once met a true intellectual, a woman called Marta from Chernovitsy. She once asked me in great surprise why all those students who thirst after truth and righteousness are always so keen on poetry. This is so, and it is peculiar to Russia. M. once asked me (or himself, rather) what it was that made someone a member of the intelligentsia. He did not use the word itself—this was at a time when it was still a term of abuse, before it was taken over by bureaucratic elements in the so called liberal professions—but that was what he meant. Was it a university education, he wondered, or attendance in a pre-revolutionary grammar school? No, it was not this. Could it be your attitude toward literature? This he thought was closer, but not quite it. Finally he decided that what really mattered was a person's feelings about poetry. Poetry does indeed have a very special place in this country. It arouses people and shapes their minds. No wonder the birth of our new intelligentsia is accompanied by a craving for poetry never seen before—it is the golden treasury in which our values are preserved; it brings people back to life, awakens their conscience and stirs them to thought. Why this should happen I do not know, but it is a fact.

My young friend who loves Blok and nourishes his own pessimism by reading him was for me the first sign of the intelligentsia's rebirth, and I find his pessimism unjustified. The new awakening is accompanied by the copying out and reading of poetry, which thus plays its part in setting things in motion again and reviving thought. The keepers of the flame hid in darkened corners, but the flame did not go out. It is there for all to see.

72

THE LAST IDYLL

Moscow drew us like a magnet all the time—we went there for gossip, news, money. . . . Each time, remembering where we were, we raced for the last train back to Kalinin, fearful of getting stranded for an extra night in the forbidden city. Occasionally people offered their seat in the train and talked with me in an oddly compassionate way. M. happened to mention this to Piast, who laughed in his peculiar way (it was like a horse whinnying) and said: "That's because they think she's the one, not you." At that time I wore a leather jacket, and Piast meant that I got all this sympathy because I was taken for an exile. As so many people in Moscow avoided us like the plague precisely on this account, the kindness of these working people was an unexpected bounty. The leather jacket, incidentally, was of secondary importance, since I got the same sort of consideration without it.

In the train M. and I always argued about whether or not to take a cab in Kalinin. I thought it was better to go home from the station on foot and save money for another day's upkeep in our Kalinin refuge. M. took the opposite view: one more day in Kalinin made no difference and we would still have to go back to Moscow again "to arrange things." This was a variation on the constant theme in the last year of his life that things "can't go on like this." We talked on such lines all the time in Kalinin, but there was nothing we could do by way of "arranging things."

Every time our argument was resolved quite simply. There were only two or three horse cabs at the station. This was one of the few remaining forms of private enterprise, but most cabbies had already been forced out of business by taxes and "liquidated as a class." They were immediately besieged by a large crowd and quickly drove off with the most enterprising clients, so we had no choice but to walk home.

On the bridges across the Volga and the Tmaka there was always a biting wind—the wind of exile and persecution. On the edge of the town where we had rented a room the streets were impassable because of mud in the fall, and in the winter we floundered helplessly in the snow. People lived here only if they didn't have to go out to work. . . .

M. got very breathless and kept on saying we should have taken a cab. I trudged along behind him.

When we knocked on our door, it was opened by our landlady, Tatiana Vasilievna, a tall, gaunt woman of about sixty. Looking at us sullenly, she asked whether we were hungry. She looked sullen not because we had awakened her in the middle of the night, but because that was just her manner. We told her we had had a meal in Moscow before leaving and were not hungry. She disappeared into her part of the house and came back in a few minutes with a jug of milk and the remains of her own dinner—some fritters, potato and cabbage. That winter she had slaughtered their pig, and she brought us a little pork as well. "Eat," she said, "it's all our own stuff, we didn't have to buy it." Our women never count the cost of their own work—anything that grows in the garden or any livestock they keep is "our own stuff," which they look on as a gift of God.

While we ate, she would stand beside us and ask how we had fared in Moscow, whether we had managed to get work, or permission to return. We talked quietly so as not to waken her other two lodgers, a married couple from Leningrad—also forced to live beyond the hundredth kilometer—who slept behind a wooden partition which did not quite reach the ceiling. The husband had once been a secretary to Shchegolev, and, after serving his sentence in a camp or in exile, was now sitting things out in Kalinin. When we first knocked on Tatiana Vasilievna's door on the advice of passers-by, the man from Leningrad had come out when he heard our voices, and he at once recognized M. Seeing us vouched for in this way, Tatiana Vasilievna let us have the room—a great stroke of luck for us. Here it is always as difficult—if not more so—to find a room as I imagine it must have been in Western Europe just after the war when all the towns were in ruins after the bombing.

Tatiana Vasilievna lived with her husband, who was a steelworker. She ruled the household with a firm hand, and her husband, a kind and gentle man, gladly left everything to her. To preserve appearances, however, Tatiana Vasilievna always consulted him, and before renting the room to us, she had invited us in for tea and said it would depend on what her husband said. He had no objections and said it was "up to the missus." He and M. soon became good friends and found common ground in their passion for music. On his silver wedding anniversary his sons (they had done very well in the Air Force, and one of them had even been presented to Stalin) had given him a phonograph and a pile of records—most of them Komsomol and army songs then in vogue. The old man was not overimpressed by this "caterwauling," as he called it, and preferred the few records that M. had managed to get hold of—the Brandenburg Concertos, a piece of church music by Dvořák, some early Italian things and Mussorgski. It was very difficult to obtain records then, and this was a quite haphazard selection, but both M. and our host got enormous pleasure out of them. In the evenings, whenever we were in Kalinin, they held "concerts," while Tatiana Vasilievna served us tea from the samovar with homemade jam. M. always wanted to have the tea brewed in his own way, and he told us that the first thing Shevchenko always bought when he had any money was a pound of tea. At tea M. generally looked through the newspaper—as a regular factory worker, our landlord was able to subscribe to *Pravda*.

As we now discovered, people talked much more freely and openly in working-class homes than in intellectual ones in those savage times. After all the equivocations of Moscow and the frantic attempts to justify the terror, we were quite startled to hear the mercilessly outspoken way in which our hosts talked. We had been conditioned to hold our tongues, and once, when M. made some evasive remark, Tatiana Vasilievna looked at him pityingly and said: "What can we do with you? You've all been scared out of your wits."

The parents and grandparents of Tatiana Vasilievna and her husband had also been factory workers and, as she told us with some pride: "We are hereditary proletarians." She remembered the political agitators they had hidden from the police in Czarist times and her comment on them was: "To think of the things they said, and look what's come of it all!" Both she and her husband were scathing about the show trials in Moscow: "See what they're doing in our name," said our host once, throwing down the newspaper in disgust. He understood what was going on as "a fight for power among themselves." They were both furious that all this went on in the name of the dictatorship of the proletariat: "They're just making fools of us with that stuff about the working class. They say the power belongs to us, but just try and interfere, and they'd soon show us our place." I told them the theory that classes were "guided" by parties, and parties by leaders. "That's very handy," said the old man. Both of them still clung firmly to their "proletarian conscience."

This family was faced, as always in Russia, by the problem of "fathers and sons." The old couple were not exactly overjoyed by the fact that their children had done so well, and didn't think it would last. As Tatiana Vasilievna put it, "There's lots of us down here at the bottom of the ladder and you're more likely to last, but once you get up top, you can really have a bad fall." The old man went even further—he didn't trust his sons and never said anything in their presence. "They'll go and report you as soon as look at you," he grumbled, "that's what children are like nowadays." But it was only after we'd got to know them really well that we learned what it was that troubled them most about their sons.

Tatiana Vasilievna kept a cow—she told us she could never have brought up her children on her husband's wages, and it was the cow that saved them. The whole family had long since become "proletarian," and this cow was their only remaining link with village life. They bought hay from collective farmers and the bargaining was always done around the samovar. Drinking tea with them, Tatiana Vasilievna heard a great deal about collectivization and life in the kolkhozes with its production targets and "labor-days."* Once, having seen her guests out and still flushed from her conversation with them, she came into our room and started telling us how her eldest son had been sent out, as a young Komsomol, to help in the mass deportation of the kulaks. He had been away quite a long time, and when he returned he said nothing to his parents and would not reply to any of their questions. "Who knows what he was doing out there? Goodness knows what I brought him up for." As she talked with the collective farmers, she kept wondering what her eldest son might have been involved in. Her husband tried to calm her by saying "They're all the same nowadays, Mother, so why should you get all worked up like that?"

We soon noticed that, for all their common sense about what was going on, our hosts had no patience with any kind of political struggle or activity. "Why did they get mixed up in all this? They were earning good money before, weren't they?" the old man said as he read about the show trials in *Pravda:* he disapproved of the very fact that the victims of these trials had involved themselves in some kind of political

---

* Labor-day: the unit by which work was measured on the collective farms, and for which the peasants received payment in kind and a small amount of cash at the end of the working year.

activity. But for us, the horrifying thing was that nobody had lifted a finger to prevent Stalin from seizing power. On the contrary, they had all helped him to pick off the others one by one. The old man remembered how the defendants had been "in the old days" and he suspected that they had been "meddling," as he put it. Both he and Tatiana Vasilievna approved of M. because they regarded him as a passive victim who had nothing to do with the regime and had simply got into trouble for writing things. They would not have been so upset if their sons had kept clear of politics, had nothing to do with the ruling group and "stuck to their own class." Any kind of resistance seemed to them futile and dishonest. They always referred to it as "meddling." In Kalinin we took part for the first time in elections.* Taken aback by the way in which they were held, M. did not know what his attitude toward them should be. At first he tried to look on the bright side by saying: "This is only the beginning—when people get used to the idea, everything will be normal." But later he said he could not possibly take part in this farce. Our hosts reasoned with him, saying, "You can't swim against the tide" and "Why should you be different from others? If everybody else votes, so will we." But their final and most telling argument was: "Don't get on the wrong side of them or you'll never hear the end of it." This was all too true, particularly for people in our position. So we all went to vote: they at six o'clock in the morning, as they had been told at the factory, and we a little later, after breakfast.

If Tatiana Vasilievna was law-abiding, it was not because she respected the law—on the contrary, she took a very dim view of it—but because of her general philosophy of life. She thought her first duty was to survive as best she could, and to this end it was essential, in her view, to avoid all needless activities. The idea of sacrificing oneself for an idea, or dying for it, would have seemed the height of absurdity to her. Her watchword was that they were "little people" who should not stick their necks out. We even sensed a certain standoffishness in this attitude: while the people "up top" fought and murdered each other, trading on the name of the proletariat (which she was so conscious of belonging to), they, as workers, would have nothing to do with it and kept their hands clean. Their business was to live and work, while the

---

* Elections with a single list of pro-Government candidates for the Supreme Soviet were provided for by Stalin's "Constitution" of 1936. Most of the freedoms and privileges "guaranteed" by it were strictly nominal.

others went to the devil in their own sweet way. But there was nothing religious about her, and she never went to church (though she kept lamps lit before the ikons, as her parents had done before her).

There were times when M. and I even seemed, in Tatiana Vasilievna's eyes, to be part, in a very small way, of the harebrained "upper crust." This was whenever she suspected that we were lacking in the will to live. Reading some horribly cynical or grotesque item in the newspaper, M. would frequently exclaim: "We are finished!" He first said this when he showed me Stalin's famous comment on Gorki's tale "The Girl and Death." It was reported in the press that Stalin had written in his copy of the book: "This thing is more powerful than Goethe's Faust. Love triumphs over Death." M. also said "We are finished!" as he showed me an illustrated magazine with a picture on the front cover of Stalin stretching out his hand to Yezhov. "Where else," M. gasped, "would the head of the State have himself photographed with the chief of his secret police?" But the worst thing about it was the expression on Yezhov's face. As M. said, "Look, you can see there's nothing he wouldn't do for Stalin." Once, at the table, Tatiana Vasilievna read out Stalin's speech at a graduation parade of army cadets when he drank a toast to "the science we need" and denounced "the science we do not need." These words were ominous: if there was a science that was not needed, then it would be uprooted and destroyed. This time, when M. pronounced his usual "We are finished," Tatiana Vasilievna and her husband were very cross with us: "You're always talking about being finished. You'll bring it on yourself yet. You ought to think about living, instead. Why don't you learn from us? We manage to live, don't we? Just keep out of things and you'll be all right." As M. summed it up: "Man's first duty is to live."

After M.'s arrest I came back to the sturdy frame house on the outskirts of Kalinin to get the basket full of manuscripts I had left there. When they heard of M.'s arrest, Tatiana Vasilievna and her husband were so upset that I broke down in tears myself. Tatiana Vasilievna, usually so undemonstrative, put her arms around me and said: "Don't cry: you'll be like the saints." And the old man added: "Your husband could never have done harm to anyone. If they're arresting people like him, things must be really bad." They both said they would tell their sons about it so they would know whom they were serving and bowing down to. "Only they won't listen to us," the old man suddenly sighed. His sons were "Stalin's Falcons"—exemplary airmen of the type so accurately portrayed by Solzhenitsyn in the person of Zotov. There certainly was no point in telling them anything—they personified the ideas that then ruled the world. Now, in the middle of the sixties, they are the fathers who complain all the time about their sons—the grandchildren of Tatiana Vasilievna's generation. They are rejected both by their parents and by their children, who have formed an alliance against them. In this connection I remember a meeting on a train with another relic of "Stalin's empire." This one, unlike the other one I have already described, was all for the Twentieth Congress. This was because he had been in trouble under Stalin—he hadn't exactly been arrested, but it had been a near thing. Now he was enjoying his retirement on a good pension as a former Party official. Not to spend his time in idleness, he had taken on the job of giving political instruction in a Leningrad technical college. As one teacher to another, he began to tell me his troubles. On one election day he had come to the college early to get all the students out to vote, but none of them wanted to. He said they should take an example from people like himself who had "made the Revolution" and told them he had got up at the crack of dawn to go and vote. To this they replied that nobody had asked him to make a revolution and that people had been better off before. This had left him speechless, and the whole of his "revolutionary" claptrap had been to no avail. "What can you make of these young people nowadays? How do you cope with them?" I told him in all honesty that I got on well with them and they never made trouble for me. These are, in effect, Tatiana Vasilievna's grandchildren—though sometimes I wonder whether they have anything in their heads apart from their negative attitude toward everything. . . .

Not long after I had been to see her, the police came to Tatiana Vasilievna's house with a warrant for my arrest. They searched the house from top to bottom, including the attic and cellar, but luckily I had taken everything away with me. They had a photograph with them, and they looked very carefully at Tatiana Vasilievna and the wife of Shchegolev's secretary. I learned all this a year later when I was about to go back to Kalinin to settle there. It was the wife of Shchegolev's secretary who had brought the story to Leningrad. I would have hesitated to return to Kalinin, but my luggage was already on the train when I heard about this, and I decided to risk it. The terror was now not quite as bad, Yezhov had fallen and the arrests were no longer on a mass scale. I lived in Kalinin nearly two years—right till the evacuation after the war broke out—and I was left alone, even though the warrant for my arrest must still have been lying, unused, in my file. It may seem fantastic, but there were many cases like this—the target figures for the man hunt had by now been "adjusted," and people not picked up under earlier warrants came through untouched. Terror was planned, like the economy, and the quotas for life and death were manipulated at will.

The effect the house search had on Tatiana Vasilievna was devastating. Three hefty fellows had turned the place upside down, and she cursed both them and me. When I saw her a year later she accused me of concealing from her that I had meanwhile been in jail. Perhaps she even suspected me of something worse: "Why did they let you out? They never let anybody out nowadays." It was more than I could do to persuade her that I had not been arrested—she just could not believe that "they" would ever fail to arrest anyone they were after, and that I had escaped because I had not been there when they came. And who, indeed, can blame her? But at last she took pity on me and asked whether I had anywhere to live: "If you have nowhere to go, you can stay here. They say God takes care of those who take care of themselves—but how anybody can take care of himself nowadays I don't know." In effect she was offering to betray her principle of non-interference in the troubled affairs of our country, but I decided not to stay in her house again: the thought of those men who had searched it would have robbed me of sleep.

73
THE TEXTILE WORKERS

During my wanderings I have met all kinds of ordinary folk and I have almost always got on better with them than with those who consider themselves the cream of the Soviet intelligentsia—not that they were so anxious for my company either.

Immediately after M.'s arrest I lived for a time in Strunino, a small cotton-mill town beyond Zagorsk. I had learned about it by chance as I was returning to Moscow from Rostov-the-Great, where I had originally wanted to settle. On the first day there I had met Efros, who went pale when I told him about M.'s arrest—he had just spent many months in the Lubianka himself. He was almost the only person during the Yezhov terror to get away with nothing more than expulsion from Moscow. When M. had heard, a few weeks before his own arrest, that Efros was out and had gone to live in Rostov, he was staggered and said: "It should be renamed Efros-the-Great." I readily believed him when he advised me not to settle in Rostov: "There are too many of us here already." In the train on the way back I got talking with an elderly woman and when I told her I was looking for a room she advised me to get out in Strunino and gave me the name and address of some good people there—the man of the house, she said, didn't drink or swear. Then she added: "And the woman's mother has been in jail, so she'll be sorry for you." The people one met in trains like this were always kinder than those in Moscow, and they always guessed what my troubles were—even though it was now spring and I had sold my leather jacket.

Strunino is on the Yaroslavl railroad along which prisoners are taken to Siberia, and I had the mad thought that one day I might catch a glimpse of M. as he went past in the prison transport, so I got out there and went to the address which had been given me. I quickly got on good terms with the people and told them exactly why I needed a place to live in the "hundred-and-five kilometer zone"—though they knew without my having to tell them. They let me have a porch which was not in use, but when it got colder later in the year, they insisted I move inside with them—they screened off a corner of their living room with cupboards and blankets to give me some privacy.

I never hid the fact that I am Jewish, and I must say that among the ordinary people I have yet to encounter any anti-Semitism. In working-class families and among collective farmers I was always treated as one of them, without the least hint of what one found in the universities after the war—and now too, for that matter. It is always among the semi-educated that fascism, chauvinism and hatred for the intelligentsia most easily take root. Anti-intellectual feelings are a greater threat than crude anti-Semitism as such, and they are rampant in all the overstaffed institutions where people are furiously defending their right to their ignorance. We gave them a Stalinist education and they have Stalinist diplomas. They naturally want to hang on to what they feel entitled to—where would they go otherwise?

I made day trips to Moscow from Strunino to hand in parcels for M., and my meager resources—I had to sell off M.'s books—soon gave out.

My hosts saw that I had nothing to eat, and they shared their tiuria and murtsovka* with me. They referred to radishes as "Stalin's lard." They made me drink fresh milk to keep my strength up—though they had little to spare, because they had to sell a good deal of what their cow gave to buy hay for it. In return I used to bring them wild berries from the woods. I spent most of my day in the woods and I always used to slow down as I came back to the house in the evening: I kept thinking that M. might have been let out of prison and one of these days would come out to meet me. It is hard to believe that someone can be taken away from you and simply be destroyed—the mind can take in the bare fact, but it is still impossible to believe.

That autumn I came completely to the end of my means and I had to think of work. My host worked in the local textile factory, and his wife's family were also textile workers. They were very upset at the thought of my taking on this drudgery, but there was nothing else for it, and when a notice about hiring new hands appeared on the factory gate, I got a job in the spinning shop. I worked on the spinning machines—each woman worker had to look after twelve of them. I sometimes volunteered for the unpopular night shift so that I could go to Moscow during the day to hand in a parcel for M. and try to get the information about him which no one would give me. Working on the night shift and running between one machine and another in the enormous shop, I kept myself awake by muttering M.'s verse to myself. I had to commit everything to memory in case all my papers were taken away from me, or the various people I had given copies to took fright and burned them in a moment of panic—that had been done more than once by the best and most devoted friends of literature. My memory was thus an additional safeguard—indeed, it was indispensable to me in my difficult task. I thus spent my eight hours of night work not only spinning yarn but also memorizing verse.

To rest from the machines the women took refuge in the washroom, which was a sort of club for us. They would stop talking and look vacant whenever some Komsomol girl intent on making a career came running in briskly. "Be careful of *her*," they would warn me. But when the coast was clear they let themselves go, giving me a picture of how their present life compared with the old days: "It was a long day then,

---

* Country dishes. Tiuria: bread soaked in kvass. Murtsovka: eggs and onion mixed with kvass or water.

but we kept breaking off for a drink of tea—you know how many machines we each had to work on then?" It was talking with them that I first became aware of how genuinely popular Yesenin is. They were always mentioning his name and he is a real legend among the ordinary people: they felt he was one of them and loved him for it.

In the morning, once they were out of the factory gates, they stood in line at the store to buy bread or cloth. Before the war, material for making dresses was very hard to get, there was never enough bread and living standards in general were extremely low. People have now forgotten what it was like, and my Stalinist neighbors in Pskov were always insisting that before the war they didn't know what poverty was and that they had only learned the taste of it nowadays. It is remarkable how willfully oblivious of the past people can be.

In Strunino I learned that a woman forced to live beyond the hundred-kilometer limit was popularly known as a "hundred-and-fiver" (stopiatnitsa). The word reminded them of the martyred St. Paraskeva, and when I later told it to Akhmatova, she used it in a poem. All the workers in the factory referred to me in this way, and they were all very kind to me—particularly the older men. Sometimes they would come into the spinning shop and offer me an apple or a piece of pie ("Eat some of this, my wife baked it yesterday"). In the factory cafeteria during the meal break they always kept a place for me and made me take some soup to "keep my strength up." Everywhere I found this warm sympathy which was shown to me as a stopiatnitsa. There was never the slightest hint of anti-intellectual prejudice among these people.

Once during a night shift two dapper young men came into the spinning shop, switched off my machines and asked me to follow them into the personnel section. This was located in another building and we had to go through several shops to get to it. Seeing us go by, other workers switched off their machines and began to follow us. As we went down some stairs leading outside, I was afraid to look around because I sensed that this was a way of saying goodbye to me—the workers knew only too well that people were often taken straight from the personnel section to the secret police.

My conversation with the two young men was quite ludicrous. They asked me why I was doing a job for which I was not qualified, and I replied that I had no qualification of any kind. And why had I come to live in Strunino? I told them I had no other place to live. "Why does an educated woman like you want to work in a factory?" At that time I still had no college diploma and was only educated in the sense that I had been to a grammar school before the Revolution and belonged to the intelligentsia—as the two men realized instinctively. "Why didn't you try to get work in a school?" "Because I don't have a diploma." To which one of them said: "There's something funny about this—tell us the truth." I couldn't make out what they wanted, but that night they decided to let me go—perhaps because of the workers who had gathered outside in the yard. They asked me whether I was working the night shift again the next day and told me to come back to the personnel section before I started work. I even had to sign a paper saying I would.

I didn't go back to the shop that night, but went straight home. My hosts were still awake—somebody had come to tell them that I had been hauled off "to personnel." The man produced a small bottle of vodka and poured out three glasses: "Let's have a drink and think what to do."

When the night shift ended, workers kept coming up to the house and stood talking to us by the window. Some said I should go away at once, and put money on the window sill for me. My landlady packed my things, and her husband and two neighbors took me to the station and put me on one of the early-morning trains. In this way I escaped a new disaster, thanks to these people who had still not learned to be indifferent. Even if the personnel section had not originally intended to hand me over to the police, I am certain they would never have let me go free after seeing how the workers had gathered to say goodbye.

The people of Strunino were sensitive to our misfortunes and knew very well what it was like to be the outlawed wife of a prisoner, a stopiatnitsa. The prison trains generally passed through at night, and in the mornings the workers from the textile factory would always look carefully as they crossed the tracks to see whether there were any notes written on scraps of paper—sometimes prisoners managed to throw them out. Anybody who found such a note put it in an envelope and mailed it. In this way the relatives of prisoners sometimes received news. If one of these trains happened to stop in Strunino during the day, everybody tried to throw the prisoners something—food or tobacco—behind the backs of the guards as they paced up and down. This was how my landlady had managed to throw a piece of chocolate to a prisoner.

There had been many arrests in Strunino itself, and this had embittered the local people. For the first time I heard Stalin referred to here as "the pockmarked fellow." When I asked why, they said: "Don't you know he had smallpox? They're always getting it down in the Caucasus." They themselves could have got something worse than smallpox for saying such things, but they were extremely careful whom they talked to, and they knew very well who all the local informers were. This is the great advantage of living in a village—in the big cities we were never sure whom we could trust.

In Strunino too they were all very law-abiding, but their inborn good nature made it impossible for them not to voice their feelings. As Yakulov once said to me, "The Russian Revolution is not cruel—the State has sucked out all the cruelty and passed it on to the Cheka."

In Russia everything always happens at the top. The people hold their peace, resisting only in the meekest way. They hate cruelty, but do not believe in fighting it actively. How these qualities can be squared with the great uprisings and revolutions of the past, I do not know. What is one to make of it?

74

THE SHKLOVSKIS

In Moscow there was only one house to which an outcast could always go. If Victor and Vasilisa Shklovski happened not to be at home when M. and I called during our trips to the city in the months before his arrest, one of the children would run out to greet us: little Varia, who always had a piece of chocolate in her hand, the tall Vasia (the daughter of Vasilisa's sister Natalia), or Nikita, their gangling son, who liked to go out catching birds and was also a great stickler for the truth. Nobody had ever explained anything to them, but they always knew what they had to do: children generally reflect their parents' standards of behavior. They would take us into the kitchen, which at the Shklovskis' was run like a cafeteria, give us food and drink, and entertain us with their chatter. Vasia, who played the viola, always told us about the latest concert—at that time Shostakovich's symphony was all the rage. Shklovski listened to what Vasia said and commented gleefully: "That puts Shostakovich right at the top!" Those were times in which everybody had to be given his precise place in the hierarchy, with everybody trying to come out on top. The State encouraged people to behave like the boyars in medieval Russia who fought each other over their place at the Czar's table, always reserving to itself the final decision as to who should sit "at the top." It was in those days that Lebedev-Kumach, who was said to be actually a very modest man, found himself elevated to the status of "top poet." Shklovski also had his ambitions, but he wanted to see things decided on the basis of his famous "Hamburg reckoning."* M. would have loved to go and hear Shostakovich's new symphony, but we were afraid to miss the last train.

With Varia the conversation was different. She showed us her school textbooks where the portraits of Party leaders had thick pieces of paper pasted over them as one by one they fell into disgrace—this the children had to do on instructions from their teacher. Varia said how much she would like to cover up Semashko—"We'll have to sooner or later, so why not now?" At this time the editors of encyclopedias and reference books were sending subscribers—most such works were bought on subscription—lists of articles that had to be pasted over or cut out. In the Shklovski household this was attended to by Victor himself. With every new arrest, people went through their books and burned the works of disgraced leaders in their stoves. In new apartment buildings, which had central heating instead of stoves, forbidden books, personal diaries, correspondence and other "subversive literature" had to be cut up in pieces with scissors and thrown down the toilet. People were kept very busy. . . .

Nikita, the least talkative of the children, sometimes said things that staggered the grownups. Once, for instance, Victor was telling us that he and Paustovski had been to see a famous bird fancier who trained canaries—he only had to give a sign for one of his birds to come out of its cage, sit on a perch and sing. On another signal from its owner, it obediently went back into its cage again. "Just like a member of the Union of Writers," said Nikita and left the room. After saying something like this, he always disappeared into his own room, where he kept the birds he had caught. But he treated his birds nicely, and didn't be-

---

* In the preface to *Hamburg Reckoning* (Leningrad, 1928), Shklovski notes that Hamburg's prizefighters were ranked once each year in a day of long, hard fighting behind closed doors, rather than by their public fights manipulated by promoters. He suggests that the same methods should be applied to writers.

lieve in training them. He told us that songbirds always learned to sing from certain older birds that were particularly good at it. In the Kursk region, once famous for its nightingales, the best songsters had all been caught, and young birds had no way of learning any more. The Kursk "school" of nightingales was thus destroyed because of the selfish people who had put the best songsters in cages. . . .

When Vasilisa with her smiling light-blue eyes arrived, she at once went into action. She ran a bath for us, gave us a change of underwear and then made us lie down for a rest. Victor was always trying to think of ways of helping M., apart from entertaining him with the latest gossip. In the late autumn he gave him an old coat made of dog skin which the previous winter had been worn by Andronikov, the "one-man orchestra." But since then Andronikov had come up in the world and had got himself a brand-new coat of the kind his status as a member of the Writers' Union entitled him to. Shklovski now solemnly handed the dog-skin coat over to M. and even made a little speech on the occasion: "Let everybody see that you came here riding inside the train, not hanging on the buffers. . . ." Till then M. had worn a yellow coat made of leather—also a gift from somebody. It was in this yellow coat that he went to the camp later on. . . .

Whenever the doorbell rang, they hid us in the kitchen or the children's room before opening the door. If it was a friend, we were at once released from captivity with shouts of joy, but if it was Pavlenko or Lelia Povolotskaya, the woman police spy from next door—the one who had a stroke when they started rehabilitating people—we stayed in our hiding place until they were gone. None of them ever once caught a glimpse of us, and we were very proud of the fact.

The Shklovskis' house was the only place where we felt like human beings again. This was a family that knew how to help lost souls like us. In their kitchen we discussed our problems—where to stay the night, how to get money, and so forth. We avoided staying the night with them, because of the women who looked after the building—the janitress, the door-woman and the one who worked the elevator. It was a time-honored tradition that these down-trodden but good-natured souls worked for the secret police. They got no extra pay for this—it simply counted as part of their normal duties. I don't remember now how we managed it, but we did go to the Shostakovich concert and stayed the night somewhere else. . . . When I later came by myself to the Shklovskis' apartment, after M.'s death, the women at the door asked me where he was, and when I told them he was dead, they sighed. "But we thought you'd be the first to go," said one of them. This remark showed me the extent to which our fate had been written on our faces, and it also made me realize that these wretched women had hearts after all, and that one needn't be so afraid of them. The ones who took pity on me soon died—the poor women didn't last long on their meager rations—but afterward I always got on well with their successors, who never informed the militia that I sometimes spent the night at the Shklovskis'. But in 1937 we were terrified of being reported and tried not to stay at the Shklovskis' for fear of getting them into trouble—instead, we kept on the move all the time, chasing breathlessly from place to place.

Occasionally, when there was no choice, we stayed the night there nevertheless, sleeping on their bedroom floor on a mattress covered with a sheepskin rug. They were on the seventh story, so you couldn't hear cars stopping outside, but if ever we heard the elevator coming up at night, we all four of us raced to the door and listened. "Thank God," we would say, "it's downstairs" or "it's gone past." This business of listening for the elevator happened every night, no matter whether we were there or not. Fortunately, it was not used all that often, since many of the writers with apartments in the building spent most of their time in Peredelkino, or in any case didn't come home late—and their children were still very young. In the years of the terror, there was not a home in the country where people did not sit trembling at night, their ears straining to catch the murmur of passing cars or the sound of the elevator. Even nowadays, whenever I spend the night at the Shklovskis' apartment, I tremble as I hear the elevator go past. The sight of half-dressed people huddling by the door, waiting to hear where the elevator stops, is something one can never forget. One night recently, after a car had stopped outside my house, I had a bad dream in which I thought M. was waking me up and saying: "Get dressed—they've come for you this time." But I refused to budge: "I won't get up—to hell with them!" This was a mental revolt against what is also, after all, a kind of collaboration: they come to cart you off to prison and you just meekly get out of bed and put on your clothes with trembling hands. But never again! If they come for me, they'll have to carry me out on a stretcher or kill me on the spot—I'll never go of my own free will.

Once during the winter of 1937 we decided it was wrong to go on taking advantage of the Shklovskis' kindness. We were afraid of compromising them—a single denunciation and they could all land in prison. We were horrified at the thought of bringing disaster on Shklovski and his whole family, and though they begged us not to worry, we stopped going to see them for a while. As a result, we felt more homeless and lonely than ever before. Soon M. could stand it no longer and while we were on a visit to Lev Bruni he phoned the Shklovskis. "Come over at once," said Victor, "Vasilisa misses you terribly." A quarter of an hour later we rang at their door and Vasilisa came out crying tears of joy. I then felt she was the only real person in the whole world—and I still think so. I should mention that I have always felt just as close to Akhmatova, but she was living in Leningrad at that time and was thus far away from us.

75

MARYINA ROSHCHA[*]

We were once sitting at the Shklovskis' when Alexander (Sania) Bernstein called and invited us to stay the night at his apartment. Nobody would have thought that the tall, frail and pampered Sania was a brave man, but he walked along the street with us, whistling as though everything was right with the world and chattering about literature, not the least bit afraid to harbor two such arch-criminals as M. and myself in his apartment. When we got there, his little daughter skipped around us and his placid wife, Niura, gave us tea and gossiped with us. He was just as calm in 1948 when he agreed to take M.'s manuscripts from my brother, Evgeni, and keep them for us. In 1938 his brother Sergei had hidden another "criminal," the linguist Victor Vinogradov, who was then forbidden to live in Moscow because he had been in prison. When Vinogradov eventually got on his feet again, became a member of the Academy of Science and was put in charge of Stalinist linguistics, he forgot this poor family that had once given him refuge and did not even go to the funeral of Sergei's wife, who had been so kind to him.

Usually, however, we went to stay the night with Vasilisa's sister, Natalia, the mother of Vasia. On these occasions Vasia would stay behind with the Shklovskis, and we slept in her mother's room in the apartment in Maryina Roshcha where Victor and Vasilisa had lived before. Another room in this apartment was occupied by Nikolai Ivan-

---

[*] A suburb of Moscow.

ovich Khardzhiev, who was good company for M. in the evenings—they always sat up talking till very late. It was with Khardzhiev that I spent the first few days after M's arrest—and then I stayed with him again after hearing of M.'s death. I just lay in a stupor, but Nikolai Ivanovich, desperately poor though he was, went out to buy food and expensive candies for me, and kept making me eat something. He was the other person who stood by Akhmatova and me at the blackest periods of our life.

I once saw in his room a drawing of Khlebnikov by Tatlin. Tatlin had done it many years after Khlebnikov's death, but it looked just like him, exactly as I remembered him when he used to come and eat kasha with us in our room at Herzen House, after which he would sit in silence, continually moving his lips. When I saw this drawing, it suddenly struck me that one day M. might similarly come to life in a good portrait by somebody, and the thought made me feel a little better. But I didn't reckon with the fact that all the artists who knew him died before it would have been safe for them to draw his portrait. The drawing by Miklashevski that appeared in the magazine *Moskva* is a very poor likeness—M. came out astonishingly well in photographs, but no artist was ever able to do justice to him.

M. used to say that Khardzhiev had a perfect ear for poetry, and this is why I insisted that he be put in charge of editing the volume of M.'s verse which was supposed to come out ten years ago in the Poets' Library but still hasn't appeared.

The tumbledown wooden house in Maryina Roshcha seemed like a haven to us, but to get to it was not so simple. When we left the Shklovskis' with Natalia, we first had to run the gauntlet of the various women looking after the building. Out in the street Natalia walked on ahead, got on tramcars first, and waited for us at the transfer stops. We always kept a little way behind, trying not to lose sight of her broad back. Obliged as we were to behave like conspirators, it would not have done for us to walk side by side. If M. had been picked up in the street—we had heard of such cases—Natalia could pretend to be a mere passerby whose papers they wouldn't even bother to check. We would thus avoid calling attention to our connection with the Shklovskis. Our precautions were ridiculous, but we had to take them—this was the penalty of living in our time and place. So we walked behind Natalia, as though hypnotized by her swaying gait. She always seemed quite imperturbable, and if we failed to get on the same tramcar, we knew she would be waiting for us at a transfer stop, or at the terminus.

Although there were other people living in her house, we always managed to slip in without being seen—Natalia went in first and had a look around before beckoning us to follow. But one of her neighbors, a certain Vaks, a member of the Union of Writers, must have known that she had people staying overnight in her room. He was evidently a decent person, however, and never denounced us. In the mornings we could hear him ringing the Union of Writers from the telephone in the passage outside, but his purpose was only to demand building materials and money for repairs to the "hovel" which we regarded as such a haven. M. even wrote some comic verse featuring Vaks—he still occasionally managed to turn out this kind of thing, though his life was now such that real poetry had come to an end. Shklovski for some reason hated humorous verse and dismissed it as a symptom of softening of the brain, if not worse—not because he thought the times were unsuitable for it, but as a matter of principle. Humorous verse is a Petersburg tradition and Moscow recognized only the art of parody—Shklovski had forgotten his youth in Petersburg.

That winter I began shouting in my sleep at night. It was an awful, inhuman cry, as if an animal or a bird were having its neck wrung. Shklovski, who heard it when I slept in their apartment, teased me that while most people shouted "Mama" in their sleep, with me it was "Osia" ["Osip"]. I still frighten people with this terrible cry at night. That same year, much to the alarm of my friends, the palms of my hands started turning bright red at moments of stress—and still do. But M. was as calm and collected as ever, and went on joking to the end.

During our trips to Moscow we sometimes had to stay on a few extra days till we could get money. The number of people able to help us got smaller all the time, and we had to wait until Shklovski was in funds—on such days he would come home with money stuffed in all his pockets. After he had given us some, we set off back to Kalinin, where we spent it on our upkeep in the house of Tatiana Vasilievna.

76

The Accomplice

In the fall of 1937 Katayev and Shklovski decided it would be a good idea to arrange for M. to meet Fadeyev, who, though not yet the boss of the Union of Writers, was already very influential. The meeting took place in Katayev's apartment. M. read some of his verse, and Fadeyev was very moved—he tended to be emotional. Apparently sober, he embraced M. tearfully and said something in a suitable vein. I wasn't present, but waited in the Shklovskis' apartment several stories up. When they came in, Victor and M. seemed pleased. They had left early to give Katayev a chance to talk privately with Fadeyev.

Fadeyev did not forget about M.'s poetry. Shortly after this, when he had to go down to Tiflis with Ehrenburg—probably for the Rustaveli anniversary—he assured Ehrenburg that he would try to get a selection of it published. But nothing came of this. Perhaps it had been hinted to him that it "wouldn't be advisable." If you approached them for permission to do something, our officials had a nice way of saying with a frown: "Of course, go ahead if you see fit." The frown was equivalent to a refusal, but since the word "no" had not actually passed the official's lips, appearances were saved and the refusal to allow something was made to look like "initiative from below" and thus entirely "democratic." Probably no other regime ever went in for such niceties in the art of bureaucratic control—apart from all its other qualities, it was distinguished by unparalleled hypocrisy. But it is even more likely that Fadeyev, fearing to "get mixed up in something," never raised the matter at all. Nevertheless, at the end of the winter in 1938, running into M. in the Writers' Union, he suddenly offered to put in a word for him "up above" and find out "what they think." He said we should come and see him again at the Union in a few days' time, when he would have the answer, or, rather, some information for us.

To our astonishment, Fadeyev actually kept the appointment on the day and at the hour we had agreed on. We left the premises of the Union with him and he invited us into his car so we could talk on the way to another place we had to go to. Fadeyev sat next to his chauffeur, and we got in the back. Turning around to us, he told us he had talked with Andreyev, but that this had produced no results: Andreyev was quite adamant that no work could be found for M. Fadeyev was embarrassed and upset that he had been turned down "point blank" (to use his own words). M. even tried to cheer him up by saying it didn't matter and everything would work out in the end. We had one good reason not to be too much put out by Fadeyev's failure: just before this M. had suddenly been received by Stavski, who suggested that we should go for a time to a rest home while the question of work for M. was being decided. On Stavski's instructions, the Literary Fund had already issued us vouchers to enable us both to spend two months in a rest home at Samatikha, and this unexpected stroke of luck had made us feel very much better. When we mentioned it to Fadeyev, however, he did not sound pleased: "Vouchers? Where to? Who gave them to you? Where is Samatikha? Why not to the Union rest home?" M. explained that the Union of Writers had no rest homes beyond the hundred-kilometer radius. "What about Maleyevka?" Fadeyev asked. We had never heard of this place, but when we asked about it, Fadeyev suddenly became evasive. "Oh, it's a pretty run-down building they've just let the Union have. I suppose it's being done over." M. then said he imagined they would not want to let him go to a Union rest home until the general question of his status had been cleared up. Fadeyev readily accepted this explanation. He was clearly upset and worried about something. Now, looking back on it, I can see that he had suddenly realized what was afoot. It is difficult for even the most hardened person to look to such things calmly—and Fadeyev was an emotional man.

The car stopped in the Kitaigorod district.* Our reason for going there, if I remember rightly, was to call at the Central Rest Homes Bureau to tell them our day of departure so they could arrange for horses to be sent to meet us at Charusti on the Murom railroad. Samatikha was twenty-five kilometers farther on from there.

Fadeyev got out of the car and gave M. a warm farewell embrace. M. promised to come and see him when he got back. "Yes, yes—you must," Fadeyev said as we parted. His elaborate farewell and oddly gloomy air made us feel uneasy. What was wrong? Everybody had more than his fair share of troubles in those years, so there was nothing all that surprising about it. Elated by our first windfall in Moscow—fancy the Union of Writers being so kind to us!—we never for a moment thought that Fadeyev's gloom might somehow be connected with M.'s fate and Andreyev's refusal to help—a terrible sentence in itself. Fadeyev, with all his experience and excellent understanding of Party affairs, could not have failed to see this.

And why, incidentally, was he not at all worried about talking to us in front of his chauffeur? Nobody ever did this. Under our system of surveillance, the chauffeurs of prominent officials always reported on their employers' every word and gesture. I happen to know that after Stalin's death, when Surkov took over the running of the Union of

---

* A district in the center of Moscow.

Writers, the first thing he did on being given Fadeyev's car was to refuse it on some idiotic pretext—saying it was too old or the wrong make—and get rid of the chauffeur that came with it. Evidently, in the new climate after Stalin's death, he hoped to avoid constant eavesdropping. Surely Fadeyev was not so fanatically certain of his immunity that he took no account of the "ears of State" in his car? Or was it, rather, that he had already given his assent to the fate prepared for M. and could therefore look bright-eyed at his chauffeur as he spoke with the untouchable in the back seat? Liuba [Ehrenburg] has told me that Fadeyev was a cold and cruel man—something quite compatible with emotionalism and the ability to shed a tear at the right moment. This became very clear, according to Liuba, at the time of the execution of the Yiddish writers.* Then also it was a case of tearful farewell embraces after he had signified his formal agreement to their arrest and liquidation—even though the Yiddish writers, unlike Mandelstam, were his friends.

But, unfamiliar as we were with the ways of officialdom in this irrational country of ours, we were just baffled by such duplicity, and certainly didn't understand how on earth a writer could behave like this, even if he held a high post in the writers' organization. We still didn't realize the extent to which people had been corrupted, nor did we know that heads of departments were always required to countersign lists of their subordinates who had been arrested, and were thus deliberately made party to their destruction. In 1938, however, this particular function would have been carried out by Stavski rather than Fadeyev—or so people say. The trouble is that we cannot be certain about anything: the past is still wrapped in mystery, and we still do not really know what they did to us.

Less than a year later, during a party in Lavrushinski Street to celebrate the award of the first Government decorations to be given to writers, Fadeyev learned about the death of M. and drank to his memory with the words "We have done away with a great poet." Translated into Soviet idiom, this meant: "You can't make an omelet without breaking eggs."

This is not quite the end of Fadeyev's involvement in our story. Shortly before the end of the war I had a chance encounter with him as I was going up to the Shklovskis' in the elevator. I was just about to

* All the leading Yiddish writers were shot, on Stalin's orders, in 1952.

close the door and press the button when the doorwoman shouted that someone else was coming—I waited a moment, and in walked Fadeyev. He did not greet me, and, being used to this kind of thing, I simply turned away so as not to embarrass a man who didn't want to recognize me. But as soon as the elevator started to move, Fadeyev bent down to my ear and whispered to me that it was Andreyev who had signed M.'s sentence. Or at least that is how I understood the sense of his words, which were roughly: "The business with Osip Emilievich was handled by Andreyev." Then the elevator stopped and Fadeyev got out. I did not yet know about the three-man tribunals* which operated then, and had imagined that sentences were passed only by the secret police. I was therefore puzzled by this reference to Andreyev. I also noticed that Fadeyev was a little drunk.

Why did he speak to me like that, and was he telling the truth? It is possible that in his fuddled brain the memory of our last conversation in his car simply sparked off an association with Andreyev, whom he had mentioned to us then. But he may have been speaking the truth. I know from the letter of the secret-police official who killed himself in Tashkent that Andreyev was one of the direct agents of Stalin's terrorist policies and came to Tashkent to brief the secret police on the "simplified interrogation procedures" required at the "new stage."†

But it scarcely matters who actually signed the sentence—in those years everybody readily signed whatever was put before them. This was not only because they feared they would otherwise at once be dispatched to the other world. It was also because we were all so well disciplined that we took part in the killing of our own kind and justified ourselves by reference to "historical necessity." The St. Bartholemew massacre lasted only one night—perhaps the cutthroats responsible for it boasted of their heroic deed to the end of their days—yet it has remained in human memory forever. The humanist ideas of the nineteenth century—no matter how ill-founded and specious they may have been—had nevertheless become ingrained in our minds, and though there is never any lack of hired killers, one cannot help wondering what old revolutionaries, dedicated as young men to the service

---

* Tribunals consisting of three officials which sentenced political prisoners behind closed doors during the terror.
† I.e., after Yezhov took over from Yagoda in 1937 and was ordered by Stalin to step up measures against "enemies of the people."

of mankind, must have thought as they sacrificed their humanist principles to "historical necessity." And is it conceivable that people will not learn from our example?

Though I can be certain of nothing, I feel that when he gave us a lift in his car Fadeyev already knew what was going to happen to M., and, what is more, that he at once understood the reason for M. being sent to a rest home not belonging to the Union of Writers.

77

The Young Lady of Samatikha

Everything went very smoothly. We got out at the station of Charusti, where there was a sleigh waiting for us with sheepskin rugs to keep us warm. It was so rare in our life for any arrangements to work out without a hitch that we were quite staggered. If they hadn't forgotten to send the sleigh down to meet us on time, there must have been very strict instructions to make sure everything was done properly. It looked as though we were being treated like guests of honor. It was a very cold March, and we could hear the pine trees cracking from the frost. The snow was so deep on the ground that at first we went everywhere on skis. As an old pupil of the Tenishev school, M. could ski and skate very well, and in Samatikha it proved easier to go short distances on skis than on foot. We were given a room in the main building, but it was very noisy there, and as soon as we mentioned this we were at once transferred to a smaller place, a quaint forest hut that usually served as a reading room. The resident doctor told us he had been instructed to create the best possible conditions for M. and he had therefore decided to let us have the reading room, temporarily barring the use of it to others, so that we could have peace and quiet. During our stay in Samatikha the doctor was phoned several times from the Union of Writers and asked how M. was getting on. He told us about these calls with a rather bemused air, and was evidently convinced that M. must be a very big fish indeed. We, for our part, were more and more confirmed in our impression that there had been a change in our fortunes and that "they" were beginning to look after us. What miracles they were, all these phone calls, inquiries about our health, and instructions to "create the best possible conditions," as though we really were people who mattered. This had never happened to us before.

The people in this rest home were quiet enough on the whole—most of them were workers from various factories. As always in such places, they were absorbed in their temporary love affairs, and nobody paid the slightest attention to us. The only person who bothered us was the "master of ceremonies," who kept wanting to arrange an evening of poetry reading by M. We eventually got rid of him by saying that M.'s poetry was banned and could not be read in public without the authorization of the Union of Writers. This he understood at once and after that left us alone. We were of course a little bored. M. had brought Dante, Khlebnikov, the one-volume Pushkin edited by Tomashevski and also Shevchenko—which had been given to him at the last moment by Boris Lapin. Several times M. had the urge to make a trip into town, but the doctor always said there was no room in the sleigh or truck that went to the railroad station. It was impossible to get horses on private hire—there were practically no villages nearby, and in any case the only ones left belonged to the kolkhozes. "You don't think we've fallen into a trap, by any chance?" M. asked me once after the doctor had refused to take us to the station, but it was only a passing thought. We were so well looked after in Samatikha that we couldn't help feeling that the worst was over—hadn't the Union itself paid all expenses (for both of us!) and given instructions to "create the best possible conditions"?

At the beginning of April—during the very first days of our stay before we asked to be moved out of the main building—a well-educated young woman of intellectual appearance arrived at the rest home. She came up to M. and started talking with him. It turned out that she knew Kaverin, Tynianov and several other completely decent people. Like M., she was—so she said—a "convicted person," and her parents had therefore had to buy her a voucher for a rest home in the hundred-and-five-kilometer zone, which was why she now found herself in such a "democratic" place as Samatikha. We felt sorry for her, and surprised that someone so young had completed a five-year sentence already. But everything was possible in this world. She often looked in on us, particularly when we moved out to the reading room—she thought it was so cozy there! She kept telling us about her mummy and daddy—how, for instance, Daddy himself had carried her into the hospital ward when she had been ill (some Daddy to have had this privilege!), about their wonderful fluffy cats which always sat on Daddy's knee, how nice and refined everything was in their house—judging by her slender arms and legs, she was certainly a well-bred young lady—and so on and so forth. Suddenly, among all this chatter she dropped a remark about her interrogation—how she had flatly refused to name the author of some poems and had fallen into a dead faint when her interrogator insisted. "What poems?" M. asked her. To this our new acquaintance babbled on about how during a search of her writing desk they had found some banned poems, but that she had not betrayed their author. On another occasion she pestered M. with questions about who was interested in his poems and who was keeping copies of them. "Alexei Tolstoi," M. replied wickedly. But it had taken him some time to see her game, and at first he had even read her one of his poems ("Gaps in Round Bays," I think it was). The young lady squealed with delight—"How daring of you to write something like that!"—and asked whether she could have a copy. I even rebuked M. for becoming so lax—I said it must be out of boredom. "Nonsense," he said, "she's a friend of Kaverin, isn't she?" He was so relaxed in the rest home that he was even willing to put up with the young lady's tales about her daddy. Later I was to hear similar idyllic tales about Mummy and Daddy from Larisa, the daughter of the police official in Tashkent who killed himself, and from other pupils of mine with the same kind of background. I had the impression that in these circles this kind of talk was thought to be "cultured."

The young lady went away two or three days before the first of May. She had intended to stay a couple of months in Samatikha, but her daddy unexpectedly telephoned from Moscow and told her to return. She was sent to the station in a truck together with the "master of ceremonies" and somebody else from the rest home who was supposed to buy supplies for the coming holiday. We asked him to get us some cigarettes, because those they sold in the local store were no good at all. M. was very keen to escape to Moscow for the holiday, away from the drinking, singing and other jollifications which could be expected during the May Day celebrations at the rest home. But the doctor said we couldn't: the truck would be fully loaded and there would be no room. The man we had asked to buy cigarettes for us—he was a worker staying in the rest home—returned from the station at Charusti by begging a lift in a peasant cart. He told us that when they arrived in Charusti, the young lady had gone on a drinking bout with the "master of ceremonies" and the truck driver. They had got blind drunk and behaved so badly that the worker just couldn't wait to get away. He was surprised that the stationmaster didn't seem to mind these goings-on and even, as soon as the young lady asked him, gave them permission to spend the night in the waiting room normally reserved for mothers and children. They went on with their drunken orgy the next morning, and the worker decided to start back on his own, without waiting for the truck driver. After all she had told us about how nice and cultured her parents were, we found her choice of drinking companions a little strange. "What if she's an agent?" I said to M. "Why should we worry if she is?" M. replied. "They don't want me any more—it's all past history." We were so sure all our troubles were over that nothing could now sow doubts in our minds. Looking back on it all, I am certain that the young lady had been sent to Samatikha on a special mission, and that the doctor was under orders not to let us leave the place. In the meantime our fate was being decided in Moscow.

78

THE FIRST OF MAY

As the first of May came nearer, the whole rest home was spring-cleaned and got ready for the holiday. People were already trying to guess what they would be given for dinner on the day itself. There were rumors that ice cream would be on the menu. M. was dying to get away, and I tried to calm him down, pointing out that he could scarcely walk to the station on foot, and that in any case it would all be over in a couple of days.

On one of the last days before the end of April, M. and I went over to the dining room—it was in a separate building not far from the main one. On the way we saw two cars standing outside the doctor's house and trembled at the sight of them—this was the effect cars always had on us. Right by the dining room we ran into the doctor with two strangers. They were large, beefy and well-groomed types—very different from the sort who came to stay in a rest home. One was in military dress and the other in civilian clothes. They were obviously officials, but not local ones by the look of them. I decided they must have come to inspect the place. "I wonder if they've come to check up on me," M. said suddenly. "Did you notice how he looked at me?" Sure enough, the one in civilian clothes had looked around at us and then said something to the doctor. But we soon forgot all about them. It was more natural to assume that they were a couple of inspectors from local Party headquarters who had come to see how the rest home was preparing to celebrate May Day. In a life such as ours we were always having fits of panic—everybody was constantly on the watch for signs of imminent disaster, and, whether our fears were justified or not, they kept us in a state bordering on dementia. We tried so much not to give way to these fears that bouts of cold terror were always succeeded by moods of recklessness during which we were quite capable of talking with police spies as though they were bosom friends.

On the first of May we didn't go out, except to the dining room for our meals, and the whole day we could hear sounds of revelry—shouting, singing and sometimes fighting. One of the other inmates, a woman textile worker from a factory near Moscow, took refuge with us. M. sat and joked with her, and I was terrified in case he said the wrong thing and she went off to denounce him. They got talking about the arrests, and she mentioned somebody at her factory who had been picked up, saying what a good person he was and how kind he had been to the workers. M. started questioning her about the man. When she had gone I told him at great length how foolish he was to be so indiscreet. He assured me he would mend his ways and never say another word to strangers. I shall never forget how I then said: "You'll have to go all the way to Siberia before you mend your ways. . . ."

That night I dreamed of ikons—this is always regarded as a bad omen. I started out of my sleep in tears and woke M. as well. "What have we got to be afraid of now?" he asked. "The worst is over." And we went back to sleep. I had never before dreamed of ikons, nor have I since—we had never possessed any ikons of our own, and the old ones which we loved had only artistic meaning for us.

In the morning we were wakened by somebody knocking quietly on the door. M. got up to open the door and three people came in: two men in military uniform and the doctor. M. began to dress. I put on a dressing gown and sat on the bed. "Do you know when it was signed?" M. asked me, looking at the warrant. It appeared that it had been signed about a week previously. "It's not our fault," one of the men in uniform explained, "we have too much to do." He complained that they had to work while people were on the spree over the holiday—it had been very difficult to get a truck in Charusti because everybody was off duty.

Coming to my senses, I began to get M.'s things together. One of them said to me in their usual way: "Why so much stuff? He won't be in long—they'll just ask a few questions and let him go."

There was no search. They just emptied the contents of our suitcase into a sack they had brought with them, and that was all. Suddenly I said: "We live in Furmanov Street in Moscow. All our papers are there." In fact there was nothing in our apartment, and I said this simply to distract attention from the room in Kalinin where there really was a basket full of papers. "What do we need your papers for?" one of the men said amiably, and he asked M. to come with them. "Come with me in the truck as far as Charusti," M. said to me. "That's not allowed," one of them said, and they left. All this took twenty minutes, or even less.

The doctor went out with them. I heard the truck start up outside, but I just remained sitting on the bed, unable to move. I didn't even close the door behind them. When the truck had left, the doctor came back into the room. "That's the way things are now," he said. "Don't despair—it may be all right in the end." And he added the usual phrase about how I should keep my strength up for when I needed it. I asked him about the people we had seen with him the day before. He said they were officials from the district center, and that they had asked to see the list of people staying in the rest home. "But it never occurred to me they were looking for you," he said. It was not the first time they had come to check the list the day before someone was arrested, and once they had called by phone to ask whether everybody was present. The great man-hunt also had its techniques: they always wanted to make sure a person was at home before coming to arrest him. The doctor was an old Communist and a very decent person. To get away from everything he had hidden away here in this simple workers' rest home where he was responsible for the administration as well as the medical treatment of the inmates. But the life outside had nevertheless invaded his refuge—there was no escaping it.

In the morning the woman textile worker I had been so afraid of the evening before came to me and wept, cursing the "sons of bitches" for all she was worth. To get back to Moscow I would have to sell off my things. I had given what little money we had to M. The woman now helped me to sell my stuff and to pack for the journey. I had to wait an agonizingly long time for the cart that was to take me to the station. When it eventually came, I had to share it with an engineer who had come to the rest home just for the May Day holiday to visit his father, who was staying there. The doctor said goodbye to me in my room, and only the woman textile worker came outside to see me off. On the way, as we rattled along in the cart, the engineer told me that he and his two brothers all worked in the automobile industry, so that if one of them was arrested, the other two would be picked up as well—they should have been more careful and gone into different things, as it would be a terrible blow for their father if they all three disappeared. I decided he must be a Chekist and would probably take me straight to the Lubianka. But I didn't care any more.

M. and I had first met on May Day in 1919, when he told me that the Bolsheviks had responded to the murder of Uritski with a "hecatomb of corpses." We parted on May Day 1938, when he was led away, pushed from behind by two soldiers. We had no time to say anything to each other—we were interrupted when we tried to say goodbye.

In Moscow I went straight to my brother and said: "Osia's been picked up." He went at once to tell the Shklovskis, and I went to Kalinin to get the basket full of manuscripts we had left with Tatiana Vasilievna. If I had delayed for a few more days, the contents of the basket would have been thrown into a sack (like the stuff from our suitcase in Samatikha) and I myself would have been taken away in a Black Maria—which at that moment I might have preferred to remaining "free." But then what would have happened to M.'s poetry? When I see books by the Aragons* of this world, who are so keen to induce their fellow countrymen to live as we do, I feel I have a duty to tell about my own experience. For the sake of what idea was it necessary to send those countless trainloads of prisoners, including the man who was so dear to me, to forced labor in eastern Siberia? M. always said that they always knew what they were doing: the aim was to destroy not only people, but the intellect itself.

79

GUGOVNA

I used to have a book on extinct birds and, looking at it, I suddenly had the thought that all my friends and acquaintances were nothing more than the last members of a dying species. I showed M. a picture of a

---

* See the note on Brik in the Appendix.

couple of extinct parakeets, and he thought they looked very much like us. I later lost the book, but I have never forgotten this instructive analogy. The only thing I did not realize then was how long-lived exotic birds can be, while the more commonplace specimens die off like crows.

The late Dmitri Sergeyevich Usov once said to me that M. was more of an Assyrian than a Jew. "In what way?" I asked in astonishment. In reply he said there was an Assyrian quality about the line "grim heliotrope suns turned full in the face." "That's why he saw through our Assyrian* so easily," he added.

Bearded, short of breath and gone to seed, like M., Usov was also afraid of no one, yet frightened by everything. As he lay dying in a hospital in Tashkent, he called for me, but I did not get there in time. I hope I may be forgiven for this. But I was able to make his last days a little easier by reading M.'s poetry to him—he was devoted to M. When Zenkevich went to the White Sea Canal on behalf of the Union of Writers, Usov was already doing the forced labor there that brought on his heart trouble. He had been arrested in connection with the "dictionary affair" and would have been shot, together with a number of others, if it hadn't been for the intervention of Romain Rolland. Some of them were released during the war, after serving five years in the camps, and came to central Asia to join their wives, who had been exiled there. Now all in their mid-forties, they died off, one after another, from the heart diseases contracted in the camps—among them my friend Usov. Every case of this kind—like the others involving the historians and the staff at the Ermitage†—was part of the systematic destruction of the country's intellectual and spiritual resources.

Usov's wife, Alisa Gugovna (or just Gugovna for short), buried her giant of a husband in the Tashkent cemetery, marked out a spot for her own grave at his side, and settled down to live out the rest of her days in central Asia, where the climate was deadly for someone in her state of health. She also managed to rescue a former official with a large family from his remote place of exile in Kazakhstan—this she did because he had helped her during her own years of exile in the same place, chopping firewood and drawing water for her. She got a residence permit for this family in her room in a building belonging to the

* Stalin.
† Museum in Leningrad, formerly a part of the Winter Palace.

Teachers' Training College—so that after her death this "living-space" obtained by Usov should not go to waste. Having arranged all this, she felt she had done her duty by the world and quietly went to her grave, first giving a little money to the beggars in the cemetery, with instructions to plant a tree over her grave—like the one over her husband's—and water the flowers as long as people remembered to bring any. She was not certain she could rely for this on the people she had put in her room.

As she gradually wasted away, Alisa Gugovna continued to react keenly to all the oddities of the life around us, and to pour scorn in the choicest language on bureaucrats, imbeciles and bogus scholars. She was completely at home in the academic world and knew exactly who was a real scholar and who a police spy, and in whose company it was all right to drink a bottle of the vinegary local wine. It was she who invented the toast which we always drank whenever any of our graduate students—whom we never, of course, dared trust—appeared at one of our modest parties. It was difficult to denounce us if we were the first to rise and propose a toast in honor of those we had to thank for this "happy life" of ours! The police spies among our graduates were quite flummoxed by this.

Despite her lame leg, Alisa Gugovna was always busily moving around her room, rearranging the piles of Usov's books and creating an effect of home comfort, quite extraordinary for us, by improvising things from broken pieces of china and tattered old blankets that must have gone back to the days of serfdom. Usov and she had a favorite drinking mug nicknamed "The Goldfinch" which nobody was allowed to use unless they could recite M.'s poem by heart. Alisa liked to massage her face with her slender fingers, remarking that Akhmatova didn't look after herself at all. She took very good care of her hands—which was important if you had spent years lighting stoves and scrubbing floors with them—and of her long, almost gray braids. She was secretly very worried that if she didn't "keep her looks" Usov might not recognize her in the next world. She had been just as concerned about her looks when she lived in exile in Kazakhstan, waiting for Usov to finish serving his sentence in the forced-labor camp: she wanted to look as beautiful to him as the night they had parted. After his death she was angry with him for a long time because he had been so thoughtless as to abandon her like this—he had, she felt, deserted her, leaving her to cope all alone with the linguistics she had to teach in order to earn her widow's daily bread.

She was one of the last few people to speak with the accent of the old Moscow aristocracy, and Usov always used to say that she could always, in any circumstances, count on being taken for an honorary Jewess rather than a born one. At the same time, account would no doubt be taken of the work she did before she was exiled: the Lenin Library employed her as a consultant to identify people in eighteenth- and early nineteenth-century portraits. She knew all the gossip there was to know about the ladies of that period, and there was no greater expert on the genealogy of the families from which the poets of the time came.

This, then, was how the beauties of my generation ended their lives—as the widows of martyrs, consoled in prison or exile only by a secret hoard of verse stored in their memory.

In those days people who read poetry belonged to a breed apart, like members of a dying species of bird. They were invariably the kindest and most honest people in the world—not to speak of their courage. Will the generation of new readers who are appearing now, in the sixties, be able to match their courage, or, rather, strength of mind? Will they face whatever ordeals life has in store for them as Alisa Gugovna did?—though she always maintained that she was just a spoiled and crotchety old woman with a bad temper. Alisa was so spoiled by fate that even in exile she managed to keep her long braids, her wonderful memory for poetry and her savage intolerance for any kind of time-serving or dishonesty.

Once at Tashkent University she was stopped by a young scholar who started asking questions about me and wanted to know whether I was keeping Mandelstam's papers. Alisa answered evasively and immediately afterward came to report to me that the young man had suggested it would be wisest to burn the lot. He was very insistent that she convey this advice to me, and referred to some mysterious source which he did not dare name. "Nonsense," I said, "I would never dream of it. If they come and take it from me, that's one thing—but I shall never destroy it myself." "That's right," said Gugovna, "but there's no point in letting it fall into their hands either. We'll make some copies for them and hide the originals." We sat up the whole of that night preparing a pile of copies. Gugovna took the originals away with her and deposited them in a safe place. We had a rule that I should never know whom the papers were with—this meant that if I was arrested, I should not in any circumstances be able to name the person who was keeping them.

We were always preparing for the worst, and that is perhaps the reason we survived. When we ran into each other at the university, where we both taught, Gugovna would tell me that the "goldfinches" were all right and singing as well as ever. The use of this code even earned her a reputation as a bird-fancier. All this happened at the time when I was being visited by the "private pupil" about whom Larisa had warned me as an employee of her father. It is possible that she was working on her own initiative rather than on direct orders—or so I judge from the fact that when the girl went to Larisa's father and complained about Larisa coming to see me and hence making it difficult for her to "work," he ordered the girl to leave me alone, explaining that M. had been a criminal, not a political offender. As he put it, M. had been "caught in Moscow after disgracing himself in some way, and he had no right to be in the city." He added that I was "in the charge of Moscow." Presumably my file, which followed me from city to city, had a note to this effect. I heard about this from Larisa. After the "private pupil" had disappeared, Gugovna brought my papers back. She did not live till Stalin's death, but, like me, she was an incorrigible optimist and knew that one day he would have to die.

80

THE TRAP

Before I learned of M.'s death I kept having a dream: I was out with him buying something for our supper and he was standing behind me; we were about to go home, but when I turned around he was no longer there and I caught a glimpse of him somewhere ahead of me. I ran after him, but never managed to catch up and ask what they were doing with him "there." . . . At this time there were already rumors about the torture of prisoners.

In my waking hours I was tormented by remorse: when we saw the two visiting officials with the doctor, why hadn't we read the writing on the wall and left at once for the railroad station? Why did we have to be so Spartan and refrain from giving way to fear—even if it had meant going on foot, leaving all our stuff behind, and perhaps dying of heart failure on the twenty-five-kilometer walk?

Why had we let ourselves be lured into a trap just because we didn't want to think about food and lodging for a few weeks, because we didn't want to go on pestering our friends for money? I have no doubt whatsoever that Stavski deliberately sent us into this trap. Evidently the police had to wait for a decision from Stalin or someone close to him—without such authorization it was impossible to arrest M. on account of Stalin's personal order in 1934 to "isolate but preserve" him. Stavski must have been told to arrange for M. to stay for the time being in some definite place so they wouldn't have to look for him when the moment came. In other words, to save the "organs" any tiresome detective work, Stavski had obligingly sent us to a rest home. The "organs" were desperately overworked and a good Communist like Stavski was always glad to help them. He had even been careful in his choice of a rest home: it was not a place you could easily get out of in a hurry—twenty-five kilometers to the nearest station was no joke for a man with a weak heart.

Before sending us to Samatika, Stavski had received M. for the first time. This also we had taken as a good sign. But in fact Stavski probably wanted to see M. only to make it easier for him to write his report—the sort of report always written on a man about to be arrested.

Such reports were sometimes written after the event, when the person in question had already been arrested, and sometimes beforehand. This was one of the formalities which had to be observed in the process of destroying people. In ordinary cases, these reports were made by the head of whatever organization the arrested man worked for, but when writers were involved, the "organs" often required additional reports and were liable to call on any member of the Union of Writers to supply one. In the moral code of the sixties we distinguish between straight denunciations and "reports" made under pressure. Who in those days could have been expected to refuse to give a report on an arrested colleague if asked to do so by the "organs"? Anybody who refused would have been arrested on the spot, and he also had to consider the consequences to his family.

People who wrote reports of this kind excuse themselves now by saying that they never went beyond what had been alleged about the victim in the press. Stavski was no doubt quite familiar with what had been written about M.—the neatly filed clippings would have been produced for him by his secretaries—and all he had to do was add a little by way of personal impressions. M. provided the material he needed during their interview by giving his views on capital punishment. He noticed that Stavski listened very intently when he talked about this—nothing, as we know, unites members of a ruling class more than complicity in crime, of which there was certainly more than enough.

In 1956, when for the first time in twenty years I went into the Union of Writers and saw Surkov, he greeted me with great expressions of joy. At that moment many people thought the revision of the past would be much more thoroughgoing than it actually was; the optimists did not foresee the recoil of the spring carefully provided for by the Stalinist system—that is, the reaction of all the myriads of peole implicated in past crimes. As Larisa, the daughter of the Tashkent police official, said: "One can't make such sudden changes—it's so traumatic for people who were in official positions." It was probably about this that she wanted to make her threatened protest abroad. . . .

Surkov at once began asking me about M.'s literary remains: where were they? He kept on telling me that he had once had some of M.'s verse written out in M.'s own hand, but that Stavski had taken it away from him—he couldn't think why, since Stavski didn't read poetry. To put a stop to this senseless conversation, I interrupted Surkov and told him what I thought of Stavski. He did not argue with me.

I later spoke in the same vein to Simonov, whom I went to see in the absence of Surkov. Simonov, great diplomat that he is, suggested I submit a formal application requesting that M. be posthumously made a member of the Union of Writers; he said I should refer to the fact that before M.'s second arrest Stavski had been proposing to have him formally elected. I rejected the idea and told Simonov what I thought of Stavski's role. He didn't argue either—he knew from his own experience how people in official posts had behaved in those fateful years. Both he and Surkov were lucky not to have been top officials then—so they didn't have to countersign lists of people to be arrested; nor were they forced to write reports on candidates for liquidation. I hope to God they didn't, anyway.

But it is pointless to mention names. Any other official would have done the same as Stavski, unless he wanted to be spirited away by car at dead of night. We were all the same: either sheep who went willingly to the slaughter, or respectful assistants to the executioners. Whichever role we played, we were uncannily submissive, stifling all our human instincts. Why did we never try to jump out of windows or give way to unreasoning fear and just run for it—to the forests, the provinces, or simply into a hail of bullets? Why did we stand by meekly as they went through our belongings? Why did M. obediently follow the two soldiers, and why didn't I throw myself on them like a wild animal? What had we to lose? Surely we were not afraid of being charged with resisting arrest? The end was the same anyway, so that was nothing to be afraid of. It was not, indeed, a question of fear. It was something quite different: a paralyzing sense of one's own helplessness to which we were all prey, not only those who were killed, but the killers themselves as well. Crushed by the system each one of us had in some way or other helped to build, we were not even capable of passive resistance. Our submissiveness only spurred on those who actively served the system. How can we escape the vicious circle?

81

THE WINDOW ON THE SOPHIA EMBANKMENT

The only link with a person in prison was the window through which one handed parcels and money to be forwarded to him by the authorities. Once a month, after waiting three or four hours in line (the number of arrests was by now falling off, so this was not very long), I went up to the window and gave my name. The clerk behind the window thumbed through his list—I went on days when he dealt with the letter "M"—and asked me for my first name and initial. As soon as I replied, a hand stretched out of the window and I put my identity papers and some money into it. The hand then returned my papers with a receipt and I went away. Everybody envied me because I at least knew that my husband was alive and where he was. It happened only too often that the man behind the window barked: "No record. . . . Next!" All questions were useless—the official would simply shut his window in your face and one of the uniformed guards would come up to you. Order was immediately restored and the next in line moved up to the window. If anybody ever tried to linger, the guard found ready allies among the other people waiting.

There was generally no conversation in the line. This was the chief prison in the Soviet Union, and the people who came here were a select, respectable and well-disciplined crowd. There were never any untoward events, unless it was a minor case of someone asking a question—but persons guilty of such misconduct would speedily retreat in embarrassment. The only incident I saw was when two little girls in neatly starched dresses once came in. Their mother had been arrested the previous night. They were let through out of turn and nobody asked what letter their name began with. All the women waiting there were no doubt moved by pity at the thought that their own children might soon be coming here in the same way. Somebody lifted up the elder of the two, because she was too small to reach the window, and she shouted through it: "Where's my mummy?" and "We won't go to the orphanage. We won't go home." They just managed to say that their father was in the army before the window was slammed shut. This could have been the actual case, or it could have meant that he had been in the secret police. The children of Chekists were always taught to say that their father was "in the army"—this was to protect them from the curiosity of their schoolmates, who, the parents explained, might be less friendly otherwise. Before going abroad on duty, Chekists also made their children learn the new name under which they would be living there. . . . The little girls in the starched dresses probably lived in a government building—they told the people waiting in line that other children had been taken away to orphanages, but that they wanted to go to their grandmother in the Ukraine. Before they could say any more, a soldier came out of a side door and led them away. The window opened again and everything returned to normal. As they were being led away, one woman called them "silly little girls," and another said: "We must send ours away before it's too late."

These little girls were exceptional. Children who came and stood in line were usually as restrained and silent as grown-ups. It was generally their fathers who were arrested first—particularly if they were military people—and they would then be carefully instructed by their mothers on how to behave when they were left completely alone. Many of them managed to keep out of the orphanages, but that depended mainly on their parents' status—the higher it had been, the less chance the children had of being looked after by relatives. It was astonishing that life continued at all, and that people still brought children into the world and had families. How could they do this, knowing what went on in front of the window in the building on Sophia Embankment?

The women who stood in line with me tried not to get drawn into conversation. They all, without exception, said that their husbands had been arrested by mistake and would soon be released. Their eyes were red from tears and lack of sleep, but I don't recall anyone ever crying while we stood in line. When they left their homes, they composed their features by some effort of the will and tried to look their best. Most of them came to hand in their parcels during working hours—they got off on some pretext or other—and on returning to their offices they had to be very careful not to show their feelings. Their faces had become masks.

In Ulianovsk, at the end of the forties, I had working for me a woman who lived in a college dormitory with her two children. She had come to the college as a technical assistant and soon made herself indispensable. She was even promoted and allowed to take courses on an extramural basis. She had practically nothing to live on, and her children were literally starving—she said her husband had left her and wouldn't give her anything for their upkeep. People advised her to sue for alimony, but she just cried and said that would go against her pride. She and her children were visibly getting thinner all the time. She was summoned by the director, who told her she should swallow her pride for the children's sake, but she would not budge: her husband had betrayed her, deserted her for another woman in a most despicable fashion, and she would not take money from him or allow him to come anywhere near her children. People tried to influence her through her oldest son, but he was just as stubborn as she. A few years later her husband suddenly appeared on the scene, and we all saw her fling herself into his arms. She then resigned from her job and began to pack her bags. Our omniscient janitresses soon learned that the husband had been refused permission to live in Ulianovsk because he had just been released from a forced-labor camp. All these years his wife had been putting it on about her pride and broken heart in order not to lose her job. If it hadn't been the most insignificant of positions, the "organs" would certainly have informed the personnel section that she was the wife of a prisoner—though it is also possible that he had been arrested not under the notorious Article 58, but on some criminal or other nonpolitical charge. He was released just before Stalin's death, so that he was not in danger of being re-arrested, and I hope that he and his family are now thriving. I can just imagine how the mother must have sat at night with her two undernourished children, telling them how careful they must be if they wanted their father to return. Their father had once been a student of political science and had shone in the realm of ideology. This was one of many cases in which the regime struck down its own supporters.

After several months of standing in line at the window on the Sophia Embankment I was told one day that M. had been transferred to Butyrki. This was the prison in which people were held before being sent off in prison trains to the forced-labor camps. I rushed there to find out on what days they dealt with inquiries about people whose names began with the letter "M." In Butyrki I was only once able to hand over something for M.; the second time I tried, I was told that he had been sent to a camp for five years by decision of the Special Tribunal.*

This was confirmed to me in the Prosecutor's Office after I had stood in line there endlessly. There were special windows through which requests for information were handed, and I did the same as everybody else. Exactly a month after putting in a request, one was always informed that it had been turned down. This was the usual routine for a prisoner's wife—if she was lucky enough not to have been sent to a camp herself. In the smooth, impregnable wall against which we beat our heads they had cut these little windows through which we handed in parcels or requests for information. I was considered particularly lucky because I got a letter—the only one—from M. and thus learned where he was. I immediately sent a package to him there, but it was returned to me and I was told that the addressee was dead. A few months after this, M.'s brother Alexander Emilievich was given a document to certify his death. I know of no other prisoner's wife who ever received a certificate like this. I cannot imagine why such a favor was shown to me.

---

* Established in 1934 to deal with "socially dangerous persons," the Special Tribunal was composed of high-ranking NKVD and militia officials and could impose sentences of exile or confinement to forced-labor camps.

Letter from Osip Mandelstam sent to his brother Alexander [Shura], and to his wife, from the "transit camp" near Vladivostok

Dear Shura,

    I am in Vladivostok—USVITL,[1] barracks no. 11.

    I was given five years for c.r.a.[2] by the Special Tribunal. The transport left Butyrki on September 9, and we got here October 12. My health is very bad, I'm extremely exhausted and thin, almost unrecognizable, but I don't know whether there's any sense in sending clothes, food and money. You can try, all the same. I'm very cold without proper clothes.

    My darling Nadia—are you alive, my dear? Shura, write to me at once about Nadia. This is a transit point. I've not been picked for Kolyma and may have to spend the winter here.

    I kiss you, my dear ones. OSIA.

SHURA: *one more thing. The last few days we've been going out to work. This has raised my spirits. This camp is a transit one and they send us on from here to regular ones. It looks as though I've been rejected, so I must prepare to spend the winter here. So please send me a telegram and cable me some money.*

[1] USVITL: "Directorate for North-Eastern Corrective Labor Camps."
[2] "Counter-revolutionary activity."

Not long before the Twentieth Congress, as I was walking along the Ordynka* with Akhmatova, I suddenly noticed an enormous number of plainclothes police agents. There was literally one in every doorway. "You needn't worry," Akhmatova said to me, "something good is happening." She had already heard vague rumors about the Party Congress at which Khrushchev read out his famous letter.† This was why so many police agents had been stationed around the city. It was at this juncture that Akhmatova advised me to go to the Union of Writers and sound out the ground. We already knew that the widows of both Babel and Meyerhold had applied for the rehabilitation of their husbands, and Ehrenburg had long been advising me to follow suit, but I had been in no hurry. Now, however, I decided to go to the Union.

Surkov came out to see me, and by the way he treated me I could see that times had indeed changed: nobody had ever spoken to me like

* A Moscow street.
† Khrushchev's denunciation of Stalin's crimes at the Twentieth Party Congress in 1956 was in the form of a circular letter to the Party organizations.

this before. My first conversation with him took place in an anteroom in the presence of secretaries. He promised to see me again in a few days' time and begged me not to leave Moscow until we had spoken. For two or three weeks following this I kept phoning the personnel section of the Union, and every time they asked me in dulcet tones to wait a little longer. This meant that Surkov still had not received instructions about what he was to say to me. So I just continued to wait, marveling at the way that strange institution known as the "personnel section" had suddenly changed its tune.

A meeting was at last arranged, and I saw how pleased Surkov was at being able to talk like a human being. He promised to help Lev Gumilev and did everything for me that I asked him. Thanks to Surkov, I was given a pension—at the moment of our interview I was again out of work, and Surkov got in touch with the Ministry of Education and told them how outrageously I was being treated. He took a rosy view of the future and promised to arrange for me to live in Moscow, getting me a residence permit and a room, and he also broached the subject of publishing M.'s work. He said that, to begin with, I should formally apply for M.'s rehabilitation. I asked him how it would have been if M. had no widow to do this for him, but I didn't pursue the matter.

I soon received an official notice clearing M. of the charges brought against him in 1938, and the woman Prosecutor dealing with the case helped me draft an application to have M. cleared of the charges brought against him in 1934 ("the accused wrote the poem, but did not circulate it"). This second application was considered during the Hungarian events* and it was turned down. Surkov, however, decided to ignore this and appointed a committee to go into the question of M.'s literary remains. I was given 5,000 roubles by way of compensation. I divided the money among all the people who had helped us in 1937.

The second stage in the ritual of restoring the names of writers who perished in the camps is the publication of their work. Here the obstacles have been manifold. I know nothing about the competition they frighten us with,† but I do know how ruthlessly people fight to keep

---

* The Hungarian uprising of November 1956, which was followed by a political reaction in Moscow.

† This presumably refers to editions of Mandelstam abroad, which are used by the Soviet authorities as an excuse for not publishing Mandelstam's work in the Soviet Union.

their entrenched positions. When the first rumors were heard about the rehabilitation commissions established by Mikoyan, many people were very upset—and not only people who had helped to dispose of their competitors. I heard whispered questions about where room could possibly be found for all the ex-prisoners returning from the camps—suppose they all wanted their old jobs back? How many new posts would have to be created in Soviet institutions to accommodate these hordes of "returnees" (as they were known)! But there was no problem: the majority of the returnees were in such poor shape that they had no thought of taking up any kind of active career again. Everything passed off very quietly, and those who had worried about having to make room heaved sighs of relief. But literature is a different matter. The carefully contrived "order of precedence" has to be protected at all cost, if many established reputations are not to collapse. This is why there is so much opposition to the publication of work by those who perished. It must be said that some of the living do not fare any better either.

A volume of M.'s poetry was scheduled by the Poets' Library in 1956. All the members of the editorial board pronounced themselves in favor. I was very pleased by Prokofiev's attitude—he said that M. was simply not a poet and that the best way to demonstrate the fact would be to publish him. Unhappily, he later abandoned this high-minded position and has since fought the proposal tooth and nail. Orlov, the editor-in-chief of the series, didn't at first anticipate any opposition, and started writing me friendly letters, but when he saw what trouble there might be with the volume, he hastily beat a retreat and broke off our correspondence. One could, however, scarcely expect anything else of Orlov, who is a high official and quite indifferent to M.'s poetry into the bargain.

Much more serious is the attitude shown by several people of real authority and independence who are anything but bureaucrats and have a real love of M.'s work. Two of them—both outstanding representatives of the generation that was destroyed—have explained to me that Orlov is right not to publish M., which technically would be quite possible for him: "It might be exploited by his enemies—there are lots of people who would like to take his place. If he goes, it will be the end of a distinguished series." By sacrificing the Mandelstam volume, they argued, Orlov would keep his position and thus be able to carry out his project to publish the poets of the twenties, thirties and forties of the last century—a project with which both of these people were concerned. It is difficult for me to make any sense of all this, with the over-lapping personal and group interests involved—not to mention the struggle to keep one's job and get a share of the cake handed out by the State. Since it is impossible, in our conditions, for me to publish M.'s work myself at my own expense, I realize that I shall not live to see his poetry come out in this country—I am now getting on in years. I am consoled only by the words of Akhmatova, who says that M. does not need Gutenberg's invention. In a sense, we really do live in a pre-Gutenberg era: more and more people read poetry in the manuscript copies that circulate all over the country. All the same, I am sorry I shall never see a book.

82

THE DATE OF DEATH

At the end of December 1938 or in January 1939, according to some journalists from *Pravda,* who mentioned it to Shklovski, someone in the Central Committee said in their hearing that it now appeared that there had been no case against Mandelstam at all. This was shortly after the dismissal of Yezhov and was meant to serve as an illustration of his misdeeds. . . . The conclusion I drew was that M. must be dead.

Not long afterward I was sent a notice asking me to go to the post office at Nikita Gate. Here I was handed back the parcel I had sent to M. in the camp. "The addressee is dead," the young lady behind the counter informed me. It would be easy enough to establish the date on which the parcel was returned to me—it was the same day on which the newspapers published the long list of Government awards—the first ever—to Soviet writers.

My brother Evgeni went that same day to tell the Shklovskis in the writers' apartment building on Lavrushinski Street. They went to call Victor from the apartment downstairs—Katayev's, I think it was—where Fadeyev and other "Fellow Travelers" were drinking on the oc-casion of the honor done them by the State. It was now that Fadeyev shed a drunken tear for M.: "We have done away with a great poet!" The celebration of the awards took on something of the flavor of a sur-reptitious wake for the dead. I am not clear, however, as to who there (apart from Shklovski) really understood what M.'s destruction meant.

Most of them, after all, belonged to the generation which had changed its values in favor of the "new." It was they who had prepared the way for the strong man, the dictator who was empowered to kill or spare people at his own discretion, to establish goals and choose whatever means he saw fit for their fulfillment.

In June 1940, M.'s brother Alexander was summoned to the Registry Office of the Bauman district* and handed M.'s death certificate with instructions to pass it on to me. M.'s age was given as forty-seven, and the date of his death as December 27, 1938. The cause was given as "heart failure." This is as much as to say that he died because he died: what is death but heart failure? There was also something about arteriosclerosis.

The issue of a death certificate was not the rule but the exception. To all intents and purposes, as far as his civil status was concerned, a person could be considered dead from the moment he was sent to a camp, or, indeed, from the moment of his arrest, which was automatically followed by his conviction and sentence to imprisonment in a camp. This meant he vanished so completely that it was regarded as tantamount to physical death. Nobody bothered to tell a man's relatives when he died in camp or prison: you regarded yourself as a widow or orphan from the moment of his arrest. When a woman was told in the Prosecutor's office that her husband had been given ten years, the official sometimes added: "You can remarry." Nobody ever raised the awkward question as to how this gracious "permission" to remarry could be squared with the official sentence, which was technically by no means a death sentence. As I have said already, I do not know why they showed such exceptional consideration to me by issuing a death certificate. I wonder what was behind it.

In the circumstances, death was the only possible deliverance. When I heard that M. had died, I stopped having my nightmares about him. Later on, Kazarnovski said to me: "Osip Emilievich did well to die: otherwise he would have gone to Kolyma." Kazarnovski had himself served his sentence in Kolyma, and when he was released in 1944 he turned up in Tashkent. He lived there without a permit or ration cards, hiding from the police, terrified of everybody and drinking very heavily. He had no proper shoes, and I gave him some tiny galoshes that had belonged to my mother. They fitted him very well because he

---

* A district in central Moscow.

had no toes on his feet—they had become frozen in the camp and he had chopped them off with an ax to prevent gangrene. Whenever they were all taken to the baths, their clothes froze in the damp air of the changing room and rattled like sheets of tin.

Recently I heard an argument as to who was more likely to survive the camps: the people who worked, or those who managed not to. Those who worked died of exhaustion, and those who didn't starved to death. This much was clear to me, though I had neither arguments nor personal observations of my own to support either side in the discussion. The few people who survived were exceptions who proved the rule. In fact, the whole argument reminded me of the Russian folk ballad about the hero at the crossroads: whichever way he goes, he will perish. The main feature of Russian history, something that never changes, is that every road always brings disaster—and not only to heroes. Survival is a matter of pure chance. It is not this that surprises me so much as the fact that a few people, for all their frailty, came through the whole ordeal like heroes, not only living to tell the tale, but preserving the keenness of mind and memory that enables them to do so. I know people like this, but the time has not yet come to name them— apart from the one whom we all know: Solzhenitsyn.

Kazarnovski had come through only with his life and a few disjointed recollections. He had arrived at the camp in Kolyma in the winter and remembered that it was an utter wilderness which was only just being opened up to receive the enormous influx of people being sent to do forced labor. Not a single building or barracks existed yet. They lived in tents and had to put up the prison buildings themselves.

I have heard that prisoners were sent form Vladivostok to Kolyma only by sea, which freezes over in winter—though quite late in the year. I am puzzled, therefore, as to how Kazarnovski could have arrived at Kolyma in winter, after the sea route was no longer navigable. Could it be that he was first sent to another camp, somewhere in the neighborhood of Vladivostok, because of overcrowding in the "transit" camp? At this period the Vladivostok transit camp, where prisoners were held temporarily before being sent on to Kolyma, can hardly have coped with the prison trains arriving all the time. Everything was too confused in Kazarnovski's disordered brain, and I could not clear this point up, though in trying to establish the date of M.'s death it was very important to know at exactly what moment Kazarnovski left the transit camp.

Kazarnovski was the first more or less authentic emissary I had met from the "other world." Before he actually turned up, I had already heard about him from other people and knew that he had really been with M. in the transit camp and had apparently even helped him in some way. They had occupied bunks in the same barracks, almost next to each other. This was the reason I hid Kazarnovski from the police for three months while I slowly extracted from him all the information he had brought to Tashkent. His memory was like a huge, rancid pancake in which fact and fancy from his prison days had been mixed up together and baked into an inseparable mass.

I already knew that this kind of affliction of the memory was not peculiar to the wretched Kazarnovski or a result of drinking too much vodka. It was a feature of almost all the former camp inmates I have met immediately after their release—they had no memory for dates or the passage of time and it was difficult for them to distinguish between things they had actually experienced themselves and stories they had heard from others. Places, names, events and their sequence were all jumbled up in the minds of these broken people, and it was never possible to disentangle them. Most accounts of life in the camps appeared on first hearing to be a disconnected series of stories about the critical moments when the narrator nearly died but then miraculously managed to save himself. The whole of camp life was reduced to these highlights, which were intended to show that although it was almost impossible to survive, man's will to live was such that he came through nevertheless. Listening to these accounts, I was horrified at the thought that there might be nobody who could ever properly bear witness to the past. Whether inside or outside the camps, we had all lost our memories. But it later turned out that there were people who had made it their aim from the beginning not only to save themselves, but to survive as witnesses. These relentless keepers of the truth, merging with all the other prisoners, had bided their time—there were probably more such people in the camps than outside, where it was all too common to succumb to the temptation to make terms with reality and live out one's life in peace. Of course those witnesses who have kept a clear memory of the past are few in number, but their very survival is the best proof that good, not evil, will prevail in the end.

Kazarnovski was not of the heroic type, and from his endless tales I gleaned only a few tiny grains of truth about M.'s life in the camp. The population of transit camps is, of course, a constantly shifting one, but the barracks in which they had been together had at first been occupied entirely by intellectuals from Moscow and Leningrad sentenced under Article 58. This had made life very much easier. As always in those years, the prisoners appointed to be "elders" in the barracks were chosen from among common criminals—generally the type who had been connected with the "organs" before they went to prison. They were extremely vicious, and prisoners sentenced under Article 58 suffered just as much at their hands as they did from the ordinary guards, with whom they had, if anything, less contact. M. had always been afflicted by a nervous restlessness and paced rapidly up and down if he was upset. In the transit camp, this tendency to run up and down in a state of nervous excitement constantly got him into trouble with the guards. Outside, in the zone around the barracks, he often ran up to the perimeter and was chased away by the sentries, who shouted obscene curses at him. But none of the dozen or so witnesses I have spoken to confirms the story that he was beaten up by criminals—that is probably a legend.

Prisoners were not issued with clothing in the transit camps, and M. froze in his leather coat, which by now was in tatters. According to Kazarnovski, however, the most terrible frosts set in only after his death and he didn't have to go through them. This detail, too, is important for the date of his death.

M. scarcely ate anything, and was afraid to—as Zoshchenko was later. He always lost his bread ration and never knew which was his own mess can. According to Kazarnovski, the transit camp had a shop where they apparently sold tobacco and sugar. But where could M. have got the money? In any case, his fear of food applied to anything he could have bought there, and to sugar as well—which he would take only if it was handed to him by Kazarnovski. One can just picture it: a dirty palm offering this last gift of a piece of sugar, and M. wondering whether to take it.... But was Kazarnovski speaking the truth? Had he perhaps invented this detail?

Apart from his fear of food and constant nervous restlessness, Kazarnovski noted that M. had a fixed idea that his life would be made easier when Romain Rolland wrote to Stalin about him. This little detail could not have been invented, and proves to me beyond doubt that Kazarnovski really did have contact with M. While we were still in Voronezh, we read about the arrival in Moscow of Romain Rolland and his wife, and about their meeting with Stalin. M. knew Maya

Kudasheva* and he kept saying wistfully: "Maya will see everybody in Moscow and they must have told her about me: what would it cost him [Rolland] to ask Stalin to let me off?" M. could not believe that professional humanists are not interested in the fate of individuals, and all his hopes were centered on the name of Romain Rolland. To be fair, however, I should add that while he was in Moscow, Romain Rolland did apparently obtain some improvement of the lot of the linguists implicated in the "dictionary affair." At least, that's what people said. But this does nothing to change my view of professional "humanists." Real humanism knows no limits and is concerned with the fate of every individual.

Another point that made Kazarnovski's account sound genuine was that M. assured him that I must be in a camp, too, and he begged Kazarnovski, if he ever returned, to find out where I was and ask the Literary Fund to help me. All his life M. had been tied to the writers' organizations like a slave laborer to his wheelbarrow, and had always depended on them for his livelihood, such as it was. However much he tried, he could never free himself of this dependence—which was so much to the advantage of those who ruled over us. Even for me, therefore, his only hope was that the Literary Fund might do something. But things turned out quite differently: during the war, when the writers' organizations had forgotten about M. and me, I managed to change over to another field of activity, and if I was able to save my life and keep my memories, it was only because of this.

Sometimes, in his calmer moments, M. recited poetry to his fellow prisoners, and some of them may even have made copies. I have seen "albums" with his verse which circulated in the camps. Once he was told by somebody that in one of the death cells in Lefortovo a line from one of his poems had been scratched on the wall: "Am I real and will death really come?" When he heard this, M. cheered up and was much calmer for a few days.

He was not made to do any work—not even such things as cleaning up inside the camp. However bad the others looked, M. looked even worse. For days on end he just wandered about, which brought down on his head threats, curses and obscenities from all the people in charge of them. He was very much upset when he was almost immediately eliminated from the transports of prisoners being sent on to the

---

* Rolland's Russian wife.

regular work camps. He thought things would be easier for him there—though people with experience of them tried to disabuse him.

Once M. heard that there was somebody in the camp by the name of Khazin and he asked Kazarnovski to go with him to find out whether this might be a relative of mine. It turned out to be simply a namesake. Many years later this Khazin wrote to Ehrenburg after reading his memoirs, and I was able to meet him. The existence of Khazin is yet another proof that Kazarnovski really was in the camp with M. Khazin himself saw M. a couple of times—when M. came to see him with Kazarnovski, and a second time when he took M. to see another prisoner who was looking for him. Khazin says that this meeting was very touching—the name of the other man, as Khazin remembers it, was Khint, and he was a Latvian, an engineer by profession. Khint was being sent back to Moscow for a review of his case (such "reviews" generally ended tragically in those years). I don't know who this Khint was. Khazin had the impression that he had been to the same school as M. and came from Leningrad. He spent only a few days in the transit camp. Kazarnovski also remembered that M. had found an old schoolmate through Khazin.

According to Khazin, M. died during a typhus epidemic, but this was something Kazarnovski never mentioned. I have heard, however, that there actually was a typhus epidemic then—several other people have told me about it. I should take steps to try and trace this man Khint, but in our conditions this is impossible: I can scarcely put an advertisement in the newspapers to say I am looking for someone who saw my husband in a camp. . . . Khazin is a primitive type. He got in touch with Ehrenburg because he wanted to tell him his memories of the beginning of the Revolution in which he had taken part with his brothers—all of them Chekists, it seems. This was the period he remembered best, and while talking with me he kept trying to bring the conversation back to his own heroic deeds at that time.

But to return to Kazarnovski's account: One day, despite the swearing and cursing of the guards, M. would not come down from his bunk. This was during the days when the cold was getting much worse—Kazarnovski could give no more precise indication of the date. Everybody was sent out to clear away snow, and M. was left by himself. A few days later he was removed from his bunk and taken to the camp hospital. Soon afterward Kazarnovski heard that he had died and had been buried, or, rather, thrown into a pit. Needless to say, prisoners were buried without coffins, and stripped of their clothing—so that it wouldn't go to waste. There was no lack of corpses, and several were always buried in the same pit, after a tag with a number had been attached to each man's leg.

This would have been by no means the worst way to die, and I like to think that Kazarnovski's version is the true one. Narbut's death was incomparably worse. They say that he was employed in the transit camp to clean out the cesspits and that together with other invalids he was taken out to sea in a barge, which was blown up. This was done to clear the camp of people unable to work. I believe that such things did happen. When I later lived in Tarusa, there was an old ex-convict called Pavel who used to get water and firewood for me. Without any prompting from me, he once told me how he had witnessed the blowing up of a barge—first they had heard the explosion and then they had seen the barge sinking. From what he heard at the time, all the prisoners on board were "politicals" sentenced under Article 58 and no longer fit for work. There are still people—including many former camp prisoners—who even now try to find excuses for everything. Such people assure me that there was only one case like that, and that the camp commandant responsible for this atrocity was later shot. This would indeed have been a touching sequel to the story, but for some reason I am not moved by it.

Most of the people I knew who went to the camps died there almost at once. Intellectuals and professional people did not last long—it was scarcely worth living anyway. What was the point of hanging on to life if the only deliverance was death? What good would a few extra days have been to Margulis, who was protected by the criminals because at night he told them stories from Dumas' novels? He was in a camp together with Sviatopolk-Mirsky, who soon died of total exhaustion. Thank God that people are mortal. The only reason one could have to go on living was to remember it all and later tell the story—perhaps thereby making people think twice before embarking on such lunacies again.

Another person with authentic information about M. was the biologist Merkulov,* whom M. asked, if ever he was released, to go to Ehrenburg and tell him about M.'s last days in the camp—he knew by

---

* Mrs. Mandelstam identifies Merkulov only by his initial, but his name is given in full in Ehrenburg's memoirs ("at the beginning of 1952 I was visited by the Briansk agronomist V. Merkulov"), which Mrs. Mandelstam may have seen before publication.

then that he would not survive himself. I reproduce his account here as it was told to me by Ehrenburg, who by the time I heard from him on my return from Tashkent had forgotten or confused some details—in particular, he referred to Merkulov as an agronomist, since, wanting to lie low after his release, he had indeed worked as an agronomist. What Merkulov told Ehrenburg substantially bore out what Kazarnovski had told me. He thought that M. had died in the first year, before the opening of navigation to Kolyma in May or June. Merkulov gave a detailed account of his conversation with the camp doctor, who was also, fortunately, a prisoner and had reportedly known M. from previous days. The doctor said that it was impossible to save M. because he was so terribly emaciated. This confirms what Kazarnovski said about his being afraid to eat anything—though camp food was such that people turned into wraiths even if they did eat it. M. was only in the hospital for a few days, and Merkulov met the doctor immediately after his death.

M. did right to ask the biologist to go to Ehrenburg with his story—no other Soviet writer, with the exception of Shklovski, would ever have agreed to see such a person in those years. As for visiting any of those writers who were treated as outcasts—nobody coming from a camp would have dared go near them for fear of being sent back again.

People who had served sentences of five or ten years—which meant they had got off very lightly, by our standards—usually stayed, either voluntarily or because they had no choice, in the remote areas where the camps were located. After the war many of them were put back in the camps, becoming what were known in our incredible terminology as "repeaters." This is why there is only a tiny handful of survivors from among all those who were sent to the camps in 1937–38—you only stood a chance if you were very young at the time—and why I have found so few ex-prisoners who met M. But stories about his fate circulated widely in the camps, and dozens of people have told me all kinds of legends about him. I have several times been taken to see people who had heard—or, rather, as they always put it, "knew for a fact"—that M. was still alive, or had survived until the war, or was still in one of the camps, or had been released. There were also people who claimed to have seen him die, but on meeting me they generally admitted with embarrassment that they knew about it only from other people (described, needless to say, as completely reliable witnesses).

Some people have written stories about M.'s death. The one by Shalamov, for example, is an attempt to convey what M. must have felt while dying—it is intended as a tribute from one writer to another. But among these fictional accounts there are some which claim to provide authentic detail. There is one about how M. supposedly died on the boat going to Kolyma. The story about his murder by criminals, and about his reading of Petrarch by the light of a campfire likewise belong to the realm of legend. Many people have fallen for the Petrarch story because it conforms so well to "poetic" convention. Then there are stories of a more "down-to-earth" kind always involving the common criminals. One of the most elaborate of these accounts is told by the poet R. Late one night, says R., some people knocked on the door of the barracks and asked for R. by name. R. was very frightened because they were criminals, but they proved to be friendly and had come with the message that he was to go to another barracks where a poet lay dying. When R. arrived he supposedly found M. lying in his bunk either unconscious or in a delirium, but, seeing R., he immediately revived a little and they spent the whole night talking. In the morning M. died and R. closed his eyes. No date, as usual, is given in this account, but the place—the transit camp of Vtoraya Rechka near Vladivostok—is correctly identified. The story was told to me by Slutski, who gave me R.'s address. But when I wrote, he never replied.

With one exception, however, all my informants have at least been well intentioned. The exception was a certain Tiufiakov, who used to come and see me in Ulianovsk at the beginning of the fifties, before Stalin's death. Tiufiakov behaved monstrously toward me. He was a member of the literature faculty at the Teachers' Training College and deputy director of it. A war veteran, he was covered with medals for his service as a political officer, and he loved to read war novels which described the execution of cowards or deserters in front of their units. He had devoted the whole of his life to the "reconstruction of higher education," and for this reason he had not had time to take any degrees himself. He was a typical Komsomol of the twenties who had then made a career as a "permanent official." He had been relieved of teaching duties so that he could devote all his time to watching over "ideological purity," the slightest deviations from which he duly reported to the right quarters. He was transferred from college to college, mainly to keep an eye on directors suspected of "liberalism." It was for this that he had been sent to Ulianovsk as deputy director—a peculiar post of a nominal kind which did not carry any teaching duties. We had two eternal Komsomols like this. Apart from Tiufiakov, there was also Glukhov, whose name should be recorded for posterity. This man had received a medal for his part in the deportation of the kulaks, and had also been awarded a doctorate for a dissertation on Spinoza. He performed his duties in quite open fashion, summoning students to his office and instructing them whom they should get up and denounce at meetings, and in what terms. Tiufiakov, on the other hand, did his work in secret. Both of them had been involved in purging institutions of higher education ever since the beginning of the twenties.

Tiufiakov's "work" with me was undertaken voluntarily, beyond the call of duty—just for his own recreation. He clearly derived an almost aesthetic pleasure form it. Every day he thought of something new to tell me: M. had been shot; M. had been in Sverdlovsk, where Tiufiakov had visited him as an act of human kindness; M. had been shot while trying to escape; M. was at the moment serving another sentence in a camp for a criminal offense; M. had been beaten to death by criminals for stealing a piece of bread; M. had been released and was living somewhere in the north with a new wife; M. had quite recently hanged himself when he heard of Zhdanov's speech, news of which had only just reached the camps. Each of these stories he relayed to me with a great air of solemnity, saying he had heard it after making inquiries through the Prosecutor's office. I had to sit and listen to him, because it was impossible to throw out a police agent. I also had to listen to his views on literature: "Our best poet is Dolmatovski.... What I appreciate most in poetry is clarity.... Say what you like, but you can't have poetry without metaphors.... Style is not only a matter of form, but a matter of ideology, too—remember what Engels said about this, you have to agree with him.... Have you ever received any of the verse Mandelstam wrote in the camp? He wrote a lot there...." Tiufiakov's wiry body was like a coiled spring. There was always a smile lurking on his face under his military mustache, which was very like Stalin's. He said he had got some real *zhenshen** from the Kremlin hospital, and that no artificial product could compare with it.

I often heard reports about poems written by M. in the camp, but they always turned out to be false—whether deliberately or unwittingly so. Recently, however, I was shown a curious collection of items

---

* A Chinese root which supposedly has rejuvenating properties.

which had been taken from poetry "albums" compiled in the camp. Most of the poems were rather garbled versions of unpublished poems, excluding all those with the slightest political undertones (such as the poem about our apartment). The bulk of them must have been made from manuscript copies which circulated in the thirties, but these were often written down from memory, which explains the large number of mistakes. Some of them appeared in old versions that M. had discarded ("To the German Language," for instance). A few can only have been written down from his dictation, since they had never existed in written copies. Among them was a poem he had written as a child about the crucifixion. Is it possible that he had remembered it and recited it to someone? These camp albums also contained a few humorous poems which I did not have before ("Dante and the Cab Driver," for example), but they are unfortunately in a badly garbled form. Such things could only have been brought to the camps by people from Leningrad, of whom there were very many.

This collection was shown to me by Dombrovski, the author of a book about our life which was written, as they used to say in the old days, "with his heart's blood." Though it has a lot about archaeological excavations, snakes, architecture and young ladies working in offices, it is also a book which gets to the very core of our wretched existence. Anybody who reads it cannot fail to understand why the camps were bound to become the main instrument by which "stability" was maintained in our country.

Dombrovski says that he met M. in the period of the "phony war"— that is, more than a year after December 27, 1938, which I had accepted as the date of his death. The sea route to Kolyma was already open for navigation, and the man whom Dombrovski took to be M.—or really was M.—was among a batch of prisoners about to be transported there from the Vtoraya Rechka transit camp. Dombrovski, who was then still very young, full of life and eager for friendship, had heard that there was someone among them nicknamed "The Poet" and wanted to see him. When Dombrovski went over to the group and shouted for "The Poet," someone came forward and introduced himself as Osip Mandelstam. Dombrovski had the impression that he was mentally ill, but still not completely out of touch with reality. It was the briefest of meetings—they talked about whether the crossing to Kolyma would be made, in view of the military situation, but then "The Poet," who looked about seventy, was called away to eat his kasha.

The fact that this prisoner looked so old—whether or not it really was M.—proves nothing one way or the other. In those conditions people aged amazingly quickly, and M., moreover, had always looked much older than his years. But how can Dombrovski's account be squared with what I had heard previously? It may be that M. left the hospital alive after all those who knew him had been sent to other camps, and that he lingered on for a few more months or even years. Or it may have been some other old man with the same name who was taken for Osip in the camps—there were lots of Mandelstams with similar first names and faces. Are there any grounds for believing that the man seen by Dombrovski really was M.?

When I told him what I had already heard, Dombrovski's confidence in his own story was slightly shaken, but I found it perplexing, and I'm no longer sure of anything now. Can one ever know anything for certain in our life? I have carefully pondered the arguments both for and against his story.

Dombrovski had not known M. previously, and though he had seen him several times in Moscow, it was always at periods when M. had grown a beard—whereas the person he met in the camp was clean-shaven. All the same, Dombrovski thought he looked like M. in some ways. This does not mean very much, of course, since there is nothing easier than to be wrong about faces. But Dombrovski learned one significant detail at the time—not, admittedly, from "The Poet" himself, but from other people in the camp: namely, that M.'s fate had been decided by some letter of Bukharin. This could mean that the letter written to Stalin by Bukharin in 1934 had played some part in the investigation after M.'s second arrest in 1938—together, no doubt, with the notes from Bukharin confiscated during the search of our apartment. It is more than likely that this was so, and the only person who could have known about it was M. himself. The only question is: Had the old man nicknamed "The Poet" himself said this to the prisoners who passed it on to Dombrovski, or was it only attributed to him as something told by a dead man for whom he was later taken? There is just no way of checking this. But the fact that there was this story about Bukharin's letter is of great interest to me: this is the only echo that has reached me about the case brought against M. after his second arrest. In his "Fourth Prose" M. wrote: "My case has not been closed and never will be closed." How right he was! Because of Bukharin's letter, M.'s case was reviewed in 1934 and then again in 1938. It was then re-examined once more in 1955, but it still remains completely obscure, and I can only hope that it may one day be properly investigated.

What of the evidence in favor of the version of M.'s death that I had previously accepted—namely, that it took place in December 1938? The first news I got came in the shape of the parcel returned "because of the addressee's death." But this is not conclusive: we know of thousands of cases in which parcels were returned for this reason, though in fact, as became known later, they had not been delivered because the addressee had been transferred to another camp. The return of a parcel was firmly associated in people's minds with the death of the addressee, and for the majority it was the only indication that a relative in a camp might have died. In fact, however, in all the confusion of the overcrowded camps, the officials in military uniform were so brazen that they wrote whatever came into their heads—who cared? People sent to the camps were in any case thought of as dead, and there was no point in standing on ceremony with them. The same thing happened at the front during the war: officers and soldiers were reported dead when they were only wounded or had been taken prisoner. But at the front it was a case of honest errors being made—nobody did it out of callousness, as in the camps, where the inmates were treated like cattle by brutes specially trained to trample on all human rights. The return of a parcel cannot, therefore, be regarded as proof of death.

The date on the certificate issued by the Registry Office also proves nothing. The dates put on such documents were often arbitrary: vast numbers of deaths, for instance, were postdated to wartime. This was a statistical device to conceal the number of people who died in the camps by blurring the difference between them and the casualties of the war period. When the rehabilitations began in the days after Stalin's death, people were almost automatically put down as having died in 1942 or 1943. How can one possibly take at its face value the date on the death certificate when one thinks of the rumor started for foreign consumption that M. was in a camp in the Voronezh region and was killed there by the Germans? Who launched this story? Clearly, one of our "progressive" writers or a Soviet diplomat, pressed on the matter by some "foreign busybody" (to use Surkov's expression), had put all the blame on the Germans. What could be simpler?

The certificate also stated that M.'s death had been entered in the register of deaths in May 1940. This entry on the certificate is more convincing as evidence that he had died by then. Though even here one cannot be absolutely certain. Imagine, for instance, that Romain Rolland, or somebody else whom Stalin wanted to keep in with, had approached him with a request for M.'s release. There were cases of Stalin releasing people because of some plea from abroad. Stalin might have decided not to listen to the plea, or he might have found that it was impossible to do anything about it because M. had been too badly beaten by the guards in prison. In either case, nothing would have been easier than to declare him officially dead, and to make me the channel for disseminating such a false report. As I have said, nobody in my position was ever given a death certificate, so what was the reason for letting me have one?

Be that as it may, the fact is that if M. really did not die until some time before May 1940—say, in April—it could be that he was indeed the old man seen by Dombrovski.

How reliable is the information given by Kazarnovski and Khazin? Most camp prisoners have only a very hazy idea of the passage of time. In their monotonous existence, dates become blurred. M. could have left the hospital alive after Kazarnovski had been sent somewhere else. Rumors in the camp about M.'s death do not mean very much—the camps lived on rumors. M.'s encounter with the doctor cannot be dated either—they might have met a year or two later. Nobody knew or could ever find out anything for certain in those zones bounded by barbed wire, or in the world outside them, for that matter. No one will ever understand what happened in the terrible shambles of those teeming camps, where the dead with numbered tags on their legs lay side by side with the living.

Nobody has said he actually saw M. dead. Nobody claims to have washed his body or put it in the grave. For those who went through the camps, life was like a delirium in which the sequence of time was lost and fact became mixed with fantasy. What these people have to say is no more reliable than similar accounts of any other calvary. Those few who survived to bear witness, including such people as Dombrovski, had no chance to check their facts at the time, let alone to weigh hypotheses about them.

I can be certain of only one thing: that somewhere M.'s sufferings ended in death. Before his death, he must have lain dying on his bunk, like others around him. Perhaps he was waiting for a parcel—a parcel which never came in time and was sent back to me. For us its return was a sign that he had died. He, on the other hand, may have concluded from its non-arrival that something had happened to us: this because some well-fed official in military uniform, a trained killer, weary of searching through endless, constantly changing lists of prisoners for one unpronounceable name, had simply scrawled on the accompanying form the simplest thing that came into his head: "Addressee Dead"—and I, who had prayed for the merciful release of my husband, received these last, inevitable good tidings from a girl clerk in a Moscow post office.

And after his death—or even before it, perhaps—he lived on in camp legend as a demented old man of seventy who had once written poetry in the outside world and was therefore nicknamed "The Poet." And another old man—or was it the same one?—lived on in the transit camp at Vtoraya Rechka, waiting to be shipped to Kolyma, and was thought by many people to be Osip Mandelstam—which, for all I know, he may have been.

That is all I have been able to find out about the last days, illness and death of Mandelstam. Others know very much less about the death of their dear ones.

83
ONE FINAL ACCOUNT

But there is still a little more to tell. The transport which took M. to Vladivostok left Moscow on September 9, 1938. Another person who was on it is a physicist called L. He does not wish to be identified because, as he says, "things are all right just now, but who knows what may happen later?" During the terror he worked in a Moscow technical college whose staff was completely decimated because one of its members was the son of a man hated by Stalin. L. was taken to join this transport from the Taganka prison. Others were brought from Butyrki, to which they had been transferred from the Lubianka just before the transport was due to leave. As the train was traveling east, L. learned from another prisoner that M. was there, too. The other prisoner had learned this after he had fallen ill and been put in the sick bay, where he had met M. He reported to L. that M. just lay on his bunk all the time, his head covered with a blanket. He still had a little money and the guards sometimes bought bread rolls for him at stations. M. always broke them in two and gave half to another prisoner, but he wouldn't touch his own half until, peeping out from under his blanket, he had seen the other man eat his. Only then would he sit up and eat himself. Terrified of being poisoned, he was starving himself, refusing to touch the soup on which the prisoners were fed.

The train arrived in Vladivostok in the middle of October. The transit camp was terribly overcrowded, and there was no room for the new prisoners, who were ordered to settle down in the open air between two rows of barracks. The weather was dry, and L. was in no hurry to get inside: he had at once noticed the half-naked people sitting near the latrines—one can imagine what they were like!—and getting rid of the lice in their ragged clothes. Spotted typhus had not yet broken out.

A few days later all the new arrivals were seen by a commission consisting of representatives of the Kolyma camp authorities. They badly needed building workers there, but it was not easy to find able-bodied people with the right skills among these hordes of prisoners worn out by nighttime interrogations and the "simplified methods" now in use. Many of them were rejected for work, including the thirty-two-year-old L., who was lame—he had broken his leg as a child. Few people were thus being taken away from the transit camp, but transports continued to arrive with hundreds and hundreds more prisoners. L. was able to make an approximate calculation as to their numbers. As a person with mathematical training, he carefully observed and analyzed everything he saw during his twenty years in the camps. But he will never pass on what he knows: worn out by his life as a prisoner and having no more trust in anything, his only wish is for peace and quiet. The whole of his existence now revolves round his new family: this sick and aging man lives only for his young daughter. He is one of the most brilliant witnesses to the past, but he will never share his knowledge with anyone. He has made an exception only for me—his meeting with M. made a great impression on him. I should have asked him whether the commissions from Kolyma did not soon start taking anybody they could get and just simply work them to death. But I forgot to ask this question.

When the rains started, there were great fights to get places in the barracks. By this time L. had been selected "elder" of a group of sixty men. His only duty had been to distribute the bread ration among them, but when the rains started, they demanded that he find a roof for them. L. suggested they see whether there was still any room in the lofts above the barracks—for the more agile prisoners these lofts were a godsend, since they were much less crowded and the air was less foul. It was not possible to stay in them during winter because of the cold, but nobody thought as far ahead as that—prisoners always take a very short-term view of their interests, and these would have been glad of the few extra weeks of comparative independence which they could gain by clambering up into the lofts at night.

They soon heard about a loft which was occupied by five criminals, though there was room for three times as many. L. and some of his comrades went to reconnoiter. The entrance was blocked by boards, but one of them was loose and L. wrenched it away to find himself face to face with the leader of the gang of criminals inside. He braced himself for a fight, but the man politely introduced himself: "Arkhangelski." They started to parley. It appeared that the camp commandant had personally assigned this loft to Arkhangelski and his friends. L. suggested they go and see the commandant together, to which Arkhangelski politely agreed. The commandant's attitude was rather surprising: he tried to reconcile the two parties. This was possibly due to an involuntary feeling of respect for L., who had not hesitated to challenge a gang of criminals; or perhaps he took L. for a criminal as well. At any rate, he suggested that Arkhangelski and his friends should make room because of the general "housing crisis," as he termed it. L. returned in triumph to his comrades in order to pick out a dozen or so of them to move into the loft, but they had all changed their minds—none of them wanted to live with criminals for fear of being robbed. L. pointed out that they had no possessions to lose, and that there would be twice as many of them, but they preferred to stay out in the open. The only result of it all was that L. had made a new friend—he and Arkhangelski henceforth greeted each other whenever they met, which was generally in the center of the camp, where the prisoners carried on a kind of barter trade among themselves.

Once Arkhangelski invited L. to come up to the loft and listen to some poetry. L. was not frightened of being robbed, since for months he had been sleeping in his clothes and his rags would not have tempted even a camp thief. All he had left was a hat, but in the camps this was of no value. Curious as to what sort of poetry it might be, he accepted Arkhangelski's invitation.

The loft was lit by a candle. In the middle stood a barrel on which there was an opened can of food and some white bread. For the starving camp this was an unheard-of luxury. People lived on thin soup of which there was never enough—what they got for their morning meal would not have filled a glass. . . .

Sitting with the criminals was a man with a gray stubble of beard, wearing a yellow leather coat. He was reciting verse which L. recognized. It was Mandelstam. The criminals offered him bread and the canned stuff, and he calmly helped himself and ate. Evidently he was only afraid to eat food given him by his jailers. He was listened to in complete silence and sometimes asked to repeat a poem.

After that evening L. always went up and spoke to M. if he saw him in the camp. L. easily got talking with him and soon noticed that M. was suffering from some kind of persecution mania or obsession. He was frightened not only of food, but also of being given "injections." Even before he was arrested, we had heard stories about mysterious injections or inoculations which were used in the Lubianka to break a person's will and make him say exactly what was required. There had been rumors of this kind ever since the mid-twenties, but whether there was anything in them, we did not, of course, know. Another thing L. noticed was that he was obsessed by the expression "socially dangerous" which always figured in the sentences pronounced by a Special Tribunal as grounds for exiling a prisoner. In his sick mind everything had got confused, and he imagined that they were going to give him an injection of rabies so that he really would be "dangerous" and have to be got rid of. He had forgotten that the "organs" didn't need to give people injections to do away with them.

L. knew nothing about psychiatry, but he very much wanted to help M. He didn't argue with him, but pretended he believed M. was deliberately spreading the story about being injected with rabies so that people would leave him alone. "But," L. said to him, "you don't want to frighten *me* away, do you?" The stratagem worked and, to L.'s astonishment, there was no more talk about injections.

In the transit camp the prisoners were not taken out to work, but building materials were being unloaded nearby and stacked on a piece of land which had been assigned to the criminals. (According to the regulations, the "politicals," arrested under Article 58, were supposed to be kept apart from the rest, but because of the congestion in the camp the rule was not strictly observed.) Anybody who worked there got nothing out of it, not even a little extra bread, but even so there were some volunteers. These were people who were tired of being penned in with the milling crowd of their half-crazed fellow prisoners. They wanted to get out, if only into the less crowded territory next to the camp, where it was at least possible to walk around more freely. The younger prisoners particularly suffered from lack of exercise. Later on, in the regular camps, nobody would ever think of volunteering for any work—but here "in transit" it was different.

Among the volunteers was L., a man who never lost heart. The worse the conditions, the stronger his will to live. He went around the camp with clenched teeth, stubbornly repeating to himself: "I can see everything and know everything, but even this is not enough to kill me." He was singlemindedly bent on one thing: not to allow himself to be destroyed, but to survive despite all the odds. I know this feeling very well myself, because I too have lived like that for almost thirty years, with clenched teeth. For this reason I have enormous respect for L.—I know what it cost to survive in ordinary conditions, let alone in the forced-labor camps where he lived throughout all those terrible years. He returned in 1956 with TB and a hopelessly damaged heart, but at least he came back sound in mind, and with a better memory than most people left at liberty can boast of.

L. took M. to help him. This was possible because there were no "work norms" in the transit camp and L. had no intention of overexerting himself. They loaded a couple of rocks on a board with handles, carted them to a place a few hundred yards away, and sat down for a rest before going back for more. Once, resting by the pile of rocks, M. said: "My first book was *Stone,* and my last will be stone, too." This phrase had stuck in L.'s memory, though he did not know the names of M.'s books, and he interrupted his story at this point to ask me whether M.'s first book really had been called *Stone.* When I confirmed this to him, he was very pleased that the excellence of his memory was thus borne out once again.

Away from the crowd, in the comparative peace of this waste lot reserved for the criminals, both of them felt in better spirits. L.'s story explained the sentence in M.'s letter about going out to work. Everybody had assured me that people did not work in transit camps, and I had never been able to understand this part of M.'s letter until it was cleared up by L.

At the beginning of December there was an outbreak of spotted typhus, and L. lost track of M. The camp authorities responded energetically to the outbreak by locking all the prisoners in their barracks and not letting them out—there was more room now because all the suspected plague cases had already been taken to a special building where they were kept in quarantine. In the mornings the barracks were opened so that the slop buckets could be emptied and everybody have his temperature taken by orderlies from the camp hospital. These preventive measures were, needless to say, quite ineffectual, and the disease spread rapidly. All those who caught it were placed in quarantine, about which there were terrifying rumors—it was thought that nobody came out alive.

Bunks in the camp barracks were in tiers of three, and L. had managed to get one in the middle. The lower ones were bad because of people milling about all the time, and in the upper ones it was intolerably hot and stuffy. After a few days L. began to shiver, and in order to get warmer he changed places with someone in an upper bunk. But he still went on shivering and he realized it was typhus. He was desperately anxious to avoid being taken off to the infirmary, and for a few days he managed to fool the orderlies by not letting them measure his temperature properly. But it kept going up and they soon took him away to quarantine. He was told that M. had been there a little while before. It appeared that he had not had typhus. The doctors, who were also prisoners, had treated him well and even given him a fur coat—they had a large stock of spare clothing because people were dying like flies. By this time M. was badly in need of it, since he had exchanged his leather coat for half a kilo of sugar—which had immediately been stolen from him. L. asked where M. had gone to, but nobody knew.

L. spent several days in quarantine before the doctors diagnosed typhus. He was then transferred to the infirmary. The transit camp turned out to have a perfectly decent and clean two-story hospital, to which all the typhus cases were sent. Here, for the first time in many months, L. slept in a proper bed. His illness brought him rest and a sweet feeling of comfort.

When he left the infirmary L. heard that M. had died. This must have been between December 1938 and April 1939—in April L. was transferred to a work camp. He met no witnesses of M.'s death and knew about it only from hearsay. L.'s story seems to bear out what Kazarnovski had told me—namely, that M. died early. I also conclude from L.'s account that, since all typhus cases were taken to the infirmary, then M., who was found not to have it, must have died in quarantine. This means that he did not even die in his own bunk, covered by his own miserable convict's blanket.

There is nowhere I can make inquiries and nobody who will tell me anything. Who is likely to search through those grisly archives just for the sake of Mandelstam, when they won't even publish a volume of his work? Those who perished are lucky if they have been posthumously rehabilitated, or if, at any rate, their cases have been "discontinued for lack of evidence." Even here there is no "egalitarianism," and there are two types of rehabilitation—M. was given the second-class one. . . .

All I can do, therefore, is to gather what meager evidence there is and speculate about the date of his death. As I constantly tell myself: the sooner he died, the better. There is nothing worse than a slow death. I hate to think that at the moment when my mind was set at rest on being told in the post office that he was dead, he may actually have been still alive and on his way to Kolyma. The date of death has not been established. And it is beyond my power to do anything more to establish it.

APPENDIX

A. Notes on Persons Mentioned in the Text

Adalis (Efron), Adelina Yefimovna (1900–1969): Poet and prose-writer.

Agranov, Yakov Savlovich (?–1939): Cheka investigator in the Kronstadt mutiny, the Tagantsev conspiracy, the Tambov uprising, the Kirov assassination, etc. Creator and chief of Litkontrol, a GPU department for the surveillance of writers. As deputy head of the NKVD under Yagoda and Yezhov, he was active in the preparation of the Moscow show trials of 1937–38. He was arrested and shot in 1939.

Akhmatova (Gorenko), Anna Andreyevna (1889–1966): Major Russian poet. Born in Odessa, she lived most of her life in St. Petersburg (Leningrad). Her verse was first published in 1911 and won immediate acclaim. Together with Nikolai Gumilev (whom she married in 1910), she became a leading figure in the Acmeist movement, with which Mandelstam was also associated. Her marriage to Gumilev ended in divorce, as did her second marriage to V. K. Shileiko, an Assyriologist. Her third husband, N. N. Punin, and her son, Lev Gumilev, were both arrested during the 1930's. She herself was never arrested, but for many years (1926–1940) she published scarcely anything and, like Mandelstam, was virtually proscribed. In 1946 she was scurrilously attacked (as a "half-nun, half-whore") by Stalin's chief lieutenant in cultural affairs, Andrei Zhdanov, and expelled from the Union of Soviet Writers. Subjected to intolerable pressures and threats of reprisals against her son, she wrote several poems in praise of Stalin in 1952. After the partial exposure of Stalin's crimes by Khrushchev in 1956 (when her son, like millions of others, was released from a forced-labor camp) she began to publish again, and swiftly won recognition from the younger generation. But her long poem "Requiem," a dirge for her husband and son and all of Stalin's victims, has still not been published in the Soviet Union. Her "Poem Without a Hero," a remarkable attempt to illuminate Russia's destiny in the last half century, was published with some cuts in the Soviet collection of her poetry, *Beg Vremeni* (Moscow, 1965). The most complete collection of her work has appeared only abroad in the two-volume edition edited by Gleb Struve and Boris Filippov (Washington, D.C., 1968). In the last years of her life Akhmatova was allowed to travel abroad for the first time since the Revolution. In 1964, at the age of seventy-five, she went to Sicily, where she received the Taormina literary prize. In 1965 she was awarded an honorary doctorate by the University of Oxford. On her way home she visited France and Italy. As she makes clear in her short memoir on Mandelstam (published in New York in 1965 in the literary almanac *Vozdushnye Puti [Aerial Ways]*, edited by Roman Grynberg), her close friendship with him was based on the natural affinity of two great poets.

Altman, Natan Isayevich (1889–1970): Painter of Akhmatova's portrait.

Amusin, Joseph Davidovich: Biblical and classical Hebrew scholar. He has published articles in Soviet scholarly journals and a book on the Dead Sea Scrolls (Moscow, 1960).

Anderson, Marian (1902–1993): American contralto. The sound of her voice inspired Mandelstam to write a poem in 1936.

Andreyev, Andrei Andreyevich (1895–1971): Member of the Central Committee of the Soviet Communist Party, 1920–61. Deputy chairman of the Council of Ministers, 1946–53.

Andronikov (Andronikashvili), Irakli Luarsabovich (1908–   ): Literary historian and critic, well known at present for his newspaper and television *causeries* on literary topics.

Annenski, Innokenti Fedorovich (1856–1909): Classical scholar and lyric poet.

Ardov, Victor Yefimovich (1900–1976): Writer of humorous stories, film scenarios and satirical sketches for the variety stage.

Aseyev, Nikolai Nikolayevich (1889–1963): Futurist poet, influenced by Khlebnikov and Mayakovski; a member of LEF. He was awarded the Stalin Prize in 1941. After Stalin's death, he helped some of the younger poets, but was very conformist in his public utterances.

Averbakh, Leopold Leopoldovich (1903–?): Literary critic, militant proponent of the concept of "proletarian" literature, and one of the leaders of RAPP. As such, he was virtually dictator of Soviet literary affairs from about 1927 until his downfall in 1932, when Stalin abruptly changed the policy in literature to one of support for all writers, whatever their background, who were willing to accept the Party line without question. Averbakh (who was married to Yagoda's sister) disappeared during the purges.

Avvakum, the Archpriest (c. 1620–1681): Leader of the "Old Believers"— schismatics who refused to accept the changes in Russian Orthodox ritual introduced by the Patriarch Nikon. Avvakum's *Life* (1672–73) is a remarkable account of his exile to Siberia with his wife.

Babel, Isaac Emanuilovich (1894–1941?): Great Soviet short-story writer, noted for his *Red Cavalry* (1923). Like Mandelstam, Akhmatova and Pasternak, he was largely reduced to silence in the 1930's (at the First Congress of Soviet Writers in 1934 he said: "I have invented a new genre—the genre of silence"). He was arrested in 1939, and fifteen years afterward, in 1954, his widow was informed in an official notification that the case against him had been "discontinued for lack of a corpus delicti." In a certificate issued at the same time, the date of his death was given as March 17, 1941.

Bagritski (Dziubin), Eduard Georgievich (1895–1934): Epic and lyric poet, translator of Burns, Rimbaud and others. After serving in the Red Army, he organized the first "proletarian" literary circle in Odessa, but moved to Moscow in 1925. He was a member of RAPP. Seva (Vsevolod Eduardovich) Bagritski (1922–1942), son of Eduard Bagritski, was also a poet.

Bakh, Alexei Nikolayevich (1857–1946): Biochemist. He was awarded the Stalin Prize in 1941.

Balmont, Konstantin Dmitrievich (1867–1943): Poet who enjoyed a considerable vogue at the turn of the century. He emigrated after the Revolution and died in Paris.

Baltrushaitis, Yurgis Kazimirovich (1873–1944): Russian and Lithuanian poet associated with the Symbolists. From 1921 to 1939 he was the Lithuanian ambassador in Moscow. He died in Paris.

Baratynski, Evgeni Abramovich (1800–1844): Major poet, contemporary of Pushkin.

Bedny, Demian (Yefim A. Pridvorov) (1883–1945): A somewhat crude versifier of great vigor who enjoyed a vogue in the 1920's and was noted particularly for his anti-religious satires. But in 1936 he incurred Stalin's displeasure by writing an opera libretto which made fun of Russia's past.

Belinski, Vissarion Grigorievich (1811–1848): Radical publicist and literary critic.

Bely, Andrei (Boris Nikolayevich Bugayev) (1880–1934): Major symbolist poet, novelist and critic. Like other Symbolists, he was at first inclined to see the October Revolution as an event of mystical significance—indeed, as the second coming of Christ. He was the leading Russian disciple of Rudolf Steiner.

Berdiayev, Nikolai Alexandrovich (1874–1948): Famous Russian philosopher and religious thinker. An ex-Marxist, he contributed to *Vekhi* (*The Landmarks*), a collection of essays (1909) in which leading Russian intellectuals critically reappraised the role of the intelligentsia, rejecting its spirit of maximalist radicalism. Berdiayev was a leading figure in the movement to revive philosophical and lay theological thinking in Russia (e.g., in the Free Philosophical Society). In 1922 he was expelled from Russia with other anti-Bolshevik intellectuals, and settled in Paris. The work referred to by Mrs. Mandelstam as *Self-Knowledge* has been translated into English under the title *Dream and Reality.*

Bernstein, Sergei Ignatievich (1892–1970): A leading linguist with a special interest in phonetics. During the 1920's he made phonograph recordings of Blok, Mayakovski, Yesenin and Mandelstam. His brother Alexander (Sania), born in 1900, is a writer of popular books on literature.

Bezymenski, Alexander Ilyich (1898–1973): Soviet poet noted for his political conformism. He was a leading member of RAPP.

Blagoi, Dmitri Dmitrievich (1893–   ): Soviet literary historian.

Bliumkin, Yakov Grigorievich (1892?–1929): Left Social Revolutionary who assassinated the German ambassador, Count Mirbach, in 1918. Sentenced to death, he was pardoned and became an official in the Cheka and a follower of Trotski. He was executed in 1929 for carrying a message from Trotski in Turkey for the opposition.

Blok, Alexander Alexandrovich (1880–1921): The leading Symbolist poet. In the first years after the Revolution he was very active in the various cultural enterprises started by Maxim Gorki under the aegis of Anatol Lunacharski, the People's Commissar for Enlightenment.

Blok, Georgi Petrovich (1888–1962): Cousin of Alexander Blok. Editor and publisher.

Borodin, Sergei Petrovich (1902–1974): Writer of historical novels, the most famous of which is *Dmitri Donskoi.* Until 1941 he wrote under the pseudonym Amir Sargidzhan.

Borodayevski, Valerian B.: A poet who wrote in *Apollon.*

Brik, Osip Maximovich (1888–1945): Friend and associate of Mayakovski. Originally associated with the Formalists, he later helped to create LEF. His wife, Lili, was the inspiration for many of Mayakovski's love poems. She is the sister of Elsa Triolet (died 1970), the wife of the French Communist poet Louis Aragon.

Briusov, Valeri Yakovlevich (1873–1924): Major poet, editor, and theoretician of the Symbolist movement. He joined the Communist Party in 1919.

Brodski, David Grigorievich (1895–1966); Poet and translator from French (Barbier, Hugo, Rimbaud), German (Goethe, Schiller), Yiddish (Perets Markish) and other languages.

Brodski, Joseph Alexandrovich (1940–1996): One of the first poets of the young generation in Russia. A protégé of Akhmatova, he was exiled to the Archangel region in 1964 as "a parasite," but was allowed to return to Leningrad the following year after a worldwide outcry. Scarcely any of his work has yet been published in the Soviet Union, but much of it has appeared abroad in Russian and other languages.

Bruni, Lev Alexandrovich: Russian artist, descended from an Italian painter who emigrated to Russia in the early nineteenth century. He painted a portrait of Mandelstam.

Bukharin, Nikolai Ivanovich (1888–1938): Member of the Bolshevik Party from 1907, of the Central Committee of the Soviet Communist Party from 1917 to 1934, and of the Politburo from 1919 to 1929. Editor of *Izvestia,* 1934–37. Expelled from the Party and arrested in 1937, he was the principal figure in the last great Moscow show trial in 1938, at which he was sentenced to be shot.

Bulgakov, Mikhail Afanasievich (1891–1940): Outstanding novelist, author of *The Master and Margarita,* which was not published till 1967, twenty-seven years after his death. His widow, Elena Sergeyevna, still lives in Moscow.

Bulgarin, Faddei (1789–1859): Writer best remembered as a police informer during the reign of Nicholas I.

Chaadayev, Peter Yakovlevich (1794–1856): Author of *Philosophical Letters,* which condemned Russia's cultural backwardness and called for her integration into the European tradition. The publication of the "First Letter" in 1836 led Nicholas I to declare him insane and to have him placed under house arrest for eighteen months. Mandelstam's essay on him appeared in the journal *Apollon* in 1915.

Charents (Sogononian), Egishe (1897–1937): Armenian poet who translated Pushkin, Mayakovski, Gorki into Armenian.

Chechanovski, Mark Osipovich: Editor and translator.

Cherniak, Robert Mikhailovich (1900–1932): Graphic artist.

Chicherin, Georgi Vasilievich (1872–1936): People's Commissar (i.e., Minister) of Foreign Affairs, 1918–30.

Chorene, Moses of: Reputed author of a fifth-century history of Armenia.

Chorny, Sasha (Alexander Mikhailovich Glikberg) (1880–1932): Talented author of satirical verse and stories. He emigrated in 1920 and eventually settled in France.

Chukovski, Kornei Ivanovich (1882–1969) Eminent Russian man of letters. His son, Nikolai Korneyevich (1905–1965), was a novelist.

Courtenay, Jan Ignacy Niecislaw, Baudoin de (1845–1929): Leading Slavic philologist, professor at St. Petersburg University.

Denikin, Anton Ivanovich (1872–1947): Commander-in-chief of the White Army in the South until he was succeeded by Wrangel in 1920. He died in the U.S.A.

Derzhavin, Gavriil Romanovich (1743–1816): Noted Russian poet.

Diki, Alexei Denisovich (1895–1955): Well-known actor and producer.

Dobroliubov, Alexander Mikhailovich (1876–?): Early Symbolist poet and mystical anarchist. He probably died during the Civil War.

Dobroliubov, Nikolai Alexandrovich (1836–1861): Radical publicist.

Dolmatovski, Yevgeni Aronovich (1915–   ): Soviet poet noted for his political conformism.

Dombrovski, Yuri Osipovich (1909–1978): Soviet writer who spent many years in a forced-labor camp. The novel to which Mrs. Mandelstam alludes is *The Keeper of Antiquities.*

Dzerzhinski, Felix Edmundovich (1877–1926): First head of the Cheka.

Efros, Abram Markovich (1888–1954): Noted art historian and translator.

Ehrenburg, Ilia Grigorievich (1891–1967): Famous Soviet novelist and journalist. After a youthful involvement with Bolshevik activities in 1906, he was imprisoned briefly. In 1908, he went abroad and lived in Paris from 1909 to 1917. He returned to Russia as an anti-Bolshevik in 1917, went back to Paris in 1921, and after some wavering became increasingly pro-Soviet. Until 1941, however, he managed to live mainly abroad (as European correspondent of *Izvestia*), making only brief visits to the Soviet Union. Notable among his vast output of novels, stories, essays, etc., are *The Extraordinary Adventures of Julio Jurenito* (1921), *The Fall of Paris* (1942) and *The Thaw* (1954). His memoirs were published in the mid-1960's and, despite the inevitable reticences, they give a fascinating picture of the fate of the Russian intelligentsia in Soviet times. His account of Mandelstam contains some inaccuracies (including the story, described as a legend by Mrs. Mandelstam, that he read Petrarch by a campfire in the days before his death in Siberia). A sardonic, gifted, and basically ambivalent figure, Ehrenburg did much after Stalin's death to promote the cultural values destroyed by the regime to which he had long paid lip-service as a novelist, journalist, and public figure. His novel *The Thaw* was of great importance as the first breach to be made in Stalinist mythology, and in his memoirs and essays after Stalin's death (such as those on Chekhov and Stendhal) he championed freedom of expression in literature and art.

Eichenbaum, Boris Mikhailovich (1886–1959): Scholar and literary critic, once a leading member of the Formalist school. He was associated with LEF.

Ekster (Grigorovich), Alexandra Alexandrovna (1884–1949): Artist and set designer. A pupil of Léger, she was active in Russian avant-garde circles, painting in a Cubist style, and illustrated books by the Futurists. After the Revolution she worked for the Kamerny Theater in Moscow, but emigrated from Russia some time in the 1920's.

Elsberg, Yakov: Soviet literary scholar, once secretary to Lev Kamenev, the Old Bolshevik purged by Stalin. In 1962 there was an attempt to have Elsberg expelled from the Union of Soviet Writers for his complicity as a secret police agent in the arrest and exile of fellow writers under Stalin, but apparently nothing came of this move (or he was speedily reinstated).

Erdman, Nikolai Robertovich (1902–1970): Playwright best known for his comedy *The Mandate* (1925), which was staged by Meyerhold. He was first arrested in 1931 and then again in the late 1930's.

Fadeyev (Bulyga), Alexander Alexandrovich (1901–1956): Soviet novelist. Author of *The Rout* (1927) and *The Young Guard* (1945), both held up in the Stalin years as models of "socialist realism"—though Stalin made him revise *The Young Guard* (revised version: 1951). From 1946 to 1953 he was Secretary General of the Union of Soviet Writers. He committed suicide in 1956.

Fedin, Konstantin Alexandrovich (1892–1977): Leading "Fellow Traveler" novelist. Fedin has been secretary of the Union of Soviet Writers (in succession to Surkov) since 1959.

Fet, Afanasi Afanasievich (1820–1892): Lyric poet.

Filippov (Filistinski), Boris Andreyevich (1905–   ): Emigré editor and poet. Collaborated with Gleb Struve in editing the works of Mandelstam (Chekhov Publishing House, New York, 1955, and Inter-Language Literary Associates, New York, three volumes, 1964–69).

Florenski, Father Pavel Alexandrovich (1882–1952): Originally a mathematician, appointed as a lecturer in philosophy at the Moscow Theological Academy in 1908, and ordained a priest in 1911. The publication in 1914 of *The Pillar and Foundation of Truth* was a landmark in the renaissance of Russian religious thinking. He was deported to Siberia after the Revolution.

Furmanov, Dmitri Andreyevich (1891–1926): Soviet writer famous for his novel *Chapayev,* about the Civil War. He served as secretary of the Moscow branch of RAPP.

Gapon, Georgi Apollonovich (1870–1906): Russian priest who in 1903 organized a Workers' Association with quasi-official support. He led the march to the Winter Palace on Bloody Sunday, January 9, 1905.

Garin, Erast Pavlovich (1902–1980): Well-known actor and producer, once an associate of Meyerhold.

Gerstein, Emma: Literary scholar, close friend of the Mandelstams and Anna Akhmatova; author of *Sudba Lermontova* (*Lermontov's Fate*) (Moscow, 1964).

Ginzburg, Grigori Romanovich (1904–1961): Pianist and professor at the Moscow Conservatory.

Ginzburg, Leo Moritsevich (1901–1966): Conductor.

Gippius, Vladimir Vasilievich (1876–1941): Poet and literary historian; director of the Tenishev school which Mandelstam attended before the Revolution.

Gladkov, Fedor V. (1883–1958): "Proletarian" writer, famous for his novel *Cement.*

Gorbunov, Nikolai Petrovich (1892–?): Executive secretary of the Council of People's Commissars; vice-president of the Lenin Academy of Agriculture.

Gorki, Maxim (Alexei Maximovich Peshkov) (1868–1936): Major Russian writer, friend of Lenin (and, later, Stalin); editor of *Novaya Zhizn* (*New Life*), which opposed the October Revolution, until it was closed down on Lenin's orders in 1918. Gorki did much to help and give material aid to intellectuals during the Civil War. He emigrated in 1921, but returned in 1929 to become the chief exponent of "socialist realism." After his death in 1936, Yagoda and Professor D. Pletnev were charged by Stalin with his "medical murder."

Grigoriev, Apollon Alexandrovich (1822–1864): Poet and critic.

Gronski, Ivan Mikhailovich (1894–   ): Journalist and critic. He was editor of *Izvestia,* 1928–34.

Gumilev, Lev Nikolayevich (1912–1992): Son of Nikolai Gumilev and Akhmatova; historian and Orientalist. He was arrested first in 1934 after the assassination of Kirov, and again in 1937. During the war he was released and served at the front. In 1949 he was arrested again and was released in 1956.

Gumilev, Nikolai Stepanovich (1886–1921): Acmeist poet and co-founder of the Poets' Guild. Before the First World War he traveled to Abyssinia. His narrative and lyric poetry and his tales were influenced by his travels, his distinguished military service in the war and his monarchist beliefs. After the Revolution he did translations for Gorki's World Literature Publishing House and taught poetry in the House of Arts. He was shot in August 1921 after he proudly confessed his involvement in the Tagantsev affair, a rather confused anti-Bolshevik conspiracy. His poetry is popular with Soviet youth, though he still has not been rehabilitated. He was the first husband of Ahkmatova.

Gusev (Drabkin), Sergei Ivanovich (1874–1933): Prominent Party official. He was head of the Press Department of the Central Committee, 1925–33.

Herzen, Alexander Ivanovich (1812–1870): Famous Russian publicist and editor of *Kolokol (The Bell)*, which he brought out in London after his emigration in 1847.

Ivanov, Georgi Vladimirovich (1894–1958): Acmeist poet who emigrated to Paris after the Revolution. His book of memoirs, *Petersburg Winters*, was first published in Paris in 1928.

Ivanov, Viacheslav Ivanovich (1866–1949): Leading Symbolist poet and classical scholar. He emigrated to Rome in 1924.

Kablukov, Sergei Platonovich: Secretary of the Religious Philosophical Society in St. Petersburg.

Kachalov (Shverubovich), Vasili Ivanovich (1875–1948): Famous actor of the Moscow Art Theater.

Kalinin, Mikhail Ivanovich (1875–1946): Member of the Politburo from 1925; chairman of the Presidium of the Supreme Soviet, 1922–46, and hence titular head of state.

Kamenev (Rosenfeld), Lev Borisovich (1883–1936): Old Bolshevik, member of the Central Committee from 1917 and one of the ruling Party triumvirate (with Stalin and Zinoviev) after Lenin's death. Arrested in 1934, he was executed after his confession at a show trial in 1936.

Katanian, Ruben Pavlovich (1881–?): Assistant Procurator General of the U.S.S.R., 1933–37.

Katayev, Valentin Petrovich (1897–1986): Prominent Soviet novelist. One of the leading "Fellow Travelers" in the 1920's. His play *The Squaring of the Circle* was often produced in the West in the 1930's. After Stalin's death, as editor of the literary monthly *Yunost* (*Youth*), he encouraged new talent. His semi-fictional reminiscences, *Holy Well* (published in English translation in 1967), contain his version of the conversation described by Mrs. Mandelstam on p. 280. His brother was the satirist Evgeni Petrov.

Kaverin (Zilber), Veniamin Alexandrovich (1902–1989): Soviet novelist who was a leading member of the Serapion Brothers in the 1920's. In recent years, since Stalin's death, he has played a courageous part in the restoration of cultural values. In 1956 he was one of the editors of the almanac *Literary Moscow,* which was a landmark in the movement for greater freedom of expression.

Kazin, Vasili (1898–?): A "proletarian" poet.

Khardzhiev, Nikolai Ivanovich: Soviet literary scholar and editor. A friend of the Mandelstams.

Khlebnikov, Velimir (Victor Vladimirovich) (1885–1922): Futurist poet noted for his linguistic experimentation. He died of malnutrition in 1922. Some of his poetry has now been reprinted after many years of suppression.

Khodasevich, Vladislav Felitsianovich (1886–1939): Poet and critic. He emigrated in 1922 and died in Paris.

Kirov (Kostrikov), Sergei Mironovich (1886–1934): Party leader of Leningrad. His assassination in December 1934, possibly with the complicity of Stalin, was used as an excuse to step up the tempo of the purges and mass terror.

Kirsanov, Semion Isaakovich (1906–1972): Poet, translator and member of LEF, influenced in his early period by Mayakovski.

Kluyev, Nikolai Alexandrovich (1887–1937): Peasant poet. He was arrested in the 1930's and died in Siberia.

Klychkov (Leshenkov), Sergei Antonovich (1889–1937): Peasant poet and novelist, arrested in 1937.

Kochetov, Vsevolod Anisimovich (1912–1973): Novelist who in recent years has become the spokesman of extreme anti-liberal forces in Soviet literature. Two of his novels, *The Brothers Yershov* (1957) and *What Do You Want?* (1969), are lampoons on the liberal intelligentsia. Kochetov is editor of the monthly *Oktiabr* (*October*).

Koltsov, Mikhail Yefimovich (1898–1942): Soviet journalist, correspondent and editor of *Pravda* who became famous for his dispatches during the Spanish civil war. Elected a corresponding member of the Academy of Sciences in 1938, he was arrested that same year, and presumably died in a forced-labor camp.

Komarovski, Count Vasili Alexeyevich (1881–1914): Minor poet connected with the Symbolist movement.

Konevskoi, Ivan (I. I. Oreus) (1877–1901): Symbolist poet of Swedish origin.

Kornilov, Boris Petrovich (1907–1938): Soviet poet influenced by Yesenin; a member of RAPP. He was arrested during the purges.

Kossior, Stanislav Vikentievich (1889–1939): Old Bolshevik, member of the Politburo from 1930; First Secretary of the Ukrainian Communist Party, 1928–38. He was arrested in 1938 and executed in 1939.

Kudasheva, Maria (Maya) Pavlovna: Daughter of a Russian father and a French mother; a friend of many Moscow writers. After corresponding with Romain Rolland, she moved to Switzerland and married him there. In 1937 she visited Moscow with him.

Kuzmin, Mikhail Alexeyevich (1875–1936): Poet whose work influenced the transition from Symbolism to Acmeism.

Lakhuti, Abolgasem Akhmedzade (1887–1957): Persian revolutionary and poet. He left Iran for Turkey in 1917, and in 1922 emigrated to the U.S.S.R., where he held positions in the government of Tajikistan and in the Union of Soviet Writers.

Lakoba, Nestor Ivanovich (1893–1936): Georgian Old Bolshevik; president of the executive committee of Abkhazia (an autonomous region of Georgia). Posthumously he was accused of a plot on Stalin's life.

Lapin, Boris Matveyevich (1905–1941): Soviet writer and translator; son-in-law of Ilia Ehrenburg. He was killed at the front as a war correspondent.

Lelevich, Grigori (Labori Gilelevich Kalmonson) (1901–1945): Soviet poet and critic. A member of RAPP until his expulsion in 1926 for opposing collaboration with the "Fellow Travelers." Arrested during the purges, he died in a forced-labor camp.

Leonov, Leonid Maximovich (1899–1994): Major Soviet novelist and playwright. A complex figure who successfully adapted to the twists and turns of Party policy while struggling to retain some integrity as a writer.

Lermontov, Mikhail Yurievich (1814–1841): Great Russian poet and author of a famous novel, *A Hero of Our Times*. He was killed in a duel at the age of twenty-six.

Lezhnev (Altshuler), Isai Grigorievich (1891–1955): Editor and journalist. Between 1922 and 1926 he edited *Novaya Rossia (New Russia)* and *Rossia (Russia)*, for which Mandelstam wrote. In 1926 he was expelled from the Party (he had joined the Bolsheviks before the Revolution) and was deported from the country by a decision of the GPU. In 1930 he "repented" and returned to the U.S.S.R., where his Party membership was restored. During 1935–39 he headed the art and literature section of *Pravda*.

Liashko, (Liashchenko), Nikolai N. (1884–1953): Novelist and short-story writer.

Linde, Fedor F. (?–1917): Bolshevik philosopher, mathematician and military commissar. He led the Finnish Guard Reserve regiment during the

April crisis in 1917, and later that year was killed on the southwestern front by soldiers under his command. His death is described by Boris Pasternak in *Dr. Zhivago,* where Linde appears as "Gints."

Livshitz, Benedikt Konstantinovich (1887–1939): Poet associated with the Futurists; translator of French prose and poetry. In his memoirs, *Polutoraglazy Strelets (The One-and-a-Half-Eyed Archer,* Moscow, 1933), he brilliantly describes the origins of the Futurist movement. He was arrested in the purges—apparently having been accused of complicity in the assassination of the head of the Cheka, Uritski, in 1919—but has now been posthumously rehabilitated.

Lominadze, Besso (?–1934): Comintern official and member of the Central Committee. He was charged in 1930 with organizing an "anti-Party Left-Right bloc," and in 1934 he committed suicide.

Lozina-Lozinski, Alexei Konstantinovich (1888–1916): Poet.

Lozinski, Mikhail Leonidovich (1886–1955): Poet and translator from Spanish, French, English and Italian; one of the founders (with Nikolai Gumilev) of the Poets' Guild. He was awarded a Stalin prize in 1946 for his translation of Dante's *Divine Comedy.*

Lugovskoi, Vladimir Alexandrovich (1901–1957): Soviet poet. He served in the Red Army until 1924. His first poetry was published in 1925. During World War II he was a correspondent.

Luppol, Ivan Kapitonovich (1896–1943): Marxist literary historian, critic and editor. He headed the Gorki Institute of World Literature, 1935–40, and was elected a member of the Academy of Sciences in 1939. Arrested in 1940, he died in a forced-labor camp and has been posthumously rehabilitated.

Lysenko, Trofim Denisovich (1898–1976): Biologist and member of the Soviet Academy of Sciences. With the support of Stalin, he tried to destroy all his opponents among the Soviet geneticists. He is now discredited.

Maikov, Apollon Nikolayevich (1821–1897): Poet.

Makovski, Sergei Konstantinovich (1877–1962): Son of the painter Konstantin Makovski, he wrote poetry, organized exhibitions of avant-garde Russian art, founded and edited the journal *Apollon* (in which Mandelstam published some of his early work) from 1909 to 1917. He emigrated to Prague and later to Paris. His memoir of Mandelstam was published in *Portrety sovremennikov (Portraits of Contemporaries,* New York, 1955). Since Mandelstam saw this before his death, it must have come out in an earlier version before the war, perhaps as an article in an émigré journal in Paris.

Malkin, Boris Fedorovich (1890–1942): Editor.

Markish, Perets Davidovich (1895–1952): Leading Yiddish poet, playwright and novelist. A member of the Jewish Anti-Fascist Committee, he was arrested in 1948 and executed in 1952 together with other Yiddish writers.

Marshak, Samuil Yakovlevich (1887–1964): Translator (Shakespeare, Heine, Burns), poet and children's writer. In 1924–25 he edited a magazine especially for children, *Novy Robinson* (*The New Robinson* [*Crusoe*]), in which some verse and translations by Mandelstam appeared. In 1925 and 1926, as head of the children's literature section of the State Publishing House, he published two books of verse for children by Mandelstam, *Balloons* and *Two Tramcars.* Though Marshak was noted for his political adaptability, he showed liberal tendencies after Stalin's death.

Mayakovski, Vladimir Vladimirovich (1893–1930): The leading figure in Russian Futurism. In addition to his vast output of poetry, he wrote two plays, *The Bedbug* and *The Bathhouse,* and edited the journal LEF (1923–25). Under attack by RAPP, involved in difficult love affairs and probably disillusioned by post-revolutionary reality (as one can judge from the two plays), he committed suicide in 1930. In 1935 Stalin said of him: "Mayakovski was and remains the best and the most talented poet of our Soviet epoch."

Mei, Lev Alexandrovich (1822–1862): Minor poet.

Meyerhold, Vsevolod Emilievich (1874–1940): Actor and producer. Prior to the Revolution he was associated with the Moscow Art Theater, and the Maryinski and Alexandrinski theaters in St. Petersburg. Joined the Communist Party in 1918. He directed the Theater of the Revolution until 1924, and then created his own theater based on his "biomechanical" system of acting. His theater was closed in 1938. Arrested in 1939 (after a defiant public refusal to accept the doctrine of "socialist realism" in art), he died in prison in 1940. Though he has now been rehabilitated as a person, there is still considerable opposition to his innovations in stagecraft.

Migai, Sergei Ivanovich (1888–1959): Singer of the Bolshoi Theater.

Mikhoels (Vovsi), Solomon Mikhailovich (1890–1948): Foremost Yiddish actor and director. Creator of the State Jewish Theater in Moscow, which was closed down in 1949 during an officially inspired campaign of anti-Semitism. The previous year *Pravda* had published a fulsome obituary of Mikhoels after his "sudden death." At the time rumors were circulated that he had been run over by a drunken truck driver, but it is now known that he was killed by the secret police on Stalin's orders (see Svetlana Alliluyeva: *Only One Year*). Evidently Stalin needed to get him out of the way before proceeding to the destruction of all Yiddish cultural facilities. His brother, Vovsi, was one of the doctors accused in 1952 of trying to assassinate Soviet leaders by medical malpractice.

Mikoyan, Anastas Ivanovich (1895–1978): Member of the Politburo from 1935 and chairman of the Supreme Soviet, 1964–67.

Mirbach, Wilhelm (Count von Mirbach-Harff) (1871–1918): German ambassador to Soviet Russia after the signing of the Brest-Litovsk peace treaty in 1918. He was assassinated by Bliumkin and Nikolai Andreyev, Left Social-Revolutionaries, on July 6, 1918.

Mirski, Dmitri Petrovich (Prince Sviatopolk-Mirski) (1890–1939?): Gifted literary historian and critic who lectured at London University, 1922–32. His *History of Russian Literature* remains the best work of its kind in English. After joining the British Communist Party, he returned to Russia in 1932, became a member of the Union of Soviet Writers, published articles onliterature and gave talks on Moscow radio. He was arrested during the purges and died in a forced-labor camp.

Molotov (Scriabin), Viacheslav Mikhailovich (1890–   ): Old Bolshevik, Soviet Foreign Minister, 1939–56. Despite his devotion to Stalin, he is believed to have been out of favor in 1936 and again in 1953 (in 1948 his wife was arrested and spent some years in a camp). Molotov was finally removed from power by Khrushchev in 1957 as a member of the so-called "anti-Party group." He now lives in retirement in Moscow.

Morozov, Alexander Antonovich (1906–   ): Literary scholar and translator.

Morozov, Pavel ("Pavlik") (1918–1932): Village boy who during collectivization denounced his father as a person of "kulak" sympathies. His father was shot and Pavel was then himself killed by a group of peasants led by his uncle. During the Stalin years Pavlik Morozov was held up to Soviet youth as a model who did not hesitate to denounce his father in the interests of the State. Books and poems were written about him, and there were many statues of him in public places.

Mravian, Askanaz Artemievich (1886–1929): Armenian revolutionary and literary figure. A Bolshevik from 1905, he was Armenian Commissar of Foreign Affairs, 1920–21, and was appointed Commissar of Education in 1923. He wrote articles about Armenian classical authors.

Narbut, Vladimir Ivanovich (1888–1944): Minor Acmeist poet who joined the Bolsheviks, but was expelled from the Party in 1928. He was editor-in-chief of the State publishing concern Land and Factory (ZIF). Arrested during the purges, he has now been posthumously rehabilitated. Sima Narbut was his wife.

Nesterov, Mikhail Vasilievich (1862–1942): Religious painter who adapted to the Soviet regime.

Nikulin, Lev Veniaminovich (1891–1967): Soviet novelist suspected of having denounced other Soviet writers, notably Isaac Babel.

Nilender, Vladimir Ottonovich (1883–1965): Poet and translator associated with the Symbolists.

Orlov, Vladimir Nikolayevich (1908–   ): Literary scholar; editor-in-chief of Poets' Library.

Oshanin, Lev Ivanovich (1912–   ): Soviet poet and playwright.

Otsup, Nikolai Avdeyevich (1894–1958): Acmeist poet. In 1923 he emigrated to Paris.

Parnok: a character in Mandelstam's "Egyptian Stamp" who personifies the raznochinets ("upstart intellectual") and is the author's "double." In real life the prototype of Parnok was a minor poet called Valentin Yakovlevich Parnakh who lived in Paris in the early 1920's. From a portrait of him by Picasso it is clear that he bore a striking physical resemblance to Mandelstam. In 1926 Parnakh published an article in the American Jewish *Menorah Journal* in which he wrote about Mandelstam (as well as Pasternak and others).

Pasternak, Boris Leonidovich (1890–1960): Poet and author of the novel *Dr. Zhivago.*

Paustovski, Konstantin Georgievich (1892–1968): Novelist and playwright. His memoirs have been translated into English under the title *Story of a Life.* His speech in defense of Dudintsev's novel *Not by Bread Alone* (October 22, 1956) was a courageous indictment of bureaucracy and philistinism.

Pavlenko, Peter Andreyevich (1899–1951): Highly orthodox Soviet novelist who was awarded a Stalin Prize for his violently anti-Western *Happiness* (1947). He wrote the scenario for the film *Alexander Nevski.*

Peshkova, Ekaterina Pavlovna (1876–1965): Legal wife of Maxim Gorki, from whom she was amicably separated. After the Revolution she founded the "Political Red Cross," a relief organization for political prisoners of all types. Because of Gorki's immense prestige it was tolerated by the Soviet secret police and allowed to exist in increasingly nominal fashion until it was closed down in 1939. Its premises were within a stone's throw of the Lubianka, the headquarters of the secret police in Moscow.

Petliura, Semion Vasilievich (1879–1926): Head of the nationalist anti-Bolshevik Ukrainian government (the Directory), 1918–20. He was assassinated in Paris in 1926.

Petrov (Kateyev), Evgeni Petrovich (1903–1942): Brother of Valentin Katayev; co-author with Ilf (Ilia Fainzilberg) of *The Twelve Chairs* and *The Golden Calf,* comic novels which still enjoy immense popularity in the Soviet Union. The two novels are about a confidence trickster from Odessa, Ostap Bender, and contain many daring satirical sketches of life in the Soviet Union during NEP.

Piast (Pestovski), Vladimir Alexeyevich (1886–1940): Poet and translator. A friend of Alexander Blok.

Pilniak (Vogau), Boris Andreyevich (1894–1937?): Prominent Soviet novelist. In his *Tale of the Extinguished Moon* (1927) he hinted that Stalin had killed the Red Army Commander Frunze by making him have an unnecessary operation. In 1929 he was chairman of the board of the Union of Writers, but was removed from this position after a violent campaign in the press because of the publication of his short novel *Mahogany* in Berlin. This attack on Pilniak signaled the beginning of Stalin's total subjugation of Soviet literature to his own political purposes. Pilniak was arrested in 1937, accused of spying for the Japanese and was either shot immediately or died in a camp.

Pisarev, Dmitri Ivanovich (1840–1868): Radical publicist noted for his extreme utilitarian approach to culture.

Podvoiski, Nikolai Ilyich (1890–1948): Organizer of the Red Guards, 1917. He was active in the military leadership of the Civil War and was a member of the Central Committee.

Polezhayev, Alexander Ivanovich (1805–1838): Poet.

Polivanov, E. D.: Leningrad philologist associated with the Formalist school of literary criticism.

Polonski, Yakov Petrovich (1819–1898): Poet.

Postupalski, Igor Stefanovich (1907–   ): Poet, translator and critic.

Prishvin, Mikhail Mikhailovich (1873–1954): Novelist and short-story writer distinguished by his love of nature.

Prokofiev, Alexander Andreyevich (1900–1971): Poet noted for his political conformism. Secretary of the Leningrad section of the Union of Soviet Writers, he was awarded a Stalin Prize and two Orders of Lenin.

Punin, Nikolai Nikolayevich (1888–1953): Art historian and critic associated with Makovski's *Apollon.* He was the third husband of Anna Akhmatova. During the purges he was arrested and sent to a forced-labor camp.

Rakovski, Christian Georgievich (1873–1941): Old Bolshevik. Sentenced to twenty years' imprisonment at the Bukharin show trial in 1938.

Raskolnikov (Ilyin), Fedor Fedorovich (1892–1939): Deputy People's Commissar for the Navy in 1918; Soviet ambassador to Afganistan, 1922–23. He defected while Soviet ambassador in Bulgaria in 1937 and committed suicide in Paris in 1939.

Reisner, Larisa Mikhailovna (1897–1928): Bolshevik heroine of the Revolution, author of *Front* (1922); wife of Fedor Raskolnikov. After divorcing him in 1922, she became a close friend of Karel Radek. According to Trotski, she had "the beauty of an Olympian goddess, a subtle mind and the courage of a warrior."

Rozhdestvenski, Vsevolod Alexandrovich (1895–1977): Poet and translator.

Rustaveli, Shota (c. 1200): Poet, author of the Georgian national epic, *The Knight in the Tiger's Skin.*

Sargidzhan, Amir: see Borodin, Sergei Petrovich.

Seifullina, Lidia Nikolayevna (1889–1954): Novelist and short-story writer well known in the 1920's for her realistic descriptions of Russian peasant life.

Selvinski, Ilia Lvovich (1899–1968): Soviet poet.

Semashko, Nikolai Alexandrovich (1874–1949): First People's Commissar of Health, and later a member of the Soviet Executive Committee.

Severianin (Lotarev), Igor Vasilievich (1887–1941): Poet noted for his flamboyance and verbal extravagance; leader of the "Ego-Futurists." He emigrated to Estonia in 1919. After the Soviet occupation of Estonia in 1940, he managed to publish in some Soviet magazines. He died in December 1941 under German occupation.

Shaginian, Marietta Sergeyevna (1888–1982): Veteran Soviet novelist and (before the Revolution) a minor poet on the fringes of the Symbolist movement. During the 1920's she was known mainly for her attempt to write thrillers and detective fiction in Western style, decried at the time as "Red Pinkertonism."

Shalamov, Varlam Tikhonovich (1907–1982): Poet and prose writer who spent seventeen years in a forced-labor camp in Kolyma. His *Tales of Kolyma* have been published in the West in Russian and French.

Shchegolev, Pavel Pavlovich (1902–): Historian, professor at Leningrad University, who helped Alexei Tolstoy with the research for his historical novels. (Probably he is the man referred to on p. 338.)

Shchepkin, Mikhail Semionovich (1788–1863): Famous Russian actor.

Shcherbakov, Alexander Sergeyevich (1901–1945): Veteran Communist official and associate of Zhdanov. He was appointed secretary of the Union of Soviet Writers in 1934, despite the fact that he had no connection with literature. Later he was in charge of purging provincial Party organizations, and during the war he was a secretary of the Central Committee (and candidate member of the Politburo) with special responsibility for political control of the army. His death in 1945 was later attributed to the Jewish doctors arrested on Stalin's orders in 1952.

Shengeli, Georgi Arkadievich (1894–1956): Poet, translator and critic.

Shervinski, Sergei Vasilievich (1892–   ): Poet, critic and translator.

Shevchenko, Taras Grigorievich (1814–1861): Ukrainian national poet, exiled for his criticism of the social and national policies of the Czarist regime.

Shkiriatov, Matvei Fedorovich (1883–1954): Major Stalinist official, a member of the Central Purge Commission set up in 1933, and a chief assistant to Yezhov during the Terror.

Shklovski, Victor Borisovich (1893–1984): Eminent literary scholar and Formalist critic, a member of LEF. Shklovski's influence in the 1920's was immense, and he continued to write articles, books and scenarios throughout the Stalinist era to the present day.

Shopen, Ivan Ivanovich (1798–1870): Author of *A Historical Memoir on the Condition of the Armenian Region at the Time of Its Union with the Russian Empire.*

Shostakovich, Dmitri Dmitrievich (1906–1975): Famous Soviet composer.

Simonov, Konstantin Mikhailovich (1915–1979): Novelist, poet and playwright.

Sinani, Boris Naumovich: St. Petersburg doctor of Karaite extraction, a confidant of the leading Social Revolutionaries. He is described in Mandelstam's *Noise of Time* (see *The Prose of Osip Mandelstam,* translated by Clarence Brown, Princeton University Press, 1965).

Sluchevski, Konstantin Konstantinovich (1837–1904): Poet.

Slutski, Boris Abramovich (1919–1986): Soviet poet and translator.

Sologub, Fedor (Fedor Kuzmich Teternikov) (1863–1927): Symbolist poet and novelist, famous for his novel *The Petty Demon* (1907). His writings of the Soviet period remain largely unpublished.

Soloviev, Vladimir Sergeyevich (1853–1900): Mystic, philosopher and poet who greatly influenced the Symbolists.

Solzhenitsyn, Alexander Isayevich (1918–   ): Russian novelist who was in a forced-labor camp from 1945 to 1953. His *One Day in the Life of Ivan Denisovich* (1962) was the first account of the camps to appear in print in the Soviet Union. A larger novel on the same subject, *The First Circle,* has been published only in the West. "Zotov," mentioned by Mrs. Mandelstam on p. 343, is a character in his short story "Incident at the Krechetovka Station."

Sosnora, Victor Alexandrovich (1936–   ): Leningrad poet.

Spasski, Sergei Dmitrievich (1898–1956): Poet. Arrested in 1936 or 1937, he was rehabilitated only after many years in prisons and camps.

Startsev, Abel Isaakovich: Literary scholar and critic.

Stavski, Vasili P. (?–1943): Prose writer. Appointed secretary of the Board of the Union of Soviet Writers in 1936, he was active in the denunciation of writers for Trotskiism and other "crimes."

Stenich (Smetanich), Valentin Iosifovich: Poet, translator (notably of James Joyce and John Dos Passos). He was evidently arrested and shot in 1938.

Stolpner, Boris Grigorievich (1863–?): Marxist philosopher and translator of Hegel.

Struve, Gleb Petrovich (1898–1985): Eminent émigré scholar, author of the standard *History of Soviet Russian Literature*. With Boris Filippov, he edited the works of Mandelstam, Pasternak, Akhmatova, Gumilev and others.

Strzigovski, Josef (1862–1941): Austrian art historian, author of *Die Baukunst der Armenier und Europa* (Vienna, 1918).

Surikov, Vasili Ivanovich (1848–1916): Russian artist whose painting "Morning of the Execution of the Streltsy" was first exhibited on March 1, 1881, the day Alexander III was assassinated.

Surkov, Alexei Alexandrovich (1899–1983): Poet, graduate of the Institute of Red Professors, war correspondent; editor of *Literaturnaya Gazeta* (*Literary Gazette*), 1944–46; secretary of the Union of Soviet Writers, 1954–59.

Syrtsov, Sergei Ivanovich (?–1938): Member of the Central Committee. He was premier of the R.S.F.S.R., 1929, and candidate member of the Politburo, 1930. In December 1930 he was accused, with Besso Lominadze, of creating an "anti-Party bloc." He disappeared in 1936 and is presumed to have died in a labor camp.

Tager, Elena Mikhailovna (1895–1964): Poet and prose writer. In 1920 she was expelled from Petrograd to Archangel by the Cheka, but returned to Leningrad in 1927. In 1939 she was arrested and accused of working for the "fascist intelligence service." She served her ten years' sentence in Kolyma, and then spent a further six years in exile in western Siberia and central Asia. In 1954 she was allowed to go and live in Moscow, but was not formally rehabilitated until 1956. A book of stories she had first published in 1929 was reissued in 1957. Her memoir on Mandelstam was published in New York in 1965 (see Tolstoi, Alexei Nikolayevich).

Tairov, Alexander Yakovlevich (1885–1950): Actor and, later, director of the Kamerny Theater in Moscow. He was dismissed from this post in 1939.

Tarasenkov, Anatoli Kuzmich (1909–1956): Literary scholar and critic.

Tatlin, Vladimir Yevgrafovich (1885–1953): Constructivist painter and set designer.

Tikhonov, Nikolai Semionovich (1896–1979): Soviet poet, influenced by Gumilev and Khlebnikov, who later adapted to the demands of "socialist realism." He was secretary of the Union of Soviet Writers, 1944–46, and from 1950 chairman of the Soviet Peace Committee.

Tiutchev, Fedor Ivanovich (1803–1873): Major lyric poet.

Tolstoi, Count Alexei Konstantinovich (1817–1875): Poet and playwright whose historical plays and humorous verse are still popular.

Tolstoi, Count Alexei Nikolayevich (1882–1945): Poet, playwright and journalist, famous for two historical novels: *The Road to Calvary* and *Peter I.* He was a prolific writer of novels and short stories and enjoyed a great vogue in the Soviet Union. In 1919 he emigrated but soon returned to the Soviet Union. Known as the "Red Count," he proceeded to adapt himself with unrivaled skill to the twists and turns of Party policy. The circumstances which led to Mandelstam slapping Tolstoi's face in 1934 are known only from E. M. Tager's memoir on Mandelstam, published in the West a few years ago (*Novy Zhurnal* [*New Review*], December 1965, New York). According to Mrs. Tager, the whole affair started with a party in the Mandelstams' apartment in Moscow during which the novelist Sergei Borodin (also known under the pseudonym Amir Sargidzhan) assaulted Mrs. Mandelstam. A writers' "court of honor" presided over by Tolstoi looked into the incident, but appears to have exonerated Borodin and suggested that the Mandelstams were themselves to blame. On a visit to Leningrad some time later (in the middle of 1934) Mandelstam slapped Tolstoi's face during a meeting in the director's office of the Leningrad Writers' Publishing House. It happened in the presence of half a dozen other writers, and when Mrs. Tager arrived on the scene a few moments later she found them all still standing open-mouthed with horror and surprise—like the cast at the end of Gogol's *Inspector General.*

Tomashevski, Boris Victorovich (1890–1957): Leningrad literary scholar and editor.

Tretiakov, Peter Nikolayevich (1892–1939): Essayist and playwright, member of LEF. He was well known for his *Roar, China!* Arrested during the purges, he died in a camp.

Tsvetayeva, Marina Ivanovna (1892–1941): Gifted Russian poet who was a friend of Pasternak, Mandelstam and Akhmatova. All four dedicated verse to one another, and are regarded as having no equals in their generation. Tsvetayeva's fate was the most tragic of all. Her husband,

Sergei Efron, whom she married in 1912, served during the Civil War as an officer in the White Army, but she was trapped in Moscow till 1922. From 1922 till 1925 she lived in Prague, and then in Paris till 1939. As a suspected GPU agent, Efron was forced to flee France and went back to Moscow. Tsvetayeva followed him there in 1939, only to find that he had been executed on his return, and that their daughter had been sent to a camp. When war broke out, she was evacuated to the town of Elabuga, where in August 1941 she hanged herself. Volumes of her selected verse were finally published in the Soviet Union in 1961 and 1965. In addition to her poetry, she wrote plays and valuable critical essays. A memoir by her on her relations with Mandelstam was published in 1964 in the *Oxford Slavonic Papers.*

Tvardovski, Alexander Trifonovich (1910–1971): Soviet poet, author of the immensely popular wartime ballad on the soldier Vasili Tiorkin. Editor of the liberal literary journal *Novy Mir (New World)* from 1949 to 1954, and again from 1958 to 1970.

Tynianov, Yuri Nikolayevich (1895–1943): Eminent Formalist critic, noted also for his biographical novels (on Pushkin, Griboyedov, etc.).

Tyshler, Alexander Grigorievich (1908–?): Painter and sculptor. He taught art to Mrs. Mandelstam.

Uritski, Mikhail Solomonovich (1873–1918): Menshevik who joined the Bolsheviks in 1917 and became head of the Petrograd Cheka. His assassination on August 30, 1919 (by the young poet Kannengiesser), and the wounding of Lenin the same day unleashed the first massive Red Terror. The Petrograd Cheka immediately shot 512 hostages.

Vaginov, Konstantin Konstantinovich (1900–1934): A little-known poet of considerable distinction.

Vakhtangov, Evgeni Bagrationovich (1883–1922): Famous Moscow theater director.

Veresayev (Smidovich), Vikenti Vikentievich (1867–1945): Novelist and literary historian.

Verkhovski, Yuri Nikandrovich (1878–1956): Translator, poet and literary critic.

Vinogradov, Victor Vladimirovich (1895–1969): Eminent linguist, professor at Moscow University and member of the Academy of Sciences.

Vishnevski, Vsevolod Vitalievich (1900–1951): Author of plays on Red Army and Navy themes who became a sycophantic supporter of Stalin. His *Unforgettable 1919* (1949) considerably enhances Stalin's role in the Civil War (and was duly awarded a Stalin Prize). In 1933, in an article entitled "We Must Know the West," he called for better knowledge of such

Western writers as James Joyce, whose *Ulysses* he extolled for its portrayal of the capitalist era.

Volpe, Caesar Samoilovich (1904–1941): Critic and editor.

Volpin, Mikhail Davidovich (1902–1988): Poet and scenario writer. He collaborated with Erdman.

Voronski, Alexander Konstantinovich (1884–1943): Old Bolshevik who edited the major Soviet literary journal *Krasnaya Nov* (*Red Virgin Soil*), which in the 1920's was the main outlet for the "Fellow Travelers." As an advocate of rapprochement between "Fellow Travelers" and "Proletarians," Voronski came under heavy fire from Averbakh's RAPP, and in 1927 he was expelled from the Party (his place as editor of *Krasnaya Nov* being taken over by Fedor Raskolnikov). Voronski finally disappeared during the purges in 1937 and probably died in a labor camp in 1943.

Vyshinski, Andrei Yanuarievich (1883–1954): A Menshevik until 1920, he was professor of law during the 1920's and later became Rector of Moscow University. He was appointed Procurator General in 1935, and as such was the chief accuser of all the Old Bolsheviks (whom he denounced as "mad dogs") during the Moscow show trials. He replaced Molotov as Minister of Foreign Affairs in 1949 and died in New York while representing the Soviet Union at the United Nations.

Wrangel, Baron Peter Nikolayevich (1878–1928): Russian general who succeeded Denikin as commander-in-chief of the White Army in the south of Russia.

Yagoda, Genrikh Grigorievich (1891–1938): Member of the Cheka from 1920, he became head of the NKVD (secret police) in 1934. He was replaced by Yezhov in 1936 and appointed Commissar of Communications. Arrested in 1937 after newspaper attacks on him, he was tried with Bukharin, Rykov and others in the last great show trial, and executed.

Yakhontov, Vladimir Nikolayevich (1899–1945): Prominent Soviet actor. Associated with the Moscow Art Theater, he was also known for his readings of literary works, and his one-man sketches. He committed suicide in 1945. Lilia Yakhontov was his wife.

Yakulov, Georgi Bogdanovich (1884–1928): Painter and set designer.

Yarkho, Boris Isaakovich: Linguist and translator.

Yashin (Popov), Alexander Yakovlevich (1913–1969): Poet and prose writer. Author of "The Levers" (*Literary Moscow,* vol. 2 [1956]).

Yazykov, Nikolai Mikhailovich (1803–1846): Poet.

Yenukidze, Abel Sofronovich (1877–1937): Old comrade of Stalin, secretary of the Central Executive Committee. Expelled from the Party in 1935, he was arrested, tried in secret and executed in 1937.

Yesenin, Sergei Alexandrovich (1895–1925): Popular lyric poet of peasant origin. He married Isadora Duncan in 1922 and traveled to western Europe and America with her. After his initial acceptance of the October Revolution, he became disillusioned and came under increasing attack for his riotous behavior. In 1925 he hanged himself in a Leningrad hotel.

Yezhov, Nikolai Ivanovich (1894–1939?): Member of the Central Committee from 1934 and chief of the NKVD, 1936–38. Stalin's Great Purge reached its height under his direction of the NKVD, and he was then made the scapegoat for its "excesses." He was succeeded by Beria in 1938, and probably was executed in 1939, although there has never been any official information about his fate.

Yudina, Maria Veniaminova (1899–1970): Eminent Soviet pianist and professor at the Moscow Conservatory.

Zadonski, Tikhon (1724–1783): Bishop, spiritual elder of the Zadonsk monastery, and author of religious works.

Zalka, Maté (1896–1937): A Hungarian who fought on the side of the Bolsheviks during the Civil War. A member of RAPP, he published a novel in the 1930's. He served with the rank of general in the Spanish civil war (under the name of Lukacz) and was killed at the front.

Zaslavski, David I. (1880–1965): Journalist. A notorious apologist for Stalinism, he made a vicious attack on Pasternak after he was awarded (and forced to renounce) the Nobel Prize in 1959.

Zenkevich, Mikhail (1891–1973): Acmeist poet.

Zhdanov, Andrei Alexandrovich (1896–1948): Close associate of Stalin who acted as his lieutenant in cultural matters. At the First Congress of Soviet Writers in 1934, Zhdanov made a speech in which the doctrine of "socialist realism" was first promulgated as the official Party line in literature. In 1946 he denounced Akhmatova, Zoshchenko, Pasternak and others for attempting to "poison the minds" of Soviet youth by their decadent, a political and "vulgar" writings which had been published in the literary magazines *Zvezda* (*Star*) and *Leningrad*. By a special Party decree of August 14, 1946, *Leningrad* was closed and *Zvezda* was ordered to "correct" its editorial policy and not open its pages again to Akhmatova, Zoshchenko "and their like." The "Zhdanov Decree" on literature was followed by similar ones on music and the cinema.

Zhirmunski, Victor Maximovich (1891–1971): Eminent literary scholar. Corresponding member of the Academy of Sciences.

Zoshchenko, Mikhail Mikhailovich (1895–1958): Popular satirist. He was attacked in 1946 by Zhdanov for his "vulgar parody" of Soviet life and, together with Akhmatova, expelled from the Union of Soviet Writers.

Zubov, Count Valentin Platonovich (1884–   ): Founder of the Institute of
the History of Arts (1912), which continued as a school and a publisher
of scholarly work until it was finally closed by the government in 1930.
Count Zubov was imprisoned, but was released and allowed to emi-
grate to Paris in the 1920's.

B. Note on Literary Movements and Organizations

In the twenty years or so before the October Revolution, Russian literature, reacting against the nineteenth-century realist tradition, went
through a period of ferment which is sometimes spoken of as the "Silver
Age." Its main feature was a revival of poetry, which in the latter half of
the nineteenth century had been almost completely overshadowed by
prose.

The first and most influential of the new movements was that of the
SYMBOLISTS (roughly 1894 to 1910), who, as Mrs. Mandelstam points out,
transformed the aesthetic standards of the Russian public. Their precur-
sor was the religious philosopher and poet Vladimir Soloviev, and among
the leading figures were: Valeri Briusov, Viacheslav Ivanov, Alexander
Blok and Andrei Bely. There were different trends within Symbolism,
but its hallmark was a certain other worldliness: poetry was often a vehicle for mystical insights which could only be hinted at in "symbolic" language.

The ACMEISTS were members of the so-called POETS' GUILD, which
was founded in 1912 by Nikolai Gumilev and Sergei Gorodetski in opposition to the Symbolists. Their aim was to restore the autonomy of poetic language; they rejected "mysticism" and strove for precision and
clarity in the use of words. Akhmatova and Mandelstam were the most
outstanding of the Acmeists, who existed as an organized group only until
1914.

Another important movement launched in 1912 was FUTURISM, which
was also a reaction to the Symbolists. The Futurists (the most prominent
of whom were Vladimir Mayakovski and Velimir Khlebnikov) espoused
modern technology and urbanism and in their poetry they were distinguished by their penchant for neologisms, slang and words of their own
invention. Temperamentally attracted to revolution, most of them were
avant-garde in politics as well as in art. Largely for this reason, Futurism
was the only literary movement to survive the October Revolution, con-
stituting itself in 1923 as the so-called LEFT FRONT (LEF) and stridently
claiming to be the only true voice of the new order.

This claim was successfully contested by the RUSSIAN ASSOCIATION OF PROLETARIAN WRITERS (RAPP), founded in 1925. Though few were true proletarians by origin, the members of RAPP, such as Leopold Averbakh and Alexander Fadeyev, asserted that the chief role of literature must be to serve the interests of the proletariat, as the new ruling class, and to reflect its "ideology." From 1929 to 1932, RAPP was given its head by the Party and exercised dictatorial powers over literature. RAPP's leaders were convinced zealots who welcomed the rigors of the First Five Year Plan and Collectivization—the relative "liberalism" of NEP (New Economic Policy) had seemed to them a betrayal of the Revolution's promise.

In line with this "liberalism," the Central Committee of the Party had in 1925 issued a famous resolution (supposedly drafted by Bukharin) proclaiming its neutrality, for the time being, as between the competing literary groups. In this atmosphere of relative tolerance, it was possible during the middle 1920's for most writers, whatever their "class" background, to carry on as "FELLOW TRAVELERS" (the name given them by Trotski). The "Fellow Travelers," who formed the largest group of Soviet writers in the first post-Revolutionary decade, were expected to give overall assent to the new regime, but were not yet forced to express positive commitment to it in their work.

Some of them, joining together in 1921 in a group known as the SERAPION BROTHERS, (Mikhail Zoshchenko, Konstantin Fedin, Nikolai Tikhonov, and others), tried to establish the independence of literature from all political and social commitment, but this position became progressively more untenable in the latter half of the 1920's. The Serapion Brothers were allied with the FORMALISTS (Victor Shklovski, Victor Zhirmunski, and others), a new school of literary criticism (founded in 1916) which concentrated on problems of form in the artistic process. Toward the end of the 1920's the Formalists came under heavy attack, and "formalism" became a standard term of abuse for any attempt to divorce literature from the political and "educational" functions imposed on it by the Party.

In 1932 Stalin made such functions paramount by abruptly decreeing the disbandment of all separate literary groups, including RAPP, which had appeared to triumph over its rivals during its three-year "dictatorship." Stalin had no use for zealots of any kind, and wanted writers to be obedient instruments of his will, without convictions of their own. They were now all forced to join the UNION OF SOVIET WRITERS, a bureaucratic machine for the imposition of strict control over literature. The doctrine of Socialist Realism, promulgated at the same time, became binding on all writers who wanted to continue being published. In effect, it meant conveying the Party's "message" in a humdrum realist style derived from the nineteenth-century Russian classics.

In the years since Stalin's death there has been some loosening of the controls imposed in 1932 (and reinforced after World War II in a series of Party decrees associated with the name of Zhdanov), but Soviet writers can still function legally only within the general administrative and ideological framework established under Stalin.

INDEX

THE MODERN LIBRARY EDITORIAL BOARD

Maya Angelou
•
Daniel J. Boorstin
•
A. S. Byatt
•
Caleb Carr
•
Christopher Cerf
•
Ron Chernow
•
Shelby Foote
•
Stephen Jay Gould
•
Vartan Gregorian
•
Charles Johnson
•
Jon Krakauer
•
Edmund Morris
•
Elaine Pagels
•
John Richardson
•
Arthur Schlesinger, Jr.
•
Carolyn See
•
William Styron
•
Gore Vidal

A Note on the Type

The principal text of this Modern Library edition
was set in a digitized version of Janson,
a typeface that dates from about 1690 and was cut by Nicholas Kis,
a Hungarian working in Amsterdam. The original matrices have
survived and are held by the Stempel foundry in Germany.
Hermann Zapf redesigned some of the weights and sizes for Stempel,
basing his revisions on the original design.